THE CHARACTER FACTORY

THE CHARACTER FACTORY

Baden-Powell and
the Origins of
the Boy Scout Movement

MICHAEL ROSENTHAL

COLLINS
8 Grafton Street, London W1
1986

William Collins Sons & Co. Ltd
London · Glasgow · Sydney · Auckland
Toronto · Johannesburg

BRITISH LIBRARY CATALOGUING IN PUBLICATION DATA

Rosenthal, Michael
The character factory: Baden-Powell and
the origins of the boy scout movement.
1. Great Britain. *Army*——Biography
2. Boy Scouts——Great Britain——
Biography   3. Generals——Great Britain
——Biography
I. Title
369.43'092'4   DA68.32.B2

ISBN 0-00-217604-1

First published in Great Britain 1986
Copyright © 1984, 1986 by Michael Rosenthal

The chapter, 'The Scout Law', first appeared in
slightly different form in *Raritan*, Summer 1984, vol. IV no. 1.

Set by Butler & Tanner Ltd, Frome and London.
Made and printed in the United States of America

For Judith
with love and gratitude

CONTENTS

Acknowledgments   ix

The Imperiled Island   1

1   The Chief Scout   15

2   Fortifying the Wall of Empire   52

3   Working-Class Lads and Public School Ideals   88

4   The Scout Law   108

5   The Specter of Deterioration   131

6   *Scouting for Boys*   161

7   "The Peace Scouts" and Edwardian Militarism   191

8   Predecessors and Successors   230

9   "Scouts, White Men and Christians"   253

The Emperor of Youth   279

Notes   284

Bibliography   318

Index   331

Photographs follow page 146

ACKNOWLEDGMENTS

This book would not have been possible without the opportunity for an unencumbered year of research, and I wish to thank the Rockefeller Foundation for awarding me the Humanities Fellowship that enabled me to spend the academic year 1978-79 in London. Once there, I benefited from the generous support of the Scout Association and its knowledgeable archivist, Peter Cooke, who permitted me access to the archives and was endlessly patient in answering my questions. Mr. Cooke's successor, G. A. Coombe, has been equally helpful in responding to my trans-Atlantic queries. Scout kindness was matched by that of the Boys' Brigade and its archivist, Muriel Ellis, who made Brigade material available to me. Librarians at the British Library were both skillful and interested in directing me to the sources I needed. During my stay in England I had the good fortune to speak with Eileen K. Wade, who had been Baden-Powell's secretary from virtually the start of Scouting to the time Baden-Powell left England for his final years in Kenya; and with Arthur Primmer, one of the original Brownsea Island Scouts. Both were wonderfully forthcoming in sharing with me their memories of Baden-Powell and the early days of Scouting.

Neither my research nor the willingness of people to foster it was confined to England. Mrs. Dee Seton Barber, Ernest Thompson Seton's daughter, not only let me examine her father's papers and his important correspondence with Baden-Powell, but also insisted that I stay in her house in Santa Fe for several days while I did so. I am extraordinarily grateful for the hospitality her entire family showed me. Darwin Kelsey, curator of the American Scout Museum, which is about to open in Kentucky, provided me with microfilms of all of Baden-Powell's papers in the American Scout Archives, which I would not otherwise have been able to consult.

A number of friends at Columbia University and elsewhere endured with good nature my interminable talk about the Scouts while also finding time to read various drafts and chapters of the book, and I wish to express my appreciation to them. Among the many who followed the project with interest I must single out Peter R. Pouncey, Alfred Palca, J. W. Smit, and Kathryn Yatrakis, all of whom gave me the benefit of tough-minded but sympathetic readings of the manuscript. I am most particularly indebted to Edward W. Said, whose formidable learning and warm personal encouragement were always present when I needed them. He was unstinting from the start in his support of book and author alike. Thomas Edwards skillfully edited a slightly different form of chapter five, teaching me in the process how I might tighten other chapters as well. Martin Macnamara tracked down elusive references as my research assistant following my return from England. During the gradual evolution of my manuscript I was fortunate to find efficient typists who could somehow fathom my scrawled illegibilities, and I want to thank Paul Lipari, Holly Williams, and most notably Deborah Poole for their contribution to the book.

A portion of chapter three and a modified version of my discussion of the Scout Law originally appeared in the *Journal of Contemporary History* and *Raritan* respectively; I am grateful to both for permission to include them here.

I am also happy to thank my editor, Wendy Wolf, for her help. She guided me through the whole enterprise with tact and care, tempering my sometimes indiscriminate enthusiasms with her firm professionalism.

Finally, and most importantly, I want to acknowledge the sustenance I received from those people who shared with me over far too many years the daily tribulations of research and writing. Erik, Stephen, and Noah were enthusiastic backers from the very beginning. Noah in particular put up with fatherless summers with characteristic understanding and a minimum of complaint. The dedication constitutes, I am afraid, a rather lame attempt to express my appreciation to Judith Rosenthal for the role she played in this book. She cajoled, criticized, and comforted as appropriate, and never wavered in her belief in what I was doing. The book is in a very real sense a cooperative achievement; it never could have happened without her participation in every phase of its creation.

THE CHARACTER FACTORY

THE IMPERILED
ISLAND

This is a book about a man, the youth movement he created, and the culture whose aspirations the two both reflected and helped shape. Neither a biographical study of Lord Baden-Powell, the founder of the Scouts, nor a narrative history of Scouting—though both biography and the organization's history are important to it—it is rather an attempt to "read" the culture of Edwardian England through one of its representative institutions and the man who started it. Scouting has for so long been a familiar and well-loved part of the Western world that it appears always to have been with us, less a man-made creation than a natural, indigenous activity of our civilization. The worldwide spread of Scouting has tended to obscure the fact that it actually began in 1908 as a quintessentially British movement arising out of a specific set of social and historical circumstances unique to Edwardian England, whose needs it addressed and whose values permeated it. That it proved congenial in a variety of other cultural contexts only documents the brilliance of a scheme that had initially been forged to serve a distinct national purpose. To examine that purpose and the innumerable ways it expressed itself in the century's most popular youth movement is my aim here.

England was preoccupied during the second half of the nineteenth century, when Baden-Powell grew up, with maintaining its
empire. For a nation with a population in 1900 of (roughly) 40
million and an area of some 120,000 square miles, according to
figures cited by J. A. Hobson, to be controlling more than 11.5
million square miles of earth with over 345 million people, such a
preoccupation was inevitable.[1] The need to manage it, protect it,
cultivate its markets, and in general use it to further Britain's varied
self-interests necessarily made its well-being a prime national concern. The empire dominated much of the political agenda—domestic as well as foreign—of the period, created attractive career possibilities for the adventurous young administrator and soldier who
wanted to see the world, and generated a complex bureaucracy to
preside over its health. Equally important, though less acknowledged, the fact of empire helped shape the moral, social, and
political sensibilities of a country in ways not many at the time
understood. To subject more than 345 million people to the will of
Her Majesty's government by threat of force, justified through the
moral imperative to bring the blessings of peace and justice to
people in need of guidance, is not an enterprise that can be pursued
without substantial implications for the imperialists. It brings with
it an inescapable set of values and a comforting—if distorted—
world picture, in which everything has its preordained place. There
are the superior races and the inferior, those who are meant to rule
and those who are meant to obey, and a host of other moral
and intellectual distinctions attached to color of skin, slope of forehead, and the nature of gods worshiped that unarguably point to
the natural superiority of the nation with the best cannon and the
most accurate rifles. And to make it all palatable, there is even a
special rhetoric to turn the unpleasant facts of conquering and
exploitation into the burdens assumed by a selfless nation altruist-
ically dispensing the glories of its civilization to those who lack
them.

Born at the moment of one major crisis in the empire—the
Indian mutiny of 1857—and achieving national eminence during
another—the Boer War—at the climax of a military career of loyal
service in Africa, India, and Afghanistan, Baden-Powell was an
authentic product of the imperial sensibility. His ideas and point of
view bear the clear label "Made in Imperial England" upon them.
He internalized its values, spoke for its ideals, and devoted his
life, from the time he joined the 13th Hussars just out of Charterhouse, to defending its claims to various parts of the world. The
greatest contribution he made to its cause, however, was not his

military prowess but his fashioning an institution intended to produce efficient recruits for the empire for generations to come.

The Scouts were born in the anxieties of an imperial power at the turn of the century beginning to feel itself threatened both from without and from within—abroad, by the commercial competition offered by the expanding industrial capacity of the United States, Japan, and Germany, as well as the development of German military might; at home by the rumblings of the labor movement, union activity, and the specter they engendered of the working classes disturbing the serenity of a highly stratified society. The Boer War (1899-1902) succeeded in focusing both internal and external threats in a visible and disturbing way, and through the trauma it inflicted on British self-confidence, helped establish the mood of national crisis that was precisely the culture in which the Scouting idea could best grow.

For Scouting was from the very beginning conceived as a remedy to Britain's moral, physical, and military weakness—conditions that the Boer War seemed to announce—especially to Tory politicians, social imperialists, and military leaders—were threatening the empire. That it ultimately required close to 450,000 troops to subdue the 40,000 or so undisciplined Dutch farmers was indeed a grave indication of military frailty, but the lessons drawn from the war were far more embracing and serious than this: the whole empire was now seen to be vulnerable, precariously tied to a mother country that was itself tottering. Military ineptitude in the field was matched by domestic and industrial inefficiency at home; both were fostered by the decline of the manly British character previously responsible for the country's greatness. "You cannot maintain an A-1 Empire on C-3 men," as Baden-Powell was fond of reiterating (the phrase was originally Lloyd George's), and Britain suddenly looked around to find itself inundated with physically deficient men with pigeon chests, bad teeth, flat feet, and slack wills, lacking the passionate loyalty to British ideals that had helped to extend the empire over so much of the world's surface. Sir Frederick Maurice's reports, based on his study of army recruiting data, that three out of every five recruits were unfit for armed service came as a terrible revelation to a country that had always prided itself on the caliber of its men. The stout yeomen of yesteryear, on whom Britain had always seemed to depend in time of crisis, appeared upon examination to be mere memories of a grander time. And if the Boers could manage as well and as long as they did, who would be available to withstand the well-trained German hordes when they attacked?

It was not just a question of an efficient army but, more critical, an efficient citizenry. How could Britain hope to compete with the evolving industrial threat of other countries—not to speak of the possible military threats to its empire—with a race of morally and physically inferior men? Concern about rising crime rates (and falling birth rates, at least among the upper classes), sickly children, seditious unions, growing masses of urban poor, lack of discipline, and erosion of imperial purpose combined with the anxiety about the empire's military capacity to form a general obsession about national deterioration.

While these preoccupations by no means entirely originated with the Boer War, they were nourished by it, and it is only in their context that we can begin to appreciate fully the impulses behind the formation of the Scouts. Although the Scouts were very much the creation of one man, they were also as characteristically a part of Britain's urgent post-Boer War self-scrutiny as were the various royal commissions—on physical deterioration, on the conduct of the war in South Africa, on physical training in Scotland, on boy labor—that the times also spawned.

One of the benign myths surrounding the origins of Scouting concerns its spontaneous, unpremeditated development. As befits the founder of a movement that stresses the natural at the expense of the artificial, Baden-Powell preferred to think of its growth as an almost organic phenomenon. Having fashioned the idea, so he claimed, he merely threw the seeds out across the English country-side, watching with amazement as Scouts sprang up everywhere. "Like Topsy, it growed," Baden-Powell would say about his move-ment, "without any guiding human agency." Scouting in fact flour-ished from the very outset, but if its instant popularity surprised even Baden-Powell, there was nothing haphazard about it. By the time he ran his demonstration camp at Brownsea Island in the summer of 1907, Baden-Powell, together with C. Arthur Pearson, the newspaper publisher and savvy public-relations expert, had labored diligently to ensure the widest possible interest in Scouting. He had lectured on his Scouting idea throughout England, obtained the support of other youth organizations, made appropri-ate contacts among the military and political establishment, and worked out an effective publicity strategy. Baden-Powell's prepar-ations were exhaustive and intelligent. When Scouting was officially given to the world, with the appearance of the first of the six fortnightly parts of *Scouting for Boys* on 15 January 1908, he had done everything he could to generate a positive public response.

No amount of entrepreneurial flair, of course, could have produced

PREVENTION BETTER THAN CURE				
NATIONAL INEFFICIENCIES	CAUSES	ORIGIN	PREVENTIVE	SCOUT TRAINING AS REMEDY
				Additional to Scholastic Education—a systemised development of:
Irreligion. Indiscipline. Want of Patriotism. Corruption. Disregard of Others. Cruelty.	Indifference to Higher Conscience.			(I) CHARACTER through Good Environment. Sense of Duty. Self-discipline. Responsibility. Resourcefulness. Handicrafts. God through Nature Study. Religion in Practice. Fair Play. Helpfulness to Others. Personal Service for the Country.
Crimes of Violence. Lunacy. Thriftlessness and Poverty.	Drink.	Want of Self-discipline	Education in: **(I) CHARACTER**	
Show Off. Loafing and Shirking. Low Moral Standards. Gambling. Illegitimacy. Disease.	Self-indulgence.		and in	
Ill-health. Squalor. Infant Mortality. Mental Deficiency. Physical Deficiency.	Irresponsibility and Ignorance on part of Parents.	Want of Hygienic and Physical Knowledge	**(II) PHYSICAL HEALTH**	(II) HEALTH through Outdoor *Practices*, not mere Drill. Responsibility for own Physical Development up to Standard. Health and Hygiene in Practice.

anything as brilliantly successful as Scouting if the movement itself had not been congenial to a broad spectrum of the nation. It was efficiently marketed but no less well conceived to meet a need— or at least a perceived need—in a way that would be enthusiastically received by adults as well as boys. The social utility that would enlist the support of the adult world had to be embodied in a fresh and exciting organization that would catch the imagination of the young. Furthermore, unlike the already existing Boys' Brigade, whose principled commitment to explicit church affiliation, Bible class, and military drill inevitably restricted its appeal, the Scouts were intended from the beginning as a mass movement with no barriers to membership. Baden-Powell wanted to catch every boy in Britain, an aim that demanded great tact and considerable political subtlety. There were to be no rough edges on which people could hang major moral or philosophical objections, no problems of Edwardian life that Scouting could not address. Baden-Powell was fond of using charts in Scouting literature to illustrate the numerous specific ways in which Scouting would remedy Britain's ills. As his schematic assurances make clear, Scout training, rightly understood and liberally applied, could bring about the regeneration of the nation. Whether the concern was poverty, drink, labor unrest, faulty education, unemployment, self-abuse, narrow chests or weak character, Scouting confronted the issues and provided the answers. In a culture that came to prize notions of "national efficiency" as the means of its salvation, Baden-Powell was shrewd enough to offer his Scouts as the safest and surest antidote to the inefficiencies plaguing the empire. It was no surprise, with this guarantee, that Scouting should have received a royal charter in 1912.

While Scouting's identification with the simple pleasures of outdoor living certainly constituted one of its attractive features, it should not lead us into overlooking Scouting's powerful ideology, an ideology intent on producing, out of the morally dubious, unformed lower-class youths, a certain kind of serviceable citizen for the empire. In a telling image, Baden-Powell cuts through the rhetoric about selfhood and the joys of woodcraft that have always been associated with the movement in the popular mind to define his sense of Scouting's purpose:

> Our business is not merely to keep up smart "show" troops, but to pass as many boys through our character factory as we possibly can: at the same time, the longer the grind that we can give them the better men they will be in the end.[2]

Factories manufacture uniform products under detailed specifications for particular uses. While the Scout factory for the turning out of serviceable citizens could not vouch for the uniformity of its finished product, its aspirations for such uniformity were nonetheless real. Both specifications and uses, in this case, were supplied by a coherent ideology stressing unquestioning obedience to properly structured authority; happy acceptance of one's social and economic position in life; and an unwavering, uncritical patriotism, for which one would be willing, if necessary, to die, as the key both to social utility and personal fulfillment.

With its emphasis on submission and discipline, on curbing the impulses of the self in the service of the community as a whole—in short, on the supreme virtue of social conformity—it is an ideology firmly rooted in the self-interest of the upper classes. There is nothing strange about this. The history of working-class reform movements in the nineteenth century, whether for boys or adults, was precisely the history of those enjoying the benefits of a class society reaching down to implant those habits of obedience, cleanliness, temperance, and loyalty that would best guarantee their own happy, stable self-perpetuation. Baden-Powell's efforts, through the Scouts, to inculcate in the lower-class boys those values and character ideals that the more privileged received in the public schools were simply another instance of that process. It is worth emphasizing, with all that has been written about Scouting's universality and apolitical nature, that an attempt to bring public school ideals to the poor was not a disembodied, altruistic exercise, but a thoroughly political act with significant social consequences. Victorian and Edwardian youth organizations—and the Scouts were no exception—clearly saw themselves as agencies of social control, designed to monitor the conduct of their members and shape it into forms acceptable to the middle- and upper-class perspectives of their founders. As R. A. Bray, one of the prominent Edwardian youth specialists, noted in 1911, "The miscellaneous associations represented by clubs, lads' brigades, boy scouts and the like, have all been called into existence for the express purpose of exerting some measure of control over the transition period of life which separates the boy from the man."[3] H. S. Pelham in *The Training of a Working Boy* (1914), shared the urgency of providing the lad with proper guidance:

He is going to be a man one day. In his hands lie the future
of the city, the country, and the church to which he belongs.
His own future, therefore, is one of paramount importance to

> Church and State.... Surely men of education and wealth
> should learn that perhaps the greatest service they can render
> to the State is to train the future citizen by bringing to bear
> upon him when he is young and unsettled the influence of a
> strong and healthy character.[4]

For Baden-Powell and the others, the basis of good character and
good citizenship—indeed, what in most cases appears to be their
sole constituent—was a firm sense of discipline. To teach a boy to
follow orders was to render him useful to both employer and nation,
thereby bringing him to the highest possible pitch of moral perfection. "A dull lad who can obey orders is better than a sharp one
who cannot,"[5] writes Baden-Powell, and all of Scouting can properly be understood—as Baden-Powell himself understood it—as an
organization expressly designed to churn out admirably obedient
lads. While the Scout Law is interesting in a number of ways, it is
above all else a marvelously variegated paean to the value of obedience. Calling for Scouts to obey orders without question, to obey
them cheerfully, and particularly to obey them when they have
pledged on their honor to do so; to be loyal to king, officers, country, and their employers; to do their duty before anything else; and,
in addition, to promise to obey all these commitments to obedience,
Scouting sought to guarantee for society the complete submissive-
ness of its members.

Glorification of discipline was crucial to the theory and rhetoric
of youth reformers, whose guiding vision was always of a well-
ordered community in which each individual happily fulfilled his
assigned role. In a world in which corporate loyalty is the highest
good, it follows that the independent, inquiring self, asking questions and searching for ways to express its own creative impulses
could only be viewed as a threat to salutary social compliance. For
Baden-Powell, the self is a source of selfishness, nothing more.

Equally threatening was the individual who wished to challenge
the social system by moving beyond his appointed place in it. One
of the delicate problems faced by all youth workers was the need to
encourage industrious work habits on the part of the lower class
while not permitting any unhealthy desires for self-betterment to
fester. People had to work hard, but also be content with their lot
and not ravaged by fantasies of moving up the social ladder. A
snob, as Baden-Powell cautions in the fourth law, is not just one
who looks down on the poor, but also a poor man who "resents
another because he is rich." As Arnold Freeman indicates in *Boy
Life and Labour*, "The working class must be taught to accommodate

themselves happily to those straitened circumstances of manual labour for which Nature seems to have fitted them."[6] Freeman's natural explanation of the poverty of the working class was matched by Charles Russell's invocation of even higher forces to account for the restricted work opportunities open to the poor. Applauding the fact that the honest working-class lad destined for the factory has come to look with scorn at the effeminate junior clerk who has pursued a more socially acceptable position, and whose "soft and ... useless hands he finds ridiculous," Russell continues,

> On the whole this is a healthy spirit. It means that working-class lads are becoming content to remain and to rise in position—an honourable position—in which it has pleased Providence to place them, and to make the best of it.[7]

In these celebrations of the natural and divine powers that have decreed that a certain segment of the population should be confined to the poorer-paying jobs, we hear the self-interested voice of the middle-class defending its turf while managing to justify the inequalities of a rigid class system.[8] It is a voice we hear repeatedly dealing with social problems in the early twentieth century, and as the founder of the century's largest youth movement, it is very decidedly Baden-Powell's as well. A number of significant metaphors occur repeatedly in Baden-Powell's writing, but unquestionably the most revealing is the exhortation to "be a brick," which brings together in one phrase the ideological tendencies I have been discussing here:

BE A BRICK

This means you should remember that being one fellow among many others, you are like one brick among many others in the wall of a house.

If you are discontented with your place or with your neighbours or if you are a rotten brick, you are no good to the wall. You are rather a danger. If the bricks get quarreling among themselves the wall is liable to split and the whole house to fall.

Some bricks may be high up and others low down in the wall; but all must make the best of it and play in their place for the good of the whole. So it is among people; each of us has his place in the world, it is no use being discontented, it is no use hating our neighbours because they are higher up or lower down than themselves. We are all Britons, and it is our duty each to play in his place and help his neighbours. Then we shall remain strong and united, and then there will be no fear of the whole building—namely, our great Empire—falling down because of rotten bricks in the wall.[9]

While the combining of bricks with his other great metaphoric cluster—the need "to play the game"—might produce minor architectural problems, it does at least indicate nicely the basic structure of Baden-Powell's social thinking. If it could be argued that the bricks high up in the wall essentially have no greater opportunities for movement or fulfillment than those lower down—a situation not altogether applicable to British society in the early twentieth century—the message was nevertheless clear: Stay where you belong, don't envy those who have more than you, and don't weaken the intricate social fabric by aspiring to climb out of your appropriate slot. Nothing is more disedifying than the spectacle of grumbling bricks, or more threatening to the stability of the wall. Unwarranted aspiration can lead to jealousy and discontent—the symptoms of the "Kultur of selfishness"[10] that Scouting was out to eliminate. Working doggedly to keep the edifice of empire from crumbling was purpose enough in life.

Although Baden-Powell always maintained that he organized the movement merely as a kind of training which might be adopted by various existing youth organizations, such as the Boys' Brigade, Church Lads' Brigade, YMCA, and others, larger ambitions for his scheme were playing upon him from the start. What Baden-Powell had in mind was never a simple set of rules and games but rather a coherent, self-contained system of education intended to shape the entire life of the boy and to implant in him a set of values and even emotional responses that would make him most useful to the state. In its ideal embodiment Scouting was not just an organization a boy joined but a total ideology that he absorbed and that thereafter determined his thinking, feeling, and acting. Aiming originally at the boy between eleven and fifteen, Baden-Powell was almost immediately chafing at the limits he set for himself. If it was the whole boy he wanted, why not begin the indoctrination sooner and extend the relationship longer, thereby assuring a product more deeply steeped in the system? The Wolf Cubs in 1916 and the Rovers in 1922 were his answers. (While Scouting was originally intended for boys only, girls enthusiastically embraced the idea from the beginning. By 1909, at the time of the Crystal Palace

Rally when eleven thousand Scouts marched, there were already six thousand girls registered as Boy Scouts. Realizing the marvelous possibilities this presented of organizing the girls, Baden-Powell set out with his sister, Agnes, to provide them with their own independent organization; in 1912, with the publication of the *Handbook for Girl Guides*—essentially a rewritten version of *Scouting for Boys*—the Girl Guides movement was officially launched.) Both the youth division and the senior wing, which also found their way into the Girl Guide movement, testified to the grand nature of Baden-Powell's vision, his desire to build a totally inclusive organization that would take the formative boy and girl and keep them there until they were ready to step into a leadership role as a young adult. In *Scouting for Boys*, he indicates that out of a total of 2 million boys, there were only 270,000 under good influences. That left 1.73 million who "are drifting towards 'hooliganism' or bad citizenship for want of hands to guide them the right way towards being useful. It is this remainder, nearly two million boys, that we want to tackle and reduce."[11] He wanted them all—and from the very beginning. During the time when plans were being formulated for establishing the Cub movement, the editor of the *Headquarters Gazette*, lamenting that there seemed to be no way to cast the net even wider, consoled himself with the thought that "It is quite possible that the genius of the Chief may invent some new order for infants, so that our training may, one day, commence with the cradle...."[12] While such a triumph was never to be, the fantasy logically fulfilled Baden-Powell's conception of Scouting's role and scope.

Scouting's therapeutic and didactic mission, the creation of a physically healthy, morally sound, and politically reliable generation of young men prepared to follow orders whenever they might be given, was eagerly embraced by a country anxiously contemplating its uncertain future. We have been comfortable with the Scouts for such a long time that it is easy to forget what a dramatic innovation they were and how much was expected of them. The reporter for the *Morning Post* was not by any means unique in suggesting, in 1913, that

> It is possible to believe that when the historian of this age comes to review its salient events he will, while passing lightly over many things that loom large upon the present day horizon, point to the Boy Scout movement as one of the most potent and significant developments of Twentieth Century civilisation—as an influence that has powerfully shaped society and helped to solve social problems; as an acorn,

sown by the passing breeze, from which a mighty oak has sprung.[13]

Hailed as a redemptive force that might well change the course of British history, it constituted, for Lord Rosebery, the moral inspiration for an entire nation:

> If I was to form the highest ideal for my country it would be this, that it should be a nation of which the manhood was exclusively composed of men who had been or were Boy Scouts, and who were trained in the Boy Scout theory. Such a nation would be the honour of mankind. It would be the greatest moral force that the world has ever known.[14]

For an institution that attempted so much, and that managed to center itself squarely in British culture almost from its conception, it is startling that so few have seriously considered what it all meant. Such immunity from critical scrutiny has left Scouting almost entirely in the hands of its own historians and publicists, a situation that is not helpful in trying to understand the origins and meaning of any movement. While affiliation with a movement does not preclude the possiblity of seeing it clearly, it can obscure matters, pitting loyalty against the need for the dispassionate view. This is particularly true of Scouting, where adult involvement has always been something of a calling and where reverence for the founder is perpetuated as a kind of sacred trust, to be protected from any taint or blemish. Thus Scout accounts of Scouting (which are effectively the only ones) are all marred by a strong hagiographical impulse, the insistence on seeing Baden-Powell in all his selflessness as a secular saint, forging an organization perfect in all its parts. Institutions, like cultures, tend to generate their own creation myths, and Scouting's official view of itself is structured around any number of them: Baden-Powell as the irrepressible boy-man,[15] gaily forming a youth movement that embodied his own exuberance about the pleasures of the outdoor life; the natural, unaided growth of the movement; its goal of fostering self-reliance among its members; its indifference to notions of color and class, to name a few.

These myths obscure what is fascinating about the Scouts: the movement's goals, values, and the fabric of assumptions underlying them; the way its ideology responded to the myriad needs of an empire in distress; the method by which Baden-Powell sold his Scouts to the public—in short, the complex relationship between the Scouts and the society around them. To look at such a relationship and take Baden-Powell's ideas more seriously than they have been taken before is itself a slightly heretical enterprise. In the most recent, comprehensive—and authorized—study of Baden-Powell, published in 1964, William Hillcourt argues that "Baden-Powell was fundamentally a man of action," so that "a book about him must therefore be mainly a book of action."[16] Such an assumption, in my view, misses what is most interesting about Baden-Powell. While by no means an intellectual or original thinker in any sense, he was certainly a man who dealt with ideas, with an exceptional ability to cull from a variety of sources those he wanted and to use them effectively in appealing to a mass audience of young and old alike. We tend to forget, for example, that by any reckoning Baden-Powell must be judged one of the most prolific and successful popular writers of the twentieth century. Author of more than fifty books and pamphlets, as well as innumerable articles and addresses, he was indefatigable in dispensing his Scout ideology throughout the country and the world. *Scouting for Boys* alone probably makes him, after Shakespeare, the most widely read British writer of all time. However daring a man of action Baden-Powell might have been, the Scouts were not fashioned through an act of will nor maintained through physical courage.

In exploring the connections between man, movement, and culture, I have avoided any strictly chronological organization, approaching the relationship instead from a variety of thematic perspectives. And while my focus is primarily on the origins and initial developments of Scouting, I have felt free to move beyond them into the post–World War I period when argument and evidence lead me there. Beginning, then, with Baden-Powell himself— and particularly his formative experiences in the Boer War—I trace the evolution of the idea of Scouting as it gradually unfolded between 1904 and 1907, looking closely at the influence on Baden-Powell's thinking of Ernest Thompson Seton, the American naturalist, who always felt that he, not Baden-Powell deserved credit as the real founder of the Scout movement. I then consider the public school ideals behind the notion of Scout character training; the major instrument of that training, the Scout Law; and the alleged state of national deterioration that the law purported to remedy. *Scouting for Boys*, of course, is the central repository of Scout values; more than a handbook of practical instruction, it is a text rich with implication, meriting the careful critical reading I next give it here. The following two chapters—on the vexed issues of Scouting's militarism, and the way in which Scouting fits into the framework of other late nineteenth- and early twentieth-century youth movements—examine some of Scouting's moral, social, and political meanings in the context of Edwardian concerns. I conclude with a discussion of how Scouting's avowed principles concerning race, religion, and color worked out in practice, and with an assessment of what the "Emperor of Youth" finally accomplished.

I have not attempted to deal with any of the varied international manifestations of Scouting, or with the large American organization. Interesting as they are, they all necessarily represent adaptations or applications into different cultures of Baden-Powell's original idea and as such are unconnected to my central purpose. I assume, of course, that readers interested in these other movements will consider for themselves the ways in which they are illuminated by British Scout ideology and practice.

I have also not felt it useful in any of these chapters to include the personal experiences of individual Scouts, however fascinating they might be in their own right. It is primarily the theory and ideology behind the movement that interest me, not the point of view of a particular Scout enrolled in a particular patrol. In a movement as large and decentralized as this, there is no way of knowing whether theory and ideology informed all parts of the organization equally. Nor is it important. It is highly unlikely that all the early Scouts felt their characters were being molded in a certain direction for a specific purpose, or even that all Scoutmasters understood precisely what was expected of them. Scouts had good and bad experiences, formative ones and otherwise, for a multitude of reasons, none of which necessarily bears on the issue of what Scouting intended to achieve or what values it expressed. Even if we could manage to digest the enormous variety of personal Scouting accounts, they would still not tell us much about the institution Baden-Powell established to catch and train the rising generation of youth. To begin to understand that we should properly start by considering the nature of the Chief Scout himself.

1

THE CHIEF
SCOUT

For the adoring biographer, the day was a watershed in the history of civilization:

> In a quiet street, on the north side of Hyde Park, that blessed breathing space of London babies and London birds, was born on the 22nd of February, 1857, a baby whose future career was destined to have perhaps more widely reaching effect than that of any man since the founder of Christianity.
>
> No "star of the east" heralded his coming. There was nothing miraculous about his birth and babyhood; yet there are literally millions of people in the world to-day who are the better for Robert Baden-Powell having been born. There are few—whether prophets, kings or statesmen—about whom as much could be said.[1]

For Henrietta Grace Powell, wife of the Reverend Baden Powell, Savilian Professor of Geometry at Oxford, on the other hand, the birth of her eighth child could hardly have been considered unusual. Since her marriage ten years earlier at twenty-one to the forty-nine-year-old professor, producing children regularly had been her major responsibility. Two more, indeed, were to follow. (Prior to Baden-Powell's birth the next three youngest children had all died: Henrietta in 1854, John in 1855, and Jessie in 1856.) The newest baby was named Robert Stephenson Smyth Powell, or "Stephe" for short. The first two names honored his godfather, son of the inventor of the first successful steam locomotive, while the "Smyth" continued Henrietta Grace's family name. Although not wealthy, the family was well connected. Henrietta's father, Adm. William Henry Smyth, insisted on seeing himself descended from Capt. John Smith of Pocahontas fame, a claim that later only Baden-Powell seemed to take seriously. Professor Powell, who wrote copiously on a range of subjects including theology, physics, mathematics and philosophy, moved with ease among the intellectuals of the day. His friends included John Ruskin, William Thackeray, Robert Browning, T. H. Huxley, Dean Stanley, and Benjamin Jowett, among others. Young Stephe treasured a shilling that Thackeray had given him one evening to cajole him back upstairs when, age three, he began a forbidden descent to an adult party. The children rode, sailed on their yacht, engaged in spirited family theatricals, and in general enjoyed the perquisites of solid Victorian respectability.

The tranquil security was threatened in 1860, when Professor Powell suddenly died, leaving Henrietta to raise not only her seven children but two of the four from his earlier marriage as well. The resources were slim but adequate, and Henrietta set out with a fierce determination to provide proper opportunities—educational and otherwise—for all of them. She was unrelenting both in her aspirations for their success and in demands from them. The close-knit family that emerged always recognized her as its shaping influence, revering her for her strength and energy. Baden-Powell remained particularly attached to her, writing her regularly (more than two thousand letters over the course of her lifetime) and keeping detailed, illustrated diaries of all that he did so that she could share his experiences. Motherhood for Baden-Powell was a sacred institution. He wrote frequently about the depth of feeling he had for his mother, seeing in that relationship a model of moral inspiration available to all men with loving mothers:

> A really good manly fellow is seldom to be found who was not also a good son to his mother. There is only one pain greater than that of losing your mother, and that is the pain your mother would suffer if she lost you. I do not mean by

death, but by your own misdeeds. Has it ever struck you what it means to your mother if you turn out a "wrong un" or a waster?—she who bore you and brought you up, she who taught you your first steps, your prayers, your straight ideas, and was glad when you showed that you could do things? .... All her loving work and expectation have been thrown away, and the pain she suffers by seeing you slide off into the wrong road is worse than if she had lost you in death. Make your career a success whatever line you take up and you will rejoice her heart. Make her happy in any way you can—you owe it to her, and, if she dies, it will be your greatest comfort to think that, at any rate, you did your best for her and were a credit to her while she lived.[2]

Under her able ministrations the family prospered. By the time Stephe was eight, Frank, Warrington, and George had left for careers and schools, leaving Stephe as the senior member of the younger triad consisting of himself, Agnes, and Baden. (The fourth older brother, Augustus, died in 1863.) The future Chief Scout demonstrated a precocious artistic ability from an early age, drawing equally well with either hand. Henrietta was concerned about this unusual talent and consulted Ruskin to assuage her anxieties that something might be wrong. After scrutinizing the young artist at work, Ruskin assured Henrietta that her son was not suffering from anything other than a legitimate case of ambidexterity. He remained a competent artist with both hands throughout his life.

In 1869, Henrietta took a step that was to have unexpected consequences for Scouting. She decided that her esteem for her late husband required that Baden be added to Powell, an act that occurred on 21 September of that year. This was fine for everybody, except perhaps the youngest son, Baden, who had now to endure Baden Baden Powell, a dreadful combination made slightly better by the subsequent addition of a hyphen, an adjustment that launched Robert Stephenson Smyth Powell on the road to Baden-Powell, thereby planting the seeds for the Scout motto, which he fashioned after his initials.

Hyphen firmly in place, Baden-Powell went off to Charterhouse in 1870 with a scholarship as a Gownboy Foundationer. Still occupying the old Carthusian monastery buildings in London where it had opened as a school more than 250 years earlier (it moved 2 years later to Godalming), Charterhouse stood proudly alongside Eton, Winchester, Harrow, Rugby, and the others as part of that great national combine of English public schools devoted to training

England's leaders. With its lack of regard for genuine intellectual development, its love of sports, and its commitment to building the character of its students in certain prescribed ways, Charterhouse found in Baden-Powell, or "Bathing-Towel" as he was popularly known, an enthusiastic disciple. Baden-Powell flourished there and carried his love of the place and its values with him all his life. In the midst of his Mafeking exploits during the Boer War he was distressed, so he wrote his mother, that he could not find a fellow Carthusian with whom to have dinner in celebration of Founder's Day.

Baden-Powell had a happy, diversified time at Charterhouse. He played goalkeeper on the football team, helped organize the rifle team, wrote for the school paper, sang in the chorus, played the violin, and in his senior year was appointed second monitor of his house. Generally popular with his schoolmates, he nevertheless managed to avoid making any close friends, a trait that, with one exception, remained true of him throughout his life. Academically he muddled through without distinction. Some sample class reports from 1874 suggest a student basically indifferent to schoolwork:

Classics: Seems to take very little interest in his work.

Mathematics: Has to all intents given up the study of mathematics.

Modern Languages: Could do well, but has become very lazy; often sleeps in class.

Natural Science: Fair—12th out of 15.

His lack of interest in his schoolwork contrasted with his passion for the stage. Baden-Powell was a natural exhibitionist, and with the explicit encouragement of Dr. Haig-Brown, the headmaster, who felt that the stage was a useful instrument in the shaping of character, he immersed himself in all kinds of dramatic activities. He sang well, was a splendid mimic, and had the capacity to project himself effectively into a range of different comic roles. *The Carthusian* in 1873 praised his performance as Cox in Sullivan's *Cox and Box* (a role he later estimated that he played on at least twenty-six occasions) and went on to note his triumphs in *Toby Whistler, or the Wandering Minstrel, Little Toddlekins*, and *Taming a Tiger*, among others. Baden-Powell endorsed Haig-Brown's view of the importance of the theater, "convinced that the play-acting which was encouraged among us boys ... was of great value to us in the afterlife."[3] He never lost interest in performing and participated not just in numerous school productions, but in a variety of amateur theatrical events throughout his army career as well. His rare ability to create a compelling public persona, especially during the critical period of the Mafeking defense, certainly drew upon those talents as an actor nourished years before by Charterhouse. In addition to instilling confidence and enabling one to handle an audience effectively, impersonation, as he points out, has another value, too: "It can in a way be educative for certain lines of life. The ability to disguise yourself to give the impression that you are someone other than yourself, and to carry it through successfully, is a gift that can be of infinite value for 'intelligence' purposes."[4]

With the move of Charterhouse out of London to the rural Godalming, Baden-Powell also discovered the joys of solitary existence in the countryside, from which he derived intense satisfaction all his life. The Copse, a densely wooded area off bounds to Charterhouse students, offered young Stephe a chance to enjoy his delicious solitude and indulge his fantasies:

> It was here that I used to imagine myself a backwoodsman, trapper and Scout. I used to creep about warily looking for "signs" and getting "close-up" observation of rabbits, squirrels, rats, and birds.
>
> As a trapper I set my snares, and when I caught a rabbit or hare (which wasn't often) I learned by painful experience to skin, clean and cook him. But knowing that the Redskins were about, in the shape of masters looking for boys out of bounds, I used a very small non-smoky fire for fear of giving away my whereabouts.[5]

The Charterhouse years from 1870 to 1876 were thus pleasant ones for Baden-Powell. He enjoyed the camaraderie and the games and imbibed the school spirit without being taxed intellectually. The dire foreboding expressed in his autobiography, that if something were not done about the tendency of the artificial to overwhelm the natural in life, "our boys will grow brains instead of brawn,"[6] did not owe anything to his Charterhouse experience. Brains were seen as properly subordinate to brawn here, and Baden-Powell's mediocre performance as a student disturbed neither the school nor himself. It did, however, interfere mightily with his plans to go to Oxford. He was turned down by the classicist Jowett of Balliol in May 1876 as "not quite up to Balliol form"—

a rejection all the more remarkable for Jowett being his godfather—
as well as by Christ Church, where his mathematics examiner,
Charles Dodgson, more popularly known as Lewis Carroll, exposed
his lamentable ignorance in that subject.

But Baden-Powell was not one to lament passively his failings,
and if Oxford were not accessible to him there were other options
to explore. In July of the same year he sat for an open examination
for direct commissions to both the infantry and the cavalry.
Baden-Powell was vacationing with his family on the Isle of Wight
when he heard the news: out of 718 candidates, he had placed fifth
for infantry and second for cavalry. While he had never been particularly interested in a military career, the opportunity suddenly
seemed attractive. His high placement on the examination meant
that he would not have to spend the customary two years at the
military college at Sandhurst; after serious family consultation,
Baden-Powell decided in favor of the cavalry as opposed to the less
romantic infantry. On 30 October, 1876, Baden-Powell sailed out
of Portsmouth on the *Serapis* to join the 13th Hussars in India,
initiating a relationship with the military that was not to end until
1910, when he retired to devote all his time to the Scout movement.

Baden-Powell embraced the life of the young subaltern enthusiastically, determined to make a success of his career. He attended
diligently to the mundane routines of his profession, turning out for
parades and mastering the drill exercises, cavalry instruction, and
rifle practice to which he was exposed. In addition to doing what
the military expected of him, Baden-Powell proved adept at
"grouping events," a form of gamesmanship Henrietta insisted all
her children master to aid their progress through life. Put simply,
"grouping events" required maximizing the benefits of all fortunate
occurrences by consciously striving to create other advantageous
circumstances around them. Writing a book for example, a good
thing in itself, can have particularly positive consequences if intel-
ligently grouped, as he reflects to his brother George when thinking
about publishing his volume entitled *Reconnaissance and Scouting* in
1854:[7]

> Moreover if it did not even sell to the extent of 20 copies it
> would be a grand advertisement for me—because I could send
> copies to all the boss quartermaster-genls., Wolseleys, etc.,
> asking if they approve of it, etc. (28 April 1884)

Writing a book and dedicating it to H. R. H. the duke of Connaught, whose favor you are currying, as Baden-Powell did in the

instance of his book on pigsticking, is an even better application of grouping. Henrietta must have been delighted to learn how well her prize pupil, just a young captain, had learned his lessons in cultivating contacts. Writing to her in February 1884, he indicates he is

> back at Meerut on account of a small event grouped. You see the regt. started to march to Muttra on the 14th. The Duke, Duchess, Lord and Lady Downe coming out to our first camp and lunching with us. Then the 3rd day out I got 3 days leave to return to Meerut to play act in "Cox & Box" & "Whitebait at Greenwich"—I am staying with the Duke for these 3 days, taking meals with the Duke. Last night after dinner en famille we all went off to a dance.... (5 February)

By 16 March, grouping has brought him even closer to the duke:

> I am getting along well & am satisfied with the result of my grouping this particular event in which fortune has helped me too, in making me ill just when Lady Downe was going away so that she insisted on my coming to live in her house—my own grouping idea ... was to get an extra month at Meerut under the Duke's eye and if possible on his staff by applying to the Staff College but luck has come to my aid in addition to my grouping ... here I'm living close to HRH seeing him every day (he was sitting in my room talking to me while I dressed this morning) .... (To Mother)

The results of this combination of grouping and good luck are conveyed excitedly to his mother four days later:

> Look at the above crest and guess where I am and what I am doing there. Well I'm sitting in the Duke's office and doing the work of his A. D. C.!
> There my dear Ma—what do you think of that? Last night I had to receive the guests to dinner and sit at the head of the table—ride out in the early morning with the Duke and Duchess ....Then I lunch with the Duke and Duchess—ask people to lawn tennis there in the evening, etc. etc. What do you think of that? But it is only for a few days while Downe is away—still it is *so* much developped at any rate.

As important for his future as grouping, he also acquired as a young officer his lifelong passion for the two activities he thought constituted the supreme achievements in sport: polo playing and pigsticking. His delight and skill in the former led to the addition of "Baden-Polo" to the list of nicknames—including "Bathing-Towel" and "Baking-Powder," among others—he had to endure through various phases of his life. Polo was an essential social undertaking for the aspiring young British officer in India, and Baden-Powell carefully managed his meager budget to build up slowly a stock of polo ponies. He became quite proficient at the game, seeing in its basic strategy an important lesson for making one's way in life—direct confrontation is always less effective than the artful approach from the side: "I have often urged my young friends, when faced with an adversary, to 'play polo' with him; i.e., not to go at him bald-headed but to ride side by side with him and gradually edge him off your track."[8]

But more satisfying even than polo was pigsticking, or boar hunting, which remained for Baden-Powell the most glorious of all sports. His infatuation with it was rapid, and he became its chief apologist as well as one of its most skilled practitioners, winning the highly sought-after Kadir Cup in 1883, and publishing his definitive *Pigsticking or Hog Hunting* in 1889. His statistics were impressive. In 1882 he managed to dispatch over thirty boars, raising that number to forty-two in 1883.

From the outset the army proved as congenial as Charterhouse had been. Baden-Powell's humor and good spirits made him popular with his men, the work was not particularly taxing, and sufficient leisure existed for sketching, writing, and of course his beloved polo and pigsticking. He traveled, hunted, and developed those Scouting techniques he had first practiced in the Copse. If he was not getting rich, he was at least living reasonably well without draining any of the carefully husbanded Baden-Powell family resources. It seemed that Jowett and Charles Dodgson had done him a favor in seeing that he did not attend Oxford.

Only one major concern disturbed this thoroughly pleasant existence: Baden-Powell's anxieties about his own career advancement. While his later exhortation to lower-class youth to "be a Brick" argued that as long as you are doing your part in holding up the wall of empire, it didn't matter where you were placed, it is clear that such advice was intended exclusively for export to the masses. Baden-Powell had no doubts whatever that he preferred a position at the very top of the wall and attempted to plot his career accordingly. He moved quite rapidly—captain at twenty-six, brevet major at thirty-one, brevet lieutenant-colonel at thirty-eight, and full colonel and commander of his own regiment (the 5th Dragoon

Guards) at forty—and never stopped thinking strategically about his own interests. Letters to his family indicate the seriousness with which he took the shaping of his own career.[9] Weighing the benefits of accepting an offer to go to Malta as a military secretary, he writes to George, "The pay, etc., is much the same as I am getting now and experiences the same. The name is, I think, better; and perhaps a stepping stone to later appointment in India, Canada, etc." (28 May, 1888).

> By and by—1891—the berth of Commandant of School of Auxiliary Cavalry will fall vacant, and although not really such a well-paid billet as this ... it gives one a field for energies—and brings one in contact (at Aldershot) with the best men and is a stepping stone to Brig. It is just *the* billet to suit me. I have told Morrison, the present Commandt. to let me know the moment he thinks of giving it up.... (To George, February 1889)
>
> As for Baker Russell—yes! His Brigade Major is just what I want to be—of all appointments in the Army. I have told him so too. (To Mother, 16 March 1889)

Explaining why he wants a change of personnel in the 13th Hussars to occur after a certain date, he writes to his mother,

> On 1st July Col. Spilling will be gazetted out of the Regt. and I shall get my majority—then Courtney will go and his successor, Close, will come in at the bottom of the majority, i.e. below me, and *there* will be a second step for me. *If,* however, Courtney goes *before* 1st July, (on Spilling's retirement) I should be *below* Close; i.e. 3rd major instead of 2nd which might put me 4 or 5 years back in getting command of the Regt. I have written to Spilling to ask him to do something for me in the way of getting the exchange between Courtney and Close postponed till after 1st July. (5 April 1891)

Having been proposed for promotion to Brigadier General in India only to find that the authorities "at home did not sanction it (on account of my youth)," he comforts his mother that "the fact of having been proposed is a great feather in my little cap—and promises well for the future.... As it is, I am very content to go on as I am for the present and to blossom out 2 or 3 years hence" (25 April 1899).

Part of Baden-Powell's concern for the development of his career had to do with his lack of active field service. From the time he joined the cavalry until 1888, with the exception of one minor incident in Afghanistan in 1881, when in the turmoil of a possible bandit raid he managed to shoot himself in the leg with his own revolver, he had seen no real action. The year 1888 brought with it an appointment in South Africa as aide-de-camp and acting military secretary to his uncle, Gen. H. A. Smyth, where he had the excitement of leading a column of mounted men against a rebel chief, who unfortunately fled before any real fighting took place, but otherwise his military career had included no genuine soldiering. Baden-Powell felt the lack of it keenly, longing to experience the exhilaration of battle as well as worrying that the absence of war service might lessen his chances of promotion.

His letters home yearn for a jolly war in which he could prove himself.[10] Writing from Cape Town, on 24 January 1885, he tells his mother that he is "happy as can be—much more pleased than I thought I should be—*but* still look out and apply for me if there is a war anywhere. Just now there seems the best chance of it here in South Africa." He confides to her on 5 February 1888, that "altogether, I am having good fun—but—it isn't work: it does not get me on: if only the Boers or Zulus would kick up a row I should be happy." And again on 15 February: "I am in constant dread of a telegram to say that war has broken out somewhere, and I am here, out of the way of it. I hope G [his brother George] will look out on my behalf whenever there *is* chance of war, and get me recalled by Lord Wolseley for machine gun duty, etc."

> You know it is disastrous to one's getting on, this want of war service: and also I have got such a beastly desire to be up and doing out of the stagnation here—while I still have the youth and activity for hard work. (15 June 1891)

Baden-Powell's great opportunity finally arrived in 1895 when he was ordered to the Gold Coast on Sir Francis Scott's staff to participate in a campaign against the Ashanti and their impudent young king, Prempeh, who had been breaking terms of previous treaties, practising human sacrifice, and, in flouting British authority, causing British prestige generally to suffer in the region. Baden-Powell also understood, with proper imperial calculation, that by going into West Africa to smash the Ashanti kingdom, the British were at once opening vast trade possibilities, and thereby gaining a significant advantage over its colonial rivals, France and Germany. In using "Prempeh as a nail to hang our cloak upon,"

Baden-Powell points out, "we have quietly beaten them in the race for the Gold Coast Hinterland."[11] Baden-Powell's job was to raise and command the native levy of some five hundred men needed to prepare the way for the British column on their march through dense jungle to Kumassi, the Ashanti capital. Baden-Powell's men had to move in advance of Scott's main force (of two thousand soldiers and twelve thousand native carriers) hacking out roads, building bridges, erecting shelters, organizing supplies, and scouting the enemy territory to avoid the unpleasant ambushes that had destroyed British columns more than half a century earlier.

Supervising five hundred indifferent natives in the steamy jungle as they inched their way towards Kumassi was not glorious work, though rumors of hostile forces readying themselves for attack added drama to the expedition, heightening Baden-Powell's expectation of a rousing skirmish at the end. After three weeks of hard work, on 17 January, Baden-Powell and his men finally broke out of the underbrush on to the clearing of Kumassi—only to find that the object of all of their exertions was not a marvelously regal, mysterious city, but an unassuming collection of motley African huts. Worse yet, the fierce Prempeh and his strong-willed mother proved perfectly docile in the face of Her Majesty's power, offering no resistance whatever to the British. Three days later the king and his mother accepted their public humiliation of kneeling before Governor Maxwell and embracing his knees with good grace, believing this to be their sole punishment. (But Maxwell had also announced that there remained an indemnity to be paid. He determined it at fifty thousand ounces of gold, an amount Prempeh claimed not to have. Maxwell then declared that the king, queen mother, and the leading chiefs would be taken prisoners to Cape Coast Castle, where they would be held as security for the payment. As the gold was obviously never forthcoming, Maxwell managed in one stroke to deprive the Ashanti permanently of their leadership. They never again posed a problem for Britain.)

Baden-Powell was acutely disappointed at the outcome. Three weeks of slogging through the jungle to Kumassi and then a week's march back to the coast, without a single shot fired against the natives. It was hardly the service he had anticipated: "I thoroughly enjoyed the outing," he wrote to his mother, "all except the want of a fight which I fear will preclude our getting any medals or decoration."[12]

But if military glory continued to elude him, the assignment was by no means without its benefits. Before leaving for Africa, Baden-Powell hired himself out to the *Daily Chronicle* as a special war correspondent for the event. As soon as he arrived in Kumassi, he sent news of their success by field telegraph to the coast, where it was duly transmitted to London. It provided the *Chronicle* with an exciting scoop, since a storm wiped out the telegraph lines shortly after Baden-Powell's report and two days passed before any other newspaper picked up the story. Upon his return to London, Methuen and Co. commissioned a book from him on the expedition. Consulting his notes, dispatches, diaries, and letters to his mother, he was able to edit them into a finished manuscript in less than a week. Complete with various sketches by the author, *The Downfall of Prempeh* was published in 1896. And even though no actual fighting had occurred, Baden-Powell came away from his month and a half of good work in Africa as a brevet lieutenant-colonel. With his reputation as a correspondent, his book, and his promotion, Baden-Powell had to consider the Ashanti campaign, despite his frustrations, a great personal success.

But the problem of battlefield experience remained: When would he have a chance to fight? In the spring of 1896 the Matabele in Rhodesia came to his rescue, rising up against British authority and killing some settlers on the way to an unsuccessful siege of Bulawayo. The British response was immediate, and in early May Baden-Powell departed for Cape Town as chief of staff to Sir Frederick Carrington, who was directing the operations against the Matabele. Baden-Powell delighted at the prospect of "having a go" at a real enemy, one moreover without much capacity to inflict damage on trained soldiers. He did not have to wait long for his first battle. On 5 June scouts reported a massing of Matabele (Baden-Powell estimated the number to be 1200) on the opposite side of the Umgusa River. Baden-Powell crossed the river with a mounted force of 250 men, and charged straight at them, gaining a stunning and total victory. Unable to resist the onslaught of the cavalry, the natives fled, remorselessly pursued by Baden-Powell's men, who picked them off with relative impunity. Baden-Powell's own figures list over 200 Matabele dead, including 15 headmen, at a cost of 4 men badly wounded (1 of whom later died) and 4 horses killed. Narrating the incident in his book that followed the campaign, Baden-Powell suddenly evinces qualms about the unequal nature of the battle and feels compelled to offer an explanation:

> Of course this was a very one-sided fight, and it sounds rather brutal to anyone reading in cold blood how we hunted them without giving them a chance—but it must be remembered that we were but 250 against at least 1200. Lord Wolseley

says, "when you get niggers on the run, keep them on the run" (this we did, for half a mile beyond the spot where we pulled up, Beal with his column cut in from the flank and bashed them from a new direction), and our only chance of bringing the war to a speedy end is to go for them whenever we get the chance, and hit as hard as ever we can: any hesitation or softness is construed by them as a sign of weakness, and at once restores their confidence and courage.[13]

While the public forum of the book may strike a somewhat sober note in describing the battle, a letter to his mother attests only to the pleasure found in it, modifying, at the same time, some of the numbers involved:

> ... and we had a grand little fight. 1500 (most people said 2000 or 3000) enemy took up a strongish looking position in thorny bush—but I went at them with the mounted troops (200) and instead of stopping to fire when they fired we charged straight into them. It was splendid—they bolted and we followed up for 3 miles fighting all the time. These Colonials are grand at it, enjoying it all like a lot of boys playing polo.
> The enemy lost about 150-200—we only had 3 badly wounded and 4 horses killed.[14]

Disasters of this sort convinced the Matabele they could not hope to engage the British in any kind of pitched battle, and large numbers of them gradually retreated to the Matopo Hills where their network of ridges and caves afforded them maximum protection against the attacking British. The campaign soon settled down into the British trying to dislodge the Matabele from their fortified positions in the Matopos, a job that required, in addition to skill and daring, detailed information as to where the various impis (armed forces) of the enemy were located. Baden-Powell excelled in the process of intelligence gathering, moving silently through the hills at night, studying the evidence of campfires and plotting the movement of the different impis. Indefatigable in his solitary reconnaissance forays, he earned the title "Impeesa"—"the beast that does not sleep, but sneaks about at night"—from the natives who knew of his behavior, a title of which he was always inordinately proud.

By mid-August the tribes occupying the Matopos stopped fighting and began negotiating, and the British forces turned their attention to those other portions of Matabeleland that were not yet pacified. Baden-Powell was ordered to take charge of a column operating in the Somabula Forest. When he joined up with it, he found that, several days before, Uwini, one of the four main Matabele chiefs, who had been actively involved in fomenting rebellion and remained implacably opposed to surrender, had been captured. Anxious to make a lesson of him and discourage further resistance on the part of his people, Baden-Powell resolved to try him by field court-martial at once, which not surprisingly found him guilty and sentenced him to be shot—a sentence Baden-Powell had carried out that very sunset. Baden-Powell had much faith in the therapeutic value of the execution:

> I have great hopes that the moral effect of this will be particularly good among the rebels, as he was the head and centre of revolution in these parts, and had come to be looked upon by them as a god. No doubt, when they have realised that he is after all but a mortal, that he has succumbed to our power, and that they have no other head to take his place, they won't delay long to surrender.[15]

What he did not anticipate was the outrage of Lord Rosmead, the high commissioner at Cape Town, that Uwini had not been given over to the proper civilian authorities. Rosmead insisted to General Carrington that he arrest Baden-Powell immediately. Carrington, a fervent supporter of Baden-Powell's, refused to do so, establishing instead a court of inquiry to look into the appropriateness of Baden-Powell's actions. The hearing, convened on 30 October, heard a defense based on two arguments: the efficacy of the execution in helping to subdue the natives and the technical right Baden-Powell had under military law to make the decision, being more than one hundred miles away from any superior authority. The not-guilty verdict that the court shortly issued delighted not only Baden-Powell but also Carrington, who praised the execution's salutary consequences in deterring rebellion in the surrounding districts.

By late fall the situation in Rhodesia was once again under control. With the exception of some continuing minor police actions, the military uprising had been crushed, British authority established, and the country pacified. In December Baden-Powell started the first phase of his long trip home, finally arriving in England, after sharing his ocean crossing with Carrington, Cecil Rhodes, and the novelist Olive Schreiner, among others, on 27 January. Returning as brevet colonel with the experience of active service he had been seeking, Baden-Powell now faced a curious career anomaly: although a colonel in the field, he still ranked as a major in his own regiment, the 13th Hussars, therefore standing below both the lieutenant-colonel who commanded it as well as the senior major. For an ambitious man this constituted an intolerable situation, from which the war office extricated him with an offer to take command of the 5th Dragoon Guards in India. It was painful to contemplate switching regiments, but it was a decision that had to be made: "Much as I hate the idea of leaving the 13th, which has been my home of 20 years," he writes his mother, "the departure would have to come some day, and I should not get command here for another seven years—so of course I must accept, for my own good."[16]

Exultant in his new command, the forty-year-old Baden-Powell initiated a whole series of measures to enhance the lives and health of his men as soon as he arrived in India. He started a regimental bakery, a mineral-water factory that produced various carbonated drinks including ginger beer, and a dairy that guaranteed properly pasteurized milk; he also insisted on strict sanitary procedures to try to keep the troops free from the enteric fever raging through the different regiments. At the same time, he began introducing his men, on a voluntary basis, to some of the tracking and surveillance techniques he had used to good effect on the South African veldt. Although he had produced a small book on the subject fourteen years earlier (*Reconnaissance and Scouting*, 1884), he had by this time developed new ideas about it as well as new ways of demonstrating its principles to those interested in mastering them.

Lecturing on this material to his men inevitably led him to decide to get it down on paper so that it would be available to everybody. By September 1898 he was ready to start dictating to a regimental clerk who knew shorthand. Tentatively called *Cavalry Aids to Scouting*, the manuscript was finished the following spring and published in the fall of 1899 under a shorter title, *Aids to Scouting*.[17] Intended originally for the military, it generated a surprising popular readership and helped stimulate the public enthusiasm that greeted the Scouting movement some eight years later. But in May 1899, oblivious to the role that the slim handbook would play in the future, Baden-Powell was simply preparing for a lengthy leave in London, unaware also of how truculent Boer farmers in South Africa were about to change his life dramatically.

*   *   *

The decisive episode in Baden-Powell's career began with a brief conversation in early July in the Naval and Military Club of London when he learned over lunch that Lord Wolseley was looking for him. He hurried to Whitehall to meet with the commander-in-chief of the British army, who told him that he was to leave immediately for South Africa. Negotiations between British and Boers had broken down, and expecting the imminent outbreak of war, Wolseley wanted Baden-Powell to raise two regiments of mounted infantry to help defend the Rhodesian and Bechuanaland borders from Boer incursions. Baden-Powell was thrilled and began preparing instantly for his journey, anxious only that the Boers might capitulate before he actually had a chance to fight. His final note to his mother from Southampton before he embarked—"I don't like the look of today's telegrams from the Cape—they seem to imply a good deal of readiness on the part of the Boers to give in before we begin work on them"[18]—suggests the dismay the possibility of a peaceful settlement caused him. Fortunately the Boers had no intention of disappointing Baden-Powell; instead, they managed to catapult him into a position of imperial prominence in a way that would not have seemed possible before.

Whatever else can be said about the Boer War, at least one of its virtues was the opportunity it gave Baden-Powell to invent himself, the necessary first step to his invention of the Scouts. From an ordinary colonel with no more national visibility than that managed by most colonels, he emerged from the war as a kind of demigod (as well as the youngest major general in the British army), the embodiment of all the noble aspirations of the British Empire. Honored by the queen, revered by the public, and even enshrined in Madame Tussaud's hall of wax immortals, he left South Africa a fully certified hero, bringing with him a mythic glory that helped guarantee the successful establishment of the Scout movement.

Certainly no opportunity could have seemed less auspicious as a launch toward national stardom than the dusty, insignificant Mafeking in which Baden-Powell permitted himself to be entrapped by the Boers in October 1899. A tin-roofed town with nothing particular to recommend it, Mafeking stood 650 miles north of Cape Town, one of a host of innocuous trading settlements dotting South Africa. In the native language, Mafeking meant "Place of Stones," and the name aptly describes its barren loneliness. Not a situation one would ordinarily have thought conducive to building a career. But Baden-Powell was a fine actor and, like any fine actor, had the capacity to breathe life into even the most unpromising of roles.

The Mafeking performance ran 217 days (from 13 October 1899 to 17 May 1900) with Baden-Powell scintillating throughout as the commander of the besieged town. Helped immeasurably by a supporting cast of stolid, rather immobile Boers reluctant to take much initiative, Baden-Powell lodged himself firmly in the center of the stage, relinquishing it to no one. While the plot was interesting enough—the large force of unkempt Boers besieging the gallant but vastly outnumbered Englishmen—Baden-Powell turned it finally into a one-man-show. For the public that watched breathlessly, Baden-Powell *was* Mafeking. It was Baden-Powell who outwitted and outfought the enemy; Baden-Powell who gave new meaning to pluck, determination, and sportsmanship. Transmitting his news dispatches through the Boer lines (the plight of the defenders, however desperate, did not preclude their sending mail regularly to England), Baden-Powell played his part with consummate skill to what was clearly the largest audience ever to witness such a spectacle of British courage. From his marvelously laconic message at the start of the siege—"All well, four hours' bombardment. One dog killed."[19]—to his superb gesture of organizing town cricket games, Baden-Powell kept the British imagination firmly fixed on his behavior. In a war steeped in British blunder and embarrassment, he helped shape an image of heroism in which nearly everyone could take refuge.

As a result of that achievement, Baden-Powell acquired an eminence that outstripped even his grandest fantasies. The arrival of the relief columns in Mafeking on the morning of 17 May unleashed a celebration in London raucous enough to leave its mark on the English language.[20] Baden-Powell was showered with an adulation that would never desert him. The hero of Mafeking, as he was immediately known, and his stirring exploits became the subject of numerous stories, biographies, and musical compositions.[21] Henceforth Baden-Powell would always carry with him the potent trappings of fame, his name capable of conjuring up the glory of the empire in the breasts of all but the most jaundiced British citizen. His Mafeking achievements constituted a source of emotional and moral capital whose assets he exploited shrewdly in putting the Scouts before the nation. A few self-deprecating remarks about how the public had exaggerated his accomplishments were invariably sufficient, in evoking them again, to compel the attention of any audience he was addressing. It is no accident that the very first sentence of the first edition of Scouting for Boys (1908) begins with a reference to Mafeking. Baden-Powell always knew what he was about.

Heroic images, of course, rarely correspond precisely to the complex reality of any human being; and the persona on which Baden-Powell and the needs of British national pride collaborated bears only a tenuous relationship to the full facts of Baden-Powell's South African activities. To begin with, it is not at all clear that Baden-Powell should ever have allowed himself to be invested in Mafeking. While Baden-Powell's account of his orders tended to change substantially after the event, his own report to Lord Roberts immediately following the end of the siege omitted any reference to his having been instructed to occupy Mafeking. According to Baden-Powell, the orders he received from Lord Wolseley in the late summer of 1889, with the likelihood of war becoming increasingly apparent, were

1. To raise two regiments of mounted infantry;
2. In the event of war, to organize the defence of Rhodesia and Bechuanaland;
3. As far as possible to keep forces of the enemy occupied in this direction away from their own main forces.[22]

The first of these tasks he accomplished with alacrity. Two regiments were promptly formed: one, the Rhodesia Regiment, to be based in Bulawayo in the north under the command of Colonel Plumer; the other, the Protectorate Regiment, under Colonel Hore, to be stationed inside Bechuanaland, about eighteen miles away from Mafeking. With these two mobile units, Baden-Powell was to harass the enemy, guard the railway lines, and help protect Rhodesia particularly (Bechuanaland being of less strategic value) from invasion. Nowhere in these orders is there any mention of Mafeking, or of the usefulness in tying up one of these mounted regiments in a protracted siege. Nor was there any ambiguity in Baden-Powell's mind when he arrived in South Africa as to the exact nature of his mission. Entries in his staff diary make perfectly clear that he saw his responsibility as exercising the mobile functions of harassment and attack, keeping the Boers off-balance and requiring from them a substantial commitment of troops to contain the threat posed by two mounted infantry regiments. On 12 August he notes, "The railway if intact would enable us to make feints and night moves to unguarded points where we could cut through, attack from unexpected direction, or raid farms and towns in rear: draw more troops of the enemy to the scene, and cut out again. With continual reliefs of squadrons at this work we might succeed in getting as many as 5,000 [Boers] detached to protect this border."[23] Lamenting the difficulty of getting volunteers to join his forces, he wishes he could tell them more of his plans, "beyond assuring them (as I have done already) that our task will be merely to watch for and seize opportunities of delivering blows at small forces of the enemy, and not to commit ourselves to big engagements, or to their traps" (27 August).

Baden-Powell had no doubts about what he was supposed to do—only about his capacity to do it with the troops at his disposal. From early September he repeatedly requested more men to permit him both to defend his supplies at Mafeking and at the same time engage in thrusts at the enemy. To these he adds another, somewhat peculiar argument: If part of his job was to keep large numbers of Boers from joining their main forces, he must himself exhibit sufficient strength to worry them so that they would not be tempted to take him lightly and redeploy where they might be more urgently needed: "They [the Protectorate Regiment] seem to draw a good force of Boers to protect this border for the present— but eventually if they do not show strength some of the enemy will be withdrawn to act elsewhere" (15 September). Appeals for more men were regularly rejected by headquarters, however, and as they were, Baden-Powell began looking longingly at the relative security offered by Mafeking. While requests for more soldiers continued, Baden-Powell also began to seek permission to move his troops into the town, something the authorities did not want to do for fear of provoking the Boers. Arguing for the necessity of reinforcements to protect Mafeking, Baden-Powell, as late as 20 September, revealed his precise understanding of the ostensibly mobile nature of his command:

> Telegraphed to CSO Capetown asking that now that troops have been sent up to occupy Kimberley and Orange River Bridge—some extra Cape Police with 2 guns, as suggested by the Defence Committee 11th inst. be sent to defend Mafeking. Until this is done the Protectorate Regt. is tied to the place in order to protect it, which is not at all in accordance with the object of the force—viz. external mobility for the defence of the border at any threatened point, and ability on outbreak of war to inflict blows sufficient to draw a strong force of the enemy against it. If say 100 Cape Police and two guns came then in addition to the townspeople and volunteers [sic] would render the town quite safe from attack on the part of the enemy and would release the Protectorate Regt. for its proper work in the frontier.

*   *   *

With negotiations at a standstill and no significant new troops forthcoming, Baden-Powell finally decided to resolve the issue on his own. Having already stockpiled huge stores of food and other supplies in Mafeking as a base for his two regiments, he now used the pretext of guarding these supplies as a means of bringing the entire Protectorate Regiment into town: "I got permission from the Cape Government to place an armed guard in Mafeking to protect these stores, but as the strength of that guard was not stipulated I moved the whole regiment into the place without delay."[24] Once in, Baden-Powell set about preparing for a comfortable and lengthy siege; the Boers happily (and foolishly) obliged, and the ingredients of a great legend were ready to be mixed.

Baden-Powell's various after-the-fact explanations for his strategy of taking his mounted infantry, whose job it was to protect the borders, off their horses and immobilizing them during a 217-day siege not only emphasized considerations not contained in his original orders but actually allude to entirely different orders as well. All attribute an importance to defending Mafeking few people would have found credible before the celebrity of the siege. Baden-Powell's report to Roberts lists six reasons why he felt he had to keep the Boers from Mafeking:

1. Because it is the outpost for Kimberley and Cape Colony.
2. Also, equally for the Protectorate and Rhodesia.
3. It threatens the weak flank of the Transvaal.
4. It is the headcenter of the large native districts of the northwest, with their 200,000 inhabitants.
5. It contains important railway stocks and shops.
6. Also large food and forage supplies.[25]

Ignoring the fact that these are really only four separate reasons (the first and second being substantially one, as are the fifth and sixth), none would seem to dictate Baden-Powell's occupation of the town. His protection of the area would have been far more easily accomplished with a mobile unit than with a stationary force surrounded by Boers. Similarly, if Baden-Powell was concerned with making sure the natives were sufficiently impressed by a display of British strength not to be tempted to join the Boers, the spectacle of a mounted regiment sitting passively in Mafeking hardly suggested Her Majesty's military might. It is indeed true that by the time he chose to enter Mafeking with his troops, the town was engorged with supplies, but the supplies were there only because Baden-Powell had been stocking the town with them. In establishing vast stores that he then felt obliged to defend, Baden-Powell had committed, in Brian Gardner's words, "a classic military blunder, the dangers of which were stressed at military colleges around the world: to allow the guardianship of stores to dictate the immobility of all those for whom the stores were intended."[26]

The reasons Baden-Powell gave for moving into Mafeking soon began to blend with the orders he claimed to have received. Unlike the three orders he initially reported to Roberts, he testified at the Royal Commission on the War in South Africa (1903), that

> I was sent to South Africa on special service in July 1899, with instructions to raise a force of two regiments of mounted rifles for the defence of Rhodesian and Bechuanaland frontier.
> In the event of war to organize the local armed forces of the countries; to keep the natives in order, and, especially, to draw as large a force of Boers as possible from opposing the British on their southern borders.[27]

Here the need to "keep the enemy occupied" has turned into the intention "to draw as large a force of Boers" to them as possible, a change that seems suspiciously like a retroactive defense of Baden-Powell's decision to avoid actively engaging the enemy in the field for the rather less dangerous enterprise of enduring a siege from within a fortified town. The self-justifying nature of these orders culminates in the version finally published in Baden-Powell's autobiography, in which they are as follows:

1. to attract Boer forces away from the coast so that they should not interfere with the landing of British troops
2. to protect British possessions in Rhodesia, Mafeking, etc.
3. to maintain British prestige among the native tribes in the area.[28]

As can be seen, these three are not the same as the three Baden-Powell received from Wolseley. Mafeking is now specifically named as a place Baden-Powell was to defend from the Boers; the charge to maintain British prestige among the natives (which Baden-Powell always equated with the need to keep the Boers out of Mafeking) is newly added; and the task of occupying the enemy has now become the order to attract as many as possible from the coast—Mafeking was over five hundred miles from the nearest port—so as not to interfere with the landing of British troops. While all three are designed to support the tactical wisdom, indeed necessity, of entering Mafeking, none is particularly compelling. And none, in any case, was a part of Baden-Powell's original orders or original understanding, as his diary entry of 20 September reveals.

Whatever the military soundness of Baden-Powell's decision, the Boers also willingly participated in a siege that was equally senseless from their point of view. Not only was Mafeking of no serious strategic value to them, but they could ill spare the troops to invest it. As their whole strategy in the war was to keep their commandos moving against the numerically superior but less mobile forces of the British, even had they taken Mafeking they would not have been able to do anything with it. It was of sufficiently little interest to President Kruger that he had instructed his general, Piet Cronjé, that if he could not capture Mafeking in a few days, he should pass on to the south, leaving only enough troops to ensure that the Mafeking garrison stayed out of the rest of the war. Under no circumstances should Cronjé run the risk of losing more than fifty men in assaulting Mafeking. But Cronjé was apparently as immune to orders as Baden-Powell; convinced that he could eventually take the town without exposing more than fifty men to risk if he just stayed around long enough, he moved his forces into position on 13 October, thus setting the stage for this most peculiar confrontation between two blundering foes, neither of whom had any good reason to be doing what they were doing.

A major feature of the epic of Mafeking's defense, from the point of view of the British public at least, was the way in which the vastly outnumbered British withstood the hordes of Boers striving to capture the town. The number of Boers actually involved therefore becomes an interesting question, not only for helping to define the extent of Mafeking's heroism, but also for assessing Baden-Powell's claim that he played a major role in the South African War by occupying Boer troops who might otherwise have been used to greater effect elsewhere. While the size of Baden-Powell's force was generally acknowledged to be approximately 1,200 men and officers, with an additional complement of some 300 armed natives, it is difficult to determine the initial strength of the investing Boers. Characteristically, Baden-Powell's own figures prove as ever-changing as his account of his orders. From an initial estimate (in a telegram sent to Roberts on 29 October 1899) of 4,000 Boers, the number expands, in his report to Roberts after the war, to 8,000, thereafter gradually swelling to 9,000 (*Sketches in Mafeking and East Africa*, 1907), and to over 10,000 in his autobiography published in 1933, culminating in *African Adventures* in 1937, in which 12,000 Boers opposed him. Most estimates by others tended to be more sober, with a figure somewhere around 6,000. The *Official History of the War in South Africa* settled on 6,750. All these figures, it is important to remember, refer to the forces Cronjé gathered outside of Mafeking in October, at the start of the siege. Five weeks later, on 18 November, Cronjé finally decided to listen to Kruger and move a substantial portion of his burghers to the south. While the estimates of the numbers left behind vary, this time the variation is much smaller, staying between 2,000 and 3,000. Baden-Powell telegramed Roberts on 25 December that there were 2,000 Boers left; Hillcourt, Baden-Powell's most reliable biographer, says about 3,000. In Baden-Powell's official report to Roberts he claims that 2,000 to 3,000 Boers were occupied for over six months.

Whatever the exact number, it is clear that the number of Boers who effectively constituted the siege force—and whose absence from other areas of the war Baden-Powell argued was so vital—was nothing like any of the estimates of those initially assembled. If drawing large numbers of Boers to Mafeking was actually what he wanted to accomplish, as he said afterwards, he was far less successful at it than he led the public to believe. The relatively modest number remaining after Cronjé departed also casts the gallant nature of the town's defense in a somewhat different light. Two to three thousand rather passive Boers, unwilling to risk the possibility of any substantial casualties, hardly posed a formidable threat to a reasonably well-fortified town garrisoned with twelve hundred armed men. With the exception of one serious attack a few days before the arrival on 14 May of the relief column, Snyman, the Boer commander who replaced Cronjé, was content by and large to shell the town desultorily with an enormous cannon that made a loud noise but did little damage. In general, Baden-Powell's defenders did not have much to do. A report filed in November by Angus Hamilton, the *Times* correspondent in Mafeking, defined conditions that stayed essentially unchanged during the entire time:

When we come to consider the siege of Mafeking in its more elemental details, the picture is not unlike those presented by the farcical melodrama. It is now nearly six weeks since Mafeking was proclaimed as being in a state of siege and, although there has been no single opportunity of any commercial reciprocity between ourselves and the outside world, the ruling prices are at present but very little above normal, distress is wholly absent, danger is purely incidental, and indeed it would seem, as Colonel Baden-Powell said in a recent order, that "Everything in the garden is lovely."[29]

The British press (Hamilton's report notwithstanding), with Baden-Powell's able assistance, orchestrated the event into a glowing instance of British pluck that the country needed in the midst of all its humiliation, but the truth remains that it was boredom rather than the Boers that constituted the gravest danger to the white inhabitants of Mafeking.

Indeed, it was in repelling boredom that Baden-Powell was at his cheery best. Life in Mafeking during the siege was enlivened by concerts, theatrical performances, football contests, pony and bicycle races, driving competitions for transport mules, baby and agricultural shows, cricket matches, and various dances (including the Beleaguered Bachelors' Ball), among other types of entertainments—all encouraged, if not actually organized, by Baden-Powell himself. He handed out prizes, sang songs, impersonated Paderewski, and participated in theatrical events. He regularly played polo on Sundays until Snyman objected to such abuse of the Sabbath, threatening to shell the town on those days if they continued to play. They stopped.

Baden-Powell had a marvelous time. He was busy, but he was happy: "I ordered a man to be shot last night and forgot to sign the warrant," he writes to Hanbury Williams, "shall he wait for tonight?; BANG-WHIZ-PHEEEUW-CRASH-clatter—a shell from a new direction—up to the look out, whistle down the tube to telephone—'send 4 men to Coole's Post to snipe that gun, get ready "Lord Nelson" and fire when I tell you'—etc., etc. It *is* rather good fun but—well, I don't exactly get fat over it all!!"[30]

He particularly enjoyed what he later described as "The fun of being a sort of Hitler in Mafeking, free from interference by superior officers."[31] His rule was absolute, and he relished the freedom to exercise his total authority. His enthusiastic letters to his mother demonstrate in part the pleasure of the competitive younger brother who has finally come into his own, breaking away at last from the psychic constraints the three older ones must have imposed:

> But it is a most interesting experience, especially as my first act was to proclaim martial law, i.e., as W. [his brother] will tell you—that all laws are in abeyance and I take the full responsibility for everything. I have already got the jail *full* of suspected spies etc. and I keep them there with no proof of guilt, etc., I forbid public houses to be open other than at

certain hours and any case of disobedience I confiscate their whole stock. I have seized every ounce of flour in the town at a price fixed by myself—and am selling it only a certain amount each day—and so on. (24 November 1899)

Yesterday a baker tried to sell more than I allow him to— I promptly seized the whole lot and confiscated it! A bar keeper has sold drink at prohibited hours. I have ordered the whole of his stock to be smashed up before his eyes. It is the only way to keep order. (30 November 1899)[32]

With the torpor of the Boers guaranteeing that they would do nothing untoward to disturb him, he gaily tended to both the morale and the defense of his people and to the fashioning of his own reputation. The rigors of the siege were not such that messengers could not pass at will through the Boer lines, so mail and dispatches were regularly sent and received with no difficulty. Early on, Baden-Powell well knew the attention Britain was lavishing on his defense of Mafeking, and he played the role of gallant defender to perfection, contriving all of his communiqués to exploit to the fullest the drama of the undauntable commander holding out against great odds. Angus Hamilton recognized the opportunity Mafeking offered Baden-Powell—and his determination to take full advantage of it. "Colonel Baden-Powell is young, as men go in the army," he writes, "with a keen appreciation of the possibilities of his career, swayed by ambition, indifferent to sentimental emotion."[33] The person Hamilton saw was not the irrepressible boyman beloved of his admirers, but someone far more calculating about himself: "Every servant in the hotel watches him, and he, as a consequence, seldom speaks without a preternatural deliberation and an air of decisive finality. He seems to close every argument with a snap, as though the steel manacles of his ambition had checkmated the emotions of the man in the instincts of the officer."[34] If Hamilton perhaps overrated Baden-Powell's decisiveness, he certainly understood his ambition. Realizing precisely what was expected of him by a nation requiring heroes, Baden-Powell catered effectively to that need even as he monitored the growth of his fame thousands of miles away in a dusty town in the middle of the veldt.

But while Baden-Powell orchestrated his popularity and helped the British in the town deal with the vague threat of the enemy and the rather more pressing danger of tedium, one constituency of the population was having trouble not amusing itself but staying alive:

the seventy-five hundred natives trapped in Mafeking. Their problem was finding enough to eat. Although the firm of Julius Weil and Co. had amassed enormous stores of food and supplies in preparation for the siege,[35] Baden-Powell's uncertainty about how long Mafeking might be invested led him to take strict measures to guarantee the well-being of the white population against any exigencies.

In addition to establishing a rationing plan for the whites that at the beginning limited them, among other things, to a pound of meat and a pound of bread daily, he effectively excluded large portions of the native population from their source of food. This latter task was accomplished, as Thomas Packenham in *The Boer War* demonstrates, in various ways—first, by charging them more money than they could afford for the meager rations they were allowed, though the indigent white garrison who couldn't pay were provided food anyway. Second, he reduced the amount of flour and meat initially designated for the blacks and added it instead to the stores for the whites, making up for some of the difference by substituting horses' rations into the native diet; and finally most decisively, by forbidding approximately two thousand of the natives, those classified as "refugee and foreign"—coming originally from outside the town—any food at all. These were told that they must leave the town and find food with Plumer's column, some seventy miles away, or starve. The problem with this alternative was the presence of the Boers, who did not look kindly on those Baralongs who sought to escape and frequently killed those they found. One particularly cruel exception was the approximately six hundred Baralong women who tried to escape the night of 7 April. Sixty-seven got away; the others were driven back to town, having been caught, stripped naked, and flogged by the Boers.

The result of all of this, not surprisingly, was misery, starvation, and death for the natives. While approximately twelve hundred made their way to Plumer, the rest suffered terribly. Baden-Powell's staff diary itself impassively records the consequences of the deprivation: "Another case of starvation occurred today making the third that has come to notice" (23 February); "Some of the local agitators have now begun to charge us with neglecting our natives. (There were four deaths yesterday from 'exposure and starvation.')" (13 March); "Dr. Hayes reports that 9 natives have been ill with starvation since 1st inst. and 2 died" (17 March).[36] Emerson Neilly of the *Pall Mall Gazette*, writing of the plight of those natives able to procure rations (as opposed to those excluded from food entirely), recorded the following impressions:

Hunger had them in its grip, and many of them were black spectres and living skeletons. I saw them crawling along on legs like the stems of well-blackened "cutties," with their ribs literally breaking through their shriveled skin—men, women, and children. I saw them, too, fall down on the veldt and lie where they had fallen, too weak to go on their way. The sufferers were mostly little boys—mere infants ranging in age from four or five upwards.[37]

Words could not portray the scene of misery. The best thing I can do is to ask you to fancy five or six hundred human frameworks of both sexes and all ages, from the tender infant upwards, dressed in the remains of tattered rags, standing in lines, each holding an old blackened can or beef tin, awaiting turn to crawl painfully up to the kitchen where the food was distributed. Having obtained the horse soup, fancy them tottering off a few yards and sitting down to wolf up the life-fastening mess, and lick the tins when they had finished. It was one of the most heart-rending sights I ever witnessed, and I have seen many.[38]

For Angus Hamilton, not all of whose views ever appeared in the *Times*, the treatment of the natives was scandalous: "There can be no doubt that the drastic principles of economy which Colonel Baden-Powell has been practising in these later days are opposed to and altogether at variance with the dignity of the liberalism which we profess and are at such little pains to execute, and which enter so much into the pacific settlement of native questions in South Africa."[39] While natives prowled about shooting dogs for food and even digging up the corpses of dogs buried outside of Mafeking, Baden-Powell continued to look after the physical and emotional health of the whites in the town. The menu for the Christmas Eve dinner at the Mafeking Hotel (*overleaf*), catering to both needs, suggests that Weil's food stores did not have to be quite that strictly managed. But Baden-Powell's concern never flagged; an entry in his staff diary as late as April finds him still thinking of ways to increase what appears to be an already sufficient ration for them:

April 20: 12th June is now what we can get to with the available meat and meal stores on present scale. But by forcing natives away from Mafeking we can get their share of horse-flesh for whites and their sowens which would improve the [white] ration in size.[40]

May Xmas find you glad and well.
In spite of Kruger's Shot and Shell.

Ye Mafeking Hotel.

BRITISH BECHUANALAND

C. RIESLE   PROPRIETOR.

MENU.

Xmas Daye 1899.

Anchovy Croûtons.
Olives.

Consommé Windsor.

Oyster Patties.

Smoked Calves Tongue.
Giblet Pie.
Tournédos Parisienne.
York Ham and Madeira Sauce.
Fricasée of Veal.

Roast Fowl and Bread Sauce.
Boiled Fowl and Bacon.

Joints.
Baron of Beef and Yorkshire Pudding.
Veal and Ham.
Roast Side of Lamb and Green Peas.
Sucking Pig and Apple Sauce.
Roast Saddle of Mutton.
Boiled Mutton and Capers.
Boiled Bacon.
Corned Beef.
Tongue and Ham.

Vegetables.
Marrow, Green Peas,
Baked and Boiled Potatoes.

Xmas Pudding.
Mince Pies.
Sandringham Jellies.
Victoria Sandwich.

Dessert   Café Noir.

RULE BRITANIA.

His success in preserving supplies for the whites can be seen in a table Baden-Powell attached to his report to Roberts indicating the difference between daily provisions allocated to them at the beginning of the siege and those dictated by austerity as the siege drew on:[41]

	At First	Latterly		At First	Latterly
Meat	1 lb.	$\frac{3}{4}$ to 1 lb.	Salt	$\frac{1}{2}$ oz.	$\frac{1}{2}$ oz.
Bread	1 lb.	5 oz.	Sugar	2 oz.	0
Veg	1 lb.	6 oz.	Tea	$\frac{1}{2}$ oz.	0
Coffee	$\frac{1}{3}$ oz.	$\frac{1}{3}$ oz.	Sowens	0	1 qt.

As the native population starved, that is, the white garrison survived the 217 days with essentially no diminution in its meat ration, and with substantial amounts of bread and vegetables as well. Seldom has a siege been endured with less hardship—for those who weren't natives. When the relief columns finally arrived, they found to their surprise that the imperiled defenders were in fact far better supplied than they were themselves, and promptly turned to the town's provisions for their own needs.

It was not simply in their inability to get enough to eat that the native population suffered under Baden-Powell's care. Lacking the protection of dugouts and shelters prepared for the whites, the natives were vulnerable to the shelling of the Boers, which otherwise posed no serious threat. Baden-Powell's figures for the siege indicate 446 native noncombatants killed and wounded, as opposed to 9 whites—stark testimony supporting Angus Hamilton's view of the unconscionable way the natives were treated in Mafeking. Justice, for the natives, was as harsh as the diet and the living conditions. Five executions of natives were carried out by Baden-Powell's court of Summary Jurisdiction for the following offenses: being outside the lines without a pass; spying; the theft of a horse; the theft of a goat; housebreaking. The only crime that might properly have incurred the death sentence during this time was the murder of Mr. Parslow, correspondent for the *Daily Chronicle*, by Lieutenant Murchison, a British artillery officer. Murchison was condemned to death but later released entirely because of his good work in the town's defense. Such was the quality of justice dispensed during the siege. In "the white man's" war, as both Boer and Briton agreed the conflict should remain, the natives did not fare well, even those under the protection of the future Chief Scout of the world.

Baden-Powell's actual performance at Mafeking, then, was considerably more complicated than most of the popular reviewers would have us believe. And while it is true that Mafeking was the sole source of the Baden-Powell legend, a complete assessment of his South African career should properly include his behavior in two other capacities: as commander of a column sent, after the relief of Mafeking, to Rustenburg; and as the head of the South African Constabulary, a military police force established to help pacify the country.

Both roles suggest a different sort of officer from the bold, dashing military genius of the Mafeking myth. Sent by Lord Roberts at the end of May to the Rustenburg district with orders to harass the enemy in the field and guard the railway lines, Baden-Powell chose instead to house his moveable columns in Rustenburg itself to invite another Boer investiture. The Boers promptly accepted, and soon Rustenburg was surrounded. Having gotten himself trapped, Baden-Powell settled in comfortably, seemingly quite pleased with his confinement. Arguing that there would be a serious loss of morale if Rustenburg fell to the Boers (the same claim he made for immobilizing his cavalry in Mafeking), Baden-Powell steadfastly resisted all entreaties from Roberts to leave. Roberts's efforts to get his unbudging commander to move into the field take on a note of almost comical plaintiveness:[42]

> As I telegraphed to you before, I think it is a mistake to scatter small detachments about the country. They cannot hold their own, and their easy capture encourages the enemy.... The efficient moveable column going from place to place would be infinitely more effective than these small garrisons. Are you still shut up in Rustenburg? (20 July 1900)
>
> Your proposal for dealing with present crisis might be the right one if there were large numbers of battalions to spare, but under existing circumstances I cannot arrange to garrison chief towns with Infantry. We must not therefore attempt to hold them, but employ the force at my disposal ... in beating the enemy in the field.... And I must ask you to leave Rustenburg as soon as the relieving column arrives here. The forces I am sending are urgently required elsewhere, and I am giving Ian Hamilton and Carrington orders not to remain at Rustenburg or to leave any troops there. (29 July 1900)
>
> As I have already explained to you it is impossible to find garrisons at present for Lichtenburg, Rustenburg and other places in that neighborhood. Moral effect of evacuating them may be bad, but this will be counteracted by our having sufficient troops to beat the enemy in the field.... You must be prepared to join him [Hamilton] with the whole of your force including the Battalion at Olifants Nek as soon as he comes within touch of you. Please see there is no delay about

the evacuation of Rustenburg as it is essential Hamilton should return here as soon as possible.... (31 July 1900)

I am afraid my decision to abandon Rustenburg for a time will be a disappointment to you, but it is unavoidable. Had I not to send Ian Hamilton's force with supplies for you, I should have employed it with Broadwood's against DeWet's, and should practically have been able to surround him. Moreover I have not a single battalion to spare to garrison Rustenburg, nor can I undertake to supply, as all troops are required for what, I venture to think, is more important duty. (1 August 1900)

Baden-Powell "seems to have a strange fancy for being besieged," Roberts writes to Lord Lansdowne on 2 August. "He is most unwilling to leave Rustenburg, but I have told him ... that Rustenburg must be temporarily abandoned."[43] And Roberts repeats on 6 August to Lansdowne that Baden-Powell "is very sad at being deprived of the chance of having to stand another siege."[44] With the arrival of Hamilton's men on 6 August, however, Baden-Powell finally relinquished his siege vision and agreed to leave Rustenburg. The difficulties involved in trying to induce one of his own officers to follow orders were not lost on Roberts and perhaps help explain why, in less than a month, he turned from suggesting Baden-Powell as the man best suited to replace him as the supreme commander of the army in South Africa to omitting him altogether from the three recommendations he makes to Milner.[45] Baden-Powell is instead proposed as the head of the police force (ultimately the South African Constabulary), possessing those requisite qualities of "energy, organization, knowledge of the country and a power of getting on with its people."[46]

It is hard to know whether Roberts's nomination of Baden-Powell to head the police force was a gentle way of easing him out of the strict chain of military command. ("He certainly is not a general," Roberts later confided to Kitchener, "but I thought he would prove to be a good organizer."[47]) Whatever Roberts's motivation, Baden-Powell jumped at the chance to establish his own police organization. The force, which was to report directly to Milner as high commissioner, was essentially charged with the civil function of policing the country. As long as the Boer resistance continued, however, Milner permitted it to be used by Kitchener as an additional military contingent. Legislated into existence in October 1900, it was to be ready in the spring of 1901.

While Baden-Powell's efforts at organizing and training ten thousand men in such a short period of time were very successful, his

actual leadership of the South African Constabulary in the field
appeared to have been less so. Kitchener's reports to Roberts on
the efficiency of Baden-Powell and his South African Constabulary
comprise one long lament:[48]

> Do you remember how we hoped for great things from
> Baden-Powell's police? Nothing has yet been done though he
> seems to have had a good many men out—I still hope, but
> they go very slowly. (29 March 1901)

> Baden-Powell does not appear to do anything with his SAC
> men beyond dressing them up. I am trying to get Milner to
> urge him on.... But I fear Baden-Powell is more outside show
> than sterling worth. (5 April 1901)

> I am still in the same state of complete disappointment
> about the work of the constabulary. They have done no-
> thing.... I think if Edwards and Nicholson had a free hand
> we should get something. They are both first rate men but
> our experience of B. P. in Rustenburg was I fear not excep-
> tional. If I could only get them to take over and hold the
> areas we clear we should soon have large areas denied to the
> enemy and I believe bring the war to an end. It is therefore
> excessively aggravating to see large numbers of men doing
> nothing but costing enormous sums and eating their heads off.
> (12 April 1901)

> Baden-Powell and the South African Constabulary are still
> very unsatisfactory. He is spending a lot of money and no
> result—I cannot get them to do anything.... Organizing is as
> far as I can see the last thing Baden-Powell can do: some of
> his officers are plainly disgusted and wishing to leave him. (24
> May 1901)

Although on 31 May Kitchener notes that at last he is getting
some value out of them, by 21 June the old complaints are back:

> I am sorry to say we do not even now get much good out
> of the Constabulary. They have not yet completed the line
> from Bloemfontein to Jacobsdal.... I wish I could get more
> out of Baden-Powell in the way of occupying cleared areas
> but they love the shelter of our garrisons and it is most difficult
> to get them out.

When queried by Roberts whether or not Baden-Powell should
be replaced, Kitchener advises that he had

> better return. I certainly do not think very highly of him as
> an organizer and his own people are somewhat dissatisfied,

but still I would not advise a change as he gets on well with Milner, and he is in a certain way distinctly sharp and clever. I daresay he will do better after the war is over than while it lasts. (17 August)

Although Kitchener's final comment refers to the constabulary's projected civil as opposed to military role, it resonates with a kind of prophetic insight about the future course of Baden-Powell's career.

If by any detailed accounting Baden-Powell's accomplishments in the Boer War were far more problematic than they appeared to be, such a fact in no way interfered with his freshly minted fame. Baden-Powell rode out of Mafeking a different man from the one who had arrived in South Africa eleven months earlier to raise two columns of mounted infantry. Henceforth he would never have to worry again about toiling in the ranks and proper advancement. However mixed the professional estimates of his talent for command, he had transformed himself into a public figure whom the army had now to treat with much delicacy. The doubts about him that Kitchener and Roberts, among others, shared could not be openly expressed, but they probably played a role in the appointments that followed the Mafeking siege as head of the South African Constabulary (1900–1903) and inspector general of the cavalry (1903–1907).

Baden-Powell liked to describe his life as falling into two distinct parts: a soldier for the first half, a man of peace for the second. The distinction, as we shall see, is not quite as neat as he suggests, but it certainly points to the total identification of man and movement from 1907 on. With the creation of the Scouts in 1907–1908 Baden-Powell inaugurated a career that would absorb all his energies up to his death in 1941.

Baden-Powell's private life, to the degree that he had one, was always very much caught up in his public role. Even his marriage to Olave Soames in 1912 took place in the public forum of Scouting. He talked about it in the Scout paper, assuring Scouts that Olave would be a great asset to the movement, and Scouts throughout the United Kingdom were permitted—and even encouraged— to contribute a penny each toward the wedding present he had indicated he wanted: a car.

The marriage itself came as something of a surprise. In the years following Mafeking, letters to his mother occasionally contain thoughts about marrying and settling down, with the financial problems that would bring, but the talk is always abstract, never revealing any particular sense of urgency. More then anything else, it seemed designated to placate his aging mother, who clearly felt there was something incomplete about his life. No evidence exists prior to the marriage of even a casual relationship with a woman, much less anything vaguely emotional. Besides bantering about various women being thrown at him in his eligible bachelorhood, he had very little to do with them. Certainly by 1912 he was well past that dangerous "rutting period," which he claimed lasted for "a few weeks or months" in which sexual temptation beseiged a young man, driving him, unless he had the strength to resist, "into the habit of immorality with women or self-abuse with himself."[49]

Indeed, the most intense relationship of his life was with Kenneth McLaren, a young officer in the 13th Hussars whom he met in 1880 and whose good looks and youthful appearance caused him always to be called "The Boy." Whether a physical relationship accompanied the deep affection Baden-Powell had for McLaren, it is impossible to determine, though it is clear that "The Boy" occupied a very special place emotionally for Baden-Powell. When McLaren was wounded and captured by the Boers during the Mafeking siege, Baden-Powell had to be restrained from rushing to the Boer lines to see him, the compelling argument being made that if he showed up, the Boers would surely take him prisoner, and Mafeking would inevitably be lost. There then ensued a peculiar correspondence between Baden-Powell and the Boers, with Baden-Powell initially proposing an exchange of Boer prisoners for the return of McLaren. As this offer was rejected, Baden-Powell next inquired whether the British physician could go to the Boer camp to examine McLaren and consult with the attending Boer doctor about the case. This, too, was refused, although it elicited a letter from the Boer doctor that McLaren was mending properly and recommending that a stiffer mattress than what the Boers had available might make "The Boy" more comfortable. Baden-Powell immediately scoured the town, and the next day an appropriately firm mattress made its way to the Boer camp. Both McLaren and Baden-Powell weathered this ordeal successfully; the arrival of the British relief forces found McLaren convalescing nicely on his stiff mattress in the Boer field hospital. When Baden-Powell started the Scouts, McLaren was right with him, attending the demonstration camp at Brownsea Island in 1907 as an officer and then taking over the position of manager of the first Scout headquarters. He left the job because of ill health in 1909 and died in 1924.

As Baden-Powell's career had been otherwise perfectly free of any close personal relationship, there was little reason to think that the fifty-five-year-old Hero of Mafeking would decide to marry, or that he would choose the twenty-three-year-old daughter of a retired but well-to-do brewer as his wife. But Olave, whom he met on board the S. S. *Arcadian*, bound for the West Indies and New York, possessed the virtues he wanted. Announcing the unexpected news of his impending marriage, he explains to his mother his fiancée's charms:

> I had been wondering what to give you as a birthday present, but I think I've got one now that will please you (I hope and believe)—and that is a daughter-in-law for you! Olave Soames, whom I met on board the "Arcadian" travelling with her father promises to make a very good one. I hope you will like her half as much as I do. She has only one fault—(and both George and Frank told me that in getting a wife you must overlook a fault or two if she is on the whole what you want)—her fault is that she is young, but she has an old head on her shoulders and is clever and wise and *very* bright and cheery.
>
> I fear I kept the idea very secret, but I did not want to worry you with anxiety about it until I knew more as to the practical possibility of this as it might have only been a dream. But it was in connection with it that I wrote lately to you asking about the expenses at No. 32 in case I shld. want to start housekeeping on my own account.
>
> So I came here [the Soames's house] ... to dine and sleep, and to have a talk with her father. He is ready to give her £1000 a year now and she will have a good deal more later— so though not exactly rich we shall be comfortable.
>
> She is the cheeriest girl possible.[50]

(As Baden-Powell was expected by his mother—along with his other brothers—to make regular payments into the family treasury at 32 Princes Gate, where his mother lived, Olave's solvency was not the least important consideration. It guaranteed that the dream could be a reality.)

Besides her cheeriness and £1,000 a year, Olave also stood ready to help Baden-Powell with Scouting in any way she could. Baden-Powell marveled on their honeymoon how conscientiously she took care of him—"looks after me like a mother," he reported to his mother[51]—and how enthusiastically she helped him in answering his correspondence. And while she continued always to lavish great attention on Baden-Powell, particularly as he grew old and increasingly fragile, her participation in Scouting soon went well beyond answering letters for her husband. By 1914 it was apparent that Baden-Powell's sister, Agnes, to whom he had entrusted the leadership of the Girl Guides, did not have the organizational abilities required to run it effectively. The movement was a shambles, more or less on the verge of being taken over by the YWCA. Baden-Powell rushed in to rescue it through various structural changes intended to lessen Agnes's power. Olave, whose first offer of help had been rebuffed by the Guides, was now made a county commissioner. Throwing her considerable energy into the movement, she proved remarkably successful both in organizing her own district and in stimulating the growth of Guiding nationally. In 1916, by unanimous vote of the executive committe, she was named the first chief commissioner. Eighteen months later an appropriate professional and marital parallelism was achieved when she joined the Chief Scout as the Chief Guide. Together they would spend their lives looking after the health and character of the rising generation of young men and women throughout the empire.

In his autobiography Baden-Powell describes the importance of picking the right guide when planning a difficult scouting expedition through hostile country. "The selection is not one that can be lightly made," he emphasizes. "It's as bad as choosing a horse—or a wife. There is a lot depending on it."[52] In the case of his wife, Baden-Powell had clearly chosen wisely. Olave did not disappoint, learning quickly to share his interests and incorporate the public stewardship of Scouts and Guides into the texture of their family life without conflict. The three children she bore him—the anomaly of the world's acknowledged youth leader being a childless bachelor must have occurred to Baden-Powell before his marriage—further graced the second half of his life, providing him with the happy family life whose values he so passionately advocated.

While Baden-Powell thought he had reached "the top of his tree" when he was appointed inspector general of cavalry,[53] it was as nothing compared with the height and embrace of the tree he ascended as Chief Scout of all the world. The international acclaim he garnered for his Scouting achievements would have assured even his most uncompromising mother that Stephe had made good:

ORDERS, DECORATIONS, AND HONORARY DEGREES

1909   Knight Commander of the Order of the Bath
        Knight Commander of the Victorian Order

1910   L L. D., Edinburgh
        Order of Merit of Chile

1912   Knight of Grace of Saint John of Jerusalem

1919   Knight of the Grand Cross of Alfonso XII (Spain)

1920   Grand Commander of the Order of Christ (Portugal)
        Grand Commander of the Order of the Redeemer
        (Greece)

1921   Baronet
        Storkos of the Order of Danneborg (Denmark)
        Order of the Commander of the Crown of Belgium

1922   Commander of the Legion of Honor (France)

1923   Grand Cross of the Victorian Order
        L L. D., Toronto
        L L. D., McGill, Montreal
        D. C. L., Oxford

1927   Order of Polonia Restituta (Poland)

1928   Knight Grand Cross of the Order of Saint Michael
        and Saint George
        Order of Amanulla (Afghanistan)

1929   L L. D., Liverpool
        First Class of the Order of Merit (Hungary)
        The Order of the White Lion (Czechoslovakia)
        The Order of the Phoenix (Greece)
        Peerage

1931   L L. D., Cambridge
        The Grand Cross of the Order of Merit (Austria)

1932   Grand Cross of Gediminus (Lithuania)
        Grand Cross of Orange of Nassau (Holland)

1933   Commander of the Order of the Oak of Luxembourg
        The Red Cross of Estonia
        Grand Cross of the Order of the Sword (Sweden)

1936   Grand Cordon of the Legion of Honor (France)

1937   Order of Merit

If honorary degrees and national decorations weren't proof enough,
the last film on which Cecil B. De Mille had begun work before he
died was to have been an extravaganza on Baden-Powell's life.
Baden-Powell died in Kenya in 1941 a happy man, content with
the precious legacy of Scouting he had left the world. Lady Olave's
final words in her diary recording his death defined the reverential
view millions the world over held of the Chief Scout: "He looked
so sweet and perfect in death as he was in life—utterly utterly noble
and good and dear and wonderful, great and faultless."[54]

2

---◆---

FORTIFYING THE
WALL OF EMPIRE

---◆---

It is a curiosity in the history of Scouting that the private moment of the idea's fertilization in Baden-Powell's mind can be more precisely dated than the actual public origins of the movement. While there are three distinct times that can legitimately be taken as the start of Scouting—Baden-Powell's demonstration camp at Brownsea Island in July 1907, the appearance of the first of the six fortnightly parts of *Scouting for Boys* on 15 January 1908, or the publication of the first complete edition of the handbook on 1 May of the same year—Baden-Powell himself noted the specific instant at which the idea began to occur to him. It was 30 April 1904, when, as inspecting officer, he attended the Annual Drill Inspection and Review of the Boys' Brigade in Glasgow. He had been to such events before, but a conversation with William Smith, founder of the Brigade, made this one entirely different. As he notes in his diary, Smith told him with pleasure of the Brigade's healthy membership, over

> 54,000 altogether.... I suggested that if the work really appealed to the boys they should have ten times that number.

He asked me how it could be made to appeal. I suggested scouting, which had proved so popular with recruits in the army. He asked me if I would not rewrite the army scouting book to suit boys.[1]

Although Smith had in mind Baden-Powell's simply making *Aids to Scouting*, the small pamphlet he had produced for the army in 1899, appropriate for the training of boys, Baden-Powell immediately began to see larger possibilities. His imagination was finally seized not by the revision of a book, but by the vision of a British society made strong by legions of well-disciplined, morally upright, patriotic youth who found their satisfaction in defending the interests of the empire and following the orders of their superiors.

If Baden-Powell needed a model for how such boys might serve the empire, the Mafeking Cadet Corps, established by Lord Edward Cecil, provided it. Since most of the adult males during the siege of Mafeking were involved one way or another with military defense, it occurred to Cecil, Baden-Powell's chief of staff, that much of the town's busy work could be carried on by its youth, thereby leaving the men free for their primary military responsibilities. With Baden-Powell's consent, Cecil organized a group of boys, nine years and older, into a cadet corps, equipping them with khaki uniforms and hats and training them into a smart, efficient unit. Carrying messages from one part of town to another, delivering mail, acting as orderlies, and sharing look-out duties, they soon were scurrying about everywhere performing their useful chores. A photograph of the cadets, standing neatly at attention in their khaki tunics, bandoliers diagonally across their chests, constituted an affecting image of what properly trained boys could do for their empire. Officially cited in the military record as part of the town's defenses, the Mafeking Cadet Corps immediately wrote itself into the mythic story of British heroism. As such, it supplied Baden-Powell in his early Scout-recruiting efforts with a telling example of the exciting role future Scouts might be asked to play in defeating Britain's enemies. Baden-Powell's reference to their usefulness in the very first sentence of *Scouting for Boys* was carefully calculated to open the book with the maximum appeal to the patriotic fantasies of its readers.

Once possessed by the vision Smith's comments generated, Baden-Powell could not free himself from its grasp. According to Hillcourt—and all of Baden-Powell's biographers before him—

Smith's challenge stayed with him for two busy years [he was at this time inspector general of the cavalry] during military inspection trips, manoeuvres in England and Ireland, France, Italy, during the establishment of the Cavalry School at Netheravon and the birth pangs of starting the *Cavalry Journal*. And it went with him on his trip to South Africa with the Duke of Connaught.

Only after he got back home in the middle of April, 1906, did he find time to sketch out some preliminary thinking. He sent a copy of his programme suggestions—which he called "Scouting for Boys"—off to William A. Smith.[2]

In fact, not two years but only eight months passed before Baden-Powell first attempted to set down in some systematic fashion thoughts on a method of organizing and training boys that were stimulated by his April exchange with Smith. Every authorized account of Scouting has overlooked the letter Baden-Powell composed on 19 December and published on 22 December in the Eton College *Chronicle*, suggesting a scheme of youth training that constitutes the first version of what was to develop into his fully hatched Scout program. Addressed to the editor of the *Chronicle*, it calls for public school boys to serve their country in a way that stamps it unmistakably as the inaugural written document in the evolution of Scouting. Unburdened by the need for any strategic discretion, which necessarily attended every phase of the formal development of the Scout movement, the Eton letter provides a more or less unmeditated view of Baden-Powell's thoughts about the need for a youth organization and the functions it might perform for the country. It should be read in its entirety:

There is an opening for English Public School boys to do their country a good turn.

In England we are a small country surrounded by nations far stronger in arms, who may at any time attempt to crush us.

The question is how can we prevent them?

We have at this moment an example of the Far East, of a small island nation like our own successfully withstanding the assaults of a far stronger one.

If we look into the causes of Japan's success we find it very largely in the soldierly spirit and self-sacrificing patriotism of the whole of the people.

We have not got anything like the same spirit in England. However much we may *talk* of our patriotism; but talking is no use: *res non verba* are the only test.

How do the Japs get their patriotism?

By the upper classes learning, as boys, the chivalry of their forefathers the Samurai (or knights of Japan), and as they grow up putting into practice and teaching it also to their middle and working classes. And they begin as children.

We in England have equally good ancestors to look back to in the Knights of the Middle Ages, but we do not imitate them as we ought to.

If we, while we were boys, learnt their patriotism, and put into practice their ideas of honour, self-sacrifice, and skill at arms, and then taught the same to all our lads throughout the country—we should be as strong as the Japs against invasion by any foreign enemy.

We can and ought to do it: but it means every young Englishman exerting himself to doing that bit of duty for his country.

The private test which every English boy ought to put to himself is this: to ask himself on the 1st of every month— 'What have I done during the past month for the good of my country, apart from what I have done for my own personal amusement or improvement?'

And here is a way by which (as I suggested to the Eton Volunteers the other day) each fellow can do a great thing for the country—now—during this next Christmas holiday.

Each one should get together and train a squad of (say) ten boys in his village or town, just as the Knights of old used to get together their 'clump' (as they called it) of armed retainers and trained them to patriotism and use of arms. The way to set about it would be to get a few boys to come in the evening and read to them a book about the knights, such as Conan Doyle's *White Company*, etc. and go on with Fitchet's *Deeds that Won the Empire*, etc., Roberts' *Adventures of Captain John Smith*, or any other interesting accounts of the battles and self-sacrifice of our forefathers.

Then teach them:

1. how to aim and shoot with miniature rifles;
2. how to judge distance;
3. how to scout;
4. how to drill and skirmish, take cover, etc.

As regards miniature rifles and ranges it is best to get advice and information about them from the secretary of the Society of Miniature Rifle Clubs, 20 Bucklersbury, Queen Victoria Street, E.C. They do not cost much.

As regards scouting, I will gladly send a copy of my little book of instruction on this subject to any member of the school who can show that he has got a clump of twelve retainers (or men-at-arms) to teach.

Uniform is not necessary. In the old days the retainers wore any kind of armour they could get hold of, and latterly we have seen that the Boers could fight well enough in their ordinary clothes.

But if it is decided to have some distinguishing badge, one kind of hat and a belt for all would do, or the crest of the commander worn as a badge.

But any expense involved in these should be borne by the members themselves—by a subscription of (say) fourpence or sixpence a month. No corps of this kind ought to be so helpless as to have to go begging for money; it must be self-supporting: and if anxious to get big funds should do it by giving a concert or gymnastic display or something of that kind, and take money at the door.

The form of the engagement, or attestation, as it is called in the army, would be a paper which every member would sign on joining—to this effect.

FORM OF ENGAGEMENT

The duties of the Knights of old and their retainers were these:

1. to fear God
2. honour the King
3. help the weak and distressed
4. reverence women and be kind to children
5. train themselves to the use of arms for defence of their country
6. sacrifice themselves, their amusements, their property, and, if necessary, their lives for the good of their fellow-countrymen.

I promise on my honour, to be loyal to the King and to back up my commander in carrying out our duty in each of the above particulars. (Each member will sign his name in the space below this.) Note—If a fellow breaks his word of honour by not carrying out the above engagement after signing it, he incurs one punishment only, and that is *Dismissal*, because he is no longer fit to be a comrade of the others.

Now, if two hundred volunteers carried out this idea and

each trained ten boys this Christmas, we should have 2,000 retainers trained and ready to defend their country the moment that Government wanted them and put rifles in their hands. If more than ten boys were got in the squad they could also form their own football, hockey, or cricket elevens.

If they make a good start other schools will of course follow their example and in a very short time England would have 50,000 or more boys training the right way.

I shall be very glad to hear from any boy who succeeds in getting together a squad as I should like to keep a register of these. And I would gladly come and inspect the one which attains the highest strength this winter.[3]

The letter is illuminating in a number of ways. Given the early Scouting movement's official position that it had nothing to do with soldiering of any kind, perhaps the most striking feature of the Eton proposal is the clearly stated military purpose behind the formation of the groups. While I will deal with the issue of Scouting's militarism in a later chapter, it is important to note here that the clumps are summoned into existence for one ostensible reason: to help defend the country by force of arms against the threat of invasion, and to be ready to do so by the end of Christmas holidays at that. Baden-Powell could hardly be more direct.

Not, of course, that he was naive enough to imagine that a group of Eton schoolboys would return to classes from their Christmas break leaving behind them in towns and villages across England trained cadres of lads ready to take on the German army. He sought less to instill any genuine fighting capability than to cultivate obedience and unswerving devotion to duty fundamental to a military organization. But if the production of a dutiful patriotism among the lower classes supplied the underlying motivation behind the knights and retainers, it is nevertheless significant that at this point Baden-Powell had no qualms at all about making their explicit military nature both the source of their appeal and the primary justification for their existence. While the soldiering is admittedly in the interests of national defense, still he makes no effort to argue for the peacetime applications of the skills being taught. Expressions of courtly concern for the weak and distressed, women and children, are noticeably less important than the activities of shooting, judging distance, skirmishing, drilling, and the rest.

Although it is difficult to believe that Baden-Powell ever really rejected the quasi-military impulses behind this proposal, it is easy to see why, in their original form, they did not find their way into the final scheme. Establishing a national organization involves more delicacy in the articulation of policy than does the rather straightforward statement of public need and remedy that Baden-Powell felt free to express in a school newspaper. A direct appeal to youth necessarily differs from a campaign requiring the backing of parents as well. Different sensibilities have to be dealt with, and Baden-Powell was careful from the start, as I will show later, not to alienate a substantial portion of the population by insisting on any overt military trappings, especially when there would be many ways to achieve the desired indoctrination once the boys were actually involved. Exchanging the miniature rifles of the 1904 retainers for the staves brandished by the Boy Scouts represents more of a change of tactics than a change of mind.

What did not change between 1904 and 1907 was the concern for invasion that Baden-Powell and other military men continually kept before the public. Whether one argued for universal military training, as did the National Service League, or for the support of the Boy Scouts, as their founder did, evoking the menace of blood-thirsty Germans ogling the meager defenses of England was designed to make the point that something had to be done. Nothing works like crisis—real or manufactured—to sell schemes for the proper indoctrination of youth, and from the beginning the Boy Scout movement was marked by a sense of urgency in the case it made for its own importance. The trope of the imperiled island with which Baden-Powell opens his Eton letter—"In England we are a small country surrounded by nations far stronger in arms, who may at any time attempt to crush us"—is part of the rhetoric common to all those calling for England's greater military preparedness and appears as a motif throughout Scout literature prior to World War I.

Another interesting feature of the Eton appeal that figured prominently in the rhetorical equipment of military-reform advocates is the exemplary instance of Japan. With the seizure of Port Arthur from the Russians in 1904, Japan suddenly thrust itself on British consciousness as the perfect illustration of what unquestioning obedience and a fervent patriotism rooted in compulsory military service could accomplish. Equating military might with moral greatness, National Service League members and others celebrated over and over again the supreme achievement of Japanese civilization. A victory in arms was transformed into a moral, spiritual, and intellectual affirmation of a culture that set itself the task of inculcating selfless patriotism in its citizens. The Japanese code of ethics, Japanese schools, Japanese discipline, Japanese physical training, Japanese cleanliness, and above all, Japanese military efficiency were seen as models worthy of emulation. In one stroke Japan had succeeded in casting off the peculiar contempt Britain traditionally maintained for non-white peoples, earning its new cultural status entirely by its fighting prowess. In his eulogistic *Great Japan*, Alfred Stead stated explicitly in 1905 how Japan has eradicated the stigma of race:

> The recognition of Japan's right to a high place among the nations of the world has also brought about a complete refutation of the formerly universal opinion as to the national superiority of those peoples living in the artificial geographic division called Europe. Japan's emergency has changed this, and in the future there is no more Asia, no more Europe, no hard-and-fast colour and race distinctions. The blood spilt on the glacis of the Port Arthur forts has for ever wiped out the colour line in national achievement.[4]

The "Britain of the East" was seen to have much to teach its Western admirer, and the pages of *Scouting for Boys* are filled with numerous vignettes of Japanese courage and patriotism. (Note that British racial contempt, however, cannot totally be obliterated by anything as simple as a military victory. For Baden-Powell they are still the "Japs"—as much a term of denigration in 1904 as it is today.)

It is also fascinating to find Baden-Powell reading as part of the Japanese lesson the role that the upper classes played in the dissemination of patriotic ideals throughout the culture. Although the Boy Scout movement prided itself from the beginning on its classlessness, ostensibly appealing to boys from all walks of life, in fact, as I will show in the next chapter, it was intended to provide for the working and lower-middle classes the character training the privileged classes were able to receive in the public schools. Public school boys were of course a welcome asset to the movement, but Scouting was never designed for them. For Baden-Powell their character and loyalty were not in doubt. Only those who stood outside the life-giving influence of the great public schools (and the wealth and social standing that gave access to them) required the help of Scouting to shape them into the same mold of useful citizenry to which their upper-class brothers were adjusting themselves in school. Baden-Powell wanted public school boys in the Scouting movement not because he felt they needed the training—for them it was essentially

superfluous—but because he thought that by having them he would
establish a strong base of future partisans of Scouting, as well as a
fine source of future Scoutmasters. That the 1904 scheme was
presented in the Eton College *Chronicle* suggests the firm sense of
class reality that underlay Scouting's egalitarianism.

The very notion of knights educating their retainers illustrates
this point, as does the praise Baden-Powell lavishes on the Japanese
samurai and English knights as purveyors of the highest ideals of
their respective cultures. Locating the principles of admirable behavior—patriotism, a sense of honor, self-sacrifice—in an artisto-
cratic, heroic (and highly mythologized) past far removed from the
imaginative world of working-class lads, Baden-Powell conferred on
Scouting an august tradition that emphasized the need for the
lower classes to look to their betters for instruction and moral
marching orders. The retainers come together to learn from their
public school knights those aristocratic values of which they have
had little experience. Baden-Powell invokes the hallowed past of
English knighthood in later Scouting literature to sell incipient
Scouts on the centrality of the movement's heritage. The attestation
the Eton proposal requires of its retainers anticipates the various
forms of the knightly code that crop up throughout Baden-Powell's
writing as precursors of the Scout Law.

For Baden-Powell, public school prefect and patrol leader shared
a common responsibility for the direction and moral growth of the
youths under them, and in this Eton scheme of "Knights and retainers" we obviously have an early version of the patrol system
that was to become a basic feature of the Scout movement. What
is particularly interesting in this plan is the range of expertise
Baden-Powell attributes to the public school boy, finding him qualified not only to transmit the lessons in patriotism in which he has
presumably been steeped in school but also to teach the basic skills
of rifle shooting, skirmishing, Scouting, drilling, and the like. A tall
order for even the most exceptional public school boy indeed, and
one that Baden-Powell will not impose on the patrol leader. Its
extravagant assumptions about the capacities of the Eton school
boy testify more to Baden-Powell's own ideal sense of class responsibility than to any realistic notions concerning the nature of the
public school student or the effects of his education.

Once formed, the "clumps" were to be financially self-sustaining,
a principle on which Baden-Powell insisted for his Scout troops. He
was always adamant about the moral dangers involved in asking
for handouts of any sort, and in suggesting that funds could be
raised by "giving a concert or gymnastic display," he defines those

very measures the Scouts would later employ to generate money for their activities.

Baden-Powell ends his letter to the *Chronicle* with the comments that he would like to keep track of any groups that are formed and that he would be happy to inspect personally the one that achieved the greatest strength by the end of the winter. Innocuous in themselves, these statements are not without their significance in pointing to the incipient kind of *organizational* thinking Baden-Powell was already beginning to do. While Smith might have challenged him simply to address the problem of training boys, Baden-Powell seems at the same time to be considering, in an admittedly rudimentary way, structure as well as method. Keeping a register of groups that are established is one bureaucratic step up from merely exhorting the Etonian to set about educating the boys in their home villages. And that he would be willing personally to attend an inspection— a not inconsiderable attraction for a group of boys, since the hero of Mafeking was still very much a hero—hints at an interest that goes well beyond mere curiosity or enthusiasm. Although it has always been Scout gospel that Baden-Powell never intended a separate movement but only a system of training designed to complement existing youth organizations, it is fair to see in this Eton document the inklings of a separate enterprise presided over by Baden-Powell himself. Although no documentary evidence exists for this interpretation,[5] I would argue that such an interpretation is certainly in keeping with what we know of his character.

However integral the doctrine of selflessness was to Boy Scout philosophy, Baden-Powell's self was always very much in view and very much in need of nourishment. To imagine that a man with his flair and egotism would be content simply to devise a system that other organizations might use hardly seems plausible. But he was also a sufficiently shrewd politician to know that it would not be prudent to enter the scene as a rival to the YMCA and those already established youth brigades. Steadfastly refusing to acknowledge any aspirations for independent status, Baden-Powell remained on good terms with the other groups, even managing during the early stages to induce them to publicize Scouting actively around the country. Finally, when the number of boys thronging to the Scouts became overwhelming, Baden-Powell was "forced" to set up his own organizational structure. It is clear that Scouting's enormous and instant popularity surprised Baden-Powell as much as anybody else, but it is difficult to imagine that he did not entertain from the start thoughts of leading his own youth movement. Considering the Eton proposal in the light of this possibility, we realize that throughout all the talk of the need for patriotism and preparedness, Baden-Powell does not mention a single word about the other youth groups that in their different ways were concerned with many of the same problems he hoped to address. Baden-Powell's silence here is not without its meaning.

The letter to the *Chronicle* is clearly Baden-Powell's first written attempt to organize his thinking about the purpose and methods of training youth. Both in specific details and in overall direction it points ahead to the fully developed Scout program of 1908.[6] As striking as are many of the resemblances between the Eton document and the final authorized version of Scouting, two major differences are equally striking and instructive. The most obvious is the relative insignificance of Scouting itself in the Eton scheme. Comprising but one of the four skills (in addition to shooting, judging distance, drilling, and skirmishing) that the public school "knights" should attempt to teach to their village retainers, it has no central or defining importance in the plan. Although part of Baden-Powell's genius lay in recognizing the enormous appeal the special activities of Scouting held for boys and in building a movement with them as a compelling nucleus, this first rough cast at an idea for organizing youth did not exploit the business of Scouting itself.

Along with the absence of the vitalizing presence of Scouting, the Eton proposal also fails to emphasize the character training that was to become such a basic part of the Boy Scout movement. Except by implication, through the injunction to the retainers to help the weak, reverence women, and in general exhibit loyalty to king and commander, the Eton letter dwells less on the issue of good citizenship than on the rather narrower problem of conferring some minimal soldierly competence on the youth of Britain. The Scout goal of training the rising generation to be exemplary citizens and useful colonists, an aspiration calculated to appeal particularly to the older generation, does not lend its tone of moral urgency to this formulation. Without the inner coherence provided by the activity of Scouting and the external allure of the insistence on proper character training, the Eton scheme lacks both the method and the mission critical to the success of the Scouts. We have no evidence that a single "clump" was ever formed in response to Baden-Powell's letter, or indeed that anyone ever paid much attention to it. Baden-Powell seems himself to have done nothing more with this particular idea beyond initially publishing it. He was not blind to its deficiencies however, though it would take him three more years before he succeeded in refining his knights and retainers into those redoubtable peace Scouts who first conquered England and then the entire world.

There still were the duties of inspector general of the cavalry to manage, however, and for much of the next two years Baden-Powell was busy traveling all over the world attending to them. But despite the responsibilities of his job, the idea of a new system of youth training continued to interest him. Returning to England in April 1906, after a period of protracted travel, he wrote a short paper entitled "Scouting for Boys", which he sent to a number of eminent men including Lord Roberts, Admiral Beresford, and William Smith. Everybody responded enthusiastically, and Smith published an abridged form of it in the *Boys' Brigade Gazette* of 1 June. Here we can see how far Baden-Powell has progressed from his "clumps" of 1904. If the overt concern of the Eton appeal dwelt on military preparedness, the aim now is the more palatable Scout concern with fashioning useful, obedient citizens: "The ulterior object of the following scheme is to develop among boys a power of sympathising with others, a spirit of self-sacrifice and patriotism, and generally to prepare them for becoming good citizens."[7] The method for achieving such goals is not yet the elaborated system of Scouting. At this point Baden-Powell emphasizes only the salutary role of developing the boy's powers of observation, his ability to draw proper conclusions from evidence. But in the process of explaining how the instructor should inculcate the principles of sound deductive reasoning in his young charges, Baden-Powell touches upon a number of those activities, skills, and concerns that would shortly form the core of the official Scouting program:

The instructor should read to the would-be scouts a detective tale from Gaboriau or Conan Doyle (Sherlock Holmes), laying special stress on the clues to the crime, and the deductions therefrom. He should examine the Boys to see that they have grasped the idea of drawing conclusions from small signs.

He should then give instruction in noticing details and remembering them; such as looking in a shop window for one minute and then moving away—to try and state all the articles in the window; noticing the difference and details of passers-by, and deducing their occupation and character; points of the compass by the sun, moon, stars, etc.; learning in the country or parks the tracks of people, horses, carriages, etc., their age and meaning; the art of lighting a fire and cooking; judging distance; knowledge of first aid, revival of apparently drowned persons; personal hygiene; ability to swim; writing brief reports, etc.; the place of Great Britain among the nations; the British Colonies; the Union Jack and its meaning. *Duty* to your country and to neighbours to be first guide in taking any step, your own *pleasure* or convenience to come second. Need of good citizens. Using your power of noticing details to spot people in every day who are wanting help, and to help them in however small a way.[8]

Topics of instruction, however, do not necessarily imply a workable organization, and a method "to make boys observant of details, and to develope [*sic*] their reasoning powers"[9] is by no means synonymous with the perfected version of Scouting that Baden-Powell finally gave the world. While a number of the individual pieces were beginning to sort themselves out in his mind, he still had a long way to go before assimilating them into the viable system embodied in the handbook, *Scouting for Boys*.

Baden-Powell never claimed that the principles behind his scheme for training youth were uniquely his. On the contrary, he always emphasized that his system drew on many sources, including his own scouting practices with the South African Constabulary. While the extent of his scholarly investigations is no doubt mildly exaggerated, Baden-Powell indicated that between 1906 and the time he started to compose the text of *Scouting for Boys* he had read Epictetus; Livy; Pestalozzi, the Swiss educator; Jahn on physical culture; as well as the *Broadstone of Honour* by Kenelm Digby; had looked into the technique for educating boys to be found among the Spartans, the Zulus and other African tribes, as well as the ancient British and Irish; had studied the Bushido of the Japanese and the educational methods of John Pounds, the Portsmouth shoemaker who founded the "ragged schools" for destitute boys; and consulted the practices of his contemporaries, such as William Smith, Ernest Thompson Seton, and Dan Beard, among others.[10] In addition to what he actually gleaned from them, the broad range of influences Baden-Powell publicly acknowledged, spanning different cultures and times, helped give credibility to Scouting, investing it with a centrality and timelessness beyond simply one man's vision. His manner of alluding to them is also meant to suggest that Baden-Powell learned equally from all of them. But in fact, of the many influences he cited, one—Ernest Thompson Seton—was appreciably more important than the others in contributing to the formation of Baden-Powell's organizational thinking in general, and to any number of specific details in particular.

Indeed, from Seton's point of view, so vital was the role he played in the development of Scouting that he always felt that he, not Baden-Powell, deserved recognition as its proper founder. Whatever the justice of the claim, the vexed relationship of the two men needs to be untangled carefully if we are to understand how *Scouting for Boys* came to be written.

Born in England and raised as a young boy in Canada, Seton came to America in the 1880s, where he became one of the great artist-naturalists of the twentieth century. The founder of the Woodcraft movement, he was far more unworldly and visionary than Baden-Powell. For Seton, the natural wisdom of the woods was the highest available to man: individuals had to learn to trust their instincts and open themselves to the promptings of nature in order to achieve their full realization as human beings. Consciousness of sin was a lamentable man-made invention that restricted the development of his potential. The woodcraft he preached was thus not in any way a narrow training for survival in the woods but rather a total philosophy of human regeneration. The aim of Woodcraft was *"to make a man,"*[11] and the perfect man for Seton was the noble Shawnee chief Tecumseh, who embodied all the virtues Seton came to associate with the outdoor ideal:

> No one now questions the broad statement that Tecumseh was a great athlete, a great hunter, a great leader, clean, manly, strong, unsordid, courteous, fearless, kindly, gentle with his strength, dignified, silent and friendly, equipped for emergencies, and filled with a religion that consisted not of books and creeds or occasional observances, but of desire to help those that had need of help....[12]

Altogether, then, "Tecumseh, besides being a great Woodcrafter, was the most Christlike character presented on the pages of American history; him, therefore, I select the model of perfect manhood held up for guidance of the young man of America."[13]

Seton began promulgating his vision of Woodcraft and the ideal Indian throughout the 1880s and '90s in magazines such as *Forest and Stream, Scribner's, Actual Friends*, and others, but it was not until 1901 that he actually attempted to fashion it into a national movement. He approached the *Ladies' Home Journal* with the idea, and in May 1902 the first of seven monthly articles appeared in the magazine with the title, "Ernest Thompson Seton's Boys: The New Department of 'American Woodcraft' for Boys," based on the assumption that, "I suppose that every boy in America loves to 'play Injun.' "[14] Seton sketched out the details and the organizational possibilities of how this could be done. Giving practical instruction on the art of tracking, tepee making, and bow-and-arrow manufacture, as well as ideas for various Woodcraft games, the seven articles succeeded both in celebrating the Indian ideal and in making that ideal accessible to all those interested in participating:

> The principal things necessary to play Indian are a tribe of the right kind of boys, woods, one or more tepees, bows and arrows, a head-dress or war bonnet for each, and of course a knowledge of woodcraft. . . .[15]

A central feature of the Woodcraft scheme concerns the symbolic significance of the Indian headdress and the different accomplishments for which feathers could be won. Seton points out the distinction between awarding the coups and awarding the grand coups to recognize various degrees of achievement and then suggests eleven separate tests for boys under fourteen for which either coups or grand coups could be earned. For example, walking one mile in fourteen minutes for a coup, or in thirteen minutes for a grand coup; running 100 yards in twelve and a half seconds for a coup, or in twelve for a grand coup; finding one's way to camp through strange woods in a requisite amount of time; and the like. In establishing absolute as opposed to competitive standards of proficiency, and in honoring performance with visibly different kinds of feathers or emblems, Seton provided an organizing structure not just for his own Woodcraft Indians but one that would also appear to have found its way into the British organization.

The symbolic headdress acknowledged merit but indicated censure as well. The Woodcraft Indians were invested with a strict code of conduct; its earliest version contained a list of six high crimes that had to be avoided: cheating, killing a songbird, setting wildfires, breaking the game laws, rebelling, and wearing honors not conferred by the council. Grave violations required the offender to wear a black feather until he could work himself back into favor with the governing council. Extreme offenders could be expelled from the tribe altogether.

With its advice on woodcraft matters, its code of behavior, and its rudimentary organization and system of merit, Seton's Woodcraft Indian scheme was for all practical purposes laid out in the series of articles in the *Ladies' Home Journal*. Helped by Seton's own proselytizing efforts, tribes began forming themselves even as the articles were appearing, so that his sixth contribution in October 1902 mentions his visit with a band—the first he knows about—that started in New Jersey.

During the next two years Seton continued to elaborate in writing on the basic scheme presented in the *Journal* while encouraging the formation of bands of Seton Indians in any way he could. In 1903 he published a thirty-two-page booklet, *How to Play Indian*, which focused his thinking along more functional organizational lines. There is now a watchword, "The best things of the best Indians"; an official object, "The Study and pleasures of woodcraft";[16] a variety of officers, beginning with Head War Chief and moving down through the ranks; and a vow that each brave had to take upon joining:

> I solemnly promise that I will obey the chief and council of my tribe, and if I fail in my duty I will surrender to them my weapons, and submit without murmuring to their decision.[17]

The six prohibitions have now been slightly altered and expanded somewhat, so that firearms are now forbidden and the braves are obliged to keep a clean camp. Interestingly, given the fact that Seton later criticized what he saw as the authoritarian character of the British Scouts, the exhortation against rebellion is emphasized. It is now the first law and more particularized than in its initial appearance: "Don't rebel. Rebellion against any decision of the Council is punishable by expulsion. Absolute obedience is always enforced."[18]

An important new organizational feature is also introduced: Each band of Indians will be identified by a totem decided by the council. For Seton, any animal, bird, tree, or flower would suffice. The totem should be something easy to draw; if an animal or bird, the band should be able to make its distinctive sound as a war cry. The resemblance between these totems and the Scout practice of naming each patrol after an animal or bird whose call the members must be able to reproduce is clearly not accidental and accounts in part for Seton's accusations that Baden-Powell stole fundamental ideas without acknowledging them.

The third version of the basic *Ladies' Home Journal* scheme, *The Red Book or How to Play Indian*, appeared in 1904. Essentially an expanded treatment of the same material, giving more games, more woodcraft lore, and a wider range of exploits for which coups and grand coups can be earned, this edition also suggests the development of a concern that, while perhaps implicit in the earlier version, was never stated directly. Part of the virtue of his plan, Seton notes, is that it gives young people "something to do, something to think about and something to enjoy in the woods with a view always to character building."[19] Seton's understanding of character is by no means the same as Baden-Powell's, but it is interesting to see Seton attributing to his Woodcraft Indians the same character-building function that Baden-Powell would also claim for his Scouts.

In addition to these various programmatic presentations of his idea, Seton also embodied his vision of the woodcraft ideal in several imaginative works, most notably *Two Little Savages*, published in 1903. Into the story of Yan and Sam living in the woods by themselves for several weeks, Seton folds the detailed, practical lessons on woodcraft and the celebration of natural life and values found in his early works. The two boys put into practice all the principles of the Woodcraft life: They play Seton's woodcraft games, set up a camp according to his instructions, make bows and arrows, traps, and tepees; award each other coups and grand coups according to their appropriate achievements; and learn the proper reverence for the sanctity of nature. The moral and even physical development they experience in the process attests to the merits of the Woodcraft way. Altogether *Two Little Savages* constitutes an applied instance of Seton's theories concerning the splendors and importance of the natural life. Its subtitle—"A Book of American Woodcraft for Boys"—suggests its intention and defines its success.

Stimulated by Seton's writings and his own personal commitment to the cause, bands of his Indians began to spring up around the country. In 1904 Seton was sufficiently encouraged by his success to bring the gospel of the ideal red man and the Woodcraft way to England. His first lecture, entitled "The Red Indian as I Knew Him," was given at the Congregational Church, Stoke Newington, in London, on 13 October, followed by talks at a number of public schools, among other places, throughout the next several months.[20] While British soil was clearly not the best place to sow the seeds of indigenous American culture, nevertheless the results of his efforts were not ungratifying for Seton. One camp was immediately established in Eccles after a lecture there on 8 November, and, according to Seton, others followed later at Hove, New Brighton, and Kent Hatch.

Seton went back to America in 1904, returning to England two years later to continue work on behalf of his Woodcraft movement. It was at this time that he made his fateful connection with Baden-Powell. Knowing of Baden-Powell's interest in Scouting, he wrote to him early in July 1906 asking if he would help popularize his Woodcraft camps in England, including with his note the most recent edition (1906) of his Indian manual, now called for the first time, *The Birch-bark Roll of the Woodcraft Indians*. Baden-Powell responded enthusiastically:

> I am sincerely grateful to you for your kindness in forwarding me your interesting Birch Bark.
>
> It may interest you to know that I had been drawing up a scheme with a handbook to it, for the education of boys as scouts—which essentially runs much on the lines of yours. So I need scarcely say that your work has a very special interest to me.
>
> I should very much like to meet you if you are at any time in England—and in any case if you should allow me to send you a copy of my scheme later on (it is not yet printed completely), and give me your criticism of it I should be very grateful indeed.[21]

They finally met on 30 October in London, with Baden-Powell indicating in his diary that Seton "told me all about his Red Indian Boys scheme."[22] On 31 October Baden-Powell wrote to Seton as follows:

> I enclose a kind of preliminary notice which I sent out early this year regarding my scheme of 'Boy Scouts'—and it has a very encouraging response—but I have to wait till this next month before I can get under way with the details of it—though I've planned them. You will see that our principles seem practically identical—except that mine does not necessarily make its own organization—it is applicable to existing ones. If we can work together in the same direction I sh'd be very glad indeed—for I'm sure that there are great possibilities before us.[23]

The 30 October meeting in fact did mark the beginning of an active relationship between the two men as they worked together to bring the possibilities of the outdoor life before the boys of Great Britain and America. They corresponded regularly throughout 1906 and 1907, exchanging ideas on techniques of tracking and effective methods of instruction, encouraging each other in their separate but similar endeavors. Baden-Powell agreed to serve as the revisor of the Scouting department for subsequent editions of *The Birch-bark Roll*; and when the Boy Scouts were established in the

United States in 1910, Seton not only revised *Scouting for Boys* into the first American Scout handbook but accepted election as the Chief Scout of the American organization.

Even as Seton and Baden-Powell pursued their common goals, however, strains began to develop between them. Seton grew increasingly aggrieved at the plaudits conferred on Baden-Powell as the inventor of Scouting, a grievance obviously exacerbated by the enormous popularity of Baden-Powell's movement as opposed to the substantially more modest success of his own Woodcraft Indians. As early as 1909 he objected to what he saw as the wholesale unacknowledged borrowings from his work that went into the writing of *Scouting for Boys*:

> The Birch Bark Roll, now in its 8th edition differs in no essential from the Scouting for Boys, it was in your possession when you formed your plans and must have contributed to helping you. Yet you give no hint of this. Next you have taken my games, Spearing the Sturgeon, Quick-Sight, Spot-the-Rabbit, Bear-Hunt, Hostile-Spy, made unimportant alterations in them, changing their names in most cases, and given them as though they were yours, in spite of the fact that these were invented slowly, developed in course of practice, and copyrighted solely by myself. This, you must admit, is not right.... But more important to me, is the fact that you do not anywhere come out frankly and make it clear that for 9 years I have been carrying on in America precisely the same movement, founding camps and teaching woodcraft and scouting to the boys as a means of developing manliness and character.[24]

By 1910, in the face of constant rebuff from Baden-Powell, Seton's claims grew more decisive and more inclusive, arguing now that, as Baden-Powell well knew, "the whole idea was originated by me and founded in England in 1904." Seton goes on, in the same letter,

> I have gone carefully over your "Scouting For Boys," and note that you grudgingly admit having got a "few details" from me. Therefore, I make this emphatic general statement: Omitting the actual stories (I always used stories) there is not an important idea in "Scouting for Boys" that I did not publish years ago in "Two Little Savages," "The Birch Bark Roll" and my Woodcraft and Scouting articles of which I furnished you with copies. The only important change you make is to

give things new names and assume their authorship for yourself.[25]

His resentment was nourished by a sense that Baden-Powell had
betrayed the purity of the woodcraft ideal, substituting for the true
woodcraft way a narrowly self-serving military training that had
nothing to do with real character building. For Seton, "Be Prepared" was transparently a prescription for war, a commitment
that in his view the entire Scout organization, in its activities,
rhetoric, and principles of unwavering obedience to Scout officers,
shared. He felt that Scouting lacked all sense of imagination or
beauty and any spiritual dimension whatever. The daily good turn
for him was guaranteed to produce an artificial, priggish character.
As Seton's antipathy toward Baden-Powell's movement developed,
it is not surprising that his role in American Scouting became
increasingly problematic. By 1915 the situation had become sufficiently intolerable for everybody that amidst a variety of unpleasant accusations, Seton left the organization entirely, still
obviously bitter at the recognition that continued to elude him.

How justified was Seton's insistence that Baden-Powell stole
many of Scouting's essential ideas from him? To answer this we
must consider first what stage in his thinking about Scouting
Baden-Powell had reached *before* meeting Seton and reading his
Birch-bark Roll in 1906. Baden-Powell had clearly been groping for
a viable organizational and conceptual scheme since that afternoon
in April 1904 when William Smith challenged him to come up with
something that would appeal to boys. While Baden-Powell's proposal in the Eton College *Chronicle* of that year still left him a good
distance away from the more detailed notion of Scouting that
emerged after his discussions with Seton, it was nevertheless iden-
tifiably the first version of that notion. In the public school knights
and their clumps, the attestation to which the village boys commit
themselves, the oath of loyalty to king and commander, and the
variety of other details contained in the Eton document, Baden-
Powell had without question started himself on the road to the Boy
Scouts.

The second piece of written evidence we have, the "Scouting for
Boys" paper that William Smith published in *The Boys' Brigade
Gazette* in June 1906 indicates, as we have seen, the substantial
progress Baden-Powell had made in shaping his understanding. But
if some specific activities and a more clearly defined purpose were
now beginning to emerge, Baden-Powell's conception still lacked,
among other things, a practicable structure. And it is at this point,

between, that is, June 1906 when Seton sent Baden-Powell the
Birch-bark Roll and February 1907, when Baden-Powell sent to a
number of people, including Seton, his outline of "Boy Patrols"[26]—
a paper that more or less marks the complete conceptualization of
the Scout movement—that Seton's *Birch-bark Roll* must have come
as a revelation to Baden-Powell, presenting as it does a coherent,
credible scheme for organizing boys into manageable self-governing
units. Its detailed system of outdoor training, its rules, honors,
games, noncompetitive standards of excellence, and even its philosophy that "manhood, not scholarship is the first aim of education,"[27] could not have failed to kindle Baden-Powell's imagination
about the possibilities for his own Scouting aspirations. However
conscientious Baden-Powell may have been about acknowledging
his sources (and in fact he was not overly scrupulous about it), the
extraordinary appropriateness of Seton's Indians to what Baden-
Powell was hoping to achieve could not easily have been resisted.
Beneath the Indian trappings, for which Baden-Powell had no use,
lurked an organizational model that provided solutions for almost
every problem he faced and that furthermore could be translated
into the language of Scouting without difficulty.

The very first sentence of the *Roll* certainly must have delighted
Baden-Powell, calling attention to that concern for national regeneration that shortly constituted the major selling point of the
Scouts: "This is a time when the whole nation is turning toward
the outdoor life, seeking in it the physical regeneration so needful
for continued national existence...."[28] It is characteristic of the
difference between the two men that while Seton never really developed the urgency of this theme for his movement, Baden-Powell
exploited it to the fullest in arguing for the importance of his Scouts.

Beyond sounding this initial note of regeneration, the opening
pages of the *Roll* were clearly important to Baden-Powell in other
ways as well. The self-governing nature of the Scout patrols, with
its members taking orders from a peer patrol leader under the
ultimate supervision of an adult Scoutmaster, is also contained in
Seton's scheme. Seton suggests there are four possible forms of
government appropriate for organizing bands of young people committed to outdoor living: the patriarchal, which is good only for
small numbers; the school system, which does not work out of doors;
the Brigade, which some people object to because of its militarism;
and the tribal or Indian form, which is vastly superior to the others.
His description of the virtues of the tribal scheme anticipate the
argument Baden-Powell would later make for the efficiency and
delights of Scouting:

Fundamentally this is a republic or limited monarchy, and has proved far the best. It makes its members *self-governing*. It offers appropriate things to do *outdoors*; it is so plastic that it can be adopted in whole or in part, at once or gradually; its *picturesqueness* takes immediate hold of the boys, and it lends itself so well to existing ideas that soon or late most camps are *forced into its essentials*, call them what you will.[29]

The flexibility, the varied program of interesting activities, and the conscious effort to catch the imagination of boys—all these ingredients of the Woodcraft Indians were essential to the appeal of Scouting as well.

While the hierarchy and symbolic systems of the two movements differ, Seton's discussion of the need for both was obviously illuminating for Baden-Powell in his efforts to turn his ideas for training boys into a successful organization:

No large band of boys ever yet camped out for a month without finding it necessary to recognize leaders, a senior form, or ruling set whose position rests on merit, some wise grown person to guide them in difficulties, and a place to display the emblems of the camp; that is, they have adopted the system of Chiefs, Council, Medicine-man and Totem-pole. Moreover, the ideal Indian, whether he ever existed or not, stands for the highest type of the primitive life, and he was a master of Woodcraft, which is our principal study. By Woodcraft we mean nature-study, certain kinds of hunting, and the art of camping, but we added all good outdoor athletics to our pursuits.[30]

The dignified, noble Indian and the grizzled trooper and frontiersman have little in common other than the exemplary metaphoric roles each played in his respective organization, embodying in his person the whole system of values Seton and Baden-Powell were espousing.

The 1906 *Roll* also contains a clear statement of what Seton calls the two "important ideas" that underlie his scheme: "The first is *personal decoration* for personal achievement; second, *no competitive honors*. All our honors are bestowed according to world-wide standards."[31] For Seton, the stress on developing champions had resulted in the neglect of the mass of Americans who needed physical development. "A great deal of this would be avoided if we strive to bring all the individuals up to a certain standard. In our noncompetitive tests the enemies are not '*the other fellows*,' but *time and space*. We try not to down the others but to raise ourselves."[32] As he did in the earlier versions of the *Roll*, Seton includes here those tests, in this instance some 150 of them, for which his braves can receive their "coups" or "grand coups," signified by the appropriate feather in the headbands or wampum medals on their coats, or both. The list includes not just athletic achievements—running, swimming, throwing, skating, rowing, and the like—but also camping skills, such as living in the woods alone, lighting a fire without matches, recognizing stars, and measuring distances, as well as demonstrating competence in nature study, fishing, archery, and mountaineering, to name a few. It also, humorously enough, includes that most characteristic of Boy Scout activities, knot making, in which a coup is awarded for tying twenty different standard knots on a rope, and a grand coup for thirty.

But in addition to listing the various exploits that yield honors, Seton describes the whole process in language and with details that appear particularly significant for the subsequent development of Scouting. To begin with, it is difficult not to hear, in Seton's statement that "These exploits are intended to distinguish those braves who are *first* considered in the *record-making class*,"[33] a clear anticipation of Baden-Powell's division of Scouts into two kinds—first and second class, depending on their abilities. (It should also be noted that Seton divided his Indians into two groups,—braves and warriors—analogous to Baden-Powell's first- and second-class Scouts. A new member is a brave until he takes a scalp, at which point he becomes a warrior.) The full panoply of badges and emblems that adorn the Scout uniform, testifying to the rank and achievements of the wearer, can also be found in Seton's scheme of feathers and wampum medals. While a feather is awarded for each coup won, Seton recognized that it would not always be appropriate to wear one's headband. Therefore wampum medals, made from shells and "engraved with the symbol or the deed for which it is given"[34] are available to be worn on a coat—surely the Indian ancestor of the Scout proficiency badge.

Detailed similarities are everywhere. For Seton, no honor can be won unless it is properly witnessed or proven, paralleling the Scout system of certification of all achievement. The Scout's badge, known as his "life,"[35] is awarded the Scout when he passes the tests necessary to enter the organization. Consider what can happen to it:

He will be called upon at some time or the other to risk his life, that is to perform some difficult task, and if he fails in it

he loses his life—that is, his badge. In such case a Court of
Honour may allow him to remain in the patrol, but he cannot
have his badge again, unless he performs some very specially
good work.[36]

Compare this with the scalp—"a long tuft of black horsehair"—
that "is presented to the brave on entering the Tribe,"[37] after he
has promised obedience and allegiance and signed the roll:

> He can lose it only in an important competition, approved
> by the Council, in which he stakes his scalp against that of
> some other brave. If he loses he surrenders his tuft to the
> winner and goes tuftless until the Council thinks proper to
> give him a new scalp.[38]

Seton's distinguishing three kinds of honors—red for heroism,
white for campercraft, and blue for nature study—appears also to
have influenced Baden-Powell, at least insofar as the highest class
for Seton, a red honor "for saving a human life at risk of one's
own,"[39] is reflected in Baden-Powell's awarding a bronze medal
with red ribbon "for gallantry in saving life, or attempting to save
life at risk of own life."[40]

In his section on animals and birds in *Scouting for Boys*, Baden-
Powell establishes a set of tests in which first-class Scouts can earn
points toward a Badge of Honor. The tests, requiring the ability to
draw the tracks of animals or birds, name and describe a number
of fish, and provide photos or sketches from life of different wild
animals, birds, or reptiles are all clearly adopted from the nature
study section of the *Birch-bark Roll*, pages 62–65. The parallels continue: If patrol leaders, corporals, and plain Scouts were naturally
available as a model to Baden-Powell from his military experience,
still Seton's Indian hierarchy of Head War Chief, Second War
Chief, and the rest must have encouraged Baden-Powell to employ
such a method of structuring his organization. The adult Scoutmaster in charge of an entire Scout troop has his predecessor in the
"one experienced grown-up person"[41] Seton saw as vital for the
successful functioning of the band, who would serve "as
Medicine-man in the Council, and as teacher when needed."[42]

I have already mentioned the totem system of Seton's Indians—
in which each band is identified by a particular animal or bird
whose distinctive cry the members must make—as undoubtedly
providing the inspiration for Baden-Powell's stricture that "Each
patrol in that troop is named after an animal or bird,"[43] and that

"Each Scout in the patrol has to be able to make the call of his patrol-animal—thus every Scout in the 'Ravens' must be able to imitate the croak of the raven."[44] In a letter of 3 November 1906, Seton also passed on the information to Baden-Powell that "Among the Indians generally the Grey Wolf is considered the ideal scout, because he sees everything and no one sees him. The Wolf, then, is the badge of their Scouting order."[45] In *Scouting for Boys*, Baden-Powell declares that a special badge and title of "Wolf" will be awarded each year for great distinction in Scouting, explaining in part that "The Red Indians of North America call their best scout 'Grey Wolf,' because the grey wolf is a beast that sees everything and yet is never seen."[46]

There are a number of ways Baden-Powell's Scouts resemble Seton's Indians that owe more to the general nature of organizations than to any specific influences of Seton upon Baden-Powell. Thus each has an entrance ritual, an oath upon joining, a set of rules to which each member must conform, and so on. Each also has a set of games designed both to instruct and to entertain its members, and it is here, in the choice of games included, that Seton felt especially abused by Baden-Powell. Seton stresses his displeasure at the stolen games in a letter to Baden-Powell in 1910:

> When first your "Scouting For Boys" appeared, in 1908, I was astounded to find all my ideas taken, all my games appropriated, disguised with new names, the essentials of my plan utilized, and not a word of acknowledgment to me, or explanation why I should be left out of a movement that I began. At once I wrote a friendly letter of protest, asking why you had used all my ideas and all my games and given me no credit.[47]

We do not have a copy of Seton's "friendly letter of protest," but we do have Baden-Powell's response to it:

> Thank you very much for your kind letter. I much regret that I should have omitted mentioning the source of several of the games, as being taken from your "Birch-bark Roll," but the truth is, I had made a general statement to that effect in the introduction of the book, which I afterwards cut out from the beginning and have inserted it at the end, where you will see it in Part VI. But in doing this I had not reflected that the remarks giving the authorship of the games, would not be read by the people until after the games had appeared

before them. I very much regret this oversight, and it is most kind of you to have taken it in the good natured way in which you have done.[48]

Seton's unhappiness—and Baden-Powell's explanation—referred to the six fortnightly parts of *Scouting for Boys*, which came out between January and March 1908. By the time of the first hardcover edition, in May 1908, Baden-Powell had rectified his omission by pointing out, on its very first page, that "Several of the games given here are founded on those in Mr. Thompson Seton's 'Birchbark Roll of the Woodcraft Indians,' called 'Spearing the Sturgeon' (Whale Hunt), 'Quick Sight' (Spotty Face), 'Spot the Rabbit,' 'Bang the Bear,' 'Hostile Spy,' (Stop Thief), etc."[49]

The acknowledgment did nothing to placate Seton:

You merely stated later that *several* of the games were *founded* on those wholly invented by me; which is an error. Not some, but *nearly all of them are taken wholly* from the games slowly perfected by much actual practice and copyrighted by myself, and nothing is said about the most important thing of all, that the whole idea was originated by me and founded in England in 1904.[50]

If we cannot blithely accept the legitimacy of the final claim, the first part of Seton's accusation seems entirely justified. With insignificant modifications, the five games Baden-Powell mentions are less founded upon than identical to games that appear in the *Birch-bark Roll*. Seton's "Spearing the Great Sturgeon," for example, involves placing a log about seven feet long equidistant between two rowboats, each with crews armed with harpoonlike spears. At the signal each crew rows toward the log (the sturgeon), trying to spear it and tow it back to its base. This is precisely the same game Baden-Powell calls "Whale Hunt," the major difference being that the sturgeon-log has been transmogrified into a whale. The fact that in the description of the game Baden-Powell repeats that it is similar to one in the *Birch-bark Roll* quite properly does not satisfy Seton; it is in fact the same game, and citing a resemblance between them finally seems more disingenuous than anything else. Similarly, Seton's "Quick Sight" and "Spot the Rabbit"—games intended to strengthen eyesight and memory—are essentially the same as Baden-Powell's "Quick Sight" and "Old Spotty Face," the Scout versions being only superficially different. "Bang the Bear," which Baden-Powell admits is "from Mr.

Thompson Seton's 'Birchbark of the Woodcraft Indians',"[51] is simply "The Bear Hunt" with another title. As is true also of "Stop Thief," which is none other than Seton's "Hostile Spy" with a few Indian trappings removed and a different name. In every case the totally straightforward tactic for Baden-Powell would have been to include these games under their original titles, acknowledging that with trivial alterations of detail they were taken directly from the *Birch-bark Roll*. To the extent that this was not done, Seton's anger at Baden-Powell's exploitation is understandable.

In addition to those games "borrowed" with inadequate acknowledgment, there are also those games Baden-Powell took from Seton with no mention at all of the fact that they first appeared in the *Birch-bark Roll*—presumably those covered by the suspiciously inclusive *etc.* in Baden-Powell's opening reference. Here is Seton's "Pole Star" game:

> Each competitor is given a long, straight stick, in daytime, and told to lay it due north and south. In doing this he may guide himself by sun, moss, or anything he can find in nature—anything, indeed, except a compass.
>
> The direction is checked by a good compass corrected for the locality. The one who comes nearest wins.[52]

Here is Baden-Powell's "Find the North":

> Scouts are posted thirty yards apart, and each lays down his staff on the ground pointing to what he considers the exact north (or south) without using any instrument. The umpire compares each stick with the compass; the one who guesses nearest wins.[53]

If it could be argued that games of this sort might properly be attributed to a common cultural authorship rather than to any one individual, the same cannot be said of Seton's consciously contrived game of "Man Hunt," in which a scout, wearing a visible badge, "is given a letter addressed to the 'Military Commandant' of any given place a mile or two away. He is told to take the letter to any one of the given houses, and get it endorsed, with the hour when he arrived, then return to the starting point within a certain time."[54] Hostiles are sent to intercept him, and thus the battle of wits commences. This shows up, with minor alterations, as "Despatch Running" in *Scouting for Boys*, in which "A scout is given a despatch to take to the headquarters of a besieged town which may be a real town (village, farm or house) and he must return with a receipt for it. He must wear a coloured rag, two feet long, pinned to his shoulder,"[55] and must elude the besiegers who will be trying to capture him. Baden-Powell spins out the details of this game without ever alluding to its clear *Birch-bark* origins.

Seton remained convinced to the end of his life that Baden-Powell had effectively stolen Scouting from him. Although he at one point grudgingly admits to Baden-Powell that "On reading over all our correspondence I can believe that you had some idea of the Boy Scouts before we met,"[56] such an admission never compromised his view that the central notions of Scouting were basically his. He cited as evidence for this not only the way *Scouting for Boys* used the material and ideas of the *Birch-bark Roll*, but also portions of the correspondence he and Baden-Powell exchanged during the formative years of 1906 to 1908. Thus he refers on several occasions to Baden-Powell's letter of 10 November 1906, to show how Baden-Powell drew on Seton's expertise:

> I am studying your article on tracks [which Seton had earlier sent him] with great interest—and will return it.
>
> I sh'd like very much to quote it in my remarks to boys on the subject.
>
> If you read my "Aids to Scouting" you will see somewhat similar ideas expressed—but not *"demonstrated"* by diagram as yours is—and that is everything in teaching the young ideas.
>
> By the way—do you use lantern slides for that purpose? I propose to do so on 22nd and 23rd when I am to lecture to some boys—but having never before attempted it I don't quite know what are the best kind of pictures to show.[57]

Seton's comments on this letter are brief: "He quoted it indeed, but gave it as his own."[58]

And it is with considerable bitterness that he mentions an exchange with Baden-Powell about his tracking irons, in which Baden-Powell inquired, "I want to know whether your tracking irons are patent or may I have some made like them calling them the 'Seton Tracking Irons.' I have so many requests for them."[59] Seton responded that they were indeed copyrighted, but nevertheless gave Baden-Powell permission to manufacture fifty pairs, without charge, with the understanding that any subsequent lots would be subject to a new arrangement. Baden-Powell thanked him on 24 February, indicating that "I am ordering a few sets to be made accordingly." The outcome of this understanding is contained in a note Seton wrote in 1940:

This he acknowledges in his of 24 Feb. 1908 ... but has continued to make and sell them, doubtless at a profit, ever since 25 years at least, and has never made any accounting or a new arrangement. I (incog.) called at his B.S. headquarters in London, 1935, and bought a pair. They were sold to me as Baden-Powell tracking irons.[60]

In 1910 Seton set down what he saw as the "nine cardinal principles" of his own Woodcraft movement, principles that he felt Baden-Powell incorporated into his Scouts. The nine provide a rather telling assessment of what animates Seton's movement. They are as follows:

1. This is recreation.
2. Camp life.
3. Self-government guided by an adult.
4. The magic of the camp fire.
5. Woodcraft pursuits.
6. Honors by standards.
7. Personal decorations for personal achievements.
8. A heroic ideal.
9. Picturesqueness in all things

And I summed up my plan in these words:—

It is something to do, something to think about, something to enjoy in the woods with a view always to character building, for manhood not scholarship is the first aim of education.[61]

Looking at these, we are struck both by how accurately they summarize the essential character of the movement and how powerfully Baden-Powell must have been affected by them. The Woodcraft Indians contained all the essential ingredients he needed to give shape to his inchoate scheme. In the specific details of games, honors, and scouting techniques, as well as in the overall conceptual framework, Baden-Powell must have recognized the solution to the problems he was facing in designing an organization that would at once work and be appealing to boys. Whether he would have arrived at the same answers without Seton, whether, in other words, Scouting would have emerged precisely as it did if there had been no Woodcraft Indians, it is impossible to say. What can be said with absolute certainty is that Baden-Powell's encounter with Seton was critical to the development of Scouting. Seton was not simply one of the many sources from whom Baden-Powell culled some specific ideas and a few games, but the vital influence who brought before Baden-Powell the model of an efficient, attractive, self-contained system toward which he had been working for two years. The lack of recognition granted Seton for his formative role in the history of Scouting is an injustice at which he was properly distressed.

But to acknowledge that role is not to assert, as Seton did, that he was the true founder of Scouting. However much Baden-Powell might have taken from Seton, Scouting is not simply the Woodcraft Indians under another name and with a slightly military flavor. If the idea stood ready to be invented, or indeed if parts of it had already been invented by Seton, nevertheless without Baden-Powell the Boy Scouts would not have existed. The noble Tecumseh and the ever-vigilant frontiersman-scout comprise entirely different ideals based on entirely different sets of values and amenable to entirely different cultural uses. For better or for worse, Baden-Powell clearly saw that his Scouts had an appeal, for children as well as adults, which far outstripped that of Seton's Indians. Seton felt that Baden-Powell had transgressed on his turf and hindered the development of his movement, but he was wrong. The Woodcraft movement was limited by the very idealism that created it. In taking the structure produced by that idealism and adapting it to his own purposes, Baden-Powell engaged in a genuinely original, creative act. Although Seton's contributions were far greater than Baden-Powell ever admitted, Baden-Powell remains the author of *Scouting for Boys* and the sole founder of the Scout movement.

At the same time that he was struggling to formulate the details of his conception on paper, Baden-Powell was already beginning to think in very practical terms about the future of his scheme. He was aware, unlike William Smith, that if his ideas were to achieve the national recognition he intended, he would have to do far more than simply offer them to the world. He would have to convince the world of their importance, and for this he would need a shrewd salesman experienced in the wiles of marketing ideas as well as personalities.

The super promoter of his time was C. Arthur Pearson, the newspaper tycoon whom Baden-Powell enlisted as his business associate, publisher, and advisor. The choice of Pearson marked the happy calculation that accompanied every phase of Scouting's development. Called by his biographer "the greatest press agent in history,"[62] Pearson had made an enormous fortune in journalism by his middle thirties. A successful manager of various papers such as *Tit-Bits* and *Review of Reviews*, Pearson branched out on his own in 1890, when he started *Pearson's Weekly*. Using a series of prize-awarding word games to boost circulation—games whose questionable legality caused them to be stopped by court order in 1893—*Pearson's Weekly* quickly had a staggering circulation. By the 51st Missing Word competition, the figures were 217,289, and by the 53rd they had exceeded 473,000. In 1900, already wealthy enough to be partially retired, he established the *Daily Express*, a newspaper explicitly designed for mass consumption, which carried the bracing reassurance, "Our policy is patriotic; our policy is the British Empire." Pearson's brand of Social-Imperialist patriotism led him, with Joseph Chamberlain, to establish the Tariff Reform League, whose chairmanship he held until 1905. As the manager of Chamberlain's ambitious publicity campaign on behalf of tariff reform, he utilized techniques of mass exposure—well-advertised motor tours, extensive lectures, and even gramophone recordings—which conveyed the message to every corner of England. For the seventy-year-old Chamberlain, Pearson's tactics were not altogether easy to manage, and in his judgment of Pearson—"the greatest hustler I have ever known"—we sense admiration mingled with a little exasperation.

But if a hustler finally proved a bit too much for Chamberlain, he offered exactly what Baden-Powell needed, particularly a hustler sporting the impeccable credentials of having started the Fresh Air Fund for sending poor children to the country, among a host of other charitable involvements. Despite an unsavory reputation brought about by some murky business and journalistic practices (*The Dictionary of National Biography* claims his career "is perhaps more alarming than edifying. Intellectually he was unfitted to guide, much less to form, public opinion...."), both the man and his publishing empire were precisely right for turning Baden-Powell's scheme into a national institution.

The Scouts have always been vaguely embarrassed by Baden-Powell's collaboration with Pearson, and the authorized version of Baden-Powell's choice stresses his spontaneous discovery of Pearson's goodness. According to Percy Everett, one of Pearson's editorial managers who joined the movement as it started, Baden-Powell's revelation about Pearson occurred during a weekend in July 1906 while he was a guest at Pearson's home. Noticing that Pearson was about to leave,

Baden-Powell strolled up beside the waiting motor car.

"Where are you off to, Pearson?"

"I am just going over to see a cripples' home. I shan't be long."

The car slid off down the road, and Baden-Powell was left thinking.

What he thought was:

Here is the man I want to help me—a lover of children, a famous organizer; a great publicity man; he will know how best to start.[63]

(How Everett knew Baden-Powell's exact thoughts at the time remains unexplained.) This rendition obscures the fact that Baden-Powell certainly knew all about Pearson and what he could do for the Scouts long before the weekend; we can safely say that Baden-Powell was drawn to Pearson less by his love of children than by his commercial acumen. The Everett version represents Scouting's best effort to cleanse its founder of the stain of associating with a character as morally dubious as Pearson.

But however questionable, Pearson provided the direction—and capital—Baden-Powell required. He orchestrated a sustained publicity campaign—which he called "the press booming"—and set up an extensive lecture tour for Baden-Powell throughout England, arranged for the publication of *Scouting for Boys* in both serial and complete form, agreed to commit £1,000 to cover Scouting's initial expenses, obtained a London office for the fledgling organization, and even sent Baden-Powell two stenographers to expedite his meeting his deadlines, in addition to supplying editorial support and advice. He participated, for example, in selecting the name of the movement. "I do not think the Imperial Scouts is a good name", he writes Baden-Powell on 10 September 1907. "For one thing I think it would get mixed up in the public mind with the Imperial League of Frontiersmen. It seems to me we should certainly use the word 'boy'. I do not think you will improve upon Boy Scouts."[64] His motives were by no means purely altruistic. Baden-Powell agreed that Pearson could publish the official magazine of the movement (*The Scout*) to which Baden-Powell would contribute a signed article each issue. (Pearson's sense of the commercial possibilities of the movement was, as usual, acute. By the end of its first year of publication, *The Scout* had a weekly circulation of 110,000 copies.)

The Scout played an important part in Scouting's early development for several reasons. Filled with the usual stuff of boys' adventure magazines—tales of intrepid explorers and dark intrigue, all celebrating the triumph of Anglo-Saxon courage and ingenuity over fiendish difficulties—along with ample instruction about the glory of the empire, the secrets of success, and the joys of outdoor living, it gave the movement the visibility and appeal necessary for its growth. It also provided Baden-Powell with a regular opportunity to communicate with his boys. More specifically, if somewhat unscrupulously, Pearson used it as an instrument to create interest in the Scouts while at the same time making money for himself. Employing the same techniques that had proved successful in popularizing *Pearson's Weekly*, he instituted, in the very first issue (18 April 1908), a competition that was guaranteed to sell Scouting (and *The Scout*) to boys everywhere. The April issue announced, without specifying details, that Baden-Powell would run a summer camp for those thirty boys who received the highest number of votes qualifying them for the privilege. Each issue of the magazine contained a coupon that could be submitted for a single vote, and boys were exhorted to get their friends to vote for them: "You must show us that you are sufficiently popular amongst your friends to justify being selected."[65] While dutiful Scouts cutting out individual coupons was one way of amassing votes, another, rather more efficient way existed. Subscriptions to *The Scout* itself were translated into votes, a three-month subscription (1s. 1d.) worth fifty, a twelve-month (4s. 4d.) worth three hundred. One's popularity therefore had less to do with the number of one's friends than with their solvency—or the solvency of their families. Every subsequent issue reminded boys of the competition, listed the leaders, and urged them on. As late as 22 August, *The Scout* declared that the winners were still not yet decided, leaving time for one last frenzied week of new subscriptions. The 29 August issue announced the lucky thirty, simultaneously opening the new competition for the following summer's camp, this time for the one hundred top vote getters (perhaps better thought of as the heaviest subscribers). By the second year the cynical nature of the competition was beginning to cause the Scouts embarrassment. Baden-Powell's response to the use of the competition was somewhat evasive. Writing in the *Headquarters Gazette*, he wished to

> premise my remarks regarding our Coupon Competition by saying that personally I do not at all like the system, but recognizing the end to which it is the means, I have felt bound to sink my personal objections for the greater good, and I may add the results have justified my action.[66]

By this time, since Scouting was solidly established in its second year and had no further need for such gimmicks, the competition was quietly dropped. In addition to his admirable charitable impulses, Pearson had once again demonstrated that he knew how to sell subscriptions.

In the summer of 1907 Baden-Powell was both working seriously on the text of *Scouting for Boys* and negotiating the terms of a contract with Pearson. At the same time, he had already determined to run a demonstration camp during the August holidays to test the efficacy of his scheme—and to exhibit it to the public. The site chosen for this historic experiment was Brownsea Island, a small island outside of Poole Harbor off the coast of Dorset, which had been contributed for the purpose by the owner, Charles van Raalte, a successful stockbroker whom Baden-Powell had met in May. Having obtained permission to use the island, Baden-Powell set about collecting a representative group of boys for his camping game. Always insisting on Scouting's classlessness, Baden-Powell wanted a constituency drawn equally from the ranks of the privileged public school boys and the less affluent working classes. For the former he chose twelve from among the sons, nephews, and contacts of his army friends; for the latter he invited the Bournemouth and Poole Boys' Brigades to nominate deserving members. In the letter he wrote to the parents of prospective campers, he outlined the seven different subjects—woodcraft, observation, discipline, health and education, chivalry, life saving, and patriotism—to each of which he proposed to devote a single day's instruction. (In practice, as his post-Brownsea Island analysis reveals, the first day was taken up with preliminary discussions and the last—the eighth—with a summary of the whole course, so that no single day was devoted to discipline, even though it was clearly included in his treatment of chivalry and patriotism.)

Twenty-two boys in all—including Baden-Powell's nine-year-old nephew, Donald—ranging in age from ten to seventeen, arrived at Brownsea for the camp, which began on 1 August. Baden-Powell divided them up into four patrols—the Wolves, Bulls, Curlews, and Ravens—each with its own patrol leader, and proceeded to initiate them into the mysteries and joys of Scouting. They played games and practised the skills of camping, cooking, tracking, and stalking; they listened to the great deeds of how the empire was won and learned the importance of loyalty to king, employers, and officers. They chanted Zulu choruses, found their way through the woods without help, and studied how to observe people without themselves being seen. With Baden-Powell, "The Boy" McLaren, and two other assistants drawn from the Boys' Brigade supervising them, the boys immersed themselves enthusiastically in all their activities. From every point of view the camp was a great success: The boys enjoyed themselves, and Baden-Powell had demonstrated that his conception was wholly viable. "The results," as he commented in his report on the Brownsea experience, "were such as to encourage the highest hopes as to the possibilities of the scheme when carried out on the larger scale."[67]

One result in which Baden-Powell took great satisfaction was that the experiment of putting public school and working-class lads together, "Succeeded beyond my expectations." "In three out of four instances, Patrol Leaders [who were all public school boys] selected as their second in command a town boy."[68] It is interesting to recognize the constraints on the social experiment: While the patrol leaders tended to select town boys as their second in command, the four patrol leaders whom Baden-Powell appointed were all public school boys. Classlessness, after all, had its limits. As Baden-Powell extolls the virtues of the two groups living together, he unwittingly reveals the stereotypic class thinking from which he never escaped:

> In this way the rougher boys were perceptibly levelled up in the matter of behaviour, cleanliness, etc.; they watched and imitated the others and improved to a remarkable degree in so short a time. And I am certain no harm was done to the other boys: indeed they gained a broader knowledge and sympathy with those whom probably they had through ignorance formerly looked down upon.[69]

The boys returned home on 9 August. For £55 2s. 8d., Baden-Powell had completed a successful trial of his program that enabled him to tell the world with confidence that it worked. His report concludes,

> I now hope to be able to organize the wider distribution of that scheme and to issue a Handbook or "Self-Educator" such as will assist schoolmasters, officers of Boys and Church Lads Brigades and Cadet Corps, and all others interested in the development of manliness and good citizenship among the rising generation by an adaptable and inexpensive means which is not only popular and attractive to the boys but is also intensely interesting to the instructors themselves.[70]

Back in London in the fall of 1907, Baden-Powell continued to work on the details of his impending lecture tour, his complicated arrangements with Pearson, and his Scouting manuscript. While he initially thought it wise to publish a single portion of the book, "Notes to Instructors," well in advance of the rest of it, Pearson argued instead that publishing small sections of the book at regular intervals was the best way to generate public interest in it. Baden-Powell accepted the advice. By the end of December he had sent material for the first two parts to the printer. On 15 January the first section appeared with its famous cover of the vigilant Scout, trusty staff and wide-brimmed hat by his side, peering from behind a rock at some suspicious but ill-defined activity in the distance. The remaining five parts followed at two-week intervals, with "Notes for Instructors," which Baden-Powell originally intended to publish first, constituting the sixth—and last—instalment.

The book was instantly successful. Its inherent appeal and identification with the hero of Mafeking, as well as the forty lectures Baden-Powell gave on Scouting during January and February, combined to create enormous enthusiasm for the book and the movement. Unofficial patrols began springing up even as the six parts were coming out; by the time of the complete text's publication in May, an irresistible momentum for Scouting had been built up throughout Great Britain. Whatever we feel about the ingenuousness of Baden-Powell's claim to have sought only to create a system of training to complement existing organizations, it became immediately clear that the proliferating number of boys wanting Scouting exceeded the capacity—and interest—of those organizations to handle them. Their needs had to be addressed directly. In September Baden-Powell started to solicit volunteers who would agree to serve on advisory committees to select Scoutmasters, award badges, arrange for camps, and in general organize the burgeoning movement. He appointed two traveling inspectors—one for the north of Britain and one for the south—to inform local advisory committees on regulations and help establish functioning councils throughout the country. With the beginnings of an effective administrative structure to direct its growth, Scouting was soon able to channel the energies of eager boys and enthusiastic adult volunteers into a coherent national movement that would develop into the most successful, most enduring scheme for youth training ever known. Baden-Powell had started on his way to becoming the Chief Scout of the world.

3

WORKING-CLASS
LADS AND
PUBLIC SCHOOL
IDEALS

Although British youth organizers tended to have little prior experience with the youth of the lower orders they wished to organize, even in this group Baden-Powell's remove from the subjects of his ultimate expertise was unusual. There could hardly have been a less likely candidate for the role of the internationally acclaimed youth specialist than the unmarried fifty-year-old inspector general of the cavalry who took twenty-two boys to Brownsea Island in the summer of 1907. It is safe to say that any previous contact between Baden-Powell and those boys on whose nature he would soon confidently proclaim was purely accidental. Having gone directly from Charterhouse into the 13th Hussars, Baden-Powell spent the whole of his army career safely insulated from any of the moral dilemmas faced by early-adolescent working-class lads.

But with his scheme to provide character training for boys—most particularly that class of boys who could never aspire to the salubrious moral atmosphere of the public schools—Baden-Powell instantly thrust himself into the forefront of those social reformers who concentrated on what the literature refers to as the problems of "Boy Nature." Responding in part to the questions of national preparedness raised by the Boer War, as well as to the potential threat to social stability embodied in the alarming growth of urban poor, "Boy Experts" grew up everywhere, devoting themselves to studying the plight of the lower-middle-class and working-class lad. The treatment of "Boy Nature," indeed, became an almost distinct subgenre of early twentieth-century social criticism,[1] and it is very much within this context that the Scouting movement must, in part, be understood.

To begin with, "boy nature" was entirely a class construct; it did not extend to all males within a certain age group but rather was restricted to those of the lower classes. The working boy was a special creature demanding special efforts to understand him.[2] Though a familiar sight, he was nevertheless altogether foreign; hence the necessary role of the expert who was qualified to characterize him, assess his weaknesses, and recommend appropriate cures. "Who is the working boy, and what is he like?" asked Henry Pelham in *The Training of a Working Boy*:

> Why is it necessary to help him? These are the questions that I desire to answer in this chapter. For it is no exaggeration to say that a very large number of people have had but little knowledge of the real nature of the cheery but grimy youngster with whose appearance we are all so familiar.[3]

Pelham then describes him in some detail. He has "an unceasing sense of *humour*. It can be somewhat shallow, and on the vulgar side, but he can appreciate a joke and can always manage to see the funny side of things." He also possesses courage, is "confident in his own powers," "wonderfully sharp," "responsive" and "loyal to his friends," with a great "willingness to be useful to others." Charles Russell saw a different specimen when he looked:

> The boy as he is in a working-class district, is indeed a puzzling, inconsistent, and often enough, exasperating creature. He has, it must be admitted, many disadvantages. He has little parental control, and resents restraint of any kind whatever. ... In his early teens he knows much of evil—and also of good, for he has seen self-denial and self-sacrifice in times of want that boys under more fortunate circumstances, know nothing of.[4]

But however disparate the characters each tended to find in the streets, whether Russell's or Pelham's or the cigarette-smoking, hollow-chested, round-shouldered wastrel preferred by Baden-Powell, all boy experts shared a thoroughly uncompromised class perspective. Facts were gathered, problems defined, and solutions proposed from one point of view—that of the dominant interest of the upper classes. Behavior and character were seen as problematic when they did not conform to their values and self-interest. This is not to impugn the idealism of the youth workers, but merely to emphasize that the ideals they were defending were those that secured the system most efficiently. Bringing to the study of youth their own biases and class needs, they wished inevitably to inculcate those principles of conduct with which they were themselves comfortable.

Although the production methods had to be different because of the difference in raw material, the Baden-Powell character factory took as its model the finely tuned artifact of that other great manufacturing combine, the public school, which supplied England with its norms of gentility and its necessary complement of leaders and statesmen. For the historian E. Wingfield-Stratford,

> The Public School may therefore be regarded as a character factory in which the raw material of what Marx called the capitalist class worked up with the finished product of a gentleman. Such factories were every bit as important a feature of the time as the great machine houses of the North. ... For this very triumph of machinery was precipitating a process of social change that might easily, if it were to get out of hand, end in a social revolution.[5]

Baden-Powell was quite explicit about the connection between public school ideals and Scout character training:

> This then is one of the main reasons for the Boy Scouts training, namely to take the place of the public school life which is only open to the comparatively few whose parents can afford it, and to give the mass of our rising generation some of the spirit of self-negation, self-discipline, sense of honour, responsibility, helpfulness to others, loyalty and patriotism which go to make "character" and in which they have no kind of education in their schools whatever they may have in the way of *instruction*.[6]

Public school boys who do not require it are nevertheless welcome in the movement in order to help spread the gospel:

> I pointed out that in the Boy Scout Movement we are trying to give the mass of boys something of the sense of honour and tone that are at present the attributes of the Public School boy. It will be the highest form of brotherhood and service for Public School men ultimately to take up and impart this training to their less well to do brothers. I don't consider scouting necessary for Public School boys themselves, but their membership in the movement and their subsequent spreading of its principles among our young citizens and their use of its ideals in their relations with employees, subordinates, etc., will have a great national value.[7]

Any assessment of the ideals of Scout character training must therefore begin with a consideration of that character ideal that the public schools pursued. How exactly did Baden-Powell want his "poorer class of boy"[8] to resemble his upper-class brother?

Whatever else they might have sought to achieve, most late Victorian public schools aspired to produce one overriding trait in their boys: an all-consuming loyalty—to side, to institution, to class, to country. This was the message they preached, the reflex they attempted to engender. As an institution committed to the perpetuation of the privileged classes who had access to it, the public schools emphasized those conservative virtues of conformity and obedience that would best guarantee the continuation of the *status quo*. In an international report on moral instruction in schools published in 1908, H. Bompas Smith, headmaster of King Edward VII School in Lytham, notes that the public schools

> aim at training their boys to become worthy members of the social group of which the function is the control and guidance of the work and thought of others. Hence in accordance with the characteristic ideals of that group, they lay stress upon the acquisition of such virtues as corporate loyalty and the fulfillment of social obligations, and the boy's conduct is largely determined by a traditional code of honour and good form.[9]

Postulated as a guiding principle of life, *esprit de corps* finally becomes synonymous with the public school spirit itself; in lamenting its absence in working-class lads, Baden-Powell can be detected thinking wistfully of the unquestioning loyalties of the well-trained public school boy.

Character, then, as shaped by the public school, consists largely in the capacity to accept unhesitatingly the values of the institution (and the class it serves) and the willingness to suppress all vestiges of self in the defense of those values. Central to such a conception is the necessity to avoid the uncertainties generated by independent critical thought. Thinking itself is subversive, inimical to that belief in corporate allegiance that distinguishes the fully matured public school character. In *Prefects: British Leadership and the Public School Tradition*, Rupert Wilkinson argues that

> In the final analysis, the education system viewed the intellect itself as hostile to loyalty. ... Loyalty itself was considered a virtue which the exercise of reason could easily destroy. ... Public school loyalties formed part of a faith rooted firmly in unquestioned assumptions about the gentleman's moral duty and his relation to the society about him. ... Self-assurance and rational inquiry were kept well apart.[10]

Membership in the public school community was by definition uncritical membership:

> Where loyalty becomes indiscriminate, it results in stifling all criticism. Loyalty to the group becomes so important that even to suggest that anything about the group could be bettered is disloyal. This trait is very observable in Public School boys in after-life when in politics, for instance, even those who have serious doubts about policy or leadership must not express them because criticism is disloyal and might break up the team.[11]

Baden-Powell was himself extremely sensitive to criticism, viewing it always as an act of hostility unacceptable under any circumstances. "Grousing," the contemptuous term he applies to any expression of dissatisfaction, is evidence of moral weakness on the part of the grouser. Addressing the men of the South African Constabulary before his departure as their commander, he cautioned them about this problem:

> ... And don't be turned aside by any difficulty or obstruction. Face it cheerfully. A difficulty ceases to be a difficulty directly you laugh at it. But there are very many individuals—I do

not call them men—who have not the pluck to take difficulties cheerfully, and they begin to shirk or grouse directly things begin to go badly, sometimes even before. They "run and tell Mother" and write to the papers.

In my experience the man who grouses most in peace-time is the first to funk in action, and the first to fail and become a "Waster" in Civil Life. He is wanting in manliness.

Therefore avoid him and his ways, and don't let him stop in the SAC. Help your officers in getting rid of him.[12]

Effeminate, incompetent, and doomed to failure, the man who is tempted to criticize had better think twice about it. The successful Scout (or adult) must never traduce his ideals by wondering about them.

The same strictures against any effort at independent appraisal applies even to war correspondents, whom Baden-Powell felt should not unsettle the public by trying to arrive at the truth. Baden-Powell had trouble with the press at Mafeking, particularly with some of the younger men who objected to the constraints imposed by Baden-Powell's press censor. In response to a memo from some of them expressing their dissatisfaction, Baden-Powell wrote on 23 March 1900, to Vere Stent, one of the more senior correspondents, asking for his help in explaining to the others the realities of their profession. A remarkable document as the credo of a war correspondent, it tells us a great deal as well about Baden-Powell's conception of the role the unfettered critical intelligence should play in civic society:

I have been a war correspondt. myself on various occasions and so I know their difficulties (as well as their opportunities).

The instances of tearing up despatches by the Press Censor have arisen from the fact that some of the correspondents have taken no notice of these warnings or hints and have tried to get the better of him by resubmitting the same, or similar copy, in the hope of getting it through.

There are some of them who do not recognise the difference that exists between the ordinary news reporter and the special war correspondent—and it would be well if they would take the advice of some of their more experienced confreres.

I hope that you will not think me presumptuous or inclined to teach my grandmother, etc., etc.,—but in the hopes that it may (if received in the spirit in which it is offered)—bring about an easier working I venture to put forward an item of my own experience as a correspt. which might serve as a hint.

Until I had been set upon by one or two of the leading press men I thought it the sure road to success to strike out a new and original line for myself, and found—I was quite wrong. That instead of taking my powers to be original my business was to write what, at the moment, the public wanted to believe. It was, at the time of the Jameson Raid, suicidal in a correspondent not to laud it to the skies whatever he may have thought or known of its defects. Labby [name of correspondent?] tried his carping system the other day on what the British Public are inclined to consider a toughly fought, glorious war which with its springing together of our colonials in arms to help the mother country, gives an unexpected vision of the strength and might of the Empire to foreign eyes, etc. and Labby went under.

A correspondent is like a doctor. He has to study his patient, the public: if things are going well—the doctor makes a mistake if he tries to dose him with bitter little pills—good, wholesome diet and the best port are what he likes then. It is only when things are going badly that the patient wants them probed into and medicine, even though nasty, administered.

That is where so many budding correspondents have failed—from acting too much as reporters, i.e. trying to combine detective acumen and flowering style, instead of watching the public feeling and giving it the food it likes—(without richness!)—and promptly.

Well—to do the latter successfully I always found it well to play up to my Press Censor's wishes—I got many extra items of news, and got them with no delays. It paid me well.

And it does not in the long run pay at all to kick against the pricks. But young genius with a loose rein, star gazing, does not see this—and gets laughed at.[13]

For T. C. Worsley, the desire to instill in its students a set of convictions free from doubt means that the public school never "even attempts to give the pupils an intelligent understanding of the modern world, a rational rather than an irrational outlook on life."[14] Sir Michael Sadler, no particular critic of the public schools, points out that "keen intellectual interest about school work is not the distinguishing mark of the rank and file in the English Public School for boys,"[15] a judgment that Bompas Smith underlines from another perspective, noting that, "I am told that when boys from these [country and municipal] schools go to Oxford and Cambridge they often show an exaggerated respect for knowledge as such." [16]

That the sustained indoctrination in narrow class loyalty that the public school offered its students had little place in it for the development of the intellect in no way perturbed the healthy product of the system. Joyful that he had the opportunity to give up his life in the Great War (which indeed he shortly did), Paul Jones, a typical Dulwich schoolboy, commented, "The Englishman doesn't like thinking; if he did, he would not be the splendid fighting man that he is." [17] For Baden-Powell himself, who went through Charterhouse thoroughly undistinguished scholastically, the lessons properly taught in the public schools had very little to do with the training of the intellect:

> Someone has bluntly said that the "main point in Public School Training is that it supplies Commonsense, Manners and Guts, even if it does not supply knowledge."
>
> At any rate it has shown that it can produce men proof against graft and bribery, men who can use initiative, discipline themselves, and take responsibility, and, as Mr. Roxburgh has said in *Eleutheros* "men who are acceptable at a dance and invaluable in a shipwreck." [18]

Such men could not learn their valuable lessons about life in the classroom. The liberating awareness of the need for discipline, the primacy of the team, and even the responsibilities of membership in a community were instead to be absorbed on the playing fields. Organized sport was perceived to be the single most important factor in the moral education of the boy, and by the 1870s had come to dominate the ethos of the public schools. Games were by no means simply games but unparalleled opportunities to master the ethical and patriotic implications of teamwork. For Cyril Norwood, headmaster of Harrow and a leading educational figure following the war, football and cricket were "a fine educational instrument":

> What, indeed, they [schoolmasters] had discovered by accident was team-spirit, which alone builds character: or rather, I should say, alone strengthens those qualities which we wish to develop. Individual excellence at games has its effect on character too, but rarely in a desirable direction. The thought of the team-spirit is a commonplace to us, but it is a recent arrival in the field of educational thought, and is indeed one

of the greatest English contributions to methods of true education. It is, moreover, the spirit which more than any other
the world wants in the twentieth century, if it is to accomplish
the work which the human race has the opportunity of achieving.[19]

Initially an effective way to organize the boys' spare time and
channel their excess energy, games rapidly achieved cult status in
the public schools. They were seen not only to be an effective
means of shaping character, but to be virtually the sole legitimate
area for human effort: "You may drudge at games—that is the
theory—that is commendable; but to drudge at the acquisition of
knowledge is pitiable and not to be endured. That is the faith of
the public school boy, which except he believe he cannot be
saved." [20] Excellence on the playing field soon provided not just the
categories but even the metaphors of moral excellence, so that the
"plucky," "self-less," "determined" forward became an exemplary
human type to be revered in every situation.

The exaltation of games above all other activities—which one
dyspeptic observer called, "an insane cult—in Tacitean phrase, 'a
pestilent superstition' " [21] corresponded at once to the fullest flowering of the public schools as well as the zenith of British Imperial
ambition.[22] It was inevitable that the obsessions with disciplined
teamwork of organized sport should ultimately be justified by nothing less sacred than their appropriateness to the very defense of
the empire itself.[23]

For the public school boys who were expected to defend British
interests across the seas, the character training supplied by sports
was seen to be the best possible preparation for that jolliest of all
sports, war. Skill in games was immediately translated into skill on
the battlefield; those who excelled in the former could also be
counted upon for inspired performances in the latter. The language
of sport frequently became the means not just of rendering the
exhilaration and challenges of warfare, but even of describing the
mundane functioning of the army:

> The army *fights* for the good of its country as the team *plays*
> for the honour of its school. Regiments assist each other as
> players do when they *shove together* or *pass the ball* from one to
> other; exceptionally gallant *charges* and heroic *defences* corres-
> pond to brilliant *runs* and fine *tackling*.[24]

The games of the schoolboy and the noblest ideal nurtured by
the public school—service to country—are thus tied together in a

web of common metaphor. It was a relationship the public school student was never permitted to forget.

The poet laureate of both playing field and public school was not, as is commonly supposed, Rudyard Kipling, but rather Henry Newbolt, whose "Vitai Lampada" articulated the relationship in its most memorable form:

VITAI LAMPADA

There's a breathless hush in the Close to-night—
    Ten to make and the match to win—
A bumping pitch and a blinding light,
    An hour to play and the last man in.
And it's not for the sake of a ribboned coat
    Or the selfish hope of a season's fame,
But his captain's hand on his shoulder smote—
    "Play up! play up! and play the game!"

The sand of the desert is sodden red,—
    Red with the wreck of a square that broke;—
The Gatling's jammed and the Colonel dead,
    And the regiment blind with dust and smoke.
The river of death has brimmed his banks,
    And England's far, and Honour a name,
But the voice of a schoolboy rallies the ranks:
    "Play up! play up! and play the game!"

This is the word that year by year,
    While in her place the School is set,
Every one of her sons must hear,
    And none that hears it dare forget.
This they all with a joyful mind
    Bear though life like a torch in flame,
And falling fling to the host behind—
    "Play up! play up! and play the game!"[25]

No single phrase more succinctly characterized the world view of the public school than the exhortation, "Play the game." At once a political ideal and a moral injunction, it constituted, for those reared in the system, an all-embracing principle of conduct applicable to every circumstance in which an individual might find himself. Good people do it and bad people don't—and these deficient ones would get better quickly if only they would. For Henry Pelham, for example, the failure to do so is what obviously ailed the working boy:

> But another weakness of the boy is his inability to "play the game." He will loudly question the referee's decision when it is against him. ... It is therefore a primary duty of the Club Helper to insist upon his boys playing a clean game and obeying the referee's decision without question or discussion. "To play the game" fairly and squarely is a lesson that is of intense value throughout life, and a club which fails to teach it neglects one of its main duties to its members.[26]

The fullest elaboration of the ideal can be found in the writing of Eustace Miles, an amateur racquets and tennis champion, editor of various books on physical fitness and popular author, whose works Baden-Powell frequently recommended to Scouts and Scout-masters alike. If somewhat extreme, his explication nevertheless brilliantly summarizes the attitudes we have been discussing here. For Miles, the phrase itself is a kind of magic talisman, evoking the noblest standards imaginable:

> In our appeal to the best self we have too often used ineffectual and futile phrases when we might have said, "Let's play the game," or "Let's be sportsmanlike." Such terms need not include all right action, but they seem the least inadequate idiom in our language, if we are to bring to the majority of Anglo-Saxon minds a clear-cut illustration and a clear sensa-tion of what we really desire them and ourselves to realize.[27]

The simple formulation thus embodies the finest aspirations of Anglo-Saxon culture, providing "a sensible test and standard for almost everything that we shall do, or say, or look, or think—or leave undone, unsaid, unlooked, unthought."[28] Although Miles suggests that it need not necesssarily include all right action, it turns out actually to do so largely because games themselves offer such an admirable and complete training for life:

> Good play is not mere recreation. It is also preparation for most if not the whole life. ... It is *preparation and education* nearly all around; physical, remedial, hygenic, aesthetic, ethical, in-tellectual, economic, social, prospective, and competitive.[29]

The lessons one derives from games are not simply appropriate for crises, invaluable as they are in times of severe difficulty:

> They are equally for the whole of life, for all its parts. When at the beginning of the day I say to myself, "I'm going to play the game to-day," I can't imagine any little crevice of my day's work or play or rest in which that play-spirit would not be a cleansing influence.[30]

Games—at least proper Anglo-Saxon games—and the salutary spirit of playing them, are ethically valuable both for the discipline as well as the true egalitarianism they engender. A group of men committed to the success of their side and loyally following their captain's orders offers, for Miles, an image of an ideal human community. Such a paradigm can usefully be applied to an understanding of our own bodies, where, as Miles suggests, each of us is a captain of his own team. The point can have practical consequences: if we tend to bolt our food too quickly, for example, Miles recommends the following:

> Speak to yourself—*unless it is likely to make you morbidly self-conscious*—in some such way as this: "It isn't the game to eat so fast: it isn't fair on the stomach and other members of my team. We've got some hard matches to play this season, and we shall all have to do our share of the work. Now then, jaws, you come on to bowl, and let stomach go back to field. Stomach has got his work cut out there, and is not a first-class bowler as you are. Now then, on you come."
> That is the way some of us may help ourselves to "play the game" as captain.[31]

And the way the individual may play the game—fairly and with the good of the whole body in mind—is paralleled on the international level by the way Britain rules its empire:

> We treat natives under our power as they are, with that same consideration which a British master of a country-house shows to his own servants in the cricket-field. There is no distinction of persons. We can express the best spirit of our Empire in those words: that we try to "play the game" with the natives; we do not try to play tricks with them or bully them, for that is not sportsmanlike; we give them a fair chance. Generally it should be a handicap game for we are bound to win if we

play level and we generally do play level; but any how we do play them, and that is something.[32]

Understood in its rich implication, then, "playing the game" is both a practical guide to daily activity as well as the most exalted ideal of human behavior. Miles's celebration of it leads him to an extraordinary, though given his assumptions, eminently logical conclusion:

> Meanwhile you are lucky to be an Anglo-Saxon. Where two or three Anglo-Saxons are gathered together, or where one stands and fights like a man alone against others or against himself, there is the sportsmanlike spirit in the midst. It is called playing the game. Its other name is God.[33]

The worship of athleticism lay at the heart of a system designed to produce sturdy sportsmen prepared to sacrifice all for the good of the team. The greatest opportunity for the system to prove itself was not the skirmishes against Afghans, Zulus, and the like in the latter part of the nineteenth century, or even the substantially more challenging campaign against the Boers, but rather the glorious crusade of World War I. The thousands of young public school officers who willingly accepted their extermination in the trenches, content with the knowledge that they were playing the game as it ought to be played, testified to the character training they had received. Their exuberance in going to be slaughtered, and the long list of names added daily to each school's honor roll, were convincing proof that the public schools were doing their jobs.

No school could have been prouder of one of its graduates than Dulwich was of Paul Jones, nor more satisfied with its ability to indoctrinate a student with the public school creed. In the words of a Dulwich master, "He was the very embodiment in himself of all that is best in the public school spirit, the very incarnation of self-sacrifice and devotion."[34] A fine athlete and loyal Dulwich citizen, Jones was thoroughly representative of the class of young men who went off gaily to be killed in the war. Possessing no special talent, his uniqueness rests in the fact that his letters home were posthumously published by his father, letters that typify his doomed generation's commitment to the public school ideal. His love for the school was matched only by his love of sports. When he entered the tank corps in 1917, having finally managed to escape from the safety of the Army Service Corps, to which his myopia had confined him for two years, he sent home all his superfluous possessions, keeping with him two prized photographs, "one of the college buildings, the other of the Playing Field," this latter depicting the cricket matches on Founder's Day. "In death as in life," his father comments, "Dulwich was close to his heart."[35] In their tone and the values they affirm, the letters could have been written by any of the multitude of credulous products of the system who perished between 1914 and 1918. Jones's letters are singular in their capacity to speak with a corporate voice.

They praise the athlete and the method of training that subsumes all to athletics:

> At present we see that the poor despised athlete or sports-man—call him what you will—is coming to the front, practically and metaphorically, in a way which makes one wonder if, for the highest purposes of duty, athletics are not really the very best of *all* systems of training. When we look at the matter in the broadest light, the explanation shines forth clearly. All learning and all business are in the end simply and solely *selfish*. For example, you work hard for a scholarship at Oxford or Cambridge—why? So that you can obtain *for yourself*—(underline these words Mr. Printer please!)—the advantages of 'Varsity' life and culture. ... In fact, it is only on our amateur playing fields that we become really unselfish. For here we play for a team or a side; and for the success of that side—which success, by the way, is in no sense material or selfish—we are prepared to take all sorts of pains. ...
>
> Nothing but athletics had succeeded in doing this sort of work in England. Religion has failed, intellect has failed, art has failed, science has failed. It is clear why: because each of these has laid emphasis on man's *selfish* side. ... But your sportsman joins the Colours because in his games he has felt the real spirit of unselfishness, and he is sworn. Besides this, he has acquired the physical fitness necessary for a campaign. These facts explain the grand part played by sport in this War; they also explain why the amateur has done so enormously better than the professional.[36]

In its insistence on selflessness, "the training of the playing-fields of the Public Schools and the 'Varsities'" is not simply as good as that of the class-rooms but in fact, "far better, if training for the path of Duty is the ideal end of education."[37]

Jones's adulation of the athlete perfectly expresses the internalization of his public school training. Even more revealingly, we see him responding to the death of a fellow officer by evoking his athletic prowess, as if that were what defined his general worth:

> Deep was my grief to read of the death in action of R. F. Mackinnon, M.C., one of the finest forwards and captains who has ever worn the blue-and-black jersey. He was captain of the first fifteen in my first year at the school, 1908-9, in which we had a pack of forwards of strong physique and whole-hearted courage.[38]

Eager to receive news of his old school, Jones rejoices to hear that rugby at Dulwich is thriving, for "All will be well with the school if the games are keen."[39]

Jones's intoxication with athletics, his unquestioned assumption of the superiority of all things British, the impatience with complex political or moral realities, the parochial loyalties—all these prime features of public school education pervade the letters. Jones's vast annoyance with the Balkan situation is a typical example:

> The Balkan business is a startling knockabout for those enthusiasts who see in the development of small states salvation for the world! If people would only accept the fact that this is a material world they would not be surprised at the situation. ... No matter; what is the fate of a few tupenny-ha'penny Balkan states, who have never done a thing worth doing, besides that of the British Empire! Why should we always play the philanthropic idiot towards all those wretched little nations? As if any of them—or anyone else, for that matter, in international politics—knows the meaning of the word gratitude.[40]

The bullying tones of the complacent imperialist can be heard in Jones's applauding the British occupation of Salonika, which required telling

> the Greeks politely to "hop it." Result, the Greeks have hopped it. How much more simple and effective this than to jaw about "the rights of the neutrals," the "sanctity of small nations," etc., etc.! No! take a strong line in this world, and you're more likely to get what you want than by cajolery.[41]

And finally, and perhaps most poignantly, a conception of life that seems to require death for its ultimate fulfillment. Jones exults in war, in the opportunity for ennobling self-sacrifice, and in the relief it promises from the quotidian affairs of daily living:

> In peace time one just lives one's own little life, engaged in trivialities, worrying about one's own comfort, about money matters, and all that sort of thing—just living for one's own self. What a sordid life it is! In war, on the other hand, even if you do get killed, you only anticipate the inevitable by a few years in any case, and you have the satisfaction of knowing that you have "pegged out" in the attempt to help your country. You have, in fact, realised an ideal, which, as far as I can see, you very rarely do in ordinary life. . . .
>
> Personally, I often rejoice that the war has come my way. It has made me realise what a petty thing life is.[42]

The deaths of Rupert Brooke, Julian Grenfell, Roland Philipps, and his other friends only serve "as a trumpet call. All the old Welsh fighting blood comes surging up in me and makes me say, 'short sight, or no short sight, I *will* prove my manhood!'"[43]

Proving their manhood by not letting down their side in battle, Jones and the others of his class graphically demonstrated the efficacy of the school system. The equivocal merits of such a system should by now be clear. It would be hard to argue with T. C. Worsley's assessment of the public schools as a

> community where a narrow patriotism is the greatest virtue; where the discipline is the discipline of the barrack square; where rods are the sign of office, where unity is more highly prized than variety—and the unity turns out to be that of sheep—or a platoon; where reason is an exile and no voice except the voice of Authority is tolerated; where Loyalty cannot suggest a single fault and where critics are denounced as "carpers or swine"; where victory by physical force is alone respected; where the individual is sacrificed to the community and freedom at a discount; where prejudice rules side by side with intolerance; where the strong are worshipped and intellectuals deemed decadent; and where justice is simply the arbitrary decision of those who have been put into power: against whose decisions there is no appeal and whose executions are summary.[44]

At the same time, it would also be hard to argue that the institution did not work. It clearly could be relied upon to produce those obedient and courageous men the country would always need. However thwarted their growth, however impoverished their emotional and intellectual lives, public school boys stood ready to serve, to play the game steadfastly to the end.

Baden-Powell's attraction to the public school character and ideology requires no complicated analysis. Not only was it what he knew through his own experience, but it also provided exactly what he needed. The discipline and patriotism in which the public school man was steeped were essential for the efficient citizenry he hoped to train. A lower order of boys with the fierce loyalty of a Paul Jones would be the answer to all problems of social unrest, industrial competition, or military threats. If Britain were to survive, these boys, too, had to be taught to play the game.[45]

In evoking standards of the public schools for his Scouts, then, Baden-Powell opted for that reliable, loyal product that these institutions attempted to engender. That such a character ideal made little sense for the lower-class lad did not seem to bother him as he promised on his honor to obey the orders of the Scoutmaster. Accepting his designated slot in life and learning not to ask unsettling questions was rather more convenient for the Eton or Harrow boy about to take his place in the world of privilege and power than it necessarily would be for the messenger boy or unskilled laborer. Nevertheless it was part of Baden-Powell's talent that he could sell the virtues of submission to authority and self-sacrificing teamwork to those not destined for the favored existence of the public schools—or for the social perquisites that followed. Wrapping his deeply conservative social ideals in an appealing and exciting movement, he achieved the formidable goal of creating an institution that could be embraced not only by those whom the social system was designed to support, but also by those largely excluded from its advantages. While instilling public school notions of character into the masses might possibly improve their moral tone, it would certainly help assure the continued existence of that elite institution and the privileged way of life it was intended to serve. For Baden-Powell, both were important.

Taking his inspiration for Scout character from the values embodied in the public schools, Baden-Powell attempted to translate them into a form appropriate for the masses of the rising generation. If the public schools were made to produce gentlemen prepared to lead, the Scouts were intended to produce young men ready to follow. One important distinction must be made here between the means each institution employed to achieve its goals. Although I have spoken of the character "training" of the public schools, that is perhaps a misleading term. The school did not provide training in the ordinary sense of that word, nor any formal program of orientation into a behavioral system to which each new student was exposed. Specific rules of conduct existed, but students were not put through their loyalty catechism or expected to explain the importance of games or the virtues of self-denial. Instead, character indoctrination occurred through indirect means, through students absorbing an ideology no less powerful for not being officially articulated. The almost mystical power of the schools' ancient tradition was an important part of this process. A public school student was aware of entering an historic community, one moreover that encouraged him to feel involved in and contribute to its growth. In such a situation, a student is inclined to take on the values of the community as naturally as he would put on a school tie. The character norms of the public schools tended to be more unspoken than explicitly available; they represented expectations of proper behavior that were primarily based on appropriate tone and style. Conformity to type was assured because few boys would have the strength to withstand the disapproval that followed from any failure to satisfy the demands of the community in which they were immersed:

> As phrases like "not done" and "bad form" suggest, the sanction behind the rules was aesthetic, appealing to group standards of good taste. In fact, the appeal was largely tacit, for aesthetic standards are difficult to articulate, to defend, or explain in rational terms.
>   Tacit acceptance of how to behave and how not to behave was, therefore, a strong public school code. It was a code well in keeping with the gentleman ideal.[46]

But whereas public school character formation could rely on the sense of tradition and the shaping powers of group standards, Baden-Powell had none of these at his disposal. No tradition existed; the boys whom he sought did not themselves share, or come from homes that shared anything like the coherence of the gentlemanly ideal; and the boys were simply joining an organization that might meet for a few hours each week, not living in an isolated community exerting total control over them twenty-four hours a day. In place of the implicit workings of the public school system, Baden-Powell had to devise an explicit code of behavior to help create the uniform character he wanted. The Scout Promise and Law became precisely such an instrument, defining the specific norms of conduct that no public school ever needed to set down in writing. Baden-Powell's character factory did not have the luxury of taking anything for granted, and the clearly articulated sanctions of the Scout Law represented his effort to create from scratch the values and assumptions that were developed over time in the public school. Once having established his code, Baden-Powell then faced the challenge of trying to authenticate it by investing it with a tradition that would add luster to its stipulations. As we will see in more detail in the next chapter, he settled on King Arthur and his round table, appropriating them for the Scouts by claiming that the Scout Law was derived from their chivalric code. Providing not simply an ethically distinguished tradition, but also one as intensely nationalistic as King Arthur and his brave knights, Baden-Powell managed to give his twentieth-century Scouts a venerable—and instant—lineage about which they could be proud. Public school boys might be able to trace their institutional ancestry back to the fourteenth (or in most cases, the fifteenth and sixteenth centuries), but Scouts could do considerably better than that, being in on the very foundation of the country.

Despite the fact that Baden-Powell always used the term himself, in its own way Scout "character training" is as much a misnomer as is public school "training." The desired shaping of character is intended to follow not from the graduated process normally associated with "training," but from the formal initiation of the Scout into an organization with a specific set of behavioral obligations to which allegiance must be sworn. Scout character training is, in a sense, the simple acceptance of the Scout Laws, reinforced by the fact that others in the organization also commit themselves to observe them. The hope is that the commitment, enhanced by ritual and community approval, will gradually become internalized in each individual and so produce the very character type Baden-Powell wanted.

The hope was never realized. No recognizable Scout species ever developed as one could say, despite its manifold individual variations, a public school species once walked upon the earth; nor has anyone ever been able to demonstrate that Boy Scouts as a group emerged from the Scouting experience significantly different from the rest of the non-Scouting world.[47] The reasons are not hard to find. While public schools catered to an elite, relatively homogeneous population already sharing common privileges and assumptions, the Scouting audience was far more heterogeneous. The difficulties of mass character imprinting in such a large and diversified group are immense and in the end impracticable. But if it is fair to say that it never managed to shape them into the uniform product sought by the movement, Scouting has at the same time been eminently successful in attracting boys. Its enormous popularity from the very beginning indicated that Scouting always "worked"—and for many of the same reasons that the public schools also did:

> The Public Schools have in the past worked as well as they have done (and it is undeniable that they have been and even still are for their specific purpose not entirely unsuccessful) for a very good reason. It is that certain features of the organisation which they employ, the kind of discipline and the kind of training in a narrow loyalty, correspond to a psychological need in most adolescent boys. The majority of adolescents somewhere between the ages of ten and fifteen ... like working and playing *in gangs*: are intensely competitive, and possibly (this is less certain) like being ordered and bossed about. ... They tend too to admire especially the military virtues, toughness, courage and endurance. This need the Public Schools ... completely satisfy. Whether it is right to gratify the need is, again, not for the moment the point. They do so, and for that reason they have been as successful as they are.[48]

Baden-Powell's own rather homier language suggests how well he understood the appeal behind both these institutions:

> Had we called it what it was, viz. a "Society for the Propagation of Moral Attributes," the boy would not exactly have rushed for it. But to call it SCOUTING and give him the chance of becoming an embryo Scout, was quite another pair of shoes. His inherent "gang" instinct would be met by making him a member of a "Troop" and a "Patrol." Give him a uniform to wear, with Badges to be won and worn on it for proficiency in Scouting—and you got him.[49]

4

THE SCOUT
LAW

Along with short pants and the wide-brimmed hat, the Scout Law was a distinctive emblem of Scouting from the very beginning. More than a code of behavior, it summarized the aspirations of an entire movement, equipped it with slogans, and provided it with the panacea for the social and psychic disfunction it was attempting to treat. If Scouting were to rescue Britain from its decline, the instrumentality of that regeneration would be the Scout Law, broadly understood and acted upon throughout the land.

Unlike the Ten Commandments, to which it was frequently compared, the Scout Law underwent a number of revisions and rewordings following its first formulation in 1908, and it is well to begin by indicating precisely which version we are talking about. As the earliest form of law and oath seems to me the most appropriate one, I accordingly reproduce both exactly as they appeared in the first edition of *Scouting for Boys* (1908), together with the important exegesis that accompanied them.

THE SCOUT'S OATH

Before he becomes a scout a boy must take
the scout's oath, thus
"On my honour I promise that—
1. I will do my duty to God and the King.
2. I will do my best to help others, whatever it costs me.
3. I know the scout law, and will obey it."

THE SCOUT LAW

1. A SCOUT'S HONOUR IS TO BE TRUSTED

   If a scout says: "On my honour it is so," that means that
   it *is* so, just as if he had taken a most solemn oath.

   Similarly, if a scout officer says to a scout, "I trust you
   on your honour to do this," the scout is bound to carry
   out the order to the very best of his ability, and to let
   nothing interfere with his doing so.

   If a scout were to break his honour by telling a lie, or by
   not carrying out an order exactly when trusted on his
   honour to do so, he would cease to be a scout, and must
   hand over his scout badge, and never be allowed to wear
   it again—he loses his life.

2. A SCOUT IS LOYAL to the King, and to his officers, and to
   his country, and to his employers. He must stick to them
   through thick and thin against anyone who is their
   enemy, or who even talks badly of them.

3. A SCOUT'S DUTY IS TO BE USEFUL AND TO HELP OTHERS.

   And he is to do his duty before everything else, even
   though he gives up his own pleasure, or comfort, or
   safety to do it. When in difficulty to know which of two
   things to do, he must ask himself, "Which is my duty?"
   that is, "Which is best for other people?"—and do that
   one. He must Be Prepared at any time to save life, or to
   help injured persons. And *he must do a good turn* to some-
   body every day.

4. A SCOUT IS A FRIEND TO ALL, AND A BROTHER TO EVERY
   OTHER SCOUT, NO MATTER TO WHAT SOCIAL CLASS THE
   OTHER BELONGS.

   Thus if a scout meets another scout, even though a stran-
   ger to him, he must speak to him, and help him in any
   way that he can, either to carry out the duty he is then
   doing, or by giving him food, or, as far as possible,

anything that he may be in want of. A scout must never be a SNOB. A snob is one who looks down upon another because he is poorer, or who is poor and resents another because he is rich. A scout accepts the other man as he finds him, and makes the best of him.

"Kim," the boy scout, was called by the Indians "Little friend to all the world," and that is the name that every scout should earn for himself.

5. A SCOUT IS COURTEOUS: That is, he is polite to all—but especially to women and children and old people and invalids, cripples, etc. And he must not take any reward for being helpful or courteous.

6. A SCOUT IS A FRIEND TO ANIMALS. He should save them as far as possible from pain, and should not kill any animal unnecessarily, even if it is only a fly—for it is one of God's creatures.

7. A SCOUT OBEYS ORDERS of his patrol leader or scout master without question.

Even if he gets an order he does not like he must do as soldiers and sailors do, he must carry it out all the same because *it is his duty*; and after he has done it he can come and state any reasons against it: but he must carry out the order at once. That is discipline.

8. A SCOUT SMILES AND WHISTLES under all circumstances. When he gets an order he should obey it cheerily and readily, not in a slow, hang-dog sort of way.

Scouts never grouse at hardships, nor whine at each other, nor swear when put out.

When you just miss a train, or someone treads on your favourite corn—not that a scout ought to have such things as corns—or under any annoying circumstances, you should force yourself to smile at once, and then whistle a tune, and you will be all right.

A scout goes about with a smile on and whistling. It cheers him and cheers other people, especially in time of danger, for he keeps it up then all the same.

The punishment for swearing or using bad language is for each offence a mug of cold water to be poured down the offender's sleeve by the other scouts. It was the punishment invented by the old British scout, Captain John Smith, three hundred years ago.

9. A SCOUT IS THRIFTY, that is, he saves every penny he can, and puts it into the bank, so that he may have money to

keep himself when out of work, and thus not make himself a burden to others; or that he may have money to give away to others when they need it.

Several distinctions between the Scout Law and the Ten Commandments readily present themselves. In the first place, as we see, there were originally only nine laws. Although Baden-Powell was as hostile to all forms of sexual indulgence—and particularly the dread sin of self-abuse—as any moralist of the time, his famous exhortation—"A Scout is pure in thought, word and deed"—was not added to the canon until 1911. Since purity would generally be considered a more urgent matter then cheerfulness, courtesy, or thrift, it might be asked why the Scouts were given three years in which they were presumably free to revel among their basest impulses and fantasies. The answer, I think, lies in the strictly social character of the original laws. Baden-Powell was intent on producing a serviceable and reliable boy, one who could always be trusted to act in certain predictable ways. The stress is on responsible functioning rather than proper states of being, and in this respect purity is secondary to the ability to follow an order cheerfully.

For Baden-Powell, the laws Moses brought down the mountain and those delivered from Scout headquarters to the youth of Britain differed significantly in the latter's lack of prohibitions. As Baden-Powell proudly and frequently pointed out, there are no negatives in the Scout Law. Where other ethical systems caution people what not to do, it tells instead what should be done:

> Moses gave the ten commandments to the Jews as to how they should behave but these were laws which all said: DON'T do this, and DON'T do that.
>
> Now I know that a real red-blooded boy is all for action, ready for adventure. He just hates to be nagged and told "You must not do this—you must not do that." He wants to know what he can do. So I thought why should we not have our own Law for Scouts, and I jotted down ten things that a fellow needs to do as his regular habit if he is going to be a real man.[1]

Stressing the positive and not blunting the boy's enthusiasm with niggling restrictions, the Scout Law, Baden-Powell insisted, was designed to exploit the opportunities for the development of the individual. In channeling the instincts of the red-blooded boy, the Scout Law addressed his particular needs in an efficient way.

Such, at least, was the argument Baden-Powell mounted. With its careful avoidance of "don'ts," the Law purported to offer the best means of guaranteeing personal fulfillment among the widest possible masses. But in fact, Baden-Powell's protestations notwithstanding, Scout Law has very little to do with the development of the individual, except as that development is seen as a product of absolute submission to all officially endorsed forms of authority. However free from any taint of prohibition, it essentially celebrates one quality only—obedience. The most succinct and telling summary of the Scout Law can be found not in any of the commentary it generated but in the closing stanza of Kipling's "The Law of the Jungle":

> *Now these are the Laws of the Jungle, and many and mighty*
> *are they;*
> *But the head and the hoof of the Law and the haunch and*
> *hump is—Obey!*

Baden-Powell's concern—which might fairly be called an obsession—with inculcating obedience can be seen in the rather peculiar structural redundancy of the Scout Oath (later known as the Scout Promise)[2] and the Scout Law. Although the Law's various explicit injunctions to do one's duty and follow orders would seem sufficient to convince even the most skeptical about the utter reliability of the Scouts, Baden-Powell felt he also had to guarantee commitment to the Law. Hence the Oath, requiring the Scout to promise to obey all the strictures of obedience contained in the Law. Given the tight control exercised by the Law, it is hard not to see the constraints of the Oath as superfluous, but Baden-Powell was clearly leaving nothing to chance:

In order to make sure that a Scout will carry out the Scout Law he makes a promise to do so.[3]

While the first two parts of the Oath merely state the ideals of duty and helpfulness on which the Law elaborates, the third, helping to ensure Scout conformity, documents Baden-Powell's vigilance.

But the oath is interesting in another way. Asking a Scout to promise on his honor to do three things, it requires only that he do *his best* to help others. The notion of holding Scouts to some absolute standard of conduct, as opposed simply to asking for their best effort, bothered Baden-Powell considerably during the early years of Scouting. The 1909 edition of *Scouting for Boys* extends doing

one's best to the entire initial promise ("On my honour I will do
my best"), and not merely to helping others; in 1910, the promise
is again absolute, with the idea of best effort associated only with
helping people; in 1911, there is no mention at all of doing one's
best; and in the 1912 regulations it returns once again to characterize all the obligations of the Oath: "On my honour I promise
that I will do my best

> To do my duty to God and the King,
> To help other people at all time,
> To obey the Scout Law,"

where it remained.

The attention Baden-Powell lavished upon the proper deploy-
ment of "doing one's best" suggests a strain basic to Scouting from
its beginning, between the principled and the pragmatic. While
Scouting built its appeal on the bedrock of unwavering standards,
it always remained sensitive to the fallibility of its members and to
the dangers of discouraging potential converts by too strict an insistence on the demands they must meet. Baden-Powell's desire to
build a mass movement that would embrace all the youth of Britain
required that he not define his ideals so strictly as to exclude large
numbers of boys interested in joining. Asking only that one do one's
best—thereby allowing the Scout occasionally to fall short in his
efforts without feeling that he had violated his Oath—is an example
of the care with which Baden-Powell looked after the health—and
growth—of his movement.[4]

What, then, precisely is the Law that the Scouts must promise to
do their best to uphold? It is above all a protracted call for obedience on a grand scale. Of the original nine laws, six have as their
essential thrust the Scout's unquestioning loyalty and his absolute
willingness to carry out any orders given him. Only the obligation
that a Scout be courteous, a friend to animals, and thrifty—three
of the rather smaller claims, by any reckoning—address other concerns. Whatever else the Scout might learn, the primary lesson is
obedience. Not only for Baden-Powell is the "dull lad who can
obey orders ... better than a sharp one who cannot," but it is only
the former who could qualify to be a Scout.

The stress on obedience begins by asserting that the Scout's
honor is to be trusted. As the commentary makes clear, the sacred-
ness of the Scout's honor is put to the test when the Scout is
charged, on his honor, to carry out an order from his Scout officer.
Under such circumstances, he must immediately do everything he

can to fulfill the order, letting nothing interfere with his task. Once
his honor has been invoked, the Scout has no choice but to do what
he has sworn to do. Although Baden-Powell mentions that a Scout's
honor should preclude the possibility of lying, the emphasis of his
brief commentary is on the carrying out of the orders. The real
value of the abstract principle lies in the rather more concrete
notion that a Scout's honor is a good guarantee that he will do
what he is told. Failure to follow orders risks disgrace and even
expulsion from the movement. Baden-Powell wraps the threat of
sanction in an effective rhetorical package. Having first declared,
in *Scouting for Boys*, that the Scout's badge "represents and is called
his 'life,'"[5] Baden-Powell then completes the grim logic of this definition: the loss of badge involved in failing to act appropriately
means the malefactor "loses his life." The metaphoric excess of
equating badge with life was designed to help the Scout cherish his
affiliation with the movement and strive to meet its demands.

The commitment to obedience implicit in the first law's notion
of honor is reinforced by the second's postulation of loyalty—to
king, officers, country and employers. The last, of course, is the
most startling constituency, one that caused Baden-Powell some
difficulty. During the next few years different versions of the Law
omitted (while others retained) mention of loyalty to employer,
and in 1917 some of its socially reactionary implications were
muted by the addition of the phrase, "and to those under him," to
the formulation. Nevertheless the matter continued to rankle, particularly as it touched upon Scouting's efforts to gain the support of
organized labor. Since the clause was introduced precisely to
counter the agitation of Socialists and trade unions, which Baden-
Powell abhorred, it was no surprise that both would object to a
stipulation of loyalty that elevated the employer to the sacred level
of king and country. The Scout Executive Committee addressed
the issue in 1930, trying to reduce the opposition to Scouting felt
in certain parts of the labor movement. At least four separate solutions were suggested:

1. To use the word "employment" instead of "employers."
2. To cut down the definition and leave the law as—"A Scout
   is loyal to King and country"—this being what is done by
   the Girl Guides Association.
3. That the Law should read after the words "King and country," "and to those over and under him."
4. To read "A Scout is loyal to his King and country and to
   others to whom loyalty is due."[6]

Baden-Powell's response to these proposals suggests how important the unquestioned allegiance of boy to employer was to his
whole conception of Scouting's regenerative role in British society:

> Re the proposal to omit from Scout Law "Loyalty to Em-
> ployer"—The objection has been raised by socialists to this.
> They maintain that the boy should be loyal rather to his
> Trades Union than to his employer. But boys don't as a rule,
> I believe, belong to Trades Unions, so there is no harm in
> their being loyal to their employers. It is their duty and they
> should be reminded of it. The fact that we do put it to them
> is the reason why so many employers prefer to give employ-
> ment to Scouts.
>
> We could, if it is considered necessary to meet socialist
> views, add: A Scout is loyal to ... his employer, his Trades
> Union and to those under him.[7]

No agreement was reached, and the formulation remained the
same, but the discussion usefully exposes some of Scouting's unacknowledged political concerns. Baden-Powell always prided himself
on the nonpolitical nature of Scouting, a subject to which we shall
return with some frequency here. It is enough for the moment to
point out that requiring loyalty to an employer during the period
of a developing labor movement is by no means the simple moral
act that Baden-Powell liked to pretend it was. Scouting was deeply
and pervasively political from the start—any large-scale effort to
refashion a segment of society necessarily has to be—and Baden-
Powell, as this exchange illustrates, knew it. His public stance of
indifference to political matters was simply one of his more effective
strategies in fostering the growth of Scouting.

Another interesting feature of this particular exchange is the way
Baden-Powell proposes to get around the criticism of the trade
unionists and socialists. We are simply dealing with boys, he reminds his committee, not adults who might be expected to belong
to trade unions, and therefore no friction should exist between us.
This is Baden-Powell at his expedient best: Since the requirement
of demonstrating loyalty to one's employer is only binding on boys,
it does not pose any threat to the labor movement.

As revealing as the inclusion of employers in the second law's
hierarchy of loyalties is the absence of any mention of parents. It
was not until 1912 that Scouts were enjoined to show loyalty to
their parents, with the new obligation inserted between *officers* and
country. What might seem a peculiar omission—parents, after all,

constitute a traditional source of august moral authority—makes sense only in the light of Baden-Powell's assumption that lower-class parents were incapable of exercising proper influence on their children. His conviction that poverty was a condition engendered by the moral fecklessness of the poor brought with it the need to remove the children from the pernicious control of those parents who were clearly unable to look after themselves. When he writes in the first edition of *Scouting for Boys* that of the 2 million boys in Great Britain "only 270,000 are under good influences outside their school walls," he implicitly denies the possibility that the remaining 1.730 million who "are drifting towards 'hooliganism' or bad citizenship,"[8] receive any adequate training from their indifferent or impoverished parents. Parents are initially omitted from those deserving Scout loyalty because Baden-Powell views them as part of the problem, not the solution. And even if working-class parents were concerned with their sons' development, Baden-Powell realized, they would not likely endorse the notion of the dutiful lad happy with his status in life that the Scouts were eager to produce. Scouting thus offers itself not as a complement to but rather as a substitute for the alleged missing or misguided home instruction.

For Baden-Powell it was essential to free the early Scouts from their malefic home environments. But by 1912, with the movement turning away from the goals of redeeming hard-core street urchins (who were never seriously recruited in any case) in favor of the more malleable and respectable sons of the lower middle class, the exclusion of parental loyalty became a public relations liability which had to be rectified. Elevating parents in 1912 to the status originally granted Scout officers and employers testifies not to Baden-Powell's changed attitudes toward the nobility of parenthood but to the sharp class consciousness that always pervaded Scout thinking.

Whether it be loyalty to employers, Scout officers, country, or parents, no commitment should be disturbed by critical inquiry. Scout loyalty is meant to breed a passionate conviction of cause that renders unnecessary any exercise of independent judgment. Even to entertain the possibility of imperfection in those one obeys is to be guilty of grave betrayal. Requiring Scouts to resist not just those who oppose revered authority but even those who speak badly of it, Baden-Powell expresses both his own striking inability to handle criticism of any sort as well as a distressing behavioral ideal.

A loyal Scout is clearly one who is useful and does his duty, and here the third and seventh laws merge with the first two in elaborating the ideal of the serviceable and obedient youth Baden-Powell seeks. Two slightly different conceptions of duty are suggested by the two laws. The third holds that the Scout's duty is to be useful, and the seventh that it is his duty to obey orders even if he doesn't like them, as any proper soldier or sailor would. Although the emphases differ, both call for escaping the confines of self-interest in order to serve the greater good of the community. For Baden-Powell, the self is always the danger to be avoided, and whether it is in automatically obeying one's Scoutmaster or in helping others, preferably at the cost of one's own pleasure, comfort, or safety, the salutary negation of self is the end to be achieved. The Scout who does his duty is not likely to shirk national service or fall prey to the seductions of socialist propaganda. The fully indoctrinated Scout was precisely that sturdy brick in the wall of empire that Baden-Powell was trying to build for Great Britain.

The whistling, cheerful Scout does not represent any trivializing of the importance of the Scout character ideal—indeed, quite the opposite, as Baden-Powell's gloss makes clear. The Scout's happy demeanor becomes the only acceptable response to receiving an order. The Scout must not only do what he is told promptly, he must do it with a smile as well. Expressions of dissatisfaction, like hostile criticism, only identify the moral weakness of the grumbler. The smiling Scout, by contrast, both shows the proper deference to authority and sets a telling model for others. The cheery exterior is important to Baden-Powell because of its practical consequences: In times of danger, it can help soothe the anxieties of less intrepid souls. Baden-Powell's own whistling insouciance throughout the siege of Mafeking, demonstrating how little the empire had to fear from the raggle-taggle Boers, exemplified what the eighth law was intended to accomplish.

The classlessness of Scouting, a purported feature of the movement about which I have already spoken, is also mandated by the Law. Like members of most fraternal organizations, Scouts are expected to help other Scouts in any way they can, though they are especially charged with extending themselves, "no matter to what social class the other belongs." Ironically, the directive to overcome class distinctions seems to stress rather than obliterate the sharp consciousness of class thinking implicit in Scouting. Not that all Scouts are actually presumed the same, but simply that they must be treated as if they were, regardless of obvious class differences that might separate them. The enjoinder not to be affected by those differences reminds us that they do exist. But since they are seen as aspects of a social order in which rigid class distinctions are simply part of the divine structure of things, Baden-Powell is worried only that the differences not be allowed to undermine the unity of the Scouts. In order for the wall to stand firm, it is necessary not only that the rich not be unkind to the underprivileged Scout, but more importantly that the underprivileged not envy the rich. "A Scout must never be a SNOB," Baden-Powell warns in his fourth law, emphasizing that a snob is not only a wealthy person who looks down upon another because of his poverty, but "one who is poor and resents another because he is rich." The distinction points to Baden-Powell's concern, which the Scouting movement as a whole embodied, that the poor be contented with their lot. Acceptance—of the social order, of one's station in life, of the privileges of others—is the key to Scout success.

Baden-Powell also insists that his Scouts be courteous, kind to animals, and thrifty—all perfectly admirable characteristics that stand at a distance from the obedience-engendering center of the Scout Law. Of these, courtesy and thrift are the more significant. While appealing in its own right, courtesy is also a particularly comforting trait for the upper classes to find exhibited by the lower. Obedience flavored with courtesy is far more gratifying than mere obedience. In addition, Baden-Powell was shrewd enough to realize that the public impression the Scouts made would be crucial in creating enthusiasm and support for them, and he was always very conscious of the usefulness of their smart, well-behaved appearance. In addition to tying Scouting to various sentimentalized notions of how the knights of yore conducted themselves, the requirement of courtesy helped guarantee that every Scout would also be a fine public relations representative for the movement.

Thrift as a virtue needs no apology, for rich or poor alike, even if it is rather more easily managed by the rich. But as Baden-Powell spells out the usefulness of thrift—primarily to build up savings so that in times of unemployment the Scout can avoid making "himself a burden to others"—we can see precisely to whom this is addressed and why. For it is surely not the public school boy who would be working or who would even know the meaning of employment, still less of unemployment. The directive to thrift is meant for the lower-class lad, who would already have left school at fourteen to take a job to help support his family. Like his fellow youth reformers, Baden-Powell imagined that it was drink, gambling, smoking, and other such expensive indulgences that accounted for the grinding poverty of the working classes. If only they would husband their resources wisely, they would avoid the desperate situations in which they frequently found themselves. And every bit as urgent, they would not constitute a problem about which the state would have to concern itself. The savings account, constituting both diagnosis and remedy, suggests the degree of complexity of Baden-Powell's social vision; and the concept of thrift, however broadly applicable, becomes a way of solving a difficult problem without having to face up to it. The ninth law implicitly defines that segment of the population Baden-Powell felt needed the moral regeneration offered by Scouting.

That a Scout should be a friend to animals is perhaps the simplest and least exceptionable of the laws, even if the caution against the needless slaughter of flies seems excessive. What is interesting here is less the admonition against hurting or killing animals than the extent to which Baden-Powell's own practices and passions violated this precept. For he was an avid hunter, and his autobiographical writings, particularly those dealing with his experiences in India and Africa, are filled with the joy of a good kill. His evident pleasure in both stalking and shooting animals belies the principles he enunciates for his Scouts. But more telling even than his enthusiasm for hunting is his absolute obsession with the joys of pigsticking, or boar hunting. Baden-Powell thought this the noblest of sports, and he frequently celebrated in painstaking detail all its many virtues. A champion pigsticker, he wrote what was perhaps the first, and certainly at the time (1889) the best book on the subject. I will not analyze the argument Baden-Powell makes for the social usefulness—indeed necessity—of the sport, beyond noting that he finds it absolutely "invaluable to our prestige and supremacy in India,"[9] a sport "at once proving and preserving our rightful claim to superiority as a dominant race."[10]

But for our discussion of the sixth law what matters is not the complicated imperial utility Baden-Powell claims for pigsticking, so much as the sheer pleasure he takes in the violent confrontation of boar, horse, and man: "It is a rough, wild sport, with perhaps a taint of barbarism about it if examined critically and in the abstract."[11] Elsewhere he admits, "I am not sure that I am not a bit of a bully myself, because I must confess to being very fond of one sport which is undoubtedly cruel."[12] Reveling in its pleasures— "Yes, hog-hunting is a brutal sport—and yet I loved it"[13]— Baden-Powell finds it fulfilling not only for the British hunter, whose lusts and manhood are realized in the bloody encounter, but even for the doomed boar himself, who ordinarily has little opportunity to express his own pleasure in the fray:

> There is no doubt that it is the most exciting work that a man can go in for. At the same time the horse without a doubt

enjoys it almost as much as his rider, and the pig, too, being endowed with a fighting and bloodthirsty nature as well as a particularly tough and unfeeling nervous system, seems to revel in the fight up to the bitter end.[14]

Making everybody happy—"Not only is pigsticking the most exciting and enjoyable sport for both the man and horse as well, but I really believe that the boar enjoys it too"[15]—it is clear why Baden-Powell honors it as "the premier sport of India."[16] Given these enthusiasms, the sixth law's caution against hurting any of God's creatures unnecessarily seems more a specific class sanction than an absolute principle, designed to ensure that the nonhunting classes treat their domestic animals—dogs, cats, and horses—with the same respect they accord their betters. Presumably the ruling class must continue to hunt as a vital (and visible) part of its self-definition.

Taken together, these nine laws, supplemented by the tenth in 1911, provided the framework for the moral redemption that Scouting promised to kindle throughout Great Britain. The Scout Law would instill that necessary quality of character so sadly lacking in the youth of the nation, and that the conventional methods of school instruction could not produce.

The Scout Law derived a considerable part of its mystique from its alleged connection to the knightly code of King Arthur and his Round Table. Drawing on the special nationalistic feeling aroused by Arthur and his knights, Baden-Powell endlessly stressed the noble lineage of his Law. Just as the modern Japanese inherited their Bushido from the ancient samurai, so the Scouts can find in the heroic exploits of Arthur and his followers the origins of their own code of conduct. Baden-Powell hammers away at this relationship, producing numerous versions of knightly behavior with which the Scout Law could be compared. While the codes he adduces tend to vary from one another, all bear a remarkable resemblance to the Scout Law. In *Scouting for Boys*, for example, these are the laws he establishes:

Be Always Ready, with your armour on, except when you are taking your rest at night.

Defend the poor, and help them that cannot defend themselves.

Do nothing to hurt or offend anyone else.

Be prepared to fight in the defence of England.

At whatever you are working try and win honour and a name for honesty.

Never break your promise.

Maintain the honour of your country with your life.

Rather die honest than live shamelessly.

Chivalry requireth that youth should be trained to perform the most laborious and humble offences with *cheerfulness* and grace; and to do good unto others.[17]

Aids to Scouting offers a generally similar knightly code as it was "republished in the time of Henry VII":

1. They were never to put off their armour, except for the purpose of rest at night.
2. They were to search for adventures wherein to attain "Bruyt and renown."
3. To defend the poor and weak.
4. To give help to any who should ask for it in a just quarrel.
5. Not to offend one another.
6. To fight for the defence and welfare of England.
7. To work for honour rather than profit.
8. Never to break a promise for any reason whatever.
9. To sacrifice themselves for the honour of their country.
10. "Sooner choose to die honestly than to fly shamelessly."[18]

In *Yarns for Boy Scouts* Baden-Powell actually gives us two complete—and somewhat different—sets of rules. The first begins by explicitly announcing King Arthur as "the founder of British Scouts, since he first started the Knights of England."[19] The association that Baden-Powell tells us (incorrectly, as a matter of fact) Arthur formed on the day of his marriage held the knights to these obligations:

To reverence God.

To be loyal to the King.

To be kind and merciful to all.

To be always courteous and helpful to women.

To keep from fighting except in a high and just cause.

To be always honourable and true.

To be always obedient in the laws of Knighthood.[20]

The commentary that follows draws the Scout parallels even closer:

> Among these laws of Knighthood it was enacted that a Knight must always "Be Prepared" with his armour on to fight for the right—to defend the poor and helpless and his country. He must never break a promise. He must maintain the honour of his country, although it cost him his life. He must do his duty with *cheerfulness* and grace, his main duty being to do good to others.
>
> If he failed to carry out these laws after swearing to do so he was considered dishonourable and unfit to wear the badge of a Knight, and could be killed, or expelled from the association.[21]

As the knight must perform his duties, so the Scout must pass his tests before he earns the right of membership. The Scout's uniform is like the knight's armour; the badge the Scout receives on joining his patrol is matched by the pair of gold spurs and shield with crest that are given to the knight when he is accepted into brotherhood; the Scout's "Be Prepared" echoes the knight's motto of "Be Ready." And just as the knight who breaks his oath is disgraced, so the Scout who fails to keep his word is "no longer an honourable, manly fellow, but merely a weak boy who makes a promise one minute and then has not the grit to stick to it. We don't want such fellows in the Scouts; we don't want them in our country."[22]

Having just presented one coherent knightly code, *Yarns for Boy Scouts* then proposes another, which, in mysteriously foreshadowing many of the Scout ideals, even includes a startling approximation to the initial Scout Oath:

> The rule of the Knights, as you know, were these:
>
> First—To be faithful to God and King.
>
> Secondly—To help other people.
>
> Thirdly—To obey the laws of chivalry.
>
> These were, to be always ready with your armour on, except when sleeping at night.
>
> To defend the poor and helpless.
>
> To do nothing to offend or hurt others.
>
> To be prepared to fight in the defence of your country.

To do all things honourably and honestly.

Never break a promise.

Maintain the honour of your country even if it cost you your life.

Die honest rather than live disgracefully.

Do all your duty cheerfully.[23]

At this point it should be evident that swearing obedience to the Scout Law or the rules of the knights comes to much the same thing. Indeed, Baden-Powell makes clear that the loyal Scout, like the honest, questing knight, will in the end find his Holy Grail, "that is, he will know what true happiness is, he will rise to great things, and he will get his reward in Heaven."[24] Bringing together Scout and knight in search of the Holy Grail, Baden-Powell invests Scouting with a hallowed pedigree in which the Scout can take pride. In becoming a Scout, the young man joins that ancient brotherhood whose mission has always been to keep Britain great, to protect it not only from external attack but from the threat of the effeminate, the grousers, the wastrels, the liars, the cowards, and the selfish who imperil it from within.

If we disregard the bogus knightly trappings with which Baden-Powell sought to enhance the moral authority of the Scout Law, we find a rather more modern, and decidedly less exalted model for it in Baden-Powell's address to the staff of the South African Constabulary upon his departure from the corps in February 1903, before he had been challenged by Sir William Smith of the Boys' Brigade to think about a scheme of youth training. Sounding the same urgent lament we hear throughout Scouting— "For all classes of society we find too little real patriotism and unselfishness, and too much looking after 'No. 1'"—Baden-Powell exhorts his men to standards of conduct that distinctly anticipate much of what will follow in the Law:

To sum up, I urge each of you, whatever your rank, to:—

A. Keep improving yourself in efficiency and smoothness in proformance [sic] of your duties.
B. Avoid doing anything low or underhand or such as might lessen your personal respect for yourself.
C. Be guided by what you know to be your duty rather than by what is easiest or most pleasant to yourself.

D. Carry out your orders or tackle differences when they arise, with willingness and cheerily.
E. Conceal nothing from your superior officers, and be loyal to them and to the Corps.
F. Be helpful and courteous to all.[25]

The emphasis on loyalty, duty, and honor, and the specific mention of helpfulness, courtesy, and cheerfulness effectively make this the first rough version of what later was to emerge as the Scout Law with its solemn Arthurian embellishments. At least six of the nine laws appear here in varying degrees of clarity. While the Scout Law is packaged altogether differently, the thinking behind the two is essentially the same. There is, of course, no reason why a person's thinking should not be consistent. But given the extravagant moral claims made (by Baden-Powell among others) for the Law, it is sobering to locate its origins not in some heroic, chivalric past but in a typewritten memo hacked out in South Africa by the retiring head of a military police force worried about the efficiency, loyalty, and appearance of his unit, and exasperated by the way dissatisfied complainers can make life difficult for administrators. However useful one may think the Scout Law for the manufacture of responsible citizens, it is important to understand that its stress on duty and obedience derives not from some potent moral code so much as from the ordinary emotional and intellectual baggage that Baden-Powell, as a public school boy and military man, always carried with him. The model is less the unique moral splendor of a Sir Galahad than the vision of corporate harmony found in a smoothly functioning South African Constabulary. Baden-Powell's view of the engine room of the steamship *Orsova* provided him with a similarly admirable example of a compelling civic ideal:

> And it is indeed an impressive sight to stand below these great monsters of steel and watch them faithfully and untiringly pounding out their work, all in order and exactly in agreement with each other, taking no notice of night or day, or storm or calm, but slinging along at all times, doing their duty with an energetic goodwill which makes them seem almost human—almost like gigantic Boy Scouts.[26]

The Scout Law remains the most explicitly didactic feature of the indoctrination that Scouting took as its mission, "the foundation," as Baden-Powell noted himself, "on which the whole of Scout

Training rests."[27] Its ten specifications of the behavior expected of each Scout were designed to structure the conduct of every new member. But if adherence to the Law promoted the character type Baden-Powell wished to encourage, the Law in itself was hardly sufficient to make that type appealing to the youth of Great Britain. For this, Baden-Powell had to rely on another set of skills, which fortunately he possessed in abundance. He wrote more than fifty books, which dispensed wisdom on every subject of conceivable interest to the adolescent—social, political, psychological, and sexual. Like every successful writer (and teacher), Baden-Powell knew how to clothe abstract principles in engaging examples. His work, particularly *Scouting for Boys* teems with dramatic vignettes that bring to life all those behavioral ideals that Scouting sought to inculcate. Through his tendentious, at times clichéd, but always readable prose, he elaborates the vision and values that are outlined by the Scout Law. Baden-Powell's writing renders a marvelously simplistic world in which boys can romp while receiving only the most bracing ethical inspiration. If in broad scope it might be likened to the work of Samuel Smiles, the Victorian apostle of success whose handbooks of moral instruction, such as *Duty*, *Thrift*, *Character*, and *Self-Help*, attempted to enlighten the Victorian middle class, it also strives for the immediate utility of a school primer such as H. O. Arnold-Forster's *The Citizen Reader*,[28] whose stated purpose of describing "the duties owed by British Citizens to their country, their countrymen, and themselves,"[29] can be extended to Baden-Powell's books as well. Common to all three is the use of the graphic example, drawn from (or at least attributed to) real history, which embodies with absolute clarity the lessons to be learned.

Perhaps the most frequently cited example, appearing in a number of his books, including *Scouting for Boys* (as well as playing a prominent role in *The Citizen Reader*), concerns the sinking in 1852 of the *Birkenhead*, a transport ship carrying soldiers, their families, and seamen. As the ship began to break up off the Cape of Good Hope, it was discovered that there were not enough lifeboats for everyone,

so the men were ordered to remain in their ranks. Then the ship broke in half and began to go down. The captain shouted to the men to jump over and save themselves, but the colonel, Colonel Seaton, said, "No, keep your ranks." For he saw that if they swam to the boats, and tried to get in, they would probably sink them too. So the men kept their ranks, and as

the ship rolled over and sank, they gave a cheer and went
down with her. Out of the whole 760 on board, only 192 were
saved, but even those would probably have been lost had it
not been for the discipline and self-sacrifice of the others.[30]

(Commenting on an early gramophone record made to celebrate
this heroic moment, British historian V. G. Kiernan caustically
notes, "Why they did not swim ashore instead [as a quarter of
them did in the end] is a question that only later, smaller minds
would think of. This was the parade-ground spirit at its subli-
mest.")[31]

The exemplary behavior of the British soldiers, going to their
deaths in disciplined ranks and with a cheer, is amplified by various
instances of Japanese self-slaughter that Baden-Powell singles out
for praise. In *Boy Scouts Beyond the Seas*, he tells the story of forty-
seven Japanese ronin who, after avenging the death of their master
by killing his assailant, commit hara-kiri together. Baden-Powell
cautions that he is not telling the story to suggest that the ronin
were necessarily right in killing their master's enemy, but rather
that

> it is interesting to see that even in those days people thought
> a lot of men who were manly and loyal to their leader, and
> who were not afraid to sacrifice themselves, even by the most
> painful of deaths, in order to do their duty. . . .[32]

The extremes to which the Japanese are willing to go to demonstrate loyalty always earn Baden-Powell's admiration:

> The Emperor, as you know, is, in the religion of the
> Japanese, their God as well as their ruler. Nogi was so devoted
> to his Emperor, that when this great man died the General
> considered there was nothing for him to live for. So the first
> gun of the salute to the dead Emperor was the signal to his
> faithful soldier to kill himself and follow him.
>
> At the General's side was also his devoted wife who took
> the same signal to stab herself and follow her husband. In this
> way they each carried out their high sense of duty, proving
> that the power of will and sense of duty are stronger than
> death.[33]

Hara-kiri seems particularly attractive to Baden-Powell as a means
of honoring the chivalric code of one's ancestors. Commenting on

the way Japanese soldiers in the Russo–Japanese war refused to surrender when overcome by the Russians, he notes that

> They did not kill themselves by the easy method of shooting themselves, but by the painful way of disemboweling themselves with their swords. They did this because it was the more honourable way in which the *Samurai* or Knights of Japan did it.[34]

The joy of giving up one's life is not limited to soldiers. In *Yarns for Boy Scouts*, Baden-Powell recounts the heroism of a Japanese boy whose father was being pursued by bandits. When the bandits finally kill the man they believe to be the boy's father, they bring the boy to identify the body. The son realizes that they have killed the wrong man—the father is presumably still safely hidden—but he must exhibit sufficient grief to convince the bandits that they did indeed kill the man they were after. The most authentic display of despair he can fashion is to kill himself—which he promptly does. Baden-Powell's approval is unqualified:

> Well, he was a plucky boy, wasn't he? He is one example for every boy, and especially every Scout, to follow in Being Prepared to give up all, even his own life if necessary, for the sake of another.
> That is what is meant by "Bushido," or self-sacrifice.[35]

Although Japanese models abound, it is not just the Japanese who can sacrifice their lives for someone else. Consider the case of Currie, a lad of eighteen, who

> saw a little girl playing on the railway line at Clydebank in front of an approaching train. He tried to rescue her, but he was lame from an injury he had got at football, and it delayed him in getting her clear. The train knocked both of them over, and both were killed.
> But Currie's gallant attempt is an example of chivalry for scouts to follow. It was sacrifice of himself in the attempt to save the child.[36]

And while dying certainly helps authenticate the act, loyalty can be demonstrated even by the living, as shown by the behavior on maneuvers of the cadet at Reigate Grammar School,

who, when posted as sentry, was accidentally left on his post
when the field day was over. But though night came on, and
it was very cold—in November last—the lad stuck to his post
till he was found in the middle of the night, half perished with
cold, but alive and alert.[37]

Together with the standard displays of British heroism—the
Light Brigade, Nelson, Sir Ernest Shackleton, General Gordon,
moments of courage during the Indian Mutiny, and others—these
samples of disciplined selflessness constitute the character paradigm
held up for emulation by the youth of the country. Boys who aspire
to mold themselves along these lines have the satisfaction of knowing they are part of that elite corps of "manly" men—not just King
Arthur and his knights or the brave British soldiers and sailors, but
also a host of intrepid pioneers and frontiersmen, trappers and
scouts—whom Baden-Powell has conjured together to appeal to
youthful imaginations. By melding them all into an ideal of true
masculinity, Baden-Powell makes clear what the consequences are
for those who don't share their values:

> Every boy ought to learn how to shoot and to obey orders,
> else he is no more good when war breaks out than an old
> woman.[38]

The brotherhood of Scouts consists of

> real *men* in every sense of the word ... they understand living
> out in the jungles, and they can find their way anywhere ...
> they know how to look after their health when far away from
> any doctors, are strong and plucky, and ready to face any
> danger, and always keen to help each other. They are accus-
> tomed to take their lives in their hands, and to fling them
> down without hesitation if they can help their country by
> doing so.
>   They give up everything, their personal comforts and de-
> sires, in order to get their work done. They do not do all this
> for their own amusement, but because it is their duty to their
> king, fellow-countrymen, or employers.[39]

In Scouting's cult of masculinity, indifference to the pleasures of
shooting, or the outdoors, or danger puts one's manhood in doubt.
What remains are old women, or squealing rabbits, or worse.
   It is easy to understand the point of this kind of indoctrination.

Obedience, a sense of duty, the willingness to sacrifice oneself in the
interests of something larger than the individual are all qualities
that most cultures in one way or another attempt to encourage in
their citizenry. And for Great Britain, concerned about the vulnerability of its vast empire and the specter of social unrest among its
own laboring classes, it is even more apparent why a system of
character training that claimed to address these national anxieties
would be given the official sanction of a royal charter. But whatever
the social utility of the Boy Scout conception of character, it is hard
not to notice its restricted emotional and intellectual premises, its
hatred of dissent, its fear of the independent critical mind. The
question of what Scout character was about was seldom asked. One
of the few to raise it was John Hargrave, originally the commissioner of woodcraft for the movement, who later left the Scouts to
form his own youth organization, the Kibbo Kift Kindred. Writing
in 1919 in *The Trail*, the magazine of the London Scout Council
that was eventually absorbed into the *Headquarters Gazette*, Hargrave
expressed those doubts that made his resignation from Scouting
inevitable:

> What exactly are we good for?
> To make boys of good character?
> But are we certain of what a "good character" consists?
> Was Tolstoy a "good character"?—the man who was up
> against his king—the man who tried to follow the Christ? Was
> William Penn a "good character"?—the man who would not
> accept the religious dogmas and creeds of his time—the man
> who broke away from the State Church and whose followers
> were imprisoned because they believed law and the slave trade
> to be wrong?
> Or is it only the Nelsons, the Drakes, the Wellingtons, and
> the Napoleons who, having stood for King and Empire by
> force, we should hold up to the Scout as "good characters"? . . .
> To-day we want men who are determined to "alter things."
> Are we training them, to think openly in every direction (even
> in the direction in which we wish they wouldn't), or are they
> bound to the same old wheel of convention upon which the
> whole world went cycling into the most bloody and unchris-
> tian war ever waged by mankind?[40]

Hargrave's questions accurately reveal the limitations in Scouting's conception of character. Committed to producing the serviceable citizen who will loyally perform his duty, Scouting neglects

the richness of individual preference and difference, closing itself off entirely from the claim of human variety. As Hargrave points out, Scouting has no room in it for dissenters, doubters, visionaries, or any other subversive individualists. Obedience to the state—and the willingness to sacrifice for it—is the sole measure by which personal worth is assessed. The questioning intelligence is a danger that cannot be tolerated; the self is perceived as something to be supressed, not nourished. Scouting envisions a world of unchanging values and simple answers; once he joins, the young Scout need not bother himself about such things again. The world is firmly divided into two distinct sides—the empire and the other—and all the Scout must do is "play the game" with pluck and good sportsmanship so that his side may win. Promising to equip Great Britain with the disciplined human resources required for its survival constituted the irresistible appeal that Scouting offered the country. Attractive as such a promise would be to a nation worried about its might, it nevertheless raises many more complicated questions about national ideals than Baden-Powell would have been willing to acknowledge.

5

THE SPECTER OF
DETERIORATION

Scouting's concern for the general mental, moral, and physical condition of the British people went beyond the need to prepare Britain's youth for the discipline of military service. About the same time that the Scouts, with their staves, hats, and shorts, started to impress themselves upon the public, an altogether different type of British lad also began to make a claim on the nation's consciousness. Even if it was not clear that anyone ever actually knew him, there was a strict consensus as to his appearance. Baden-Powell described him thus: "pale, narrow-chested, hunched-up ... smoking endless cigarettes,"[1] and even provides us with an illustration of him. The *Nation in Arms* had also seen him, the "weedy youth with hollow chest, slouching shoulders, weak knees, and slack muscles,"[2] a lamentable physical specimen well known to Colonel G. Malcolm Fox: "We do not want them bandy-legged, knock-kneed, or flat-footed, narrow-chested, stooping, pale, anaemic, short-sighted, or blear eyed, stuttering or hard of hearing.... What sort of a fate will fall upon the nation composed of units like these—and they are alarmingly on the increase."[3] C. F. G. Masterman noticed him everywhere in the pestilential city, "stunted, narrow-chested, easily wearied; yet voluble, excitable, with little ballast, stamina, or endurance."[4] Lord Beresford looked to military training as a way of bridging the gap between "the stunted, narrow-chested recruit—rejected, town-bred hobbledehoy of our English streets today, and the young up-standing, keen-eyed colonial."[5] Inhabiting cities almost exclusively, lingering around music halls, and watching (instead of participating in) football games, this corporate wastrel, with his decaying teeth and meager chest, not only constituted the obvious antitype of the healthy and purposeful Scout, but provided the strongest argument for the importance of Scouting as well. He appears throughout Baden-Powell's work, as potent a trope (for he is primarily that) as the frequently invoked "imperiled island." Both island and wastrel emphasized the need for the Scouting cure Baden-Powell proposed.[6]

In pointing out the prevalence of these young men, whose scrawny physiques were understood to be merely the visible forms of their scrawny characters, Baden-Powell was doing more than making the case for the importance of Scouting, though he was certainly doing that. He was expressing the view—broadly shared in certain social and intellectual circles—that Britain itself was in decline, and that in the great struggle that inevitably characterized national and international existence, it no longer had the manhood to compete. The call for efficiency, which was heard from these same circles, grew in part out of the claim that Britain was a nation collapsing from within. Universal military training was seen as vital not only because it would enhance the country's ability to defend itself, but because it would—or so it was argued—turn wayward British youth into physically capable, socially responsible citizens of trustworthy character. As a guaranteed shortcut to the goal of social regeneration, it had no equal.

It is not easy to distinguish between the legitimate conviction of Baden-Powell and others that Britain was being overrun by hordes of the inefficient and narrow-chested and their deliberate insistence on this vision for their own social and political purposes. Fortunately a neat distinction isn't needed, and the truth, in any case, certainly lies somewhere in the middle. The insistence on a deteriorating Britain—something unquestionably more than a fiction—enabled Baden-Powell, the Fabians, the Eugenicists, the Liberal-Imperialists, the military conscriptionists, the social Darwinists, and a host of conservative politicians, historians, and philosophers calling for a renewed patriotic commitment and a more tightly disciplined society to base their arguments on the alleged data available to every sensible person. One had only to glance down the streets of any city to see demonstrable evidence of Britain's peril.

The grand historical exemplar of a powerful empire succumbing to internal rot, of course, is Rome, and it is not surprising to find Baden-Powell drawing the analogy explicitly on several occasions between the moral and physical deterioration of the Romans and those lamentable tendencies discernible among the British. An unwillingness to take an active role in the defense of one's country, a debilitating reliance on the generosity of the state to feed and take care of its people, a growing dependency on the passive enjoyment of the spectator to the exclusion of healthy exercise for one-self—all these are symptomatic for Baden-Powell of the way Britain was pursuing the same self-destructive course as that of the Roman Empire.[7] Baden-Powell was fond of quoting the words of George Wyndham, a Tory Imperialist, that "The same causes which brought about the fall of the great Roman Empire are working to-day in Great Britain."[8]

Although Baden-Powell made good use of the cautionary instance of Rome, the idea was not his. He derived the detailed parallelism from a pamphlet published anonymously in 1905 entitled, *The Decline and Fall of the British Empire: Appointed for use in the National Schools of Japan. Tokio, 2005*. Its author, Elliot Mills, an enthusiastic National Service League supporter, applied Gibbon to an analysis of Britain's failure, so that Japan—presumably the next great empire to replace Britain—will not repeat the same mistakes. Gibbon's analysis of Rome's demise accounts for Britain's as well, and as Mills touches upon all the areas of British decadence that proved fatal to the maintenance of the empire, we can hear Baden-Powell's concerns: the movement of the population from the country to the town, the replacement of the hearty British yeoman by effete and self-indulgent men lacking in patriotism, the increase in the number of unhealthy parents, the obsessive interest in professional athletics, the inability of the nation to protect itself against its enemies. Like the invasion literature of William LeQueux (see Chapter 7), Mills ends with a reference to the wisdom of Lord Roberts, who sought to alert the nation to the dangers it faced. From the vantage point of the twenty-first century, it is clear that Britain would have survived had it only heeded Roberts's message that "Four months under canvas, a rigid discipline, and a sound education in the most bracing of all schools, the school of war, would have given a new tone to the community, and compelled every man to realize what it meant to be the citizen of an empire which strove to direct the aspirations of the world."[9] Failing to learn from Roberts, however, the country was finally engulfed by its enemies, and the obligations of a peace-loving empire, once entrusted to England, fell to Japan:

> In many points we resemble the English: we have the same sturdy physique which was theirs in the days of Queen Elizabeth; the same faith in God and ourselves. Like them we are an Island Race on the verge of a great continent with an increasing trade and a boasted Navy.... Let us study the Decline and Fall of England as the English should have studied the Decline and Fall of the Roman Empire. *For the Good of the Race.*[10]

If Mills provided a specific analogy between Rome and Great Britain that Baden-Powell used to good effect, he could not lay similar claim to the preoccupation with "the good of the race," which the Scouts also exploited from the beginning. The concern about the purity and the continued vitality of the Anglo-Saxon race, which Baden-Powell did so much to foster, was commonly expressed throughout Edwardian England. The alarm was publicly sounded in the autumn of 1903 by the establishment of the Inter-Departmental Committee on Physical Deterioration, with its original charge,

> To make a preliminary enquiry into the allegations concerning the deterioration of certain classes of the population as shown by the large percentage of rejections for physical causes of recruits for the Army and by other evidence, especially the Report of the Royal Commission on Physical Training (Scotland), and to consider in what manner the medical profession can best be consulted on the subject with a view to the appointment of a Royal Commission, and the terms of reference to such a Commission, if appointed.[11]

Credit for getting the investigation launched belongs to Lord Meath, a man particularly committed to assuring the durability of the empire. Drawing attention in the House of Lords in July 1903 to the problems of the physical well-being of the people as seen in the Report of the Commission on Physical Training in Scotland and on recruiting statistics for the army, Meath argued for the importance of a committee to determine "whether the poorer populations in our large towns are exposed to conditions that, if continued, must inevitably contribute to a low national standard of physical health and strength, seeing that if such be the case it would constitute a grave national peril."[12] His concern, Meath emphasized, was not for the physical condition of the sons of the well-to-do, which he assumed was improving all the time, but specifically the "less favoured classes"[13] who lived in cities—precisely those for whom Baden-Powell intended his Scouts. Meath cites a variety of data about the disparity between the height and weight of public school as opposed to working-class boys, the infant mortality rates of the poor, and the incidence of ear and throat infections that afflict the unhappy denizens of the city slums. Meath ends his part of the discussion with a kind of exhortation to patriotic battle, which constituted the rhetorical appeal on which the Scouting movement was based as well. The subject must be pursued, Meath argues,

> so that future generations may be able fearlessly to face the burden which fierce foreign competition and the ever increasing responsibilities of extending Empire have placed and will place, on the shoulders of the subjects of King Edward.... I firmly believe in the capabilities and energy of the Anglo-Saxon, and have confidence that, with the ancient pluck of their race, the future of the Empire will be made by its sons and daughters even more glorious than its memorable past, if only we, the fathers of the rising generation, do not neglect our duties, but give our sons and our grandsons a chance to equip themselves properly for the contest, and see that, in founding the mightiest Empire the world has ever known, we do not, by our indifference and carelessness, hinder nature in her efforts to people that Empire with an Imperial race.[14]

Certainly the Imperial race appeared to need some help if the army recruiting figures, or at least those as interpreted by General Frederick Maurice, could be believed. Maurice's role in nourishing the national anxiety about deterioration cannot be overstated. His two articles in *The Contemporary Review*—"Where to Get Men" (1902) and "National Health: A Soldier's Study" (1903)—gave the public the simple and distressing formula that "out of every five men who are willing to enlist only two are fit to become effective soldiers."[15] The 60 percent unfitness rate was adopted by all those pushing for various kinds of social, military, and racial reform as compelling documentation for the urgency of constructive action. Predictably, Lord Meath referred to it in his speech in the House of Lords, just as Baden-Powell frequently employed it as part of his recruiting efforts for Scouting. Given its wide acceptance as a touchstone of degeneration, it would be well to look briefly at how Maurice derived it.

Maurice begins by saying that at first glance the recent report of the inspector general for recruiting would seem to be encouraging, "for whereas in 1896 42 percent of the men who offered themselves were rejected by the doctors as unfit for soldiering, in 1900 only 28 percent were so rejected."[16] But this decline is misleading, Maurice points out, on two grounds: The quality of recruiting generally tends to improve with the allure of war, accounting for the 1900 (Boer War) improvement, and recruiting officers were warned not to bring up men before the doctors who where seen to be physically marginal candidates. On the basis of these two reasons, therefore, Maurice concludes, in a rather startlingly intuitive way, that it would "be a moderate estimate to take about 35 percent as the ordinary figure of the doctor's rejections in quiet times, and to add to these at least 10 percent more for those who are not brought up before doctors, though willing to enlist if they had been fit to become soldiers."[17] But having moved without benefit of a single fact from 28 to 45 percent of the potential pool who are now physically unfit to serve, there still remained one constituency un-accounted for: the men who are accepted into the army but after one or two years are discharged as unlikely ever to make satisfac-tory soldiers. Without burdening his argument with data, and with-out any effort to distinguish among the various reasons, medical and otherwise, for which soldiers might be dismissed from the ranks, Maurice decides that it is a "far too moderate estimate to say that another 15 percent must be added for those who for one cause or another disappear as unfit for soldiering by the end of their first two years of service."[18] Such is the evolution of the dramatic 60 percent that helped call the Inter-Departmental Committee into existence and that sounded a warning repeated throughout Britain. Interestingly, while the figures Maurice cites were more or less accepted by everyone as accurate, those supplied to the Inder-De-partmental Committee by the director general of the Army Medical Service suggest that Maurice's figures are substantially exagger-ated. [19] The director general's reasons for the rejection of recruits point to a somewhat less dire situation than Maurice would have us believe exists. According to these data the three largest causes for rejections in 1900 were insufficient chest measurement, defective vision, and inadequate weight—problems, to be sure, but not neces-sarily indicative of the impending national catastrophe that Maur-ice invokes at the conclusion of his "Where to Get Men": "What I want to insist on is, that till we can develop a population out of which more than two in five of those who wish to enlist are fit to become soldiers, we are in face of a far more deadly peril than any that was presented by the most anxious period of the South African War. It would not, nevertheless, be easy to exaggerate what that was."[20]

The Inter-Departmental Committee began its hearings on 2 September 1903 and gathered evidence for twenty-six days, examining in the process sixty-eight witnesses. Taking testimony from a variety of experts on the conditions of cities, the health of schoolchildren, and the problems of feeding them; on the role of boys' clubs and employment difficulties of the poor; on infant mortality and physical exercise and the need to educate working-class mothers about the principles of sound nourishment, the committee explored the social and medical issues attached to the notion of deterioration. In so doing, it played a substantial role in popularizing the idea of deterioration throughout the country, the committee's very existence presumably documenting the gravity of the problem. In fact, despite the extensive evidence it compiled on the insalubrious nature of working-class life in cities and the consequences for the health of the urban poor, the committee concluded that there were no grounds for the belief "that progressive deterioration is to be found among the people generally."[21] Not only did the witnesses not share the view that there was any noticeable degeneration, but, more important, all acknowledged that no reliable figures existed to compare the physique and well-being of the current population with those of any previous time. The lack of a statistical base made allegations about degeneration (or for that matter improvement) logically impossible. But this technical disclaimer notwithstanding, the committee turned up disturbing material regarding the infirm condition of those poorer classes that normally provided the army with its recruits. If degeneration as such was not an inference easily substantiated, nevertheless there was ample evidence that the poor working-class inhabitants of city slums were not prospering, physically or any other way. Detailing the crowded, filthy conditions in which the poor were forced to struggle, and the dangers to health and morality that such conditions posed, the committee argued the case for the Boy Scouts even before Baden-Powell was prepared to do so himself.

In this regard the committee was astoundingly prescient in addressing the plight of the lower-class lad—the member of the "rough classes"—who lived his life outside the morally uplifting influences of a middle-class home, school, or church. What was to happen to him, and how could society look after his character development, not to speak of his chest? Voluntary youth organizations seemed to provide the best possibility, but as various witnesses made clear, no club or association had the complete answer. The mandatory religious element in the different brigades—Boys', London Diocesan, Church Lads', Jewish, and others—guaranteed that their enrollments would never be very large, while the clergy was reluctant to lend its support to any movement lacking a significant religious component. And with or without religion it was still hard to get the "roughest element" to join any sort of club. But despite the difficulties, the need to train both character and body remained, a problem the committee thought might best be solved by asking all boys to attend continuation classes in which "drill and physical exercises should take a prominent place,"[22] or else join a cadet corps or club that would stress the proper development of their physiques. Groping for a viable training method, the committee looked to results that were much like what Baden-Powell was soon to argue his Scouts would provide:

> By these means, without recourse being had to any suggestion of compulsory military service, the male adolescent population might undergo a species of training that would befit them to bear arms with very little supplementary discipline. The older lads could actually be familiarised with the use of the rifle, an exercise of no inconsiderable value from the point of view of general education, and a great deal might thus be done which would not only provide partly prepared material for absorption in the army or reserved forces, but would give a tone and carriage to all that came under the influence of the system.[23]

The committee's principal conclusion—that there were no signs of physical deterioration among the population—was the one finding to which people paid least attention. The evidence it revealed on the way to its conclusion only heightened the general feeling that a grave problem existed. And its various recommendations to improve the condition of the working class, such as mandatory medical inspection of schoolchildren, school meals for the underfed, the establishment of milk depots, the training of mothers in the principles of proper hygiene and nourishment, the insistence on adequate exercise for the young, among others—also suggested that despite the assertion that England was not suffering from deterioration, all was by no means well.

The social pathology the committee addressed, it must be emphasized, was defined as an almost exclusively urban phenomenon.

It was the polluted city, teeming with pernicious aliens, that de-
formed the character and body of the British worker. Youth clubs,
and the Scouts in particular, saw themselves as treating a set of
problems specifically caused by the population's shift from the
country to the cities in search of industrial opportunities. Along
with the potent "sixty percent" figure for those unfit for military
service, "seventy-seven percent" also became a mythically charged
statistic, evoking in a different way the imperiled condition of Britain. This represented the percentage of the population residing in
cities at the turn of the century, an increase from the 50 percent of
the 1870s. Seventy-seven percent summoned up the overcrowded
hovels, the disease, and the moral decay alleged to be synonymous
with city living in the early twentieth century. The city's density
and pestilence became the metaphoric opposite of all the life-
enhancing qualities found in the country:

> The evil existing in the number of human beings huddled
> together in an acre—built up towards the sky in barracks, so
> many hundred persons all being hived in one small spot of
> ground; even if the actual room accommodation be sufficient,
> this evil is distinct and remains. Closely connected with this
> idea is the absence of open spaces; the enormous distances that
> must be traversed before a man can get out of the sordid
> streets of the city to the restful green of the country—to the
> soft, moist fields, the gentle restfulness of trees. The moral,
> aesthetic, physical loss that all this implies![24]

The Committee on Physical Deterioration even included the deliberate proselytizing in favor of country life as one of its recommendations:

> With a view to combatting the evils resulting from the con-
> stant influx from country to town, the Committee recom-
> mends that every effort should be made by those charged with
> the conduct and control of rural schools to open the minds of
> the children to the resources and opportunities of rural exist-
> ence.[25]

Such a suggestion was by no means unusual. While the committee
wanted to restrict the human flow into the city, A. W. Smyth argued for the urgency of encouraging those already trapped in the
city to move back to the country:

In order to raise the national physique, it will be necessary to produce boys and girls possessed of sound bodies and minds and until the children of the poor are raised out of the gutters and slums, their mental and physical health will continue to fail. The objects of the Garden City Association, or any other association which seeks to encourage townspeople to move to healthier surroundings, cannot be too highly commended.[26]

In its implicit as well as explicit repudiation of urban culture, Scouting expressed a set of values common to all reformers in the early part of the century. Bad citizenship and sunken chests were seen as uniquely city products. For Smyth it is obvious that "the evidence of vital statistics proves beyond cavil that the effect of town conditions is to cause premature death."[27] Reginald Bray, one of the Edwardian boyologists, details the consequences of urban existence for the survivors:

Physically it tends to rear an unhealthy race. Mentally it tends to create a people of quick, superficial intelligence. Morally it tends to bring about three results. First, the absence of the nature element, the lack of all that is beautiful, the overcrowded homes, and the influence of the street all co-operate in producing an excitable disposition. Secondly, poverty, while encouraging a love of the weak, incites all to fight for themselves when their opponents are their equals.... Lastly, the habit of regarding the external character and of neglecting the internal causes the untruthfulness which exists among the poor.[28]

The rejection of urban culture goes beyond the realistic perception of the problems posed by slums, overcrowding, and unemployment. The moral and spiritual pestilence attributed to the city represented in large part a judgment rendered by the upper classes on the way of life of the lower. Little attempt was ever made to understand the characteristic institutions or values of the urban poor. Everything connected with urban life was suspect, and the enterprise of moral reform was largely to convince the poor of the superior standards, amusements, and manners of their betters. As the poor obviously would not have the option of escaping to the country as the affluent middle class did, they had to be protected against the contamination of city living. Hence the concern shown by Baden-Powell and other youth workers over the malefic influences of ice-cream parlors, music halls, cinemas, professional football contests, and the

various forms of spontaneous street life—in short, all those opportunities for entertainment and relaxation spawned by an urban
culture. Denying the possibilities of character growth to be found
in the cities, they looked to the country as the source of all ethical
instruction. The pleasures of outdoor living—real, to be sure—were
suddenly invested with an almost mystical capacity to shape
character in desirable ways. Summer camping sessions for the
young were not merely a diverting escape from the city heat but a
crucial opportunity to expose the city urchin to the edifying moral
impulses to be found in nature. "The myth was spread and
accepted that Nature contained the greatest purity and could be
used to save every young person,"[29] a myth which Scouting certainly helped propagate.

The distance separating the cramped city from the open country,
a distance that for Pethick Lawrence had metaphoric significance—
"The towniness of the towns, on the other hand, is to be regarded
as an evil on account of the sheer geographical concomitant of
overcrowding to the acre, and also on account of the moral, physical, and aesthetic degradation which is implied by the denial of
access to the country"[30]—also represents the distance between what
is properly English and what is not. Separated from the life-giving
rhythms of rural England, the city was seen by many as something
suspiciously foreign, exposing its inhabitants to all manner of noxious, non-British influences. James Cantlie, an active crusader for
social reform, draws a firm distinction between the well-nourished
country-bred man, eating British vegetables and British beef, and
the rootless, thwarted city dwellers, digesting imported goods:

> The flour for his bread is probably American, his eggs are
> possibly French, the bacon he eats is likely imported from
> Chicago, butter from Denmark, beef from Argentina pastur-
> age or from some "foreign" source.... There is little British in
> his composition in a physical sense. Mentally his efforts are
> mainly directed to the newspapers, and the pabulum for his
> consumption is mostly concerned with foreign politics and the
> doings and opinions of every country under the sun.... En-
> vironment has little to do with his existence, his body is mostly
> composed of materials derived from any source except British.
> Appeals to his patriotism have another basis than in times
> gone by when the Briton was the product of British pastures.[31]

For Cantlie, who embodies the purest strains of British insularity,

"Physical deterioration and consumption of foreign-grown foods came in together about thirty years ago, and it is possible the inferior quality of the food we now consume may have directly to do with our falling off in physique. British prowess cannot be maintained on the dumped refuse of the Chicago slaughterhouses canned for British consumption."[32]

Cantlie's obsessions about the deleterious effects of city life may have led him to adopt certain extreme positions, but the obsessions were themselves not unique to him. The inferior quality of city air, for example, was a major issue for those concerned with the well-being of the urban masses. "Our health is largely determined by the character of the air we breathe," Thomas Oliver writes in his massive study of industrial maladies. "Indoor occupations contrast unfavourably with a life spent in the open air."[33] Bad air not only deposited effluvia into the system, but mitigated the potential benefits of any exercise taken in the city, accounting in part for the critical value attached to the camping experience in the Scouts and Boys' Brigades. The moral uplift of country living also brought with it a respite from fetid city air. If it was only Cantlie who was prepared to solve the problem of impure air by seriously proposing "to bring fresh air into the town by pipes laid down for the purpose,"[34] nevertheless this rather extraordinary recommendation defined a problem that everyone agreed was severe.

The harsh vision of urban degeneracy not only spawned a variety of organizations and committees designed to counter its effects, it also helped push into prominence the career—and the fortunes—of a man who dramatically embodied the physical ideals toward which the nation could look for inspiration. More than simply a carnival strong man, which was how he began, Eugen Sandow captured the imagination of a country that imputed to him a moral grandeur consonant with his physical perfection. In addition to parlaying his strength into a vast commercial success with his gymnasiums and personal exhibitions, Sandow became a spokesman for that proper cultivation of the body that was mocked by the stunted products of the city. Speaking from the pulpit of the gymnasium, he argued the case for the commitment to physical excellence as passionately as any preacher would the value of the moral life. Indeed, for Sandow, there was no difference between them:

All 'Varsity men will know from their own experience that the moral degenerates among the undergraduates are not to be found among the athletes, and that where the subsequent life of the athlete is followed up, it is very rare indeed that he is found among the "legion of the damned," that ignoble crowd of men, who, starting apparently with every advantage, have "gone under." Obscure parson or distinguished judge, under-paid schoolmaster or wealthy merchant ... whatever the athlete's comparative success or failure in life, he will rarely be found to have lost the self-respect and the willpower that he acquired when he was taught by those who trained him to respect and to care for his body.[35]

Celebrated as an exemplary figure by those involved in the physical regeneration of the British race, Sandow achieved a cultural status rarely afforded strong men. Arthur Conan Doyle, a friend of Baden-Powell's who shared his concern about the deterioration of the British, put the case for Sandow's importance in the preface to his *The Construction and Reconstruction of the Human Body*. For Conan Doyle, "the man who can raise the standard of physique in any country has done something to raise all other standards as well."[36] Opposed to compulsory military service, Conan Doyle nevertheless extolled the role it allegedly played in most continental countries in curing its physical degenerates, a role that in Britain necessarily had to be left to voluntary agencies. And herein lay the immense contribution of Sandow:

It is my appreciation of the national quality of his services, and the really vital aim towards which they have been directed, which must be my excuse if for a moment I have intruded upon the patience of his readers. It is my firm conviction that few men have done more for this country during our generation than he, and that his gymnastic schools have appreciably improved our physique. Every word which he writes upon the subject deserves the most careful consideration not only of the general public, but also of the medical faculty with whom he has always loyally worked.[37]

The perception of the city as an alien place, inimical to traditional English values and ideals, was heightened by the conviction that the major cities were in fact being inundated by hordes of East European immigrants. The cities were malign not merely by virtue of their remove from country manors but as a result of the foreign element in them. It was these unwashed foreigners of questionable character who were responsible for overcrowding in the slums, for the high rents, for the unemployment of good British workmen, for the sickness that inevitably followed from their hygienic ways. The facts, which were that "Russian and Polish immigrants comprised in all merely one-third of the total foreign population, and therefore an even smaller one-third of one percent of the whole population—hardly a figure calculated to inspire alarm,"[38] had little effect on the zeal of the anti-aliens, who pressed their case with remarkable tenacity. For people like Admiral Beresford, the earl of Dunraven, William Evans-Gordon, and Arnold White, the corruption of sturdy British stock through the influx of morally inferior and undesirable foreigners was nothing less than a national hazard. Organizing themselves around the British Brothers League, the body established to do battle with the menace, they did their best to attribute to the immigrants every evil that might plague those unhappy people trapped in a city slum.[39] The immigrant, or Jew—"'Immigrant' and 'Jew' became synonymous terms"[40]—was blamed for all the difficulties in which the poor British workers found themselves. The agitation eventually precipitated the formation of the Royal Commission on Alien Immigration (1903) to study the matter and recommend ways to deal with it. For our purposes the commission's importance was less in the specific conclusions it reached than the fact that, like the Committee on Physical Deterioration, it called attention to the problems of urban degeneracy. The greater the plight of the cities and the hapless "native race"[41] imprisoned in their slums, the greater the need for the teaching of good citizenship, obedience, and healthy exercise—and for organizations like the Scouts.

Baden-Powell's efforts at race regeneration shared both the rhetoric and the goals of the National Council of Public Morals (for Great and Greater Britain), whose stated purpose—"The Renewal of the Race—Spiritual: Moral: Physical"—was similar to his own. Established in 1910 with its explicit aim "to help to raise the quality and to maintain the purity, stability, and strength of the British race, at home and in our Dominions beyond the seas. We are out to promote the permanent racial and moral welfare of an Imperial Race-to-be,"[42] the council charged itself with examining those social and moral problems that might interfere with such a development. In their investigations of the obstacles to full imperial glory they functioned as a kind of nongovernmental royal commission, sponsoring lengthy reports based on the evidence of witnesses taken at hearings on the "manifold evils and diseases of society."[43] While Baden-Powell's Scouts can be regarded as a kind of populist solution to the challenge of "race-renewal,"[44] theirs was the intellectual response, bringing before the public in carefully documented studies the difficulties that would have to be overcome in the process of national regeneration. If the council never proposed a specific, practical program for society's ills, as Baden-Powell did, nevertheless their diagnosis of the disease, and the ideals that they promulgated as remedies, closely resembled those on which Scouting was built. Indeed, the common interests of the two can be seen in the fact that Baden-Powell served as a member of two of the commissions the council sponsored—on the educational possibilities and perils of the cinema (1917), and on *Youth and the Race* (1922) which examined the training that might best ensure that adolescents would develop into good citizens and responsible parents. He also gave testimony before the Commission on Youth and the Race.

Whether the subject under scrutiny was venereal disease or the suppression of the sexual impulse or the infant mortality rate or the connection between food and morality, the various commissions never wavered from the council's great mission "to save the British race."[45] The rather weighty rhetorical question Sir Rider Haggard, a member of the Commission on Youth and the Race, put before Baden-Powell about the purposes of his Scouts suggests the council's own commitment:

> The great objects of your Association are to inculcate honour and patriotism and love of country and devotion to duty and all those things which have in the past distinguished our race or a large proportion of it?[46]

(To which Baden-Powell, needless to say, answered, "Yes.")

In addition to the reports they issued through the agency of their different commissions,[47] the council promoted a number of books—with titles, for example, like *The Problem of Race-Regeneration, The Methods of Race-Regeneration, The Cleansing of a City, The Menace of the Empty Cradle, National Ideals and Race-Regeneration, Education and Race-Regeneration*, among others—which testified to their particular absorption with the perpetuation of the imperial race.

Of the different issues that they engaged on behalf of the ascendency of the British race, few were thought more urgent than the declining birthrate, the subject of its first report published after three years' work in 1916. Anxiety about Britain's birthrate was a common theme among social reformers early in the century, a powerful component of the overarching fear about national deterioration. It was, in a sense, the other side of the peril to British wellbeing posed by the alleged wave of alien immigration. If the country were being deluged by morally questionable foreigners of infirm constitution, what was happening to the sturdy British stock that had made Britain great? The question not only involved the internal health of the country, but equally importantly its colonial duties as well. The white races—and particularly the British—had the enormous obligation of tending to the well-being of the colored races whom they were protecting throughout their beneficent empire. To fulfill the responsibilities of this trust, Britain needed numbers of self-sacrificing, efficient administrators, soldiers, and statesmen to help preserve the white domination of the world. As the council argued after World War I,

> But, as the world-war revealed, the whole of the white races must, in the end, stand together to maintain their position in the world, or they may be overwhelmed in racial competition. Of the 1,800,000,000 human beings in the world, 1,300,000,000 belong to the fertile coloured races which are increasing at an overwhelming rate, protected by our own civilizing operations, and 500,000,000 are white, which in almost all countries show a persistently declining birth-rate.
>
> And the world-war has further depleted the white stocks of several millions of their best men and many more millions of women and children. We do not write of this matter in an ebullition of jingoism, but we do note it is a sensible factor in the trend of racial development.
>
> It behoves the white races to end their differences and to unite in establishing durable civilizations which, by reason of moral and intellectual supremacy, will be able to set up a bulwark against the brute force of mere numbers. In our humble fashion we are also helping towards this desirable end.[48]

The commission's report, *The Declining Birth Rate* (1916), was the most extensive study at the time, but it was by no means the first. Writing in 1907, Sidney Webb devoted Fabian Tract No. 131[49] to an analysis of the depressing reality that the decline was not uniform, but was more pronounced among the wealthier, educated classes, upon whom the nation counted for leadership. Webb makes clear what the inevitable consequences were of such inappropriate breeding habits:

> In Great Britain at this moment, when half, or perhaps two-thirds, of all the married people are regulating their families, children are being freely born to the Irish Roman Catholics, and the Polish, Russian and German Jews, on the one hand, and to the thriftless and irresponsible—largely the casual

Colonel Robert Baden-Powell during the siege of Mafeking. *British Scout Association*

Wolf Gun, made in Mafeking during the Siege. Colonel Baden Powell on the extreme left

Published by Halls & C.
Port Elizabeth.

ILLUSTRATED WAR SPECIAL   NOV. 26, 1899

MALCOLM PATERSON

"I'LL LET YOU KNOW WHEN WE HAVE HAD ENOUGH."
Colonel Baden-Powell's answer to Commandant Cronje's demand for the surrender of Mafeking.

ABOVE: Mafeking defense force
Baden-Powell is on the far left. *Br*
ish Scout Association
LEFT: Popular magazine depiction *
Baden-Powell responding to Bo
demands at Mafeking: "I'll let yc
know when we have had enoug!
British Scout Association

LEFT: Baden-Powell (second from left) on the Wimbledon rifle team in 1874. *British Scout Association*
BELOW: Baden-Powell with officers of Colonel Hore's Protectorate Regiment, Mafeking. *British Scout Association*

ABOVE: 1st New Barnet Company of the Boys' Brigade, 1905. *Brigade House*
BELOW: Mafeking Cadet Corps. *British Scout Association*
OPPOSITE, TOP: Baden-Powell in Matabeleland, 1896. *British Scout Association*
OPPOSITE, LEFT: Front cover of part I of the fortnightly edition of *Scouting for Boys*, publishe
January 15, 1908.
OPPOSITE, RIGHT: Scouts practicing first-aid drill in the early years. *British Scout Association*

ABOVE: Baden-Powell inspecting scouts at Amesbury, circa 1909. *British Scout Association*

BELOW: Ernest Thompson Seton. *Boy Scouts of America*

OPPOSITE, TOP: Crystal Palace Rally, London, 1932. *British Scout Association*

OPPOSITE, BOTTOM: Baden-Powell (right) telling a story at Scout Camp at Humshaugh, August 1908. *British Scout Association*

LEFT: Lord Baden-Powell, circ
1930. *British Scout Association*
BELOW: Lord and Lady Baden-Powe
with their children returning
Southampton from their tour
South Africa, 1927. *Girl Scouts
the U.S.A.*

labourers and the other denizens of the one-roomed tenements of our great cities—on the other. 25 per cent of our parents, as Professor Karl Pearson keeps warning us, is producing 50 per cent of the next generation. This can hardly result in anything but national deterioration; or, as an alternative, in this country gradually falling to the Irish and the Jews. Finally, there are signs that even these races are becoming influenced. The ultimate future of these islands may be to the Chinese.[50]

(It is worthwhile noticing in passing the racist pecking order implicit in Webb's alternative. Even the most unacceptable of the whites—Jews and Irish—are preferable to any of the yellow race. It goes without saying that the most terrible vision Webb could imagine is the British Isles dominated by the Chinese. He obviously could not permit his imagination the apocalyptic leap to a future belonging to the blacks.)

Even allowing for the higher death rate among the lower classes, it still remained true that they were reproducing at a considerably greater rate than those people whom Webb variously defined as the "servant-keeping class," or, more wonderfully, as composing "those sections of the population which give proofs of thrift and foresight." Webb's analysis of the causes of this unhealthy decline in births among the reasonably well-off, however, gives him some hope. For it was not, he discovered, a result of any physical degeneracy among "the best classes," but rather "a deliberately volitional interference, due chiefly to economic motives,"[51] which can itself be influenced by any number of economic measures that would encourage larger families among the respectable classes. Webb then suggests steps that the government might take to achieve this goal, including schemes for the endowment of motherhood, school feeding programs and a vast increase in maintenance scholarships for secondary, technical, and university education, as well as the multiplication of tax-supported higher schools. By lightening the financial burden imposed by children, the economic reasons behind the constraints on family size would be removed, thereby enhancing the possibility of an increase in the birthrate from those classes Webb looked to for the salvation of the country. Such was the way out of the dangerous situation that Webb feared was sapping the greatness of the nation:

Once the production of healthy, moral, and intelligent citizens is revered as a social service and made the subject of deliberate praise and encouragement on the part of the government, it will, we may be sure, attract the best and most patriotic of the citizens. . . .

To the present writer it seems that only by some such "sharp turn" in our way of dealing with these problems can we avoid degeneration of type—that is, race deterioration, if not race suicide.[52]

The commission's 1916 report did not, for the most part, reach conclusions fundamentally different from those in Webb's tract. Its significance rested in its thoroughness and the public recognition it earned during the three-year period of its hearings and preparation. Reviewing it for *The New Statesman*, Sidney Webb concluded that "The National Council of Public Morals has done a great public service. The Commission has produced the most candid, the most outspoken, and the most impartial statement that this country has yet had as to the extent, the nature, and the ethical character of the voluntary regulation of the marriage state which now prevails over the greater part of the civilised world."[53]

Summarizing relevant statistical data, the commission demonstrated the varying birthrates (per thousand) of a given year— 1911—in England and Wales, showing the range from 119 in the upper and middle classes to 213 among the unskilled workmen. Against these figures stand the mortality rates of the same groups for the first year of life, moving from 76.4 to 152.5. An examination of the data yielded findings that both supported and amplified Webb's: The birthrate declined by approximately one-third over the previous thirty-five years; the decline was not uniform over the population or a result of alterations in the marriage rate or anything that diminished the proportion of fertile, married women in the population; the heavier infant mortality of the lower classes did not reduce their effective fertility to the level of the wealthier classes. While not based on the same statistical evidence as these other conclusions, the commission also argued that "Conscious limitation of fertility is widely practised among the middle and upper classes, and there is good reason to think that, in addition to other means of limitation, the illegal induction of abortion frequently occurs among the industrial population."[54]

The commission, in the body of its report, responded more calmly to the evidence than did Webb. While he saw the decline in the birthrate of the better classes as tantamount to race suicide, the commission took no stand on whether the decline in the birthrate posed a threat to the well-being of Britain or the world:

Here the prime question arises, "Have we any reliable criterion of desirability in respect of races and race-blends. Is there any evidence that a mis-population of the earth is taking place, in the sense of a refusal of 'higher' and intrinsically fitter races to multiply, while lower and intrinsically less fit peoples are spreading more numerously over the earth?" The necessary limitations of our knowledge about human qualities and their relative values for the civilisation of the future, as well as our racial and patriotic biases, render it impossible to give a confident answer to these vital questions. There is recent evidence to indicate that the supposed differences in inherent racial qualities are much slighter than has been alleged, and that education and cultural environment explain the greater part of what are considered ethnical differences.[55]

But the commission's refusal to judge the decline did not satisfy all of its members. In an "Addition to the Report", in which only four—the chairman, W. R. Inge; the secretary, James Marchant; a physician, James Crichton-Browne; and the liberal historian and political scientist, J. A. Hobson—did not join, a major question omitted in the body of the report was taken up: "Is the present decline of our national birth-rate regrettable?"[56] The unequivocal answer—it was very much to be deplored: "The decline in the birth-rate at present is not eugenic, but dysgenic."[57] Britain required more people both for its own economic growth as well as for the special needs of the world as a whole. With a logic characteristic of Britain's socially committed imperialists, the commission argued for the exalted obligation to perpetuate the British race so that it could further the development of the rest of the world:

Can we resist the pressure of Asiatic immigration without provoking antagonism, if not worse, while we are not making full use of the lands which we are resolved to keep "white"? If we value our national type should we not desire its diffusion? For the sake of the backward types even that they may be advanced by our influence to a better standard of life and thought, should we not desire the preservation and expansion of our people? Without any desire for imperial domination or commercial exploitation, or military subjugation of other races, Britain must, in view of what has been advanced, regard with gravest concern her falling birth-rate, and take such practical steps as may be within her power to arrest the decline, and if possible restore the rate to a *higher figure*.[58]

The addition concludes with a number of proposals to halt the decline, such as a minimum wage, bonuses for low-income families when their children reach the age of fourteen, alterations in the income tax to encourage the birth of children, inexpensive secondary schools, and increased scholarship opportunities for the poor, among others.

Through its various commissions and its unending proselytizing on behalf of Britain's moral crusade and imperial mission, the council played a major role in making sure that, in its own words, "Race-Renewal is on the lips of all, in every daily paper; and the most hard-headed, practical man realises that the next thing to do is to regenerate our national life."[59] In its efforts the council drew on the logic, rhetoric, and intellectual leadership of the eminent theoreticians and statisticians of the eugenics movement, who supplied much of the "scientific" data on the threat of racial deterioration and the means to counter it. As a measure of their influence, it is worth remembering that the addition to the commission's main report chose to lament the decline in the birthrate by calling it "not eugenic, but dysgenic." In the cultural climate of the early twentieth century there could hardly have been a more definitively damning judgment.

The eugenics movement was founded in 1904 by the distinguished psychologist Sir Francis Galton, who defined it, in a lecture to the Sociological Society on 16 May of that year, as "the science which deals with all influences that improve and develop the inborn qualities of the race."[60] Eugenics grew out of developments in three major—and interrelated—areas: advances in biometry, the application of statistical methods to the study of biological phenomena; the germ plasm theory of August Weismann, the German biologist, who argued that germ cells were independent of the somatic cells and therefore immune to any modification of the bodily organs; and a new understanding of Mendel's work in genetics. Fashioning all of these into a method for approaching the problem of human diversity and social usefulness, Galton offered eugenics as a solution to those who were concerned with the erosion of national power:

> All would agree that it was better to be healthy than sick, vigorous than weak, well-fitted than ill-fitted for their part in life. In short, that it was better to be good rather than bad specimens of their kind, whatever their kind might be. There are a vast number of conflicting ideals, of alternative characters, of incomparable civilisations, which are wanted to give

fulness and interest to life. The aim of eugenics is to represent each class or sect by its best specimens, causing them to contribute *more* than their proportion to the next generation....[61]

Holding out the promise of national regeneration at a time when fears of decay were everywhere, eugenics was embraced by a culture eager for salvation:

The Boer War panic about possible physical deterioration, the preoccupation with "National Efficiency", and despondency about the apparent failure of "environmental" social policies, had between them created a political atmosphere highly congenial to eugenics.[62]

The aim of improving the racial stock of a nation was for Galton one of the highest human aspirations imaginable. In suggesting to the members of the Sociological Society the urgency of disseminating the principles and national importance of eugenics across Britain, Galton argued that

It must be introduced into the national conscience, like a new religion. It has, indeed, strong claims to become an orthodox religious tenet of the future, for Eugenics cooperate with the workings of nature by securing that humanity shall be represented by the fittest races. What nature does blindly, slowly and ruthlessly, man may do violently, quickly and kindly....[63]

Galton called for a society to further the work of eugenics by informing people about the laws of heredity, by systematically collecting facts about the origins of successful families, by conducting an historical analysis into the contributions different classes have made to society, and by studying the influences affecting marriages, to see if there were not some way of discouraging eugenically unsuitable unions. In 1908 the Eugenics Education Society was developed out of the Moral Education League to take up the challenge of bringing before the public the significance of this new science. Through its quarterly, *The Eugenics Review*, it made an effort to realize Galton's dream of seeing eugenics become "a religious dogma among mankind."[64]

Although Galton created the "science" of eugenics, it was primarily his disciple, Karl Pearson, who shaped it into an influential movement and helped spread its ruling assumptions throughout the country. [65] An eminent biometrician and philosopher, whose major work, *The Grammer of Science*, was a significant contribution to the philosophy of science, Pearson developed Galton's ideas into a rigidly applied theory of biological determinism (a predecessor in some ways of today's fashionable sociobiology), which held that intelligence in particular and human capability in general were a result of genetic endowment independent of environmental influence. For Pearson, attempts to address social problems without giving "due weight to the biological factors controlling human communities"[66] were misguided. The failure to recognize the workings of the laws of heredity accounted, in Pearson's view, for much of the muddled thinking about social issues:

> Have we not for the last seventy to eighty years devised all our social reform on the conception that we had but to improve the environment, to better the nurture of the nation, and we should progress indefinitely? Has not the assumption that nurture, not nature, is the chief factor in national progress been the key to all social legislation, to factory acts, building acts, sanitation acts, education acts, and a multitude of other enactments devised to raise the state of the people? ... It appears to me, therefore, that the whole of the liberal and philanthropic social reform of the past half-century and more has been based not on the hypothesis that *both* nature and nurture contribute to the progress of the race, but solely on the assumption that improving the environment would indefinitely raise us in the scale of nations.[67]

Social legislation based on the possibilities of nurture cannot, therefore, come to much more than sentimental dreams. Racial or national progress can only occur within the context of the implacable transmission of genetic material from one generation to the next, hence Pearson's concern, like that of Sidney Webb and the National Council for Public Morals, over the declining birthrate among Britain's better classes. Given the unalterable genetic differences between races and even social classes, maintaining the fecundity of the well-to-do was the highest national priority: "To insure that fertility shall in the rough be correlated with social value—as it has ceased to be since 1878—is the greatest political problem of the near future; it is the sole condition whereby modern European civilisation ... can hope to save itself."[68] Only by a conscious effort to insist that wages directly reflect social value as "measured by physique and mentality," and that "the size of the family ought to be proportional on the average to wages," can national progress "be assured by the continuous propagation of the superior physical and mental elements in the community at the expense of the inferior elements."[69]

Couching a variety of racial and class assumptions in the unassailable jargon of the scientist, with his tables of correlations and impeccable statistical methodologies, Pearson lent scientific credibility to Britain's fears of national degeneracy. If talent were purely a product of genetic inheritance, as could be demonstrated by his scientific studies, and if the pool of qualified breeders was neglecting its obligation to propagate at a sufficient rate, then clearly the country was in imminent danger of falling to the lower types. Two steps had to be taken: The worthy had to be encouraged to reproduce their kind, and the unfit to be prevented from doing so. In this latter effort, the country had been undermined by its own charitable impulses. As a strict social Darwinist, Pearson was concerned about any measure taken by society that might interfere with the racial cleansing power of natural selection. Racial efficiency requires that a nation keep its benevolent instincts under control:

One factor—absolutely needful for race survival—sympathy, has been developed in such an exaggerated form that we are in danger, by suspending selection, of lessening the effect of those other factors that automatically purge the state of the degenerates in body and mind.

Do I therefore call for less human sympathy, for more limited charity, and for sterner treatment of the weak? Not for a moment.... But I demand that all sympathy and charity shall be organized and guided into paths where they will provide racial efficiency, and not lead us straight towards national shipwreck. The time is coming when we must consciously carry out that purification of the state and race which has hitherto been the work of the unconscious cosmic process. The higher patriotism and the pride of race must come to our aid in stemming deterioration.... To produce a nation healthy alike in mind and body must become a fixed idea—one of almost religious intensity, as Francis Galton has expressed it— in the minds of the intellectual oligarchy, which after all sways the masses and their political leaders.[70]

From the hereditarian point of view, ameliorative social measures to deal with misfits were necessarily trivial, helpless as they were to affect the rotten gene pool that guaranteed that the problems would return in future generations. Only careful monitoring of the racial stock, avoiding the pitfalls of sloppy, sentimental thinking, could accomplish the task of racial evolution:

> We cannot reform the criminal. Nor cure the insane from the standpoint of heredity.... Education for the criminal, fresh air for the tuberculous, rest and food for the neurotic—these are excellent, they may bring control, sound lungs, and sanity to the individual; but they will not save the offspring from the need of like treatment, nor from the danger of collapse when the time of strain comes. They cannot make a nation sound in mind and body. They merely screen degeneracy behind a throng of arrested degeneracies. Our highly developed human sympathy will no longer allow us to watch the state purify itself by aid of crude natural selection. We see pain and suffering only to relieve it, without inquiry as to the moral character of the sufferer or as to his national or racial value.[71]

Degeneracy, then, cannot be significantly resisted by traditional kinds of social legislation, effective as they might be in a local and ephemeral way. In the long term the fight against racial deterioration required a policy ensuring that only the fittest stocks be permitted to proliferate. In the past, or so Pearson argues, the rigors of natural selection provided this safeguard. But since the civilized world has more or less suspended the gross workings of natural selection—a development with which Pearson has no quarrel—Britain's concern must be to supervise the growth of the population, making sure that the fit outnumber the unfit. Thus the right to reproduce must be controlled by the state:

> As Eugenists we assert that the right to live does not connote the right of each man to reproduce his kind. Step by step, as we lessen the stringency of natural selection, and more and more of the weaklings and the unfit survive, we must increase the standard, mental and physical, of parentage.[72]

The road to national salvation demands "that the fit shall not only be parents, but have a fertility which entirely dominates the fertility of the unfit."[73]

Acknowledging that the problem of defining "the fit" is not entirely uncomplicated, Pearson nevertheless has no serious difficulty with the notion. The end result of an effectively implemented eugenics policy would be a breed of men designed to do their duty and keep the empire intact.

A clean body, a sound if slow mind, a vigorous and healthy stock, a numerous progeny, these factors were largely representative of the typical Englishman of the past; and we see today that one and all these characteristics can be defended on scientific grounds; they are the essentials of an imperial race.[74]

Especially as articulated by Pearson, who was the most uncompromising hereditarian among his eugenical peers, eugenics provided the scientific theory to support every variety of conservative social thought. Whether the issue was class, race, or empire, Pearson's eugenics, with its formidable correlations and closely reasoned assumptions, shared a social vision essentially the same as that of the National Service League, the Duty and Discipline movement, and the Earl of Meath (see Chapter 7). Basic to that vision was the rightness of the British class system, which was seen to represent the immutable workings of the laws of nature. Reflecting the predictable differences in genetic inheritance, social classes followed the lines of biological revolution, and indeed were to be understood primarily as biological phenomena. Scientific law justifies the existence and perpetuation of a rigidly stratified society:

> The differentiation of men in physique and mentality has led to the slow but still imperfect development of occupational castes within all civilised communities. ... In a perfectly efficient society, there would always be castes suited to specialised careers—the engineer, the ploughman, the mathematician, the navy, the statesman, the actor and the craftsman.[75]

In such a neatly categorized world, people are delighted to stay in their castes and marry others of their kind. For Sir William Bateson, a physician and active hereditarian, the great difference between democracy and eugenics is that "democracy regards class distinction as evil; we perceive it to be essential."[76] Bateson goes on to spell out the implications of regarding class distinction as scientifically justified:

> The aim of social reform must be not to abolish class, but to provide that each individual shall so far as possible get into the right class and stay there, and usually his children after him. Men rise from below and fall from above, and the fact is sometimes appealed to as evidence that such vicissitudes are a normal and wholesale phenomenon. The naturalist sees that

the convection currents to which such displacements are due must indicate special kinds of disturbance. These disturbances are mainly due to interbreeding between the social grades, and between sections of the population formerly isolated.... Just as numbers of the population tend always to reach an equilibrium in which births balance deaths, so do the differentiated elements of the population tend always to find their particular level, near which they would stop till the mass is again disturbed.[77]

Baden-Powell's exhortation to be a brick and not envy those fellow bricks that appear to be more advantageously placed, in short, elaborated into an impressive social theory with all the genetic trimmings.

The defense of the class system as biologically determined was but one feature of Pearson's thinking that helped sustain conservative social theorizing early in the century. His assumption of the superiority of the Anglo-Saxon race was another. Pearson argued that the races moved through clearly defined stages from higher to lower, with the whites at the top and the "negro"—"nearer to the childhood of man,"[78] as could be amply demonstrated by their cranial capacity—at the bottom. Asians of various sorts occupy the middle range, superior to the blacks but at the same time not quite the equal of the whites. Like class distinctions, these sharp gradations reveal the unalterable laws of heredity, which remain immune to all efforts of benign human interference:

What I have said about bad stock seems to me to hold for the lower races of man. How many centuries, how many thousands of years, have the Kaffir or the negro held large districts in Africa undisturbed by the white man? Yet their intertribal struggles have not yet produced a civilisation in the least comparable with the Aryan. Educate them and nurture them as you will, I do not believe that you will succeed in modifying the stock.[79]

Nurture and education were powerless to affect the vitality of a stock that owed everything to the purifying rigors of natural selection. To tamper with those stern workings on which all racial progress depends was to run grave risks:

If you bring the white man into contact with the black, you too often suspend the very process of natural selection on which the evolution of a higher type depends. You get super-ior and inferior races living on the same soil, and that coexist-ence is demoralizing for both.[80]

It is preferable for the white man not to venture out at all "than that he should settle down and live alongside the inferior race. The only healthy alternative is that he should go and completely drive out the inferior race."[81]

The social vision emerging from Pearson's eugenics is of a world in which ceaseless struggle based on harsh Darwinian selection is the necessary condition for progress, for both a race and a nation. It follows in such a world where conflict produces growth that readi-ness is all. Or to use Baden-Powell's apposite language, a nation had better be prepared for warfare of all kinds—military as well as commercial. Accepting not only the inevitability but even the de-sirability of conflict, and calling for efficiency on every level if Britain is to survive, Pearson's fully articulated model of national existence embodied that network of assumptions and priorities out of which the Boy Scout movement emerged:

> You will see that my view—and I think it may be called the scientific view of a nation—is that of an organized whole, kept up to a high pitch of internal efficiency by insuring that its members are substantially recruited from the better stocks, and kept up to a high pitch of external efficiency by contest, chiefly by way of war with inferior races, and with equal races by the struggle for trade-routes and for the sources of raw material and of food supply. This is the natural history view of mankind, and I do not think you can in its main features subvert it.[82]

In spite of the fact that Baden-Powell and Pearson inhabited two entirely different cultural universes, they shared strikingly similar concerns for the viability of an imperial race that could sustain the empire both through its strength of arms and through its industrial and commercial success. Baden-Powell never tired of reminding the public immediately after the end of World War I that the real winner would not be apparent until years later, when the economic health of the combatants could be assessed. For both Baden-Powell and Pearson, the commercial struggles of peacetime were no less important or intense than the battles that armies fought in the field.

The intellectual affinity between two such oddly disparate figures can further be seen in Pearson's endorsement of Baden-Powell as a practitioner of the scientific method, at least as regards his Scouting techniques. Writing of the importance of teaching people "the power of observing and reasoning upon observation," Pearson singles out Baden-Powell for his work:

> There is a very excellent little book which many of you may have read recently, Baden-Powell's *Aids to Scouting*; it is a capital introduction to the true scientific method. The man with a scientific training *scouts* through nature, including under nature mankind itself. You may sum up his conduct just as I think Baden-Powell's booklet may be summed up—Keep your eyes open and apply commonsense.[83]

I do not want to give the impression that Pearson's strict hereditarian obsessions were necessarily shared by every eugenicist. Although it is true that Pearson was the most influential member of the movement, a number of his colleagues allocated to the animating power of "nurture" a much larger social role than Pearson ever allowed. Perhaps the best known of the anti-Pearsonians was the distinguished physician C. W. Saleeby, who wrote widely on the importance of eugenics. Saleeby argued that while "nature" was logically primary, "nurture" was equally important in shaping an imperial race: "The asserted opposition between eugenics and social reform, eugenics and education, eugenics and philanthropy, does not exist. The eugenist must welcome all agencies that make for better nurture, alike for rich and poor, born and unborn."[84]

Saleeby attacked Pearson for a simple-minded application of Darwinian selection to human social problems that could maintain that a heavy infantile death rate was good because it purified the race of weaklings. Saleeby's brand of eugenics was gentler than Pearson's, claiming that every human being, regardless of his genetic stock, deserves the best possible kind of nurture. Eugenics, as properly conceived, should attempt to eliminate the causes of degeneracy wherever they are found:

> When Eugenists understand this, we shall have not more arguments concerning the relative value of "nature" and "nurture." We shall see that the nurture of the future parent may affect the nature of the offspring, and that eugenics consists in much more than the mere practice of selection, regarding all individuals as immutably good or bad for parental purposes, and ignoring their individual nurture altogether.[85]

Despite the sharp differences between them, it is interesting to see Pearson and Saleeby come together in their admiration for Baden-Powell. Pearson found in him a man who preached some primitive form of the scientific method; Saleeby saw him as an educator, indeed, "the greatest educator of our time."[86] However moderate Saleeby was in making claims for the cleansing powers of natural selection, he was unrestrained in his praise of Baden-Powell and his Scouting achievement. The Scout movement was, in his judgment, "the greatest step towards the progress of eugenics since 1909,"[87] and he credited Baden-Powell with what is "incomparably the greatest constructive idea of our century."[88] Saleeby thought the Scouts a prime agency in his quest for developing a program of national eugenics that would combat the forces of degeneracy by instilling sound educational principles throughout the land:

> ... If national eugenics is ever to be achieved in Great Britain it will come through the Boy Scouts and the Girl Guides, who almost alone, of all our young people, are being made ready, by "training in citizenship, character discipline, and patriotism," for education for parenthood, which must be the beginning of national eugenics. This movement is what national education in Great Britain has tried and failed to be for forty years.[89]

Saleeby's conscious embracing of the Scouts as an institution pursuing the same goals as the eugenics movement points to the similarities between the two. Indeed, Scouting's passionately avowed patriotism, its commitment to fashioning a race of men able to defend the country in time of war and enhance its commercial position in time of peace, is finally what drives eugenics as well: "Eugenics becomes a method of patriotism. The worker in this science is now a greater national benefactor than the soldier or the captain of industry."[90] In their various ways, then, Scouting, eugenics, and the other organizations, committees and movements discussed in this chapter were all responding to the specter of deterioration observed menacingly on the horizon following the debacle of the Boer War. Plagued by the vision of Britain defended by the narrow-chested and the pigeon-toed, and troubled by their sense of a disintegrating social fabric, they took refuge in the thought of a new "national efficiency" that might prove the country's salvation. None of these efforts was precisely the same, but all shared a similar diagnosis of the problems, a common rhetoric, and a strong disposition for a kind of discipline and training that at the very least bordered on the militaristic. Arnold White, the leading apostle of national efficiency, as well as a fervent eugenicist, put the case nicely for this sensibility in an article written in 1909:

> Further, complete revision of our educational system is needed with the view, instead of decanting indigestible facts into brains unnourished by good red blood, of enforcing on boys and girls alike through physical (I might say military) training, and so creating a body of citizens not only fit to reproduce their kind, but to do their duty to themselves. Only by such measures as these, not by maudlin philanthropic sentiment, can we reach national efficiency.[91]

Despite the insistence on the part of almost all of the official organizations examined here that they were entirely apolitical, committed only to the well-being of the nation in a way that took no notice of the pettiness of party politics, the ideology behind their concerns was decidedly conservative.[92] In stressing those old-fashioned virtues of obedience, loyalty, and selflessness, they argued for the ideal of a higher patriotism that was generally inimical to the aspirations and seething individualism they perceived to be on the rise among the rapidly proliferating working classes. A disciplined imperial race, strong in body and united in resolve, was the common goal, requiring vigilance on the part of those in power and willing self-sacrifice on the part of the others. Constructed on sound eugenic principles and carefully supervised by wise builders able to make difficult choices, Baden-Powell's wall of dedicated bricks toiling productively in their place became a cultural metaphor for a significant part of Britain's response to those uncertainties—social, military, and economic—that seemed to threaten its stability early in the century.

6

SCOUTING FOR BOYS

The Scout handbook, often dismissed today simply as a repository of useful information concerning camping activities, merit badges, knot tying, and the like,[1] was viewed rather differently by Baden-Powell. For him it was very decidedly the sacred text of the brotherhood, arguing for the importance of what it was doing even as it initiated people into its mysteries. The first edition (1908) of *Scouting for Boys* is less a practical guide to outdoor living than a thoroughly didactic introduction to Scouting's ideology. In a sense the handbook *is* the movement, defining the total universe of the Scouts, its priorities, practices, and principles. It diagnoses problems, establishes remedies, and makes the case for its own centrality. A detailed understanding of it is vital for any appreciation of the movement it at once advertises and embodies.

Not uncharacteristically, Baden-Powell himself makes the strongest claim for mastering its contents. In the preface to the eighth edition he indicates that even he finds it instructive to go through it once each year, and suggests a day—appropriately enough Empire Day, established by his friend Lord Meath to celebrate those

glories of the empire to which Scouting is so ardently committed—
on which this might be done.

The book is divided into ten chapters, but within the chapters
the operative unit of organization is what Baden-Powell calls
"Camp Fire Yarns," the homey, outdoor quality of the title
specially intended to fit in with the whole concept of the Scouting
life. Following some preliminary notes for potential Scoutmasters,
the opening sentence of the opening campfire yarn begins the Scout
movement on a revealing note: "We had an example of how useful
Boy Scouts can be on active service, when a corps of boys was
formed in defence of Mafeking, 1899–1900."[2] Although Baden-
Powell always protested about the exaggerated importance of Mafeking, he makes sure here to evoke the memory of the exciting
217-day siege as he starts to unfold his scheme. Mafeking, as
Baden-Powell well knew, remained firmly lodged in the pantheon
of British mythic memory, and the hero of Mafeking was not above
tapping those associations in the interests of selling his Scouts to the
British public.

But it is also fascinating to see him discuss his Scouts in terms
not only of their usefulness, but particularly of their usefulness in
times of war.[3] For as I have suggested, the notion of the Scout as
a serviceable citizen trained to follow orders in wartime is at the
heart of Scouting. Whether this makes him a war Scout or a peace
Scout, or whether a willingness to defend one's country is the best
way to express detestation of war is beside the point; what matters
is simply that Scouting holds out before us a model of human
excellence in which absolute loyalty, an unbudgeable devotion to
duty, and the readiness to fight, and if necessary to die for one's
country, are the highest virtues. In short, as Baden-Powell repeats
throughout the book, manliness and good citizenship are the aims
of the movement; in more practical terms, as our opening yarn tells
us about Mafeking, "Every boy ought to learn how to shoot and
obey orders, else he is no more good when war breaks out than an
old woman" (3). Baden-Powell's reverence for his mother did not
extend to old women in general. All references to them in his work
stress not the wisdom and dignity he found in Henrietta but only
their chronic inability to defend themselves.

Baden-Powell's summary of the role Lord Edward Cecil's cadre
of messengers (they were not, after all, Boy Scouts) played during
the siege of Mafeking immediately plunges the reader into Scouting's ideological universe, in which courage and patriotism were
effectively mobilized to preserve a piece of the empire. But the
Mafeking story contains other meanings as well, which Baden-

Powell also exploits. For just as Mafeking was besieged by hostile Boers, so by analogy Britain is surrounded by a variety of enemies, all prepared to strike. The vulnerability of Mafeking stands by metaphoric extension for the vulnerability of Britain itself. Readiness is all: "and so, too, we ought to be prepared in Britain against being attacked by enemies; for though it may not be probable, it is quite as possible as it was at Mafeking; and every boy in Britain should be just as ready as those boys were in Mafeking to take their share in its defence" (3). The Mafeking analogy to the imperiled island is repeated, and made more emphatic, later in the book, where the possibility of attack has now become a likelihood. Baden-Powell points out that nations coveting the wealth of the empire know that the only way to achieve it is to conquer England:

> For this reason every Briton who has any grit in him will
> Be Prepared to help in defending his country.
>
> When Mafeking was attacked by the Boers the boys of the
> town made themselves into a Cadet Corps, and did very useful
> work in the defence. It is quite likely that England will some
> day be attacked just as Mafeking was, unexpectedly, by a
> large number of enemies.
>
> If this happens every boy in the country should be prepared
> to take his place and help in the defence, like those Mafeking
> boys did. (246)

Linking the defenses of both town and nations is the classic Scout injunction to be prepared, the phrase that Baden-Powell officially established from the outset as the Scout motto and placed on the Scout badge. The similarity between Baden-Powell's initials and the first letters of the motto is not accidental; indeed, in the fortnightly edition of the handbook Baden-Powell insists on stressing, on two separate occasions, that "The Scouts' motto is founded on my initials."[4] He obviously thought better of—or at least was cautioned against—calling attention to this fact subsequently, and omitted all reference to it in the first complete edition. But regardless of the splendid narcissism of its source, the phrase has succeeded in taking on an independent life of its own, embedding itself in Western culture as a readily identifiable—and easily parodied—characteristic of Scouting.

Our familiarity with it, however, should not blind us to recognizing its significance to the movement. In addition to immortalizing the initials of the founder, it addresses a multitude of Scout aspirations, as any reading of *Scouting for Boys* will reveal. A Scout "must always be prepared at any moment to do his duty, and to face danger in order to help his fellow man."(24); you must "*Be Prepared in Mind* by having disciplined yourself to be obedient to every order"; you must "*Be Prepared in Body* by making yourself strong and active and *able* to do the right thing at the right moment"(34); the Scout must "prepare himself by previous thinking out and practising how to act on any accident or emergency so that he is never taken by surprise"(11); you must "'be prepared' for what is going to happen to you in the future"(212) in terms of your career; and you must "BE PREPARED, even at most ordinary moments of strolling along, talking to a friend, to spring at once to the assistance of a fellow-creature who is in danger"(225); "you must be prepared to work, and to work hard, and to turn your hand to any kind of job"(237) should you find yourself in one of the Colonies; instructors of Scouting "must 'Be prepared' ... for disappointments at first"(27) as well as "from the first 'Be Prepared' for the prevailing want of concentration of mind on the part of boys"(271) (though if the boys have in fact prepared themselves in mind properly, this should be no problem). And so on. In short, there is hardly anything for which the Scout or his instructor should not be prepared. But the broad array of interpretations Baden-Powell assigns to his motto are relatively trivial in comparison with the one central meaning on which he insists throughout the book: Above all the Scout must be prepared to defend his country, indeed "Be PREPARED to die for your country if need be; so that when the moment arrives you may charge home with confidence, not caring whether you are going to be killed or not"(256). As Baden-Powell points out, it hardly makes any difference anyway:

> We have all got to die some day; a few years more or less of our lives don't much matter in the history of the world, but it is a very great matter if by dying a year or two sooner than we should otherwise do from disease we can help to save the flag of our country from going under. (255–56)

The willingness to serve without regard for one's safety in time of war is thus the most exalted state of preparation from which, in a sense, all the other forms derive their value. It establishes the criterion for judging the good citizenship and manliness the book attempts to inculcate on every page.

The readiness for self-sacrifice requires a consciousness of imminent threat to keep it sharply honed. A complacent sense of a stable universe is antithetical to the state of eternal vigilance—mental, moral, and physical—that the Scout is expected to maintain, and from the opening campfire yarn about Mafeking, demonstrating how we "must be prepared for what is *possible*, not only what is *probable* in war"(3), the world of *Scouting for Boys* teems with threats, enemies, violence, sudden catastrophes. Such a world can only be negotiated at great peril, and only then if one is capable of looking over one's shoulder and round the next corner simultaneously, all the time keeping an eye peeled for the covetousness of foreign nations. While war is the specific dominant threat in *Scouting for Boys*, it also constitutes the central metaphoric conception of the vision of human life implicit in the book. Out of the wealth of detail concerning matters as diversified as baking bread and brushing teeth, tying knots, building bridges, and breathing through one's nose emerges a coherent view of life and set of assumptions that place struggle and violence of all kinds squarely at the heart of things.

Scouting for Boys introduces us to a world of danger and adventure in which the best people, regardless of age or national origin, are "accustomed to take their lives in their hands, and to fling them down without hesitation if they can help their country by doing so"(5); a world in which boys like Kim, the hero of Rudyard Kipling's novel, stand as a model of "what valuable work a boy scout could do for his country if he were sufficiently trained and sufficiently intelligent"(10). Baden-Powell devotes almost five pages to summarizing Kim's exploits as he travels throughout India working for British Intelligence, saving agents from assassination, helping to capture Russian spies, and in general risking his life in the service of empire. Kim's life of roaming across India playing spy looms as an exciting possibility for all those who master Baden-Powell's Scouting lessons.

If a boy can't be a spy, Scouting still remains important as a technique in solving the various murders he might tend to come across in his daily activities. Early in *Scouting for Boys* Baden-Powell recounts the tale of the Eldson murder, in which a brutal murderer "was caught, convicted, and hanged through the scoutcraft of a shepherd boy"(19). The value of the tale is clarified in a note Baden-Powell appends for the use of the potential Scout instructor: "[*The following story, which in the main is true, is a sample of a story that should be given by the Instructor illustrating generally the duties of a Boy Scout*]" (19). It is a simple story of a young boy who, on his way home, passes a tramp sitting on the ground eating his food. Being observant, he notices everything about the tramp, including the nails on his boots, registering the details in such a way as not to alarm him. When he gets near home, he learns that an old woman was killed, and in walking around her garden detects some boot-prints that match the peculiar configuration of nails he glimpsed on the tramp's boots. Outraged—"The fact that it was a helpless old woman who had been murdered made the boy's chivalrous feelings rise against the murderer, whoever it might be"(19)—he resolves to risk incurring the enmity of the tramp's friends by telling the police and bringing them back to the tramp, an act requiring substantial physical endurance. The Gypsy (for it was he) is in due course hanged, and the lad is "overcome with misery at having caused the death of a fellow-creature"(20). But he is assured by the magistrate that he has in fact saved the lives of others by getting rid of such a dangerous criminal, and in any case is to be congratulated for having done his duty, which "'must always be carried out regardless of how much it costs you, even if you had to give up your life'"(21). Baden-Powell concludes that the tale is exemplary because the boy did every part of a Scout's duty, without even being taught. He exercised:

> Woodcraft.
>
> Observation without being noticed.
>
> Deduction.
>
> Chivalry.
>
> Sense of Duty.
>
> Endurance.
>
> Kind-heartedness. (21)

The powers of observation and deduction revealed by the shepherd boy in bringing the Gypsy, Willie Winter, to justice, are crucial. The ability to take in details and reach proper conclusions produces not only astute Scouts, skilled in assessing the strength of the enemy, but responsible citizens as well, able to sift evidence and reach appropriate conclusions. As Baden-Powell suggests to his instructors, "When once observation and deduction have been made habitual in the boy, a great step in the development of 'character' has been gained"(51). Although these skills might appear less useful in the city than in the country, we have the example of Sherlock Holmes to indicate the contrary. Holmes's manner of proceeding in his investigations is precisely the model of behavior Baden-Powell admires. In keeping with the particular nature of the universe in *Scouting for Boys*, it also demonstrates the kind of behavior a Scout might well have to exhibit himself:

> It may happen to some of you that one day you will be the first to find the dead body of a man, in which case you will

remember that it is your duty to examine and note down the smallest signs that are to be seen on and near the body before it is moved or the ground disturbed or trampled down. Besides noticing the exact position of the body (which should, if possible, be photographed exactly as found) the ground all round should be very carefully examined—without treading on it yourself more than is absolutely necessary, for fear of spoiling existing tracks. If you can also draw a little map of how the body lay and where the signs round it were, it might be of value.

Twice lately bodies have been found which were at first supposed to be those of people who had hanged themselves; but close examination of the ground round them—in one case some torn twigs and trampled grass, and in the other a crumpled carpet—showed that murder had been committed, and that the bodies had been hung after death to make it appear as though they had committed suicide. (56–57)

A declaration about the importance of fingerprints then follows, as well as a brief incident concerning the way in which a careful scrutiny of teeth marks on a cigar holder was sufficient to arrest a nephew for the murder of his banker uncle.

If the exact relationship between such skills and the formation of good character appears tenuous, it remains nevertheless characteristic of the method of *Scouting for Boys* that the value in the presumably benign virtues of keen observation is illustrated by responsible behavior when in the presence of murder victims. Danger lurks everywhere in Baden-Powell's world, so that it is not enough for a Scout to have good eyesight, he must also be endlessly alert to use it properly: "Often by suddenly looking back you will see an enemy's scout or a thief showing himself in a way that he would not have done had he thought you would look round"(59).

Again and again the campfire yarns justify mastering the techniques of peace Scouting in terms of a world that is peopled by enemies against whom one must use every conceivable resource at one's disposal. Thus the art of spooring is introduced by a description from the American General Dodge of "how he once had to pursue a party of Red Indians who had been murdering some people"(63). With the the expert help of Espinosa, his splendid tracking scout, General Dodge gets his man.

"On another occasion some American troops were following up a number of Indians, who had been raiding and murdering whites, and they had some other Red Indian Scouts to assist them in tracking"(63). Utilizing good tracking methods, they surprised them the following morning. Then there are the exploits of Burnham, the famous American scout, who escaped with a dispatch when his party was massacred in Matabeleland and by feeling his way along tracks at night made his way to safety—not to speak of Baden-Powell's own varied achievements in tracking the enemy in Rhodesia and Matabeleland. No specific anecdote is particularly significant in itself, but together they establish a context in which warfare, crime prevention, and crime detection implicitly become the normal, everyday activities in which human beings engage. The hero of civic Scouting is thus more the conventionally civilized Sherlock Holmes than the more exotic Selous or Burnham, and it is not surprising that Holmes and his adventures are frequently mentioned in the handbook.

Details contributing to the sense of a world in perpetual strife requiring constant vigilance to survive appear everywhere. A Scout's capacity to smell acutely is important, "in order to find his enemy at night"(167), and this capacity can be considerably helped if the Scout will learn to breathe through his nose, one of Baden-Powell's minor obsessions. In addition to developing the sense of smell and filtering disease germs so they don't get into the stomach, breathing through the nose "prevents snoring and snoring is a dangerous thing if you are sleeping anywhere in an enemy's country"(167). Cleanliness hardly needs any argument to be made for it, but Baden-Powell points out that "In the war in South Africa we lost an enormous number of men dying from disease as well as from wounds"(174). The performance of the Japanese in their war with Russia contrasts sharply with that sorry record: "There was very little sickness among them, and those who were wounded generally very quickly recovered because their skin was clean and their blood was in a healthy, sound condition"(166). Similarly, the virtues of endurance are seen in the performance of Selous, the great scout and hunter, who managed to survive alone in the countryside of Barotseland for three weeks after his party had been assaulted by a hostile tribe of natives. Stalking wild animals in the bush involves great subtlety, and stalking people in order to weed out the guilty from the innocent requires comparable care:

> If a guilty person finds himself being watched it puts him on his guard, while an innocent person becomes annoyed. So when you are observing a person, don't do so by openly star-

ing at them, but notice the details you want to at one glance or two, and if you want to study them more, walk behind them; you can learn just as much from a back view, in fact, more than you can from a front view, and, unless they are scouts and look around frequently, they do not know that you are observing them. (83)

In the section entitled "Duties as Citizen-Soldier," in which he elaborates on the responsibilities of all citizens to defend their country, Baden-Powell cites approvingly a passage from another great outdoorsman he admired, Theodore Roosevelt, on the resemblance between good scouts and good hunters:

> The qualities that make a good scout are, in large part, the qualities that make a good hunter. Most important of all is the ability to shift for one's self—the mixture of hardihood and resourcefulness which enables a man to tramp all day in the right direction, and, when night comes, to make the best of whatever opportunities for shelter and warmth may be at hand. Skill in use of the rifle is another trait; quickness in seeing game, another; ability to take advantage of cover, yet another; while patience, endurance, keenness of observation, good nerves, and instant readiness in an emergency, are all indispensable to a really good hunter. (247)

The attributes of the Scout would seem also to be shared by the soldier, and in fact it turns out that the original comparison was precisely between the soldier and the hunter, not the Scout and the hunter. Baden-Powell simply crossed out Roosevelt's soldier and substituted his own Scout.[5] What Baden-Powell actually endorses here is Roosevelt's celebration of the wartime soldier, not the peace Scout, an endorsement in keeping with the nature of the world defined by *Scouting for Boys*. Baden-Powell concludes this section of the book with a warning that explicitly addresses the dangers of such a world: "So make yourselves good scouts and good rifle shots in order to protect the women and children of your country if it should ever become necessary"(47).[6]

Such is the universe of *Scouting for Boys*. Its central facts are struggle, threat, and uncertainty—conditions demanding the utmost watchfulness and discipline to counter. Given this reality, *Scouting for Boys* can perhaps best be thought of as a manual of survival, attempting to equip those enmeshed in a dangerous world with the necessary tools to endure. Accepting the premises of the world as portrayed in *Scouting for Boys* leads inevitably to the importance of the Scouting system, and to those values that it espouses. Logic, rhetoric, and example all work together to compel assent both to the dangers Scouting perceives and to the solutions it proposes.

Foremost among those solutions is the absolute necessity to stand together against the common enemy—whoever or whatever it may be. The challenges and treacheries in life call for a total commitment to every institution of which one is a part—family, team, Scout patrol, school, business, and finally, of course, country and empire. The self on its own is both vulnerable and a source of selfishness, hence something prone to breeding dissension and weakness. Appropriately, then, the essential concern for the education of the Scouts is to inculcate in them an unquestioning loyalty. It is both morally correct and, in a thoroughly practical way, the key to survival. Celebrating the individual initiative of the plucky frontiersman, trapper, and explorer accustomed to living on their own does not undercut the importance of this precept. For their splendid work in isolation, Baden-Powell emphasizes, is not escapism or self-indulgence but always service in a higher cause: "They give up everything, their personal comforts and desires, in order to get their work done. They do not do all this for their own amusement, but because it is their duty to their King, fellow-countrymen, or employers"(5).[7]

From the opening description of how useful Lord Cecil's boys were in doing their duty at Mafeking, *Scouting for Boys* stresses in a number of ways the personal salvation to be gained in following orders and in risking one's life for the good of the country. To begin with, there is much explicit argument about the current state of the empire and the supreme effort required to keep it strong. The glories—as well as the obligations—of the empire are put before the reader early and kept there throughout. Instructors are enjoined from the start to underline the relationship between the individual Scout novitiate and the empire of which he is a part and from which he derives his strength:

> You belong to the Great British Empire, one of the greatest empires that has ever existed in the world.
> (*Show on the map.*)
> From this little island of Great Britain have sprung colonies all over the world, Australia, New Zealand, South Africa, India, Canada.
> Almost every race, every kind of man, black, white, or yellow, furnished subjects of King Edward VII.

This vast empire did not grow of itself out of nothing; it was made by your forefathers by dint of hard work and hard fighting, at the sacrifice of their lives—that is, by their hearty patriotism. (18)

The patriotism of the forefathers is something to emulate, but this can only be achieved by the suppression of the pleasure-seeking, narcissistic self.

"Country first, self second," should be your motto. Probably if you ask yourself truly, you will find you have at present got them just the other way about.

I hope if it is so that you will from this moment put yourself right and remain so always. Patriot first, player second. Don't be content, like the Romans were, and some people now are, to pay other people to play your football or to fight your battles for you. Do something yourself to keep the flag flying.

If you take up scouting in that spirit you will be doing something; take it up, not merely because it amuses you, but because by doing so you will be fitting yourself to help your country. Then you will have in you the true spirit of patriotism, which every British boy ought to have if he is worth his salt.

(*Show the Union Jack. Explain its history and composition, and which is the right way for flying it.*) (18)

In addition to the intellectual appeal of its argument and the power to sanction behavior of its law, *Scouting for Boys* offers for emulation innumerable instances of men and boys who embodied in their own actions the values Baden-Powell sought to inculcate in the rising generation. Their individual feats of daring, self-sacrifice, and devotion to duty are all specific applications of the larger principles that inform Scouting. Almost any one of them can be unraveled to reveal the ethical system of the entire movement. Baden-Powell finds a splendidly mummified instance of the "Loyalty to duty," for example, in the figure of the Roman soldier in Pompeii who stood at his post even as the ashes from Vesuvius descended upon him: "His remains are still there with his hand covering his mouth and nose to prevent the suffocation which in the end overcame him"(199).

I have already mentioned the edifying modern parallel to this that Baden-Powell notes in the Reigate Grammar School cadet who, assigned to sentry duty during daytime maneuvers, stayed on through the night when authorities forgot to tell him the exercises were over. Instruction can be derived from the lives of the great and humble alike, so that if King Richard I, "who was one of the first of the Scouts of the Empire"(191), demonstrates the virtue of self-sacrifice by leaving everything to "go and fight against the enemies of the Christian religion"(191), so also does the eighteen-year-old Currie (191), who gives up his life in an effort to save a little girl from being hit by a train.

Willingness to die for one's country represents the most sublime form of self-sacrifice, and we have copious illustrations of this. Particularly gripping is the instance of some courageous Japanese soldiers in the siege of Port Arthur:

> In the late war between Japan and Russia some Japanese pioneers had been ordered to blow up the gate of a Russian fort so that the attackers could get in. After nearly all of them had been shot down, a few of them managed to get to the gate with their charges of powder. These had to be "tamped" or jammed tight against the door somehow, and then fired. The Japs "tamped" them by pushing them against the door with their chests; they then lit their matches, fired the charge, and blew up the gates, but blew up themselves in doing so. But their plucky self-sacrifice enabled their comrades to get in and win the place for the Emperor. (201)

Although it didn't involve any battle on behalf of the empire, the disciplined way the soldiers on the *Birkenhead* met their end as the ship went down off the Cape of Good Hope is meant to provide inspiration for every British lad.

Baden-Powell also lauds the commitment to duty shown by the chief magistrate of Galway in 1493, an act that gave to posterity its "'Lynch-Law,' by which is meant stern justice by hanging an evildoer"(206). Walter Lynch's son had been sentenced to death for killing a Spaniard.

> The murderer had been properly tried and convicted. His mother begged the citizens to rescue her son when he was brought out from jail to suffer punishment, but the father, forseeing this, had the sentence carried out in the prison, and young Lynch was hanged from the prison window.
>
> The elder Lynch's sense of duty must have been very strong

indeed to enable him to make his feelings as a father give way
to his conscience as a magistrate. (206)

Beyond those celebrated by history, however, *Scouting for Boys*
also records those less public acts of heroism worthy of emulation.
Thus Police-Sergeant Cole, who won the Albert Medal for snatch-
ing up a dynamite bomb he found in Westminster Hall and running
outside to throw it away, rather than simply fleeing from it before
it exploded and allowing "the place to be smashed up"(225). Or
John Smith, who also won the Albert Medal for dragging a fellow
workman in a steel-casting factory out of a pit containing a
twenty-six ton red-hot ingot into which he had fallen. "Stanley
died of his burns two days later, but Smith, though badly burnt
himself, recovered to wear the Albert Medal"(225). Runaway
horses, drowning children, sudden fires, and oncoming trains provide numerous opportunities to test the mettle and preparation of
any Scout, and *Scouting for Boys* testifies to those who have met the
challenge. We are told of Albert Hardwick, who earned the Albert
Medal by jumping in front of an approaching train to hold a
woman who had fallen on the tracks between the rails so that the
train could pass safely over them both; of Cyril Adion, age thirteen,
and Newlyn Elliott, age seventeen, who rescued people from
drowning, and David Scannell, age nine, who saved a child at a
fire; of Albert Abraham, who rescued a boy fallen from a cliff near
the seashore; of Kate Chapman, herself only nine, who was badly
injured dragging two children out of the path of a runaway cart;
of Sir Thomas Buxton, who subdued a mad dog at great personal
peril; of Private Davies, who diverted the horses of an artillery
wagon from running over a number of children; of a man named
Gray, who helped calm a serious panic at a theater in which eight
children were crushed to death and more certainly would have lost
their lives had it not been for his efforts; of Miss Edith Harris, Miss
Bessie Matthews, and Mrs. Langley at Brentford, all of whom came
to the aid of constables who were having difficulties with violent
The values of Scouting that emerge from the combination of the
argument of the text, the Scout law, and the multitude of examples
thus form a self-evident, self-confirming set of assumptions about
the world that one disavows at great peril to oneself. The different
parts of *Scouting for Boys* work together to generate acceptance of its
total system; adherence to the system determines human worth; to
question some part of it is to place oneself outside the context of
human norms entirely. The consequences of such behavior are
addressed in an incident Baden-Powell recounts about the siege of

Malta, in which General Elliot successfully defended the rock against the French and Spanish by maintaining the very strictest discipline:

> Every man had learnt to obey orders without any hesitation or question.
>
> One day a man disobeyed an order, so General Elliot had him up before him and explained that he could not be in his right senses; he must be mad. So he ordered that he should be shaved, and that he should be blistered, bled and put into a straight waist-coat, and should be put into the cells, with bread and water, as a lunatic, and should also be prayed for in church! (200)[8]

It is an interesting commentary on Scouting's obsession with obedience that the man who questions an order is treated like a lunatic, while the Reigate cadet who stays at his post throughout the night until he almost freezes to death, long after he had been forgotten, becomes a model of steadfastness.

As we have seen, Scouting attempted to authenticate the traditional values it defended by connecting them explicitly with Britain's noble chivalric past. In addition to deriving the Scout Law from presumed knightly predecessors, Baden-Powell is quite direct in *Scouting for Boys* about the salutary role chivalry might play in the moral regeneration of the young.[9] Chapter 7, "Chivalry of the Knights," opens with the following hints to instructors:

> One aim of the Boy Scouts scheme is to revive amongst us, if possible, some of the rules of the knights of old, which did so much for the moral tone of our race, just as the Bushido of the ancient Samurai Knights has done, and is still doing for Japan. Unfortunately, chivalry with us has, to a large extent, been allowed to die out, whereas in Japan it is taught to the children, so that it becomes with them a practice of their life, and it is also taught to children in Germany and Switzerland with the best results. Our effort is not so much to discipline the boys as to teach them to discipline themselves. (188)

The vision of chivalry Baden-Powell offers his boy audience is, in fact, the total child's vision, complete with all the standard paraphernalia of shining armor, damsels in distress, and good deeds:

> "In days of old, when knights were bold," it must have been a fine sight to see one of these steel-clad horsemen come

riding through the dark green woods in his shining armour, with shield and lance and waving plumes, bestriding his gallant war-horse, strong to bear its load, and full of fire to charge upon an enemy. And near him rode his squire, a young man, his assistant and companion, who would some day become a knight.

Behind him rode his group, or patrol of men-at-arms— stout, hearty warriors, ready to follow their knight to the gates of death if need be. They were the tough yeomen of the old days, who won so many of her fine fights for Britain through their pluck and loyal devotion to their knights.

In peace time, when there was no fighting to be done, the knight would daily ride about looking for a chance of doing a good turn to any wanting help, especially woman or child who might be in distress. When engaged in thus doing good turns he was called a "Knight Errant." His patrol naturally acted in the same way as their leader, and a man-at-arms was always equally ready to help the distressed with his strong right arm. The knights of old were the patrol leaders of the nation, and the men-at-arms were the scouts. (189)

In these small communities of men bound together by strict loyalty and motivated by the highest ideals, Baden-Powell finds the perfect analogue for his Scout patrols. Returning to the rhetoric of knights and retainers he first proposed in the Eton College *Chronicle*, he points out that

You patrol leaders and scouts are therefore very like the knights and retainers, especially if you keep your honour ever before you in the first place, and do your best to help other people who are in trouble or who want assistance. Your motto is, "Be Prepared" to do this, and the motto of the knights was a similar one, "Be Always Ready." (189)

Admiring the authoritarian societies of Germany and Japan, Baden-Powell attributes the efficiency of their citizens and their fierce patriotism to the inculcation of chivalric training in the young. We have already noted his high regard for the principles of Bushido. German chivalry, lacking any special code, is less useful, though it, too, accounts for much that is happily disciplined about German youth. Baden-Powell's enthusiasm for exemplary German discipline caused him some editorial problems at the moment when that discipline was directed against Britain in World War I. Baden-Powell was up to the challenge, however, so that the chivalry that, for seven editions of *Scouting for Boys*, had been "also taught to children in Germany and Switzerland with the best results", turns out in the eighth, published in 1916, to be simply "taught to children in other countries with the best results"(217). So much for the chivalry of the Hun. (It is also worth noting that Scout visits to museums and armories, which until 1916 were modeled on "what is regularly done in Germany as part of the training of the boys while at school" [236], plays no part in the instructional methodology of the eighth edition.)[10]

While manufacturing loyal and obedient youths to serve the empire is Scouting's essential mission, instilling in them a proper pride in the splendor of that empire is also central to its purpose. From the beginning *Scouting for Boys* insists that the British nation is "one of the best and greatest that the world has ever known"(14), and misses no opportunity to document this obvious postulate of existence: "Of all the different kinds of government in the world ours is the easiest and fairest for everybody"(256). Achieved through the efforts of the heroes and scouts of the past, men like Captain Cook, Lord Clive, Wellington, John Smith, and others, the empire represents for Baden-Powell the noblest aspiration of a people determined to do their duty to the world at large:

> And now in all these countries [of the Empire] we are spreading the blessings of peace and justice, doing away with slavery and oppression, developing commerce, and manufactures, and prosperity. (239)

The blatant nationalism of *Scouting for Boys* is no different from that served up in any of the primers of boys' histories and accounts of heroic exploits that Baden-Powell includes in his various suggestions for further reading, such as Fitchett's *Deeds That Won the Empire*, H. O. Arnold-Forster's *History of England*, and countless others. It is no different, indeed, from the celebration of national greatness in which every culture engages while indoctrinating its youth. It becomes a problem for the Scouts, however, when the insistence on British superiority clashes with the notion of the equality of all people that is so much a part of Scouting, and more particularly with the movement's worldwide ambitions that rapidly developed. That the British are more equal than other men is not necessarily an assumption guaranteed to please everybody in an organization committed to international brotherhood.

Two brief plays in *Scouting for Boys*, intended to be performed by Scouts, indicate the nature of the difficulty. The first—and less problematic—dramatizes the capture of Captain John Smith and

Pocahontas's role in saving his life. Captain Smith, a jolly adventurer of great exuberance, possesses the supreme self-confidence of knowing himself to be British. Brought as a prisoner before Powhatan, he greets the king enthusiastically, "Hail, King! I am no witch nor devil—nothing but a man—an Englishman, which is something more than a mere man," and in answer to Powhatan's naive question concerning the possibility that he might be afraid, reminds him, laughingly, "Forget not—I am an Englishman—an Englishman knows no fear"(44). Powhatan continues to try to make him quail before his power, but Smith continues insouciantly to emphasize that in doing his duty to extend the blessings of British rule to Powhatan he hardly cares what may happen to him:

> What brought me here was duty to my King and God and countrymen; to spread his powerful sway over all the earth, that you and yours may know of God, that trade may spread to carry peace and wealth throughout the world. If you accept these views all will be well; if you accept them not then do your worst, but use your haste; our mission is to *clean* the world! (46)

Unconvinced, the king gives the order to kill Smith. But the intervention of Pocahontas, and the report of more white devils arriving offstage, sufficiently confuse things so that Smith manages to take Powhatan prisoner, offering to him and his warriors the opportunity to better themselves by serving the king of England:

> If you would live in peace, your only way is now to join with us. Our God is stronger than your idols, and our King is King of many tribes far greater and more powerful than your own. But if you join with us your wicked ways must cease; no more to kill your people for no crime, no more to steal their goods or beasts, no more to make them slaves against their will. Beneath the British flag all men are free. (48)

Powhatan negotiates with his warriors, and all agree that "to join this mighty power whereby we shall ourselves be strong"(49) is the better part of valor. They then swear an oath of allegiance and are given in return "the flag of St. George and Merry England"(49), which Smith removes from his coat and, tying it to a Scout's staff, presents to them. The warriors salute, and the band plays "Rule Britannia."

The ebullient good spirits and transparently mythic quality make this basically a benign instance of nationalistic puffery, despite some assumptions of superiority that in a different context might well be offensive.

The second play—or display, as Baden-Powell calls it—is quite another matter. It celebrates an incident in which General John Nicholson, who served in India during the mutiny, quelled some potential unrest by shaming a chief (the term is Baden-Powell's) who was trying to dispute Nicholson's authority in front of his fellow chiefs. Celebrating Nicholson in any way is a questionable procedure for a book that seeks to put before its readers models of unimpeachable British fairness, decency, and responsibility. Although Baden-Powell cites him as "one of the finest among many fine Britons who helped to rule India"(241), the portrait drawn by Christopher Hibbert in his study of the mutiny is of a rather different sort. Hibbert's Nicholson is an erratic, tormented soul who ruled the areas under his control with a ferocity that went well beyond British administrative efficiency: "He stamped out lawlessness ... with the utmost severity, pursuing criminals personally and displaying their severed heads upon his desk. His strange and forceful personality so impressed the natives that numbers of them worshipped him as their spiritual guide and deity, falling down at his feet in reverent submission."[11]

Rather than viewing the Indians he ruled with appropriate colonial paternalism, he detested them, "so Ensign Wilberforce said, 'with a hatred no words could describe!' "[12] The mutiny gave him a chance to express those feelings:

> Let us propose a Bill for the flaying alive, impalement, or burning of the murderers of the women and children at Delhi. The idea of simply hanging the perpetrators is maddening. I wish that I were in that part of the world, that if necessary I might take the law into my own hands. ... If I had [the wretches] ... in my power today and knew that I were to die tomorrow, I would inflict the most excruciating tortures I could think of on them with a perfectly easy conscience.[13]

If he couldn't in fact torture them to his satisfaction, he could at least hang them without paying overmuch attention to the niceties of a trial, which he apparently did with some frequency. To help restore proper regard for the British, he also issued an order that "no native should pass a white man riding, without dismounting and salaaming."[14]

Baden-Powell's display centers on the moment Mehtab Singh, the dissident chief, enters a meeting with Nicholson wearing his shoes: "(It is the custom in India for natives to take off their shoes on entering the presence of a superior, just as in England you take off your hat on coming in.) And he did so. He walked in before them all with his shoes on"(242). Nicholson conducts the meeting as if nothing unusual had happened. As the chiefs are about to depart, however, he summons them back:

> Stay, gentlemen, one moment. I have a matter with you, Mehtab Singh. Thou camest here to show contempt for me, who represent your Queen. But you forget that you are dealing with a Briton—one of that band who never brooks an insult even from an equal, much less from a native of this land. Were I a common soldier it would be the same; a Briton, even though alone amongst a thousand of your kind, shall be respected, though it brought about his death. That's how we hold the world. (243)

And glaring at Singh, he orders him to remove his shoes, which after a moment's defiance he obediently does, walking slowly out of the room, shoes in hand.[15] Issued without any of Captain Smith's gay bravado, Nicholson's extraordinary assertion of British superiority at the expense of a lesser breed—"never brooks an insult from an equal, much less from a native of this land"—and his undisguised contempt for the Indians—"alone amongst a thousand of your kind"—document a set of racial attitudes markedly out of keeping with the professed brotherhood of Scouting.

Whatever his reasons for including the incident, Baden-Powell either understood he went wrong here or was so advised: The Nicholson display is omitted from the second and all subsequent editions of *Scouting for Boys*.

Even though it disappears after the first edition, the scene points to a problem in *Scouting for Boys* that does not go away so easily: the blurring of the thin line between creating a healthy pride in the genuine achievement of one's country and inducing instead a smug sense of the superiority of the true Briton. It is a blurring that the great public schools of Baden-Powell's time fostered, and it is not surprising that a movement that is as explicitly a product of the public school system as Scouting should share not only the ideals of that system but also its prejudices. The two come together in the creation both of a desirable character type, whose selflessness, devotion to duty, loyalty, and the like are already familiar to us, and, more astonishingly, a physical type as well. If words cannot render accurately this best embodiment of empire, images can, and fortunately Baden-Powell himself has provided us with an illustration of what he looks like. The context is important. In his section on observation and deduction, Baden-Powell has been arguing for the importance of noticing detail in the process of reaching judgments of people:

> It has been said that you can tell a man's character from the way he wears his hat. If it is slightly on one side, the wearer is good-natured; if it is worn very much on one side, he is a swaggerer; if on the back of the head, he is bad at paying his debts; if worn straight on the top, he is probably honest but very dull. (54)

HOW THE WEARING OF A HAT SHOWS CHARACTER

He comments on the different and revealing ways in which people walk, indicates his distrust of wax moustaches, and comes to his central formulation:

> Certainly the "quiff" or lock of hair which some lads wear on their forehead, is a sure sign of silliness. The shape of the face gives a good guide to a man's character.
>
> Perhaps you can tell the characters of the gentlemen on the next page? (54)

The page in question presents us with the following:

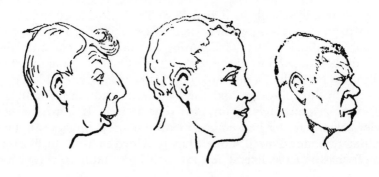

Inferring character from physiognomy, of course, is one of the standard activities of nineteenth- and twentieth-century racist theorizers. Although Baden-Powell doesn't provide us with the cranial measurements and specious scientific data found in classic racist works, his caricatures of the large-nosed, weak-chinned, witless creature on the left and the frowning, low-browed troglodyte on the right, framing the clear-eyed, sculpted face of the public school lad in the middle constitute a genuine, if modest, contribution to early twentieth-century racist thinking, all the more significant for being part of the Boy Scout handbook. It is, to be sure, the unconscious racism of the public school elite preferring its own select kind to all others rather than anything consciously programmatic on Baden-Powell's part, though it is no more admirable for that. However innocent, the clean-cut Aryan, with his strength and intelligence, bracketed by suspiciously inferior beings reminds us of cultural uses of similar stereotypes in this century that were anything but benign. While obviously Scouting is guilty of no such abuses, the assumptions behind those three faces nevertheless have to be understood if we are to make sense of the movement. It is worth noting that the faces make several appearances in *Scouting for Boys*, most notably in distinguishing the slacker, with his bad posture and narrow chest, who smokes, from the healthy, upstanding athlete who doesn't.

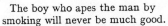

The boy who apes the man by smoking will never be much good.

A strong and healthy boy has the ball at his feet.

The glowing presence of the public school countenance that irradiates the pages of *Scouting for Boys*, reminding us of the values and ideals Baden-Powell cherishes, also helps us appreciate the perspective from which *Scouting for Boys* approaches some of the broad social issues it addresses. Although Baden-Powell does not devote as much time in the handbook as he does elsewhere to a discussion of poverty, it is clear from *Scouting for Boys* that he views it as a moral defect among those afflicted by it, rather than in part as a social problem requiring some kind of social action. Drink, lack of thrift, and a slack will are responsible, and the remedy lies in stimulating the poor to take a more active, prudent role in their own interests:

> A very large proportion of the distress and unemployedness in the country is due to want of thrift on the part of the people themselves; and social reformers, before seeking for new remedies, would do well to set this part of the problem right in the first place; they would then probably find very little more left for them to do. Mr. John Burns, in a recent speech, pointed out that there is plenty of money in the country to put everyone on a fair footing, if only it were made proper use of by the working man. (278)[16]

The working man must thus be helped to help himself, primarily by encouraging him to save his money and to renounce drinking and smoking, two activities Baden-Powell sees as entirely unnecessary for his well-being or pleasure. The gain would be enormous:

> £166,000,000 were spent last year on drink, and £25,000,000 on tobacco. This alone would be enough, if divided amongst our thirty-five millions of poor, to give £22 a year to each family; and we know that this is only part of the extravagance of the nation. . . .
>
> The wastefulness in Great Britain is almost inconceivable, and ought to be made criminal. . . . If they had thrift a large majority of our working men and their families might be in prosperous circumstances to-day, but they have never been taught what thrift may be, and they naturally do as their neighbours do. If the rising generation could be started in the practise of economy, it would make a vast difference to the character and prosperity of the nation in the future. (279)

Ignoring William Beveridge's important study, *Unemployment*, published in 1905, which demonstrated how seasonal fluctuation in various trades produced an inevitably high rate of unemployment, and Seebohm Rowntree's analysis of how the poor manage their meager incomes, which turns out to have nothing to do with lavish consumption of beer and tobacco,[17] Baden-Powell lays the blame squarely on the wasteful habits of the poor themselves. His impatience with their plight can be inferred from the thoughtless comment he includes in a discussion of bees, noting "They are quite a model community, for they respect their queen and kill their unemployed"(101). Scouting's commitment to educate the rising generation in thrifty ways—symbolized by the fact that every first-class Scout had to have six pence in the savings bank—must be judged one of its less efficacious solutions to the challenge of Britain's regeneration.[18]

Baden-Powell's conviction that the poor themselves possessed the key to their own financial salvation comforts him, obviating as it does the need for any radical social action. Admiring above all the strictly disciplined society in which everybody is content to play his appropriate role, he viewed with anxiety any threat to the established social order. Despite his insistence that both he and Scouting were above politics of any sort, both regard the world from the perspective of that scrubbed public school face: What is good for him is clearly good for the country, and Baden-Powell can condemn with a clear conscience any extreme idea, of the sort promulgated by socialist agitators, that might threaten his privileged existence:

> Extreme ideas are seldom much good; if you look them up in history you will see almost always they have been tried before somewhere. The Socialists are right in wishing to get money more evenly distributed so that there would be no millionaires and no paupers, but everyone pretty well off.
>
> But they go the wrong way to work; they want to fight all other people to get themselves up, instead of joining in with everybody in doing a great thing for the whole country by a way which is fair and good for all. They do not read history, which shows that their plans have been tried before, and failed, because they made life a kind of slavery for everybody, and left the country an easy prey to another stronger one.
>
> More thrift rather than a change of government will bring money to all. And a strong united Empire, where all are helpful and patriotic will bring us power, peace, and prosperity such as no Socialistic dream could do. (257)

The bogey of Socialism troubled Baden-Powell enormously; acknowledging in this passage that Socialists might be right in some of their aspirations actually represented a daring sort of concession that later came to disturb him. It does not survive into the third edition of *Scouting for Boys*, which drops the entire discussion of Socialist goals. By this time Baden-Powell cannot bring himself to mention the dread word at all, and in place of the last sentence about the Socialistic dream we find, "And a strong united Empire ... will bring us power, peace, and prosperity such as no visionary politician's remedies could do."[19] Such was the untimely end of Baden-Powell's earlier subversive impulses.

In addition to recommending to the poor a fiscally responsible, abstemious existence, Scouting also claimed for itself a more practical role in treating the problems of youth unemployment, specifically the problems caused by the so-called "blind alley" jobs. Requiring no skills and leading to no careers, these marginal positions—messengers, clerks, newsboys, and the like—would take boys in at twelve or fourteen and occupy them at small salaries for several years. At the point at which the boys were old enough to command full-time salaries and begin a serious trade, they would be turned out, so that the process of cheap employment of the young could begin all over again. The older boys were left stranded, without training of any kind or hope for the future. The "blind alley" predicament was a source of concern to all boyologists, Baden-Powell included, who shrewdly helped market Scouting to the public by stressing its capacity to alleviate the problem through the skills acquired in earning various proficiency badges. The first edition of *Scouting for Boys* only begins to touch on this, advising instructors to "Encourage him to take up 'hobbies' or handicrafts"(204), but it shortly developed into a central part of the argument for the importance of Scout training. Earning badges thus becomes not a disinterested exercise but rather a means of vocational preparation, so that the Scout who earns his carpenter's or mason's or tailor's or textile worker's badge will at the same time have opened up a career possibility for himself. Baden-Powell stressed this part of Scouting to good effect, declaring the training in handicrafts, or what he calls, in the Fifth Annual Report (1914), "Equipment for making a Career,"[20] to be as essential a feature of Scouting as instilling good character or propagating the principles of service to others. Despite the calculated appeal of this claim, it is not at all clear that the rudimentary nature of the training involved in earning a proficiency badge ever seriously affected the problem of "blind-alley" employment. The theory behind the awarding of badges, in fact, runs counter to the notion that substantial, exploitable skills are mastered in the process of gaining them. Baden-Powell emphasizes, in the second edition (1909), that

The mistake usually made is for scoutmasters and examiners to require too high a standard of proficiency before awarding a badge. Our real object is to instill into every boy and encourage an idea of self-improvement. A fair average standard of proficiency is therefore all that is required. If you try higher than that you get a few brilliant boys qualified, but you dishearten a large number of others who fail, and you teach them the elements of hopelessness and helplessness, which is exactly what we want to avoid.

Scoutmasters will remember that our policy is to get numbers. We don't want a select "corps d'elite," but we want to put a taste of the right spirit into every boy we can possibly get hold of. There are three million boys wanting it.[21]

Baden-Powell's admonition to Scoutmasters was taken seriously. It drops out of the third edition, obviously no longer necessary. The flexibility he wants in awarding badges to Scouts he extends to the qualifications for Scoutmasters as well, and for the same reasons. As he writes to Percy Everett, "I don't think we ought to make the test of Scoutmasters too stringent for fear of putting them off. ... All that examiners and candidates need bother themselves about would be the simple tests shown on my list of 'Tests for Scoutmasters.'"[22]

Though character training remains its essential underlying business, the book's larger purpose is to touch upon every aspect of a boy's life, to establish itself as a kind of indispensable moral and practical handbook for the young. In addition to the vast amount of information it contains about wildlife and camping, *Scouting for Boys* offers useful wisdom on a dazzling array of subjects: on the proper way to breathe, eat, sleep, and clothe oneself; on how to fight disease, keep clean, and brush one's teeth; on the necessity of keeping one's blood clean by having at least one bowel movement a day—known as a "rear"—or sometimes even two; on the correct way to fly the flag, combat snakebite, remove grit from the eye, carry an unconscious person, make buttons out of bootlaces; on how to talk a suicidal person out of killing himself, how to choose a career (with a disproportionate amount of proselytizing about the benefits of the army and the navy), and how to bake bread, to name a few.

Of all the specific areas of a boy's education with which the book deals, there is, by Baden-Powell's own admission, "scarcely one more important" (279) than the subject of continence, which "under advice" (279), he has removed from an earlier place in the text and included in the final section, "Notes for Instructors." Like all psychologists, moralists, and boyologists at the turn of the century, Baden-Powell was impassioned about the mental and physical dangers of masturbation. Expert testimony, if one needed it, was available everywhere, but none more expert or adamant about the horrors that followed touching "the racial organ" than G. Stanley Hall, whose massive two-volume work on adolescence (1904) provided indisputable scientific evidence of the grisly consequences of self-abuse.[23] Baden-Powell's view of it as the worst of all vices, bringing "with it weakness of heart and head, and, if persisted in, idiocy and lunacy" (280), was not unique. What is interesting is the way he formulated his advice for presentation in *Scouting for Boys*. Two points are particularly striking about his discussion of this vital subject: The first is his insistence that the issue be treated openly, without any of the fudgy circumlocutions and delicacy that have obscured clear understanding of it in the past; and the second is the careful way he avoids doing this.

Four strong sentences at the start herald the absolute frankness of his approach:

> The training of the boy would be very incomplete did it not contain some clear and plain-spoken instructions on the subject of continence.
> The prudish mystery with which we have come to veil this important question is doing incalculable harm.
> The very secrecy with which we withhold all knowledge from the boy prompts him the more readily to take his own line, also secretly, and, therefore, injuriously.
> I have never known a boy who was not the better for having the question put to him frankly and openly. It can quite well be done without indelicacy. (279)

After such a promisingly candid introduction, however, we learn only that "indulgence" or "self-abuse" (279) is a contemptible vice, avoided by manly men; that the temptation to engage in it may come from physical causes, "such as eating rich foods, sleeping on the back in a soft bed with too many blankets on, or from constipation" (280); and that washing in cold water and exercising the upper part of the body can help resist the desire for it. If all else fails, the boy is cautioned to speak to his Scout officer, "who can then advise him what to do"(280). At no point does Baden-Powell define the vice, so that the reader emerges from the "frank and open" discussion with no more knowledge about what precisely should be avoided than he would have possessed had he not read it in the first place. The prudish mystery, in short, remains heavily veiled.

Such was not Baden-Powell's initial intention. The original typescript of this section, in its detailed fervor, indicates exactly how powerfully Baden-Powell wanted to put the case:

> You all know what it is to have at times a pleasant feeling in your private parts, and there comes an inclination to work it up with your hand or otherwise. It is especially likely to happen when you see a dirty picture or hear dirty stories and jokes.
>
> Well, lots of fellows from not knowing any better please themselves in this way until it often becomes a sort of habit with them which they cannot get out of. Yet I am sure that every sensible boy, if he were told in time of the danger of it, would have the strength of mind not to do it.

The consequences of engaging in this habit are considerably more severe than those spelled out in *Scouting for Boys*:

> And the result of self-abuse is always—mind you, always— that the boy after a time becomes weak and nervous and shy, he gets headaches and probably palpitation of the heart, and if he still carries it on too far he very often goes out of his mind and becomes an idiot.
>
> A very large number of lunatics in our asylums have made themselves mad by indulging in this vice although at one time they were sensible cheery boys like any of you.
>
> The use of your parts is not to play with when you are a boy, but to enable you to get children when you are grown up and married. But if you misuse them while young you will not be able to use them when you are a man; they will not work then.
>
> Remember too that several awful diseases come from in- dulgence—one especially that rots away the inside of men's mouths, their noses, and eyes, etc.

Altogether a grim specificity more wide-ranging and far-reaching than the relatively straightforward weakness of heart and head, possibly leading to idiocy, which afflicts the unwary abuser in the published handbook. It is also worth noting that the physical causes of the wet dreams in the typescript (which become the causes of temptation in *Scouting for Boys*) include eating meat but not constipation. Adding constipation obviously helps legitimate Baden-Powell's principle of the need for a daily rear, as well as possibly involving in an almost mythic way a commitment to keeping the blood clean not only of waste products but also of impure thoughts.

Since this original version clearly embodied the tone and the honesty that Baden-Powell was after, how did the muted, less emphatic discussion of the handbook come about? As Baden-Powell mentions in *Scouting for Boys*, he inserted the section on continence at the back "under advice," the advice in part being that of the reluctance of the printer of the fortnightly edition to include it in its initial form. In a letter to Peter Keary, one of C. Arthur Pearson's managers who was assigned to help Baden-Powell get his handbook into print, Baden-Powell argues that

> I can't say that I have the slightest feeling myself against putting in the whole paragraph on continence—because I think there is far too much prudery on the subject, with disastrous consequences to thousands every year. ... If, however, the printer cannot put it in, the best course will be to insert a heading of this kind:

CONTINENCE

The Dangers of Self-Indulgence and How to Avoid Them.
These points are gone into in a separate paper which will be forwarded to anyone applying for the same and enclosing one penny stamp.[24]

When the fifth part came out, however, Baden-Powell discovered that all mention of continence was omitted, distressing him considerably "because the promotion of continence is one of the main reasons for starting the scheme: and letters which I have had from some high authorities encourage me to think that it is perhaps the most important of the whole lot."[25] But negotiations between Baden-Powell, Keary, and the printer soon resulted in Baden-Powell relinquishing his initial vision for the more respectable solution that would cause no offense:

> I have rewritten Continence and I think that as it now stands there can be no objection to its going in [at] its proper

place. ... I don't think it can now shock anybody's suscepti-
bilities, and cannot possibly do any harm to girls. I have taken
my mother's opinion on it.

I see now that to put it at the end of the book (among the
games!) would be so out of place—and would accuse me of
inconsistency in putting too much prudish importance on it
myself!

In its present form the paragraph can't do any harm as one
of the Hints to Instructors.[26]

The discarded version, in addition to articulating Baden-Powell's
feelings about masturbation in the way he originally intended, also
contains a fascinating insight into his social thinking. Following his
advice to consult with a Scout officer if the temptation for self-
abuse persists, Baden-Powell concludes the entire section with this
observation:

Restrain yourself while you are young and you will be able
to restrain yourself when you grow up. It is at present a
disgrace and a danger to England that from want of self-
restraint among men and women thousands upon thousands
of children are born every year for whom there is no work
and no money—and so we get such an enormous crowd of
poor people and unemployed.

I walked round the other day with some of the unemployed
to see if they were really anxious to get work. They were.
They tried several places but no hands were wanted. Then
one of them made the remark which seemed to me very true.
"There's not enough work to go round. The truth is there's
too many of us in the world."

The logic and implications of this passage are disturbing in a number of ways—perhaps accounting for its being dropped from the
published book. In the first place, if, as Baden-Powell argues, private parts are not to play with but only to use for procreation in
marriage, then criticizing the lack of self-restraint of those who
presumably use them properly to have children is at once contra-
dictory and, more importantly, a transparently class-determined
sanction. We are thus firmly in the world of Sidney Webb and the
Eugenicists, calling for a proliferation of the birthrate of the superior classes and a diminishing of the rest—for the good of the race.
While I don't think there can be much doubt that this represents
Baden-Powell's view, it was clearly not a view, upon reflection, that

he was prepared to assert publicly. The leader of a youth movement could not finally make such invidious distinctions, however compelling he might have thought them. The logical muddle of the passage is further seen in the fact that if self-abuse in the young leads, as Baden-Powell claims, to malfunction of parts in the mature man, then it appears indisputably the case that healthy excesses of this vice would seem to offer the best remedy to the swollen birthrate among the poor. It should be encouraged, not suppressed.

Most important, of course, is Baden-Powell's attributing poverty and unemployment to the sheer number of the poor, for whom no jobs exist. This is precisely the opposite position he emphatically maintains throughout all his published work, where he explicitly states that opportunity and money abound, the plight of the poor resting solely on their own wasteful habits and lack of self-discipline. The bathos of the unemployed worker's remark, which Baden-Powell quotes approvingly, thus undercuts the entire social analysis Baden-Powell promulgates officially through the Scout movement.[27] In a world in which obedience and thrift are meant to guarantee satisfaction for all, it is not surprising that Scouting will never again entertain such a heresy.

Having begun the first Camp Fire Yarn with a reference to the vital contribution the boys of Mafeking made in its defense, Baden-Powell ends *Scouting for Boys* by calling upon all interested men to take an active part in the scheme of youth training, thereby "doing a great thing for your country, for your younger brothers, and for yourself" (282). Trying to attract boys to the excitement of the movement while at the same time selling its merits as an instrument of character instruction to the men on whom the organization would depend to make it run, *Scouting for Boys* sought an almost impossibly broad audience of boys and adults alike. To have appealed to only one constituency at the expense of the other would have been disastrous, and it must be said that Baden-Powell managed with extraordinary skill to do both. An effective blend of inspiration, indoctrination, and information, providing a total system of moral education and character training, *Scouting for Boys* was very much the book the movement required, fascinating for the values and attitudes it deliberately espouses as well as for what it unwittingly reveals. If immersion in it once a year is perhaps a bit excessive, it is nevertheless worth the serious attention of anybody interested in early twentieth-century British society in general—and obviously essential for an understanding of the Boy Scout movement in particular.

7

"THE PEACE SCOUTS" AND EDWARDIAN MILITARISM

From its very beginning Scouting always defined itself as staunchly antimilitaristic. The opening pages of *Scouting for Boys* distinguish between war scouts and peace scouts, emphatically making the point that the Scout movement is devoted entirely to training the latter, a position from which no public Scout statement or policy document ever wavered. At the same time, the major charge brought against Scouting from its very beginning was pre-precisely that it did serve as a kind of paramilitary organization, bent on preparing Britain's youth to fight ably in defense of the empire. Accusations of Scouting's secret agenda have been as impassioned as the protestations of innocence from official Scout spokesmen, with each side earnestly repudiating the claims of the other.

Whatever precisely was meant by militarism—and everyone had a different idea—it was important to large numbers of people that the Scouts not be guilty of it, and most importantly to Baden-Powell himself. Too many parents, Baden-Powell feared, would refuse to let their sons join if they felt Scouting were a military organization. Always shrewdly expedient when it came to charting policy issues, Baden-Powell was explicit about the need to maintain a peaceful profile: "The Boy Scout movement is non-military. ... That fact appeals to a very large number of parents.... Anti-military parents will allow their sons to join the Boy Scouts but prohibit them from joining a Cadet Corps."[1] In response to a letter from Percy Everett asking him (in 1909) about the status of the Scout in wartime and wondering if it might be possible to get Scouts recognized by the War Office, Baden-Powell noted in the margin, "No—not yet—when we are firmly established."[2]

Before examining in what ways militarism does or does not describe the nature, or practice, or ideals of the early Scouting movement, let me first provide a warning. There is a sense in which any effort to analyze the specific strands of militarism behind the formation of the Scouts, to attempt to discriminate finely between facade and reality, misses the point. However deliberately the Scouts were fashioned, it is also true that the Scouting movement grew out of a coherent ideology that Baden-Powell did not seem to have questioned. While it is important to try to determine what he consciously intended for his Scouts, we must also understand that for a man of his class, profession, and era, certain kinds of distinctions we might insist upon would have puzzled him. For a cavalry officer from Charterhouse, reared in the skirmishes against Afghans and Africans, military ideals of service and behavior inevitably constituted the basis of human excellence. Warfare was not an aberrant condition but a natural fact of existence and a legitimate test of the moral stature of those engaged in it. Hence the training that turned people into successful soldiers was also the best training for developing successful, productive citizens. The virtues of the soldier and the virtues of the citizen were the same; Baden-Powell would have found difficult the notion that civic society might properly esteem values different from those cherished by the army.

Like so much else in post-Darwinian Victorian culture, the Scouts developed out of an implicit understanding of the world as a place of ceaseless struggle in which military might and moral worth were equated. Behind the niceties of Scout doctrine, that is, with its studious avoidance of military drill and its distinction between war and peace Scouts, lies a sensibility that Baden-Powell shared with others of his generation and class, which saw "all human activity in terms of warfare, and warfare was presented not only as an unavoidable feature of international life, but also something inherently desirable, since it helped develop a courageous and resourceful community."[3] In an era that saw the British flag planted over a substantial portion of the earth's surface, bringing the benefits of British civilization to lesser breeds through its fighting prowess, the establishment of military virtues as the most important criterion by which one evaluated the health of societies and of individuals is not surprising.[4] At this level of unconscious cultural assumption, modes of expression are as revealing as explicit policy stipulations, and none more so than the famous motto of the Boy Scouts, "Be Prepared."

As a civic injunction, the admonition is practically without meaning. Be prepared for what? Against whom? Whatever we take to be life's demands on us, being endlessly on edge for the arrival of the unexpected is not normally one of them. While we should all learn to suffer disappointment calmly, work hard, and help others—interpretations that in the course of *Scouting for Boys*, as we have seen, Baden-Powell attaches to his maxim—in fact none of them can sensibly be embraced by the advice. Peacetime existence as we know it does not necessarily involve holding oneself in a constant state of readiness to do one's duty; indeed such a posture might produce not health but gnawing anxiety. In a world of threats and ambushes, however, with enemies hovering everywhere ready to attack, it constitutes the minimal gospel of survival. And as I indicated in the last chapter, this is precisely the universe the Scouting movement inhabits. The images, illustrations, and anecdotes of *Scouting for Boys* are unselfconsciously drawn from the military, not only because Baden-Powell knows it well and knows the ways such exploits can be made to appeal to the young, but also because it represents the most accurate model he can fashion of the world as he understands it. It is a simple model, beset with a variety of simple problems to which a state of chronic preparation provides adequate remedy. In postulating such a universe of struggle in which the prizes will go only to the most disciplined, Baden-Powell expressed a broadly held view, confirmed by the popular social Darwinism of the time, that no doubt seemed to him an obvious fact of everyday experience.

Militarism, of course, is not a concept with a single meaning. It can sensibly be used in various ways: to describe the tendency to regard military efficiency as the chief interest of the state or the deification of military values and training as the ideal models for civic life; to characterize the prevalence of military sentiments of a people or the power of the military as the chief interest of the state. The major thrust of Baden-Powell's disavowal of Scout militarism, however, rests on a narrow, almost technical conception of the term. The Scouts cannot be construed as militaristic, Baden-Powell emphasized repeatedly, because they do not include military drill in any part of their approved activities. "Militarism is a word like 'Mesopotamia'," Baden-Powell writes, "which many people like to flourish and talk about hotly without understanding it very deeply. Still, even those people cannot accuse us of being militarists, since we do not go in for military drill."[5] And certainly when compared with the rigidly prescribed drill program insisted upon by the Boys' Brigade, the Scouts might appear the very model of pacifism. But the issue is considerably more complicated than this. In the first place, the absence of explicit military exercises is hardly definitive proof about an organization's values. It is true that the presence of such drills inescapably suggests a strong militaristic bias (as, for example, in the Boys' Brigade); the lack of them, however, does not argue convincingly for its opposite.

Second, although official Scout policy did not embrace drill, the decentralized workings of the movement permitted individual Scoutmasters substantial autonomy in deciding what particular training methods they wished to employ. So that what Scout theory rejected, Scout practice was free to include. Describing the nature of Scouting to a Captain MacIlwain in 1909, Baden-Powell explains,

> To the Scout master is left the method of carrying out the training—in each case according to the class of boys, local conditions, and his own abilities. To him is left full power as to their religious training, and to make his troop, if he likes, into sailors (as is done in a good many cases) or missioners, or firemen, or marksmen, etc. . . .
>
> 2. As regards a section of a troop or even a whole troop taking up military training, it is only what is being done elsewhere—that is, the troop directs its training according to the Scout Master's ideas and qualifications. I am hoping soon to see "Missioner" troops at work, for instance. We have already a number of "Sea Scout" troops and a few equipped with carbines, others with fire hose, and two of them with field guns, etc. . . .
>
> 4. As regards military ranks and uniform, I do not personally approve of them except in the case of a corporal of a patrol unless the troop becomes a cadet company, but for this at present no provision exists.[6]

Baden-Powell elaborated on this point the same year in the *Headquarters Gazette*. Commenting on the charge that "the Boy Scout of today is the Territorial of tomorrow," Baden-Powell argues that the methods of Scout training are all consistent with our work as Peace Scouts and do not tend very much to militarism. At the same time the form of training is very much left in the hands of Scoutmasters, and if they like to train their lads to become gymnasts, marksmen, farmers or mechanics, they are free to do so according to their individual ability.[7]

Under these circumstances, it should be clear that the absence of prescribed drill in the Scouts does not even address—no less resolve—the question of Scouting's militarism. Putting aside the issue of drill, let us ask instead if Baden-Powell harbored any principled objections to militarism in youth organizations before he founded the Scouts.

We can begin with the Boys' Brigade, and Baden-Powell's review of their annual display in the Albert Hall on the night of 5 May 1903. The *Times* reporter echoed his colleagues on other papers present that evening in noting the enthusiasm with which the audience greeted the boys' skill in drill and gymnastic exercises, in musical dumbbell and ambulance work. When Baden-Powell, who was presiding at the demonstration, rose to speak, he was received with tremendous cheering. He was warm in his praise of the movement, mentioning in particular the importance of its mission and the dedication of its officers. According to the account in the *Times*, Baden-Powell went on to insist that

> people certainly ought to know more about it and appreciate the wonderful work it was doing. Whatever its promoters intended, it certainly had a military tendency. A country like ours had largely to depend on Volunteer forces, and its enemies were carefully watching to see what these Volunteers could do. He was sure that, if the brigade increased, as he hoped it would, such a mass of boys, well organized and all carefully taught to discipline themselves to be the slaves of duty, would be a strong force behind the Volunteers and the Army. But, apart from that incidental effect, the movement had a much grander value in training boys to become the best type of citizen.... In Mafeking (cheers) they had had a very small garrison, and the boys formed themselves into a cadet corps, which was of very great value ... setting all the men free to take their places in the fighting line. If all the boys were organized and disciplined like those of the Boys' Brigade they would form a most valuable back line.[8]

The strict emphasis on close-order drill was, along with Bible class, the fundamental activity of the Brigade, the method by which

Sir William Smith hoped to bring all his members "towards a true Christian manliness."[9] The efficacy of such exercises in fashioning loyal "slaves of duty" commended them, without apology or hesitation, to a wide variety of socially concerned people. In celebrating its reliance on military drill and the virtues of obedience that were seen to follow from it, Baden-Powell was merely paying tribute to the most obvious point of the movement. It was perhaps less the explicit military preparation induced by the drill that was important than the overall aim of the character training, the production of that dependable, "best type of citizen" on whom one could count in times of peace as well as war. Before the formation of the Scouts made militarism a sensitive political matter requiring deft handling, Baden-Powell had no difficulty finding the Brigade's military tendencies not only defensible but even crucial. Discipline, the essential prescription for the healthy soldier, was necessarily the treatment of choice for any moral or civic weakness. For Baden-Powell, the soldier, more than any other human type, embodied the fullest range of essential virtues.

It had not, of course, always been the case that the soldier was regarded as an agent of impeccable and even heroic moral splendor. He began the nineteenth century as a lout of low degree, not a character to emulate. His climb out of disreputableness, stimulated by the Crimean War, is a complex one that Olive Anderson has examined,[10] but it satisfies our purposes to say that by the end of the century the military life offered redemption where previously it smacked of sin. Nurtured by various strains of Christianity, both evangelical and muscular, Christian heroes and intrepid Tommy Atkinses emerged from the bloated, rather seedy chrysalis of their dubious predecessors. The soldierly life now taught a potent blend of service and selflessness that guaranteed not only military strength but civic greatness as well. The citizen, it was obvious, had much to learn from the soldier.

The enthusiasm for the soldier as moral exemplar was heightened by the Boer War. It was not the fact that the British army returned in glory but, on the contrary, its difficulty in subduing the Boers that emphasized the importance of the individual fighting man. If he conducted himself admirably, he was let down by an inept, unprepared general staff. Imperial might turned out to be far less mighty than anyone had previously thought. One of the disturbing statistics to come out of the war was the frequently cited discovery of Sir Frederick Maurice's that only two out of five recruits were physically qualified to be in the army.[11] The methodological murkiness of the formulation notwithstanding,[12] the 60 percent failure rate became a kind of metaphoric statement of Britain's difficulties, capable of conjuring up in a single number the most awful specter of imperial collapse. The words "60 percent" defined the peril of the empire; "60 percent" helped initiate the Inter-Departmental Committee on Physical Deterioration in 1903, which sought to examine the serious questions raised by Maurice's report. Although the conclusions of the report found no evidence of any deterioration in the population at large, the title of the committee seemed to say that there was, and the existence of the committee itself was generally taken as documentary proof of that fact. Together the "60 percent" and the Inter-Departmental Committee sounded an ominous warning that was picked up by reformers of every sort.

National renewal through a vast effort at national efficiency[13] became the theme permeating nearly every sphere of British life— political, social, economic, and military as well. Vital to all these efforts was the perceived need for a freshly disciplined nation ready to meet the challenges of urban decay, foreign military power, and industrial competition through a race of citizen–patriots prepared to make sacrifices for the good of the empire. The trope of the imperiled island figured heavily in the rhetoric of military and social reformers alike as they evoked the vulnerability of their nation in an effort to elicit popular support. Besieged by slackers and socialists within and aggressive, covetous empires without, Britain required loyal service, which made distinctions between civilian and military seem trivial. "Good citizens and useful colonists," Baden-Powell had said; above all, men who knew how to obey, whether in the field or at home. As his own initial response to his nation's crisis, Baden-Powell's Eton proposal of 1904, with its two thousand armed retainers ready to fight by the end of Christmas vacation, certainly indicates no reluctance to avow a conscious military purpose.

Ironically Baden-Powell had to contend not just with his critics who objected to the militarism they found in the movement, but also with those fervent supporters who arrived at the same conclusions about Scouting but were in fact delighted at the rudimentary military readiness it conferred. If the opposition—disaffected former Scout officials like Ernest Thompson Seton, John Hargrave, and Francis Fletcher Vane, as well as various pacifist organizations, socialist journals, and the like—could be dismissed as failing to understand Scouting's real mission, it was obviously more difficult to temper the enthusiasm of friendly advocates of the movement. And so we rarely find Baden-Powell addressing himself to the misguided approbation of those who took for granted the paramilitary nature of Scouting. Ian Hamilton, an old Boer War colleague of Baden-Powell's who preferred compulsory cadet training in the schools to conscription, argued that the voluntary youth groups were already preparing Britain's youth for its military responsibility:

> ... open your eyes, be bold, be honest, school cadet corps, boys' brigades, church lads' brigades, and boy scouts have a direct bearing on war and the defense of the country. Those serving in them are not playing a silly game. They are doing something quite intensely real, more real perhaps than the things the fathers and mothers of those cadets and scouts are doing.[14]

The country needed to further the efforts to train boys in the proper way:

> Were their neither competitors nor menace we could afford to relegate this task of leavening the vast lump of selfishness, slackness, and anaemia to the efforts of the small band of amateur enthusiasts who are now giving real education to some 8 percent of our boys—the numbers of boys I mean now enrolled in the corps having *some* sort of military flavour with them, from Baden-Powell Scouts at one end of the scale to corps recognized by Territorial Force County Associations at the other. *But there is no time.* We must help General Baden-Powell by giving him some schooltrained and disciplined boys to work upon with his voluntary system.[15]

For Hamilton, the most effective way of combatting the selfishness fostered by Britain's commercial and political system was through "organisations either frankly military like the Territorial Force, or trained on a military pattern like Boys' Brigades, Church Lads' Brigades, Baden-Powell Scouts, and the Salvation Army."[16]

Eric George, who wanted to require military training of all boys between the ages of fourteen and sixteen, pointed out that such training was currently being made available on a voluntary basis:

> Again, there is the analogy of the Boys' Brigades and Boy Scouts, to which organisations there are few who take exception. Perhaps this is because they are often connected with some particular sect or church, and consequently some such casuistry is employed to salve the anti-militaristic conscience,

as that the possible harm of mock-soldiering is more than counter-balanced by the immense amount of good that is instilled into the boys with their sectarian prejudices.[17]

George had no doubts at all about what the Scouts were doing:

> Give the boy the art [of military training], and he will himself wish to continue to have an opportunity to practice that art, whether in the Regulars or Territorials. The argument is amply supported by the reports of the Industrial Schools and similar semi-military institutions. The percentage of boys who join the Regular Forces therefrom is very high, and almost any noncom will agree that they make the best soldiers. They supply numbers; they also supply quality. Similarly the number of young men who, having been members of the Boys' Brigades and Boy Scouts, show their appreciation of camp life and military training by proceeding from these to the ranks of the Territorials, goes to prove Lord Roberts's statement [The possession of an art ... stimulates the wish to practice that art].[18]

The pages of *The Nation in Arms*, the journal of the National Service League (see below), which called for universal military training, were filled with praise for the role of the Scouts in indoctrinating British youth with the proper ideals and practices:

> On Friday evening, 20th March ... Lord Brassey ... inspected 376 of all ranks of the Cadet Corps companies attached to the 1st Sussex Royal Engineers, the Boys' and Church Lads' Brigades, the Hastings and St. Leonard's Cadet Corps for Working Lads, and the Boy Scouts for the Hastings District. The smart appearance and soldierly bearing of the lads was most noticeable, and the quiet and systematic way in which each unit moved showed the careful training the lads had received, which must go to prove the advantage of the system advocated by the League, that every boy at school should receive military training.[19]

A reporter for the Newcastle *Journal* was enthusiastic about the possibility that the War Office might take a number of youth organizations under its wing:

> There are the Boy Scouts, numbering about 200,000; the Boys' Brigades, 65,000; the Church Lads' Brigade, 47,000; the

Catholic Boys' Brigade, 4,000; and the Jewish Lads' Brigade, 3,000.... The reason of this proposed grouping of various Boys' Brigades is the inculcation of a military spirit in the youth of the land. It is in opposition to the teachings of the Socialists, little Englanders, and the peace-at-any-price folk, but for many reasons it is much to be commended. It will mean much for the defence of the Empire ... and besides, there will be a tremendous impetus given to the military ardour of our boys if their efforts are regarded as part of our military system.[20]

Roger Pocock, the commissioner of the Legion of Frontiersmen and a great admirer of the Scouts, pointed out in a letter to Ernest Thompson Seton that his scheme of the Woodcraft Indians "closely resembles that of Baden-Powell's Boy Scouts, the main difference being that the American Organization is civil, and the British military in conception. Both of them are of the highest educational value."[21] In short, no one concerned with the military strength of the country could fail to see the possibilities generated by Baden-Powell's obedient Scouts:

But we are here to-night only as members of the National Defence Association, and our immediate question is, What are the more direct results of this Boy Scout movement likely to be, so far as regards National Defence? Well, Sir Robert has told us that so far as experience has gone they contribute a large percentage of their numbers to our military service. I think we may look forward in the future, when the movement has grown to its full dimensions, to our drawing the bulk of our recruits, both for the Regular Army and for the Territorial Force, from Sir Robert's boys.[22]

The usefulness of Scout training, by which Baden-Powell largely means the experience of following orders, in preparing boys to be soldiers provided him with one of his major assets as he began his campaign to arouse public interest in the movement. Although his argument for concerned parents assured them that Scouts had nothing to do with soldiering, his appeal to the military establishment whose support he always sought was precisely that Scouting produced the best possible material for the army.

Addressing a meeting of the National Defence Association in 1908 on the training of men for the Territorial Forces, Baden-Powell surveyed the various groups available for home defense:

In the same way I think a potential recruiting ground or reserve lies in the enormous number of Boys' Clubs, Cadets, Rifle Clubs, Boys' Brigades, Boy Scouts, etc., where the fellows are only too willing to learn a little of soldiering. Even though some of them are religious organisations, they all seem to like drill and shooting; and I think it is a pity not to encourage them whenever one can. I am myself associated with one particular lot, and I am told that if we could only find Officers we could get at once thousands of them in every town; and they are nearly all anxious to do something in the way of soldiering. This would be a splendid thing, and only wants a little encouragement.... I venture to think that parades of Veterans, Homeland Defence, Rifle Clubs, and Boys' organisations on certain holidays and other occasions, in public, might be of the greatest assistance; they would do a good deal towards putting the spirit of soldiering into their counties, and would certainly be of very great help in training the Force with which we have to deal.[23]

For Baden-Powell, Scout training was effective in encouraging interest in the army precisely by its avoidance of military drill. Not only does it keep boys from bogging down in routinized work, but it also attracts those who would not willingly associate with anything overtly militaristic:

We do not take up soldiering as part of our main policy, not only on account of the drill, but because we find that we get in a large proportion of boys who would otherwise escape any of these organisations—whose parents object to military drill in any form. They think if we drill them that we are going to make soldiers of them at once ... so by not insisting on military drill we catch a lot of boys who would otherwise have no idea of coming into the education that we are trying to give. We put patriotism and self-sacrifice into them, and there is no doubt that after they have learnt a certain amount of that, and of their duty to their country, they will feel bound to take up the defence in one form or another, should it be necessary, when the time comes.[24]

The consequence therefore would be a large number of boys eagerly embracing national service—further reason why the Scouts were preferable to the Cadet Corps or the Boys' Brigade:

> Although our policy is not to make the boys into soldiers,
> but as a first aim to make them good citizens, the results show
> that a very large proportion of our boys who have left us have
> gone into the Service.[25]

Baden-Powell demonstrates the efficacy of his peace Scouts in attracting people into the army by claiming that only 10 percent of
Cadets went on to join in contrast to about 70 percent of his Scouts.
Whatever the accuracy of the figures, it remains a curious justification for a nonmilitaristic movement to make, regardless of how
much it stressed national defense only.

The most persistent and important organization pressing for Britain's enhanced military might was the National Service League—
founded in 1902 by Lord Newton—which called for universal military training for all able-bodied men between eighteen and
twenty-three. The League was the single most influential voice in
putting Britain's vulnerability before the nation.[26] Speaking
through its own journal (first the *National Service Journal*, later *The
Nation in Arms*), the National Service League kept up a steady
barrage of concern about Britain's weakness and the steps necessary
to rectify it. Its goals, its rhetoric, and its analysis of national peril
all appeared in various forms in the program and rationale of the
Scouting movement.

The League was for all practical purposes launched with the
publication of George Shee's *The Briton's First Duty* (1901). Shee,
later its secretary, was "as a citizen of this empire, speaking to my
fellow citizens, as one dearly loving his country to the millions who
share that feeling,"[27] to explain to them their dire predicament.
Invoking his love of Britain at every turn, he details with much
statistical evidence the rapid decline in Britain's military strength
over the course of the nineteenth century. From a population in
which one man in ten could bear arms, Britain had deteriorated to
a population in 1898 in which only one in twenty-four was so
capable, leaving the army dangerously undermanned:

> Thus, while the area of the British Empire has increased
> more than tenfold and its population eightfold, the total of
> the regular army was only about 30,000 more in 1898 than in
> 1805—excluding the army in India it was 30,000 *less* than in
> 1805—while there were 125,000 *less* men "in arms" in the
> United Kingdom.[28]

Shee finds the army absolutely inadequate both in regard to the enormous expansion of the empire and to the vast armed forces (and covetous impulses) of the continental powers. After criticizing the "blue water" school of military thinkers, who held that England required only a strong navy to ensure that it would never be invaded, Shee depicts the grim international scene, where "It is an undeniable fact that at the present time we are regarded with more or less openly expressed hatred and distrust by nearly every important European power."[29] The imperiled island is never more so than in Shee's analysis. Beginning with the French, who "hate us far worse than they hate the Germans,"[30] he runs through practically every other major power, including Japan, to show how unfriendly all are to Britain. With a navy that can't guarantee safety from invasion and an army that is too weak to protect the vast empire, Britain is in a dire state indeed.

Shee locates the solution to the crisis in a system of universal military training in which every able-bodied man will undergo a period of active service, followed by a period in the Reserve. Although the specifics of Shee's proposal differed in some minor details from the proposals finally adopted by the League, the call for military training for every qualified male constituted its essential program. The League devoted itself for the next fourteen years to implementing this goal. But beyond equipping the League with its object, Shee also endowed it with its basic justification, which, for understanding Scouting, is as important as its aim. Shee's system did not merely render Britain secure from invasion and its empire immune from attack; it engendered true patriotism by bringing together all classes, improving the health of the nation, and inculcating a true sense of duty. This last is perhaps the most interesting for our purposes:

> The training of the whole manhood of the nation in discipline, duty, obedience to authority, manliness and self-mastery would prove a *moral* and *intellectual* factor of untold value in the life of the people, which our officers, knowing that they were forming not merely soldiers, but citizens, would by precept and example place before their men in a high ideal of duty.... During his period of military service every man learns the lesson of discipline, ready obedience to authority, absolute devotion to duty, and thoroughness in the performance of the smallest detail.... Above all, he realizes that he, mere unit though he be, has a real share in his country's fate; he knows that at any moment he may be called upon to defend that

country; in a word, he feels the warm glow of true patriotism which comes with the liability and the readiness to lay down his life in his country's service.[31]

Baden-Powell himself could not have written a more succinct appreciation of what the Boy Scout movement hoped to achieve. Point by point it summarizes the ideals behind the Scouts. Shee's view of what ailed the nation was Baden-Powell's as well: people who

> think less of *duty* and more of *pleasure*, especially in its more expensive and unhealthy forms.... The increased facilities of communication, the cheapness and wide dissemination of a very low type of "Literature"... the growing extravagance and vulgarity of dress among the working classes, the large number of low-class music-halls, the undoubted *decrease* of *bona-fide* athletic sports, coupled with the debatable development of professionalism, and of contests which are rapidly degenerating into gladiatorial shows—all these things are at once the causes and the outward symptoms of a tendency to seek amusement in vicious and unhealthy forms.[32]

What might appear a major distinction—the League's aim of universal service—is in fact altogether minor, for the essential ingredient of the League's program was that same indoctrination of discipline and patriotism central to Scouting. Eschewing all military drill as they did, the Scouts nevertheless provided exactly the sort of training that the League found most valuable for its goals. As Lord Roberts maintained,

> The training of the rank and file for war consists in teaching three things—drill, musketry (or gunnery) and discipline. But of these essentials, discipline is by far the most essential, for discipline, even more than drill or musketry, leads to victory, and discipline cannot be imparted in small doses.[33]

Although George Shee provided much of the early inspiration, for the League, it was Roberts, Baden-Powell's former commander-in-chief during the Boer War, who became its vitalizing presence. Taking up the presidency of the League in 1905, following his resignation from the Imperial Defence Committee, "old Bobs" was indefatigable in proselytizing for its goals. Britain's most distinguished general, he commanded great respect as he stumped the country lecturing on the imminent threat of invasion, the moral decay sapping the strength of the nation, and the need for the compulsory military training that would solve both. At a time when purveyors of crisis abounded, few spoke with the passion or the certitude—or expertise—of the country's greatest soldier. Listening to Roberts, it was hard not to think that at that very moment Germany was about to set sail for England:

> Our German friends ... in their heart of hearts they know, every man of them, that just as in 1866 and just as in 1870, war will take place the instant the German forces by land and sea are, by their superiority at every point, as certain of victory as anything in human calculation can be made certain. "Germany strikes when Germany's hour has struck." That is the time honoured policy of her Foreign Office.[34]

Far from decrying such a policy, Roberts saw it as necessary and inevitable, "the policy of every nation prepared to play a great part in history. Under that policy Germany has, within the last ten years sprung, as at a bound, from one of the weakest of naval powers to the greatest naval power, save one, upon this globe."[35] Like Japan, whose seizure of Port Arthur from the Russians immediately elevated it, in the eyes of the National Service Leaguers and others, to a model for the British, Germany was always admired for the fanatical patriotism and discipline of its people. Though regarded as dangerous and potentially hostile, Germans were nevertheless esteemed for their military efficiency:

> How impressive is this magnificent and unresting energy. It has the mark of true greatness; it extorts admiration even from those against whom it is directed.[36]

For Roberts, the greatness of a nation was embodied in the greatness of its armed forces, which "should be the measure of the nation's devotion to whatever ends it pursued."[37] His message to the people of Manchester—and the citizens of Great Britain—was finally a simple one: "Arm and prepare to quit yourselves like men, for the time of your ordeal is at hand."[38] It was a message to which Baden-Powell was particularly sensitive, and the connections between League and Scouts went beyond a common ideology. In 1911, the Boy Scout Council, the policy-making body of the organization, included six men who were at one time or another prominent members of the National Service League: Vice Admiral

Charles Beresford; General Edmund Elles; Major General Sir Ronald Lane; the earl of Meath; the headmaster of Eton, Reverend Lyttelton; and Lord Roberts. Baden-Powell, we remember, originally sent his 1906 prospectus on the Boy Scouts to Beresford and Roberts for their comments. The presence of National Service League members on the council represented what some took to be symptoms of a larger problem. As an ex-military man, Baden-Powell would naturally have had recourse to other former officers when it came to appointing his Scout officials. And as he pointed out, retired army officers would be likely to have the leisure and interest to involve themselves in youth work. Nevertheless, the fact that

> in 1910, out of the 250 Presidents and Commissioners of Boy Scouts, 140 were classified as military officers, both serving and retired; by 1912, out of a total of 352, there were 247 military men running the Scouts in Britain,[39]

cannot be explained by mere convenience and familiarity. It is easy to see why Sir Francis Vane, the first Scout commissioner of London, who was later driven out of the movement, thought that Scouting had to be rescued from degenerating "into simply a recruiting ground for the army."[40] For him it was all too clear that

> the militarists who had made no appreciable success of their crusade in favour of universal military training, wisely saw that by this flourishing organisation they might arrive at their aims under the cloak of Peace Scouting.... The Council of the Baden-Powell movement, as soon as General Baden-Powell had been permitted to have a council at all, was almost entirely recruited from ex-generals or colonels, and among them such eminent "Peace" Scouts as are Lord Roberts, Lord Charles Beresford and General Elles, all of whom are leading members of the National Service League. In fact it became a military cabal controlling a great educational movement.[41]

While there is no evidence that the League ever attempted to influence Scout policy, it was certainly not surprising that when the League went out of existence in 1921, following the achievement of conscription during World War I, it donated its assets of £12,000 to the Scouts as the organization that "most successfully teaches the ideals of citizenship of which Lord Roberts' scheme was a part."[42]

*   *   *

The National Service League was the most influential organization lobbying for a militant patriotism, but it was not the only one. The concern for Britain's moral and physical decay and the solution that a disciplined citizenry seemed to offer were shared by any number of groups at the start of the century. Lord Meath, who was passionately committed to the notion of military training for youth and whose name appears on the executive committee of almost all these organizations, founded his own, the Lads' Drill Association in 1899, whose object was the "Systematic Physical and Military Training of All British Lads."[43] Meath was totally convinced of the redemptive powers of military training. The Association tried to "emphasize the importance, if the Empire is to be maintained, of training to arms, during the educative portion of their lives, the entire male youth of the British race, confident that in time of real danger the great mass would voluntarily offer their services to the state." Such training would not only bolster the armed forces, it would "be of inestimable advantage in reforming the loafing elements to be found amongst all classes, and would implant in the youthful mind a respect for the manly virtues which tend towards the manufacture of good and useful citizens."[44]

The affinity between Association and the National Service League (and their two leaders) was such that Roberts permitted the Association to publish his important admonitory address, "Defence of the Empire", with an introduction by Meath. In it Meath makes clear that he hopes that the publication of Roberts's speech "may hasten the time when by the adoption of the above proposals, supplemented by the detailed recommendations of so eminent an authority as Lord Roberts, the British nation and people may be effectually safeguarded against all danger of hostile attack." The similarities of the two organizations ultimately resulted in the Lads' Drill Association merging with the National Service League in 1906.

Founded in 1904 to keep tabs on veterans of the Boer War so that they would be available for service in any emergency, the Legion of Frontiersmen soon came to define itself as a "Self-Governing, Self-Supporting, Patriotic and Private (but not secret) Organisation, consisting of members—either unable or ineligible to serve in his Majesty's Forces—enrolled and organised with a view to their being utilised during emergency, for the maintenance of Imperial Prestige and Peace."[45] The Legion was anxious not to interfere with enlistment in the regular forces, including the Territorials, which accounted for the curious restriction of limiting membership to those with prior military training who were unable or ineligible to serve elsewhere. There were three classes of membership—those

pledged to take up active service anywhere; those pledged to undertake home defense if called upon; and those merely sympathetic
to the aims of the Legion. Providing a pool of experienced men
prepared to augment His Majesty's forces in time of war, the
Legion also set itself to address the alleged lack of discipline and
sense of duty that were undermining Britain's greatness:

> Conscious cowardice, conscious meanness, are foreign to the
> British character. But as to the unconscious kind, the burden
> of it lies heavily upon England at this moment. Its existence
> must be realised before it can be removed. . . .
>
> Our people are more in need of the advantages to be gained
> from discipline, self-denial, and a clear sense of grave responsi-
> bility than anything else. The lesson which, I believe, Fron-
> tiersmen could help us to teach is, that the able-bodied man
> who declines to undergo any form of military training is not
> quite a complete man. England expects and needs that every
> able-bodied man should do his duty, and fulfill honourably
> the responsibilities of citizenship, instead of thinking only of
> the privileges.[46]

The Legion was officially recognized by the British War Office in
1906, and shortly thereafter started publication of its own journal,
The Frontiersman.

In their efforts to indoctrinate the nation with the need for loyalty and military preparedness, the Legionnaires understandably
and actively supported the Scout movement, whose aims they saw
as identical with their own. The pages of *The Frontiersman* are filled
with laudatory references to the qualities of Scout character-training, and to its role in the "making of a good citizen and ... the
making of a possible young soldier and defender of the Empire."[47]
Indeed, regulation 77 in their official constitution requires every
Legionnaire to support the Scouts in any way he can:

> 77. All members of the Legion are directed, as far as lies in
> their power, to assist the Boy Scouts, the Boys' Brigade, and
> the Church Lads' Brigade, on the ground that by encouraging
> training of the kind involved in these movements respectively,
> they are promoting the essential conditions to an early con-
> ception of discipline, of technical knowledge, and of the value
> of organised and united effort, upon which the Defence Forces
> of the British Empire must ever rely for success in emergency.

(The Legion's admiration for the Scouts was reciprocated. A footnote to regulation 77 reads, "Lieut.-General Sir Robert Baden-Powell, K.C.B., K.C.V.O., the 'Chief Scout,' desires, in connection with this regulation, to state that, as members of the Legion of Frontiersmen are greatly respected by all Boy Scouts, the Legion is capable of exercising an immense influence for good in this direction.")[48]

While hardy frontiersmen and waiters might appear to have little in common with one another, the Loyal British Waiters Society, founded in 1910, shared the Legion's patriotic ideals. With its motto, "Loyalty is Strength," the Society sought, in addition to finding employment for British-born waiters, "to inculcate a correct conception of duty towards employers and in relation to the Empire." As an article states in *The Frontiersman*, the Society is committed to "maintaining and preserving the peace and promoting the prosperity of the Empire."[49] In response to the threat to England posed by hordes of genetically dubious aliens, the Society staunchly stood up for the rights of the besieged natives: "We do not want official England overcome by foreigners to the prejudice of national and Imperial prosperity.... We want England ... to be a land of loyal freedom."[50] Their effort to train and place waiters prepared to serve both customers and king with zeal was closely followed by the Loyal British Hairdressers Society, which wanted to further the interests of the same kind of deserving men. Both organizations were clearly in sympathy with the aims and rhetoric of Scouts and Legionnaires alike.

Another symptom of the era's anxieties was the Duty and Discipline movement. Designed to bring England back to a proper respect for authority, it issued in 1911 a bulky volume of essays lamenting the severe deterioration of behavior, particularly children's behavior, and extolling the salutary glories of discipline:

> This series is being published, not for profit, but with a view to counteract the lack of adequate moral training and discipline, the effects of which are so apparent in these days amongst many British children, in rich as well as in poor homes.
> The writers feel strongly that the present juvenile indiscipline is a serious social danger, and a peril to the permanent security of the Empire. In this view they are supported by many men and women eminent in varying lines of thought and action....[51]

The eminences, 192 in all, read like a list of who's who among the morally concerned: Baden-Powell, Roberts, Admiral Beresford, Meath, Churchill, Conan-Doyle, Kitchener, Roseberry, Cromer, Curzon, Milner, Arnold White, General Booth, and the like. In a note following the table of contents the publishers indicate that their contributors are unified in their shared distress at the "very generally acknowledged growth of indiscipline amongst British children of all classes, the decay among many of them of a sense of duty, and ... the apparent gradual disappearance of the ancient British determination to overcome difficulties by the force of a strong will, which declined under all circumstances to recognise even the possibility of defeat."

The titles of some of the entries suggest the overall character of the book: "The Early Training of Boys in Citizenship," "Have We the 'Grit' of Our Forefathers?" "Endure Hardness," "Discipline and Training in the Prevention of Nervous Diseases," "Responsibility for the Moral Education of Youth," and "The Model Childhood," among others, including a piece by Baden-Powell on "British Discipline" and "An Appeal to British Boys and Girls" by Lord Roberts. All the usual lamentations and remedies are here. The complaint that the diminishing birthrate "shows that women are showing the 'white feather,' that they prefer amusements, sports, and idleness to the sweet toils and endless duties of motherhood";[52] the weakness and effeminacy of modern educational ideals that stress joy at the expense of duty and compulsion; the dangers of individualism; the greatness of the Japanese principle of self-sacrifice; the need for military training. Fleet Engineer Quick, R.N. Retired, believing in the "sanctifying power of the whip,"[53] recommends "flogging in lieu of imprisonment in certain cases, so that, in the case of a married man, the wife and family shall suffer as little as possible."[54] Lady Massie Blomfield, disturbed by the lack of obedience in children, argues for the salutary effects of instituting morning drill in the nursery for even the youngest children:

A morning drill, before the children are dressed, is an excellent way of beginning the systematic training of the will of the child, and this is particularly useful when begun at an early age. By this morning drill, which ought to last from five to thirty minutes—according to the age of the children—you get them accustomed to obey smartly the words of command, and so train brain and limbs to work quickly and easily together. These baby soldiers will quite enjoy their lesson in obedience and alertness. . . .

Now, the first words of command are "Stand up" (and insist on a smart obedience), then, "Attention" (heels together, head up, shoulders back, hands by side), "Salute" (hand to the forehead), "Hands behind head," "Hands on shoulders," "Quick march," "Right turn," "Left turn," "Right about turn" (turn right around), "High step," "Double" (running), "Half," etc. During this morning drill do not scold the child, nor even talk to him, nor must you allow the child to talk during the drill lesson. If the child, however, wishes to speak to you, it must first salute, and then you give it leave to do so.... You will soon find that this morning drill will give you the control over your children which you lack. It will, therefore, help you as well as your boys and girls, and when you have once obtained obedience the rest will follow naturally.[55]

The earl of Meath calls attention to the "general slackness amongst all classes of our population in regard to the performance of duty—a slackness which is weakening to the moral fibre,"[56] and Magistrate Horace Smith attributes crime among the lower classes to the tendency among poor parents to spoil their children: "Be they ever so poor, they contrive to indulge their babies and treat them merely as pets to be spoiled."[57] In short, the book seeks to help bring about "the creation of a public opinion favourable to a *stricter* discipline in the training of British children,"[58] which the Most Reverend J. F. Peacock feels is desperately needed if Britain is to survive. With such aspirations, it is easy to see why Scouting found an adult audience eager to support it. Secretary of State for War Haldane spoke for the society as a whole when he welcomed Scouting, "from the point of view of education; I welcome it from the point of view of the War Office; I welcome it from the point of view of the national good."[59]

If National Service League members were instrumental in dispensing throughout Britain that invasion panic on which the Scouts capitalized, they by no means invented the idea or alone were even responsible for popularizing it. Similar scares had periodically broken out in Britain well before the League directed its energies to popularizing the German threat of the early twentieth century. In *The Six Panics and Other Essays*, F.W. Hirst[60] argues that there were at least three major ones earlier in the nineteenth century—those of 1847-48, 1851-53, and 1859-61—all of which were exclusively French and, in his view, as hysterical and unfounded as the German threat. W. T. Stead, the influential editor of *Review of Reviews*, managed to induce a minor one involving the Germans in 1884. Not as significant as the others, it nevertheless did manage to stimulate again the expansion of naval armaments that had essentially been dormant during the noncrisis period of 1862–84.

As Hirst indicates, those occurring during the late forties and fifties were French, but as early as 1871 George Chesney anticipated with remarkable accuracy the National Service League's anxieties of a German invasion in his fictional *The Battle of Dorking*. Chesney, a retired army officer, detailed the consequences of a German surprise attack on an unsuspecting nation that had too long been complacent in the security afforded it by its unmatched navy. Although the interest of the book, insofar as it has any, lies in the sensational subject matter and the narrative details of the battle, it is in fact a polemic in the guise of a novel, railing against the same apathy, ignorance, and lack of will power from which the League sought to save Britain some thirty-five years later. Chesney's analysis might well have appeared in the pages of *The Nation in Arms*:

> The warnings of the few were drowned in the voice of the multitude. Power was then passing away from the class which had been used to rule, and to face political dangers, and which had brought the nation with honour unsullied through former struggles, into the hands of the lower classes, uneducated, untrained to the use of political rights, and swayed by demagogues; and the few who were wise in their generation were denounced as alarmists, or as aristocrats who sought their own aggrandizement by wasting public money on bloated armaments. The rich were idle and luxurious, the poor grudged the cost of defence. Politics had become a mere bidding for radical votes.... But when I reflect how a little firmness and self-denial, or political courage and foresight, might have averted the disaster, I feel that the judgment must really have been deserved. A nation too selfish to defend its liberty, could not have been fit to retain it.[61]

Chesney's fantasy was the predecessor of a substantial number of novels and plays written prior to World War I that can almost be thought of as constituting a subgenre of invasions literature.[62] If Britain was fortunate enough to have the German plans scuttled by the enterprising hero of Erskine Childers' *Riddle of the Sands* (1903), it had no such savior in William LeQueux's extraordinary bestseller, *The Invasion of 1910*, written in 1906. LeQueux believed fervently that only Lord Roberts and universal military training stood between England and the German occupation; the book constitutes a warning to the British people of what they must do to avoid catastrophe:

> The object of this book is to illustrate our utter unpreparedness for war from a military standpoint; to show how, under certain conditions which may easily occur, England can be successfully invaded by Germany; and to present a picture of the ruin which must inevitably fall upon us on the evening of that not far-distant day.[63]

LeQueux actually discussed with Roberts, the naval writer H. W. Wilson, and others the most likely scenario for an invasion, so that the details in his book represent the best wisdom of "the highest authorities on strategy."[64] That the attack begins on a Sunday, for example, was not accidental but established strategic consensus that as Sunday was the time of least national readiness, it would unquestionably be that day on which the Hun would arrive on England's shores. (Some tactical adjustment had to be made for sound commercial motives, however. Alfred Harmsworth, who was serializing portions in the *Daily Mail*, insisted that the German approaches to London pass through centers of larger newspaper circulation than had originally been planned. The German high command adopted his suggestions.)

LeQueux documents in minute detail the course of the battles and the inevitable path to London that the well-armed, well-disciplined German soldiers beat against the courageous but uncoordinated, poorly trained British resistance. National Service League moralizing punctuates the defeats, bringing home the message of why this happened:

> "Who, then, was responsible?" it may well be asked. The answer is simple. The British public, which, in its apathetic attitude towards military efficiency, aided and abetted by the soothing theories of the extremists of the "Blue Water" school, had, as usual, neglected to provide an Army fitted to cope in numbers and efficiency with those of our continental neighbours.[65]

> Everywhere people were regretting that Lord Roberts's solemn warnings in 1906 had been unheeded, for had we

adopted his scheme for universal service such dire catastrophe could not have occurred. Many had, alas! declared it to be synonymous with conscription, which it certainly was not, and by that foolish argument had prevented the public at large from accepting it as the only means to our salvation as a nation.[66]

In London we fail because we have so few riflemen. If every man who now carries a gun could shoot, we could compel the Germans to fly a flag of truce within twenty-four hours. Indeed, if Lord Roberts' scheme of universal military training in 1906 had been adopted, the enemy would certainly never have been suffered to approach our capital.[67]

English forces finally manage to save the situation at the end, but not before untold damage had been done and the lesson of unpreparedness brought home to the public in graphic terms.

The Invasion of 1910 was the most successful and influential work of this rather specialized genre, translated into twenty-seven languages and selling over 1 million copies in all. It helped disseminate anxieties about Britain's vulnerability, stimulating public interest in organizations like the National Service League and the Boy Scouts.

Another popular work that sought to raise public consciousness was *An Englishman's Home*, a play written in 1909 by Guy du Maurier. An officer in the Royal Fusiliers, du Maurier demonstrated the tragic results of the absence of compulsory training. The *Spectator* commented that "The country is in excitement over a play which sets forth the physical horrors of invasion and the moral horror that comes to those who are crushed by a great disaster which a little care and forethought might have prevented."[68] The invaders from "Nearland," a country in the north whose highly disciplined soldiers seem suspiciously Prussian in character, encounter no real resistance from an unprepared and physically deficient group of British citizens who can do little to defend themselves. The volunteers who try to drive them out are no more successful, and it is only with the arrival of the regular British army at the end that things begin to improve. Unequivocally bad, the play was nevertheless a commercial success—suggesting the degree to which it caught the anxiety of the period. According to the *Times*, it encouraged an increase in the number of recruits joining the London Territorials. Despite this, and despite the fact that the play clearly sounds the call for compulsory military training, the National

Service League thought it a failure, artistically and educationally, because of its conventional happy ending. The costs of an untrained citizenry were too grave to be vitiated by the dramatic appearance of the British army.

In response to this misdirected effort, B. S. Townroe, an ardent National Service Leaguer, wrote a play, *A Nation in Arms*, which toured various cities in England from September to November 1909. Here there was no escape from the failure to be prepared. The young bridegroom who had resisted joining the Territorial Force is found by the invading forces with a gun in his hand and, as a civilian, is condemned to be shot. His wife is driven mad with despair. Amidst all the misery the point of the play emerges clearly, as *The Nation in Arms* emphasized:

> But the chief lesson to be brought home is that invasion is possible; that an undefended nation practically invites it, and deserves all the horrors that invasion invites. It is no use locking your door after the steed is stolen; it is no use declaring yourself ready to defend your country when the enemy are on your shores.... Why should you not take common precautionary measures in defending your country? It is a simple lesson, as old as the hills, that the new play is trying to teach. It surely cannot fail to make a permanent impression on many of the audience.[69]

Townroe's view of the crisis and the importance of the Boy Scouts in solving it was summarized later the same year in *The Nation in Arms*:

> In this respect the Boy Scouts promise to be an enormous strength to our cause. Once let the advantages of military training be apparent, not in cold argument, but in the smart keen little body of a Boy Scout, and we have won over the Fathers and Mothers. The nightly experience of public opinion, as shown by the clapping of unconverted hands, may be summed up in these sentences—
>
> 1. The man in the street is not deceived by the present make believe of a citizen army.
> 2. Every Territorial and Boy Scout is a stepping stone to national service.
> 3. The way League arguments are appreciated, even by those who have never heard of the League, shows that, given time, we are on the road to victory.[70]

As grim as Townroe's play—and as devoid of literary value—is W. Douglas Newton's *War*, a novel published in 1914. Bearing with it a cautionary introduction by Rudyard Kipling, who inveighs against England's vast indifference to its own security and the lies and delusion by which it chooses to remain blind to imminent catastrophe, it stresses, like the others, the consequences of unpreparedness. Its unprepared protagonist, Rafael Bruns, witnesses the devastation that a highly professionalized (if unnamed) army wreaks upon an unsuspecting England. In addition to its gory details and preposterously clotted rhetoric, a unique feature of *War* rests in its entrusting the standard assault on English apathy to an *enemy* officer. Following one of the many bloody skirmishes, Bruns tries to enlist an enemy physician to look after some of the badly wounded British women. Bruns is horrified when he refuses, claiming he must attend to his own men. In response to Bruns's agonized cry that "Nobody ever told me it was like this,"[71] the officer delivers a scathing attack that might have been written by Lord Roberts himself:

> Ay, they never told you. It wasn't nice. It wasn't good form. The horrors are too revolting to put before comfortable, domestic people. You mustn't be shocked. All the same the horrors *are*. They always are, they always have been, they always will be. And you never know. It would be bad taste to shock you. Bah—you precious, comfortable, sit-at-home hypocrites make me sick. You never know, you don't try to know, and so you don't care. It's because you didn't care that they've happened. You're the cause of all this—you—*you*. Why didn't you find out all about it and try to prevent it happening to you? [72]

Bruns's punishment for his complacency is not limited to a painful insight. Losing his mind after his gentle wife, Agnes, is raped, Bruns kills several enemy soldiers, and as a civilian is condemned to death. He realizes, after all, that it was his own fault—as well as the fault of all those who did nothing about the possibility of war coming to their shores. The final sentence sounds the message of the entire novel: "A thin rip of rifles slashed out in the quiet air. Another wretch had paid the price of ignorance."[73]

Perhaps the most convincing evidence of the widely acknowledged role these works played in the culture is the brilliant parody they inspired in P. G. Wodehouse's "The Swoop, or How Clarence Saved England," written in 1908. Wodehouse weaves the skeins of

invasion panic and the artistic motifs it stimulated into a marvelously wrought spoof of both the genre and the anxiety:

> Not only had the Germans effected a landing in Essex, but, in
> addition, no fewer than eight other hostile armies had, by
> some remarkable coincidence, hit on that identical moment
> for launching their long-prepared blow.
>
> England was not merely beneath the heel of the invader. It
> was beneath the heels of nine invaders.
>
> There was barely standing-room.
>
> Full details were given in the Press. It seemed that while
> Germany was landing in Essex, a strong force of Russians,
> under the Grand Duke Vodkakoff, had occupied Yarmouth.
> Simultaneously the Mad Mullah had captured Portsmouth;
> while the Swiss navy had bombarded Lyme Regis, and landed
> troops immediately to westward of the bathing-machines. At
> precisely the same moment China, at last awakened, had
> swooped down upon that picturesque little Welsh watering-
> place, Lllgxtplll, and, despite desperate resistance on the part
> of an excursion of Evanses and Joneses from Cardiff, had
> obtained a secure foothold. While these things were happening
> in Wales, the army of Monaco had descended on Auchter-
> muchty, on the Firth of Clyde. Within two minutes of this
> disaster, by Greenwich time, a boisterous band of Young
> Turks had seized Scarborough. And, at Brighton and Margate
> respectively, small but determined armies, the one of Moroc-
> can brigands under Raisuli, the other of dark-skinned warriors
> from the distant isle of Bollygolla, had made good their foot-
> ing.[74]

If only an effective parody of such concerns, "Clarence" would still
deserve mention, but in fact Wodehouse plays with something far
more interesting for our purposes, namely the paramilitary aspirations that he perceived behind the Scouts. For Clarence Chugwater,
the savior of his country, is nothing less than a Scout, and it is as
a Scout that he rescues Britain. The invasion of nine hostile armies,

> disturbing enough in itself, was rendered still more disquieting
> by the fact that, except for the Boy Scouts, England's military
> strength at this time was practically nil.[75]

With the abolition of the army, "the land defence of the country
was entrusted entirely to the Territorials, the Legion of Frontiersmen,

and the Boy Scouts."[76] But with the disbanding of the Legion and
the Territorials,

> in the end England's defenders were narrowed down to the
> Boy Scouts, of whom Clarence Chugwater was the pride, and
> a large civilian population, prepared at any moment to turn
> out for their country's sake and wave flags.[77]

Writing the same year in which the Scouts were officially launched,
Wodehouse engaged with a deft ironic touch their nationalism and
militarism. "England, my England," Clarence endlessly moans,
appalled that "Not a single member of that family was practising
with the rifle, or drilling, or learning to make bandages."[78] Even
without the considerable pleasures of Wodehouse's wit—

> He could do everything that the Boy Scout must learn to
> do. He could low like a bull. He could gurgle like a wood-
> pigeon. He could imitate the cry of the turnip in order to de-
> ceive rabbits. He could smile and whistle simultaneously in
> accordance with rule 8 (and only those who have tried this
> know how difficult it is)—[79]

"Swoop" would still remain valuable as a penetrating contemporary view of the manufactured ethos of panic and the movement
it helped to spawn.

The salvation offered Britain by the Scouts, which Wodehouse
parodies in the figure of Clarence Chugwater, plays a central and
serious role in the work of a writer with a different sensibility, H. H.
Munroe, better known as Saki. His 1913 novel, *When William Came*,
portrays a country in which the price of ignorance has already been
paid by complete capitulation before the efficient German military
might. When Murrey Yeovil, the craggy representative of the in-
domitable British gentry, returns home after an illness in Siberia
that has rendered him oblivious to world events, he finds the nation
comfortably settling into an acceptance of what everybody thinks
of as the *fait accompli*. Outraged, he learns from his physician friend
how quickly a country that had not looked to its own defense had
fallen to the scheming Germans:

> "War between two such civilized and enlightened nations is an
> impossibility," one of our leaders of public opinion had de-
> clared on the Saturday; by the following Friday the war had
> indeed become an impossibility, because we could no longer

carry it on. It burst on us with calculated suddenness, and we were just not enough, everywhere where the pressure came. Our ships were good against their ships, our seamen were better than their seamen, but our ships were not able to cope with their ships plus their superiority in aircraft. Our trained men were good against their trained men, but they could not be in several places at once, and the enemy could. Our half-trained men and our untrained men could not master the science of war at a moment's notice, and a moment's notice was all they got. The enemy were a nation apprenticed in arms, we were not even the idle apprentice: we had not deemed apprenticeship worth our while.[80]

"Bred and reared as a unit of a ruling race" (198), Yeovil refuses to accommodate himself to the apathy with which the rest of the country seems to greet German signs, German flags, German-speaking cab drivers. But resistance is futile; even if the people should rise up in rebellion, as the shrewd student of human affairs Fritz von Kwarl points out, German control of the sea and air would permit only a temporary British victory. In the short run the Germans have nothing to fear. For von Kwarl, there is but one possible obstacle to complete and permanent German control:

> The youth of the country, the generation that is at the threshold now. It is them that we must capture. We must teach them to learn, and coax them to forget. In course of time Anglo-Saxon may blend with German, as the Elbe Saxons and the Bavarians and Swabians have blended with the Prussians into a loyal united people under the sceptre of the Hohenzollerns. (195-96)

Should the Germans fail to entrap the minds of the rising generation, however, all would be vulnerable:

> On the other hand, the younger generation of Britons may grow up in hereditary hatred, repulsing all our overtures, forgetting nothing, waiting and watching for the time when some weakness assails us, when some crisis entangles us, when we cannot be everywhere at once. Then our work will be imperilled, perhaps undone. There lies the danger, there lies the hope, the younger generation. (196)

While the novel's main thrust is to excoriate, through Yeovil, the passivity, effeteness, and moral triviality of the British that made the disaster inevitable, its drama centers on the issue of the future generation's commitment. The decisive event of *When William Came*, serving as an index to the attitude of the young, is to be a massive Boy Scout parade past a reviewing stand of dignitaries in Hyde Park. The stakes attending the parade's success are clearly spelled out by the countess of Bailquist, one of the many advocates of the *fait accompli* whom Saki pillories:

> It's going to be an historical occasion ... if it miscarries it will be a serious set-back for the *fait accompli*. If it is a success it will be the biggest step forward in the path of reconciliation between the two races that has yet been taken. It will mean that the younger generation is on our side—not all, of course, but some, that is all we can expect at present, and that will be enough to work on. (283–84)

Lady Bailquist estimates that probably two-thirds of the Scouts will not participate, but even a third or a sixth would be sufficient to indicate the support the *fait accompli* has among the young. Every conceivable encouragement has been given to the Scouts to enlist them in the new order: A decoration of merit has been specially designed for them; a gymnasium and hostelry for their use established in Westminster; an athletic meeting scheduled each year for them with valuable prizes; a free holiday for several hundred of them every summer in the Bavarian highlands and the Baltic seaboard; and selected tax exemptions for the parents of all Scouts who earn the medal of efficiency. As Lady Bailquist points out, though costly, these inducements are worth creating, for the Scouts

> are going to be the Janissaries of the Empire; the younger generation knocking at the doors of progress, and thrusting back the bars and bolts of old racial prejudices. I tell you, Sir Leonard, it will be an historic moment when the first corps of those little khaki-clad boys swings through the gates of the Park. (284)

The scene is set for the great affirmation. The emperor and his retinue move to their places, along with the king of Württemburg, two Bavarian royal princes, an Abyssinian envoy, and assorted military attachés. Imperial banners flutter in the wind, and trumpets and kettledrums establish the triumphant mood. But the parade ground remains empty, and as Lady Bailquist, Cecily Yeovil, Sir

Leonard Pitherby, Grafin von Tolb, Herr Rebinok, and their companions scan the distance desperately, looking for a sign of the advancing Scouts, Murrey Yeovil, standing at the back of the crowd to witness the sad moment, realizes the magnificent truth: discouraged though he has become,

> in thousands of English homes throughout the land there were young hearts that had not forgotten, had not compounded, would not yield.
> The younger generation had barred the door. (290)

A symbol of national pride that will not submit to foreign domination, the Scouts, by their absence, make clear that Britain's rescue is at hand. Approaching the motif of Britain's vulnerability from entirely different points of view and for entirely different artistic purposes, both Wodehouse and Saki attest to the widespread nature of the concern, as well as to the role that Scouting was seen to play in a culture beset with such anxieties.

However disorganized Britain's army, it is certaintly difficult to take seriously the severity of the crisis as propounded by the National Service League. The naval authorities were perhaps somewhat professionally parochial (and committed to their own goals of expansion) in arguing that they were capable alone of guaranteeing the security of the island, but a realistic appraisal of Britain's naval strength would tend to support their position. The baroque scenarios fabricated by League supporters, showing how the British navy could be lured away from Britain's shores and deterred by clever configurations of mines and sunken obstacles from returning in time to prevent an invasion, could only suggest to all but the most credulous the unlikelihood of such a possibility. The argument that a home defense force made strong by compulsory training supplied the only real protection on which the country could rely was not easily supported by any reasoned analysis of the logistics of invasion or the naval capabilities of the Germans. The possibility, in any case, had been carefully studied by the Invasion Sub-Committee of the Committee of Imperial Defence and found decidedly implausible. Writing in 1928, Asquith looked back on the earlier notion of a surprise German invasion as a

> chimerical danger with which the authority of Lord Roberts alarmed the public imagination, and which, in deference to him, received careful and protracted investigation in 1907–08

by the Committee of Imperial Defence under my chairmanship. The report of the Committee ... demonstrated that such
an enterprise was out of the range of practical warfare.[81]

But whether or not the concern for the German peril had any
legitimate basis, the League's agitation on behalf of compulsory
military training embodied a vision of civil society that went well
beyond the realities of an invasion threat. The National Service
League saw in a nation that submitted itself to military training
and discipline an answer to the problems of political unrest,
social dissension, and moral decay afflicting it.[82] More than a response to a presumed crisis of military unpreparedness, the call for
training expressed a specific set of moral and political values that
sought to rescue England from its slide into a kind of sloppy democracy that was turning its back on the great achievements of the
empire. Although Chesney's rhetoric is perhaps too shrill even for
the League, his denunciation of Britain's failures neatly anticipated
the political posture of its supporters. The wresting of power from
"the class used to rule" by the uneducated lower classes; the degeneration of politics into a craven "bidding for radical votes"; the
inability of the few strong and wise men to beat down the shouting
of the multitude—all these views define the pure strains of Tory
conservatism that underlay the purportedly nonpartisan stance of
the League. As much as the threat from outside, it was "the countless evils within"[83] that military training—and the concurrent
training in patriotism—was seen to remedy. Opponents of the
League stressed its commitment to suppressing social dissent and
supporting Tory interests. J. A. Farrar, one of its harshest Liberal
critics, argues that

> The League, in fact, is saturated through and through with
> Toryism. It is nothing more than the military wing of the
> Tory party, consisting almost entirely of the same chauvinist
> spirits which applauded the Jameson Raid, made the Boer
> War, and are always on the side of a warlike policy and of
> increased armaments.[84]

Farrar goes on to state:

> There is nothing like military pressure and influence for the
> furtherance of Tory aims. Once get all the young civilians into
> the barrack atmosphere, once knock the conceit out of them
> by drill and discipline, once inspire them with a wholesome
> dread of the penalties of military law, and in a few years,

where there are now only hundreds of Tory votes, there will be thousands.

Is not this the real explanation of the Tory attachment to Compulsory Service?[85]

For J. Bruce Glasier, the National Service League transparently embodied the needs of "the Lord Northcliffes, the Lord Milners, Lord Derbys, and their kind,"[86] to maintain their control of the people, to defend the ascendancy of their class. "They are obsessed with the militarist idea. It profoundly appeals to their class system, to their own material interests, to their craving for power over people."[87] Military training, for both Farrar and Glasier, had more to do with the social control and manipulation of the lower classes than the ostensible urgency to protect England from the threat of invasion.

Whatever one thinks of the values it stood for, it is important to recognize that the League, despite its avowals to the contrary, was very much a political organization whose program had vast social implications. Roberts always expressed contempt for the petty bickering of politics, seeing himself as a patriot concerned for the health of the nation rather than the parochial interests of the party, not unlike Baden-Powell, who allegedly replied when asked to run for Parliament, "Delighted, which side?"

Under the determined leadership of Roberts, the League was unrelenting in its efforts to convince the country of the merits of military training: "Probably there was no other propaganda pre-war organisation which permeated the social life of England to the same extent as the National Service League."[88] The pages of the League's journal elaborated not just the critical need for such training, but also its broad social usefulness. With minor rhetorical adjustments, Roberts's explanation of the all-inclusive virtues of military training could serve as justification of the Scout program as well:

If we look to the effect on the men who would actually undergo the training, there is little doubt the wholesome food and healthy exercise in good air would do much for the development of their bodies; and that the moral training they would receive from subjection to judicious discipline, and the habits of endurance, self-restraint, and method they would acquire, would greatly increase their industrial efficiency, and lead to the recognition of a higher standard of behaviour. The general acknowledgement, too, of the duty that all owe to the community, together with the increase of self-respect that membership in the national Army would bring, would not only strengthen their power of resisting evil influence, but would also prevent many a youth from drifting to join the host of unemployable wastrels, whose existence renders so difficult the problem of assisting the genuinely deserving unemployed.[89]

For League enthusiasts, the splendors of military training in the process of character development were finally absolute, actually transcending any particular social role assigned them. T. C. Horsfall, an active campaigner for the League's proposals, held that 'If there was no war in the world, and it was not necessary to think of the chance of invasion, military drill would still be a desirable kind of training.'[90] Of a grander, cosmological sweep, rivaling Cecil Rhodes's sublime desire to colonize the stars, was the passion of H. Miller Maguire, another active League supporter: "'Peace or no peace,' he commented to Robert Blatchford, editor of *The Clarion*, 'I'd have every man trained to arms. If there was never to be another fight, I'd drill every male thing. By George, I'd have universal military service in Heaven.'"[91]

In addition to the common ideal of a docile, disciplined youth, ready to sacrifice all for the good of the empire, Scouts and League also shared an enthusiasm for the many virtues of marksmanship. Acquiring skill with a rifle was desirable not only because it would make a soldier more effective in the field, but because it would make him a better human being—more conscientious, disciplined, and even moral than he would otherwise be. Indeed, the claims made for the benefits of rifle shooting were no less exalted than those for military training as a whole. *The Nation in Arms* cites the scientific evidence of the medical officer from the London County Council to show that the movements involved in aiming a rifle

are more highly specialised and educational than anything at present taught in school, meaning the training and coordination to very high perfection of a large number of nerve centers and muscular masses. The result of the shot ending in a bull's eye affords greater educational perfection and finish than anything else that boys of 12 can be expected to do usefully. The effects of any excess lends itself to immediate demonstration. The result of even a single cigarette could no doubt be made evident at once in the smoked paper. For these reasons, as well as its highly moral influences, rifle-shooting seems one of the best educational subject for boys from the age of 12 and upwards, and is free from any unduly fatiguing effects.[92]

The National Service League actively pushed to have shooting adopted in schools. Requiring the firm hand that only temperate habits can confer, shooting, "which improves the character, intelligence, and physique of the children ... should be included in the curriculum to the exclusion of some of the subjects which do not bear so directly on the boys' future welfare."[93]

The exact relationship between mastery of the rifle and moral greatness was never really made clear; it was simply the assumption from which all League discourse on the importance of shooting proceeded. Shooting straight, thinking straight, and living straight were all part of one central core of character strength; weakness in any one of these was necessarily reflected in the other two, resulting in a less capable and reliable human product. Rifle shooting must therefore not be regarded simply as an amusement or a sport; on the contrary, it was vitally important to the country's well-being. The National Service League invested a substantial amount of energy in trying to establish rifle clubs across Britain. "The proposed system of rifle clubs and physical training," Roberts argued, "must prove of the greatest possible benefit to the nation, for they would greatly increase the intelligence of the masses, develop their physique, and inculcate habits of order and discipline, besides providing a reserve of efficient marksmen."[94] In 1906 Roberts established his "Lord Roberts' Boys," a shooting club for boys, and while miniature rifle clubs flourished with the active support of the League, the attempt to establish rifle shooting as a full-fledged and fully underwritten "national pursuit"[95] never materialized.

If an obsession with accurate shooting made perfect sense for a movement explicitly intent on readying the country for war, it might be thought peculiar for an organization insisting on its non-militaristic character. And yet Baden-Powell's celebration of the rifle was as effusive as any found in *The Nation in Arms*. It was an important part of the manliness the Scouts always stressed, an indispensable skill for every boy who wanted to contribute to the defense of the nation:

It is not much fun to have to face an enemy who means to kill you, when you have never learned to shoot.

Every boy ought to learn how to shoot and to obey orders, else he is no more good when war breaks out than an old woman.[96]

The ability to handle a rifle was central to Baden-Powell's conception of the *real* man—the hunters and trappers, frontiersmen and soldiers—whom the Scouts offered for emulation. Those who can't are not only useless in time of war, they are milksops and tenderfeet—contemptible objects of questionable value:

> "We don't think much of a fellow who is no good at cricket or football, and who only loafs about trying (without success) to look like a man by smoking cheap cigarettes. But we ought really not to think too much of any boy, even though a cricketer and footballer, unless he can also *shoot*, and can *drill* and *scout*."[97]

We remember that "how to aim and shoot with miniature rifles" is the first activity the knights of Baden-Powell's Eton proposal were to teach their retainers. "Manliness can only be taught by men, and not by those who are half men, half old women,"[98] a distinction that certainly depends in significant measure on one's ability to shoot. In addition to helping confer the gift of manliness, "rifle practice is a good preparation and does a boy no harm morally, on the contrary, it does him good, since it promotes concentration, steadiness of nerve, eyesight, exactness, etc."[99] Exemplary as a means of "physical and mental training",[100] encouraging moderation, self-reliance, loyalty, and discipline, rifle shooting emerged as the ideal instrument for proper character training.

Baden-Powell, of course, was sensitive to the possible anomalous appearance of his peace Scouts arguing for the importance of accurate marksmanship. He ridiculed the "grumpers who, not knowing how to shoot, are against rifle practice. They say it makes you bloodthirsty and anxious to be shooting other people", pointing out that marksmanship never "made me particularly bloodthirsty or anxious to shoot anybody. I hate war and look upon it as a disgrace to civilisation."[101] But the fact remains that however admirable the rifle as an instrument of moral instruction, *Scouting for Boys* must surely be the only handbook of peace Scouting that gives detailed advice on how to shoot a man, as opposed to a fixed target:

> Shooting at a fixed target is only a step towards shooting at a moving one, like a man. Firing at moving objects is, of course, more difficult, but more real, because you will not find a deer or an enemy as a rule kind enough to stand still while you shoot at him, he will be running and dodging behind cover, so you have to get your aim quick and to shoot quick.

The very best practice for this is always to be aiming at moving objects with your staff, using it as if it were a rifle.

Aim first at the man, then, moving the muzzle a little faster than he is moving, and fire while moving it when it is pointing where he will be a second or two later, and the bullet will just get there at the same time as he does and will hit him.[102]

Baden-Powell's detestation of war, in short, seems only to be matched by his enthusiasm for it, and his eagerness to inculcate that enthusiasm in the youth of Britain. "Better than football, better than any other game, is man-hunting,"[103] he emphasized, spelling out the details in his autobiography, *Lessons from the 'Varsity of Life*:

Shalimar, writing in Blackwood's Magazine, quotes an American soldier who says: "War is *not* Hell, and any young fellow who thinks it is is dead from the neck up. I know of no more glorious feeling on land or sea than that of leading— under the sure touch of such a general as Stonewall Jackson— a hundred men such as mine in action...."

But apart from the glamour of the surface, apart from its comradeship and its sports, apart from the adventure of pioneering and fighting in far-off corners of the world—all of which have their strong appeal to any red-blooded man— there is a higher call and opportunity for the young men who pass through his hands for future citizenhood for their country.[104]

Bloodthirsty or not, Baden-Powell welcomed the outbreak of World War I as an excellent chance for the Scouts to demonstrate their usefulness to the nation:

The sudden involvement of the country in the European War has brought to our movement its great opportunity.

... It has been put to the highest possible proof—namely, the test of war—and has not failed.[105]

(That the test of war should be seen as the highest proof of the movement's worth, of course, was not insignificant in itself.) As soon as hostilities were declared, Baden-Powell leaped into action, mobilizing his Scouts for all sorts of activities, such as guarding bridges and railroads, handing out notices, carrying messages, and the like, as well as lobbying for recognition from the authorities for these enterprises. By September 1914 he had obtained, from the parliamentary undersecretary of war, in view of the different services rendered by the Scouts, permission to publish the announcement that the Boy Scout uniform was now officially recognized by the government as the uniform of a public-service, nonmilitary body. Baden-Powell immediately established a war services badge for those Scouts who performed twenty-eight days' special voluntary service of at least three hours a day. In his enthusiasm for having Scouts busy serving the nation in a visible way, he tried to convince school authorities and employers to excuse Scouts from school or work so that they could pursue this higher calling. This venture failed, however, and Scouts were forced to serve after hours or on weekends.

Baden-Powell also took the opportunity offered by the war to establish a Scout Defense Corps, in which Scouts between fifteen and seventeen would receive special training in shooting, signaling, entrenching, and basic infantry techniques (a throwback to the training the knights of the Eton proposal were to give their retainers), with the object "to form a trained force of young men who would be immediately available for defence of the country, should their services be required during the war."[106] After passing their course of recruits' training, members were entitled to wear a single red feather on the left side of their hats. Obtaining the red feather counted fourteen days toward the twenty-eight for the War Service badge.

While Baden-Powell was anxious to take advantage of the war spirit to form his Defense Corps, he remained sensitive to the need of keeping Scouting free from any obvious connection with the military. Consequently he proceeded with great care to emphasize that the existence of the Defense Corps in no way changed the movement's strict antimilitarism:

> So, too, on the outbreak of the war the minds of the boys are obsessed with warlike ideas. It is of little use to fight against this when the fever is on them. We, therefore, utilise it and allow those boys who are eager to help in the defence of their country to take up public services, preferably of a peaceable nature under the police and municipal authorities; but where they have more military aspirations we allow them to learn the details of drill and musketry with a view to their taking up home defence should they ever be required for it. But our Scoutmasters and Commissioners, in carrying out this branch of training, do not fail to take the opportunity of using it for the higher aims of education....

It need not be assumed that we are, therefore, binding ourselves to this military training as part of our permanent policy for it is not so.... We merely utilise the present occasion for the further development of their education, and so soon as the war fever has died down we shall resume our former attitude eschewing military drill and training as being forms of education which are bound within narrower limits than those of the Scout Movement generally.[107]

Allowing Baden-Powell to show his Scouts in action—guarding, drilling, helping, and in the case of those old enough to do so, giving their lives in battle—the war was a great boon to the Scout movement. The efficacy of Scout training in patriotism and self-sacrifice was eloquently demonstrated by the growing number of Scouts and Scoutmasters added to the honor role as the war progressed. The Scouts had come a long way in showing what they could achieve since the rather limited challenge afforded Lord Cecil's boys in dusty Mafeking. Baden-Powell's jaunty assessment of what the war did for the Sea Scouts epitomized his sense of how the movement as a whole benefited from the opportunities European conflict provided:

I say Scouts, we really must put up a statue to that old———. Well, I won't say what I think of him—but I mean Kaiser Bill. He did such a lot for us by bringing on that war.

Thanks to the war, the Sea Scouts got their chance of doing really valuable war service for the country in taking over the coast watching duties, a chance they would never have had otherwise....

Thanks to the war, the Mercantile Marine came up in the world instead of being sunk to the bottom by German submarines....

Thanks to the war, a very large proportion of our old ships were sent to the bottom, and are being fast replaced by new ones.[108]

The one thing that would have to be admitted by both admirers and detractors of the Scouting movement was that when war came, both Baden-Powell and his peace Scouts were ready for it.

8

PREDECESSORS AND
SUCCESSORS

Unquestionably the most significant youth movement of the twentieth century, the Boy Scouts, as we have seen, were by no means the first in Britain to attempt to organize the leisure and—more important—the character structure of Britain's rising generation by involving them in a uniformed youth organization. Nor were they the last. Developing out of the various youth brigades, particularly William Smith's Boys' Brigade, the Scouts in turn provoked the establishment of several others, which sought to provide British children with an alternate ideology to that espoused by the Scouts. Though none even vaguely rivaled the Scouts in size or influence, together they constitute an important context in which to understand Scouting's achievement.

My focus on some of these other youth organizations does not imply that they alone represent the totality of the middle- and upper-class reformist impulse to lend a helping—and shaping—hand to lower-class youth. The nineteenth century is filled with such efforts, for adult and young alike. Working men's clubs, boys' clubs, General Booth's Salvation Army, the YMCA, the Saint John's Ambulance Brigade, to name the most prominent, attest to the growing concern of the upper classes for the moral well-being of the less fortunate. But since none of these were specifically youth movements,[1] with the organizational structure and strict ideology found in the Scouts, the Boys' Brigade, and the woodcraft organizations generated in response to the Scouts, I will simply note here that they are a part of that larger cultural sensibility out of which the youth movements themselves grew.

Unlike the Scouts, which were only launched after much careful planning and publicity, and with a national program in mind, the Boys' Brigade emerged without fanfare from the mainly personal interest of one earnest Sunday school teacher to find a method to tame his unruly charges.[2] As the founder not only of the Boys' Brigade but indirectly of all British youth movements, William A. Smith could not have been more different from Baden-Powell. A stolid Glasgow businessman, he lacked the flair and capacity for self-promotion that Baden-Powell possessed in such abundance. At the time of the Brigade's inception, in 1883, Smith was running a small business with his brother and teaching at the North Woodside Sunday School, a Mission school run by the College Free Church of Scotland. The school was located in a basically working-class district of Glasgow, and Smith was having difficulty getting the boys to behave and do their work conscientiously. He had for nine years been an enthusiastic member of the First Lancashire Rifles, a Glasgow Volunteer Regiment, and while it is not entirely clear who actually made the initial suggestion, Smith began in the fall of 1883 to think about utilizing the discipline of the Volunteers as a means of controlling and interesting his Sunday school pupils. After discussing the possibilities with two friends, John and James Hill, Smith opened the 1st Glasgow Company for enrollment on 4 October.

The organization's goal was unambiguously stated from the start: "The Object of the Brigade shall be the advancement of Christ's Kingdom among Boys, and the promotion of habits of reverence, discipline, self-respect, and all that tends towards a true Christian manliness."[3] The method to achieve this—as well as what Smith calculated would constitute the major part of the Brigade's special appeal—was military drill. Drill was the essential requirement and activity of the Brigade. Its efficacy in character training is proclaimed throughout Brigade literature. The first *Boys' Brigade Handbook* in 1886 makes quite clear that

> The fact that drill is a stimulating and binding attraction to most boys is taken advantage of and turned to good account

in attaining the one great object announced in the constitution
of the Brigade, and experience has shown (the testimony of
superintendents and teachers being to the same effect) that a
military organization in drill and discipline is a most legitimate and effective way of dealing with boys in our efforts for
their religious and moral improvement.[4]

The opportunity to engage in military drill, as Smith had anticipated, was not without its attractiveness. Fifty-nine boys enrolled
within the first three nights, and by November thirty-five of them
had accepted membership and actually received membership cards.
As befitted an organization committed to the therapeutic powers
of Close Order Drill, the brigade was run in a fiercely disciplined
way. No boy could fall in if a single minute late, and nobody was
permitted to miss two consecutive drills without an adequate explanation. The strictness of both drill and discipline not only revealed something about Smith's authoritarian nature, but more
importantly demonstrated that true Christian manliness was not
for the faint at heart but rather the tough, feisty boy who could
handle what the officers had to give out—in short, for precisely the
working-class lads who made up the population of Smith's Sunday
school.

The very first sentence of the first handbook—"Among the benefits derived from the Volunteer movement we are entitled to claim
as last, and surely not least, the institution of the Boys' Brigade"—
underlines its military origin. Although it generated criticism from
some directions, military drill comprised such a basic feature of the
movement that there was at least no ambiguity involved in how
the Brigade presented itself. The Brigade was transparently an effort to apply the virtues of the good soldier and his training to the
manufacturing of good Christian citizens, "not to make soldiers for
the Crown, but for Christ."[5] Military titles provided the organization's structure. The Brigade was composed of companies, three
or more of which could form themselves into battalions, under the
leadership of Captains, with junior officers called Lieutenants. The
boys drilled with dummy rifles; the characteristic uniform of "pill-
box" cap, belt, and white haversack was introduced after the first
year.

The movement developed slowly, in part because Smith, unlike
Baden-Powell, was not an inspired salesman and had no initial
aspirations for a national organization embracing all British youth,
in part because of the built-in limitations of the Brigade itself. No

youth movement calling for military drill and requiring of all members an official connection with some Christian organization could reasonably hope for immediate success, and on these points Smith allowed no possibility of compromise. (The Brigade did address the requirement of an explicitly religious affiliation by instituting, in 1884, its own Sunday Bible class for those aspiring soldiers of Christ who lacked any other church connection. This cast the net considerably wider, opening the movement to boys outside Smith's regular Sunday school and other traditional Christian organizations.) Given these constraints, what is striking is not the slowness of the movement's growth but the fact that it achieved the popularity that it did. While the 1st Glasgow Company remained the only one for a year, gradually other companies began to form in Glasgow, spreading to Edinburgh the next year. In 1885 Smith set up a governing council and a formal constitution to structure what he realized was the beginning of a national movement. By 1886 companies appeared in England and Wales, and thereafter the movement continued to expand slowly but steadily. We remember that when Baden-Powell reviewed their annual drill demonstration in 1904, he was told by Smith that there were some 55,000 boys enrolled throughout the United Kingdom.

With the appeal of the uniform, the fascination of the military, and the delicious pleasure, particularly for the underprivileged, of the summer camping experience (introduced in 1886), Smith created the model for structuring the leisure time of boys from which all future youth organizations would borrow heavily. Above all, the Brigade appeared to define a method by which that unquestioning obedience so dear to the hearts of youth workers could be inculcated in the potentially unruly young:

> They are taught that, to be true Brigade Boys, they must be *through and through* with no sham about them; that they must carry the spirit and principles of the Brigade into every part of their lives; that they must not only obey their officers on parade, but their parents at home, their masters at work, their teachers at school, and, above all, that they must give prompt and unwavering obedience to *God's will* in whatever *He* commands them to do.[6]

This alleged capacity to shape the amorphous working-class lad into a disciplined, serviceable citizen led G. A. Henty, the popular boys' novelist who was also an honorary vice-president of the Brigade, to praise it as one of the most important and useful features of the time. It is to my mind a most happy thing that the authors of the movement conceived the idea of forming it, to some extent, upon military lines, for thus they not only added a great attraction to the movement, but it enabled them, at the most critical period of a Boy's life, to inspire him with invaluable habits of discipline.[7]

Smith's nondenominational Boys' Brigade eventually spawned a variety of sectarian offshoots, the first and most important of which was the Anglican Church Lads' Brigade, founded in 1891 by Walter Mallock Gee. A devoted temperance worker and, like Smith, an officer in a Volunteer regiment, Gee established his first company in London after Smith had refused to consider the possibility of a separate Anglican section working within the Boys' Brigade. The Church Lads' Brigade followed essentially the same program as the Boys' Brigade, putting its members through their military paces as the best way of guaranteeing their moral and social well-being. They were, if anything, more explicitly militaristic than the Boys' Brigade, a consequence of Gee's intense admiration for the army. His fervor led him to the politically unsound decision to accept the Army Council's recommendation in 1911 that the Church Lads' Brigade apply to their local Territorials to be granted official cadet status, a step that Smith wisely avoided for the Boys' Brigade. In giving in to the temptation to be more closely involved with the army, Gee was ultimately seen by the public to have compromised the religious thrust of the movement in favor of the purely military. Membership in the Church Lads' Brigade, which was as high as 70,000 in 1908 (as opposed to 64,000 for the Boys' Brigade), plummeted after the war in the midst of the antimilitarist feeling that swept England, and the Church Lads' Brigade was never again to rival the Boys' Brigade as Britain's second-largest youth group.[8]

In many ways more interesting than the Church Lads' Brigade—and certainly more poignant—was the Jewish Lads' Brigade, established through the efforts of Colonel A. E. Goldsmid, a Zionist British army officer who was so impressed when he inspected a company of Church Lads that he resolved to establish a similar scheme for Jewish boys. Enlisting the support of the Maccabeans, an influential group of Jewish professional men and intellectuals, he organized the first meeting of the Jewish Lads' Brigade in February 1895. Its social goals were more complicated than those of the other brigades. For although the use of military drill to ensure disciplined, healthy citizens was the same, its special hope was that in producing well-trained, strong Jewish lads able to follow orders and hold their own physically, the Jewish Lads' Brigade would not only be aiding the individual Jewish boy assimilate himself into the mainstream of British society, but would at the same time be combatting whatever anti-Jewish sentiment was prevalent in Britain. The aim of creating admirable *representatives*, a burden no other brigade shared, is announced in the Jewish Lads' Brigade's statement of its purpose: "The object of the Jewish Lads' Brigade is to teach its members habits of Orderliness, Cleanliness, and Honour; so that in learning to respect themselves, they will be a credit to their community."[9] Working largely with the immigrant Jews of the East End, the Jewish Lads' Brigade thus sought to shape them into acceptable English products, and by so doing mitigate some of the stigma attached to the Jewish community generally. Lionel de Rothschild, at an annual prize-giving ceremony of the Free School company of the Jewish Lads' Brigade in 1908, emphasized the obligation he hoped the Lads would feel toward their beneficent host nation, exhorting them,

> After leaving school, if they had the time, and it did not interfere with their careers, [to] join some branch of the Territorial Army and help England which had done so much to help the Jews. ... At the present time the strength of nations depended upon armaments and England was just because she was strong. Justice and strength went hand in hand, and it was England's strength they must all help to maintain.[10]

The number of Jewish boys receiving this training was small, perhaps no more than 4,000 throughout England in the early 1900s[11]—but the Jewish Lads' Brigade is nevertheless interesting in its use of the Brigade model not only to achieve the social control desired by all youth brigades, but also as an agency to facilitate the integration of its members and the community they represented into the nation as a whole.

In 1896 a Catholic Boys' Brigade was formed by the local Catholic curate in charge of a boys' club in southeast London. Begun primarily to keep boys interested in church activities, the Brigade employed the familiar combination of religion and military drill to maintain their involvement. The idea gradually spread beyond Bermondsey, the site of the original Brigade, and by 1906 it was estimated that about eight thousand boys were enrolled.

Perhaps the most unusual brigade was the Boys' Life Brigade, started in 1899 by the Reverend John Paton. An admirer of the Boys' Brigade, Paton nevertheless recognized the objections many parents and noncomformist churchmen had to its militarism and resolved to establish a youth brigade without any of the military trappings of the Boys' Brigade. In place of the military drill, Paton substituted a life-saving drill—instruction in saving people from death through drowning, fire, and other accidents—which became the means of establishing discipline. The idea was endorsed by the National Sunday School Union, which adopted it as a national organization with which it remained formally connected for the duration of its existence. By 1914 it had a membership of fifteen thousand; in 1926 it merged with the Boys' Brigade.[12]

It was into this network that Baden-Powell introduced his Scouts in 1908. He did so, as we have seen, with great tact, fully aware that it would be neither politic nor productive to enter the business of youth training by antagonizing those already in the field, particularly William Smith, its acknowledged leader. Offering his Scout training simply as a method that could be adopted by all existing organizations certainly helped calm anxieties that Baden-Powell had any independent aspirations in mind. While everybody has taken at face value Baden-Powell's claim that all he ever intended was to fashion an attractive program of training that the Brigades, YMCA, boys' clubs, and other such groups could use in appealing to boys, such a claim, as I suggested earlier, seems to me utterly unconvincing. It makes no sense given the extraordinary preparations behind the launching of the Scouts—the lectures across the country; the complicated arrangements with Pearson, including the establishment of the separate Scout magazine; securing the support of a variety of military, church, and government leaders; setting up the demonstration camp at Brownsea Island; producing *Scouting for Boys*—and disregards entirely the sort of man Baden-Powell actually was. With his intense ambition and well-developed narcissism, it is hard to believe that he did not all along imagine that his training program might lead to a national youth movement with the hero of Mafeking at its head. Baden-Powell never regarded himself as a selfless toiler in the service of others; his disclaimers about a separate movement must be understood as basically strategic, aimed at enlisting the support of Smith and others rather than incurring their enmity by appearing to intrude on their turf. In this, as in so much else connected to the origins of Scouting, Baden-Powell was totally successful. The *Boys' Brigade Gazette* helped publicize the Scouts at the start, and the Brigade even introduced a Scouting branch within its own movement, describing it in the 1910 Brigade manual.

Though they were obviously rivals, the relationship between Baden-Powell and Smith was, at least superficially, always cordial. Baden-Powell went so far as to invite Smith, in 1909, to become a member of the Scout Advisory Council, in order to ensure "friendly cooperation" between the different youth organizations. On 20 December Smith politely demurred, convinced, after much deliberation, that "it would not be appropriate for me to do so, as I am sure that being on the Advisory Council of the Boy Scouts while Brigade Secretary of the Boys' Brigade would lead to much misconception."[13] Baden-Powell asked again on Christmas Day, and again Smith refused, noting that

> Scouting is an excellent thing as taken up within the Boys' Brigade or other organizations, as an interesting and helpful adjunct to its regular work, but when you take the Boy Scouts as a separate organization, and propose to include all the other service organizations within an Advisory Council of the Boy Scouts directed by the heads of the other organizations, it seems to me that from both points of view the thing would be unworkable and would tend to create the very difficulties which you seek to avoid.[14]

Once Scouting entered the lists to redeem boys' souls for the good of the empire, there was little any of the brigades could do to match it. Stripping the basic brigade idea of its obligatory religiousness and drill, and investing it instead with the romance of chivalry, the delight of woodcraft, and the excitement of mastering the skills of the best game, that of "man-hunting," Baden-Powell devised a marvelously appealing opportunity for boys that no brigade could equal. And having taken pains to encase the movement's militarism in a rhetoric that strictly denied its presence, he also managed to deflect from the Scouts much of the adult objection to the militarism of the other brigades. A movement that was fun for the boys; promised the production of disciplined, loyal, and serviceable citizens for the empire; and was peaceful to boot was hard to resist. The brigades couldn't seriously compete.

But if the brigades posed no threat to Baden-Powell's dream of processing a rising generation through the Scout character factory, he was quite concerned about one institution whose status occupied a good deal of his attention, namely the Cadet Corps. Originally established in the 1859 panic over the invasion threat mounted by Napoleon III, the Cadet Corps had, by the start of the twentieth century, developed roots throughout the country's great public schools as well as powerful backing from numerous people as an ideal kind of training in the molding of responsible citizens. In the wake of the post-Boer War anxiety about the physical fitness and discipline of the British male, renewed interest developed in the possibility of requiring Cadet training for all British boys as an official part of the school curriculum. Ian Hamilton's proposal to put Cadet training on a mandatory national basis elaborated advantages that were distressingly close to what Baden-Powell argued the Scouts were best qualified to achieve:

A. A course of military training for all boys as the best antidote to excess of individualism. The cadet corps as part of our school curriculum giving cohesion to the nation.

B. Military training giving definite shape to a sense of citizenship now vague and formless. The cadet corps serving as a constant object lesson in the subservience of the boys to the group—of the group to the company.[15]

Baden-Powell viewed with some alarm the enthusiasm for Cadet training—in 1908, for example, the government encouraged the formation of Cadet units by extending a grant of five pounds to every company—seeing its possible adoption as a scheme of national training for twelve- to eighteen-year-olds as a severe constraint, even a death blow, to his aspirations for the Scouts. It was a ticklish position to be in, as Baden-Powell was reluctant to say anything unkind about a sacred British institution in which he had himself been enrolled while at Charterhouse and that had strong support from those same military men who also liked the Scouts. Moreover, one of the virtues claimed for the Cadet scheme was its success in preparing boys both physically and emotionally for the armed services. As Baden-Powell had always maintained that the Scouts did not provide military training, it was awkward to argue that they could in fact fashion boys for military service more efficiently than the Cadets. Nevertheless something had to be done, and from roughly 1911 on, Baden-Powell was indefatigable in publicly (and privately) arguing the case for the superiority of the Scouts over the Cadets. He first set out all the basic points of comparison in a lecture at the Royal United Services Institute in 1911; thereafter it was simply a question of playing variations—and many repetitions—of the theme in all the appropriate places. As reprinted in the *Headquarters Gazette* of October 1911, it outlines the strategy he pursued in resisting any effort to base a national training program on Cadet principles.

He prefaces his analysis of Cadet problems, of course, with a glowing evocation of how valuable the corps is:

> Character training for our boys, then, is the essential ground-work for making our men into a nation of good citizens. It is equally essential for making them into soldiers. Now, one great organisation which is doing a great good for the boys, in addition to those I have referred to is that of the Cadet Corps. It gives them an outdoor life and physical development, it gives them the training of soldiers, the love for their country, and a sense of duty and discipline, which, as I say, is not given them inside the school walls. I have been an ardent cadet-man since I was a bugler in the Charterhouse Cadet Corps; I have had cadets under me on active service; I have held the rank of Honorary Commander of several Cadet Corps; and I have seen their great expansion in our over-sea Dominions; but gradually, as I have got older and studied their ways and looked around, I have detected many shortcomings and many defects in the cadet system.[16]

There turn out to be nine points that Baden-Powell is forced "re-gretfully to acknowledge against my beloved Cadet Corps." To-gether they make clear that there is very little benefit indeed to be derived from Cadet training:

1. First of all, there is need for specially capable officers for training the boys, because it is not every man who has the peculiar gift of training a boy, and these are very hard to find, good officers preferring the more serious form of soldiering.
2. The expense limits the Cadet training to only a certain class of boys.
3. A very considerable portion of our citizens conscientiously object to their sons being taught soldiering, and the idea of fighting and bloodshed, before they are of age to judge for themselves, and therefore bar their sons from serving as Cadets. Well, that is a thing you have to take into considera-tion.
4. The principle of the Cadet Corps is only applicable to popu-lous centres, where you can raise a company. Out in the country districts a boy gets no chance of becoming a cadet.
5. The physical training is only a nominal thing. While they are on parade they get a certain amount of exercise, but the parades are very few and far between.
6. It is the same with the discipline. They only obey orders while

they are on parade; the discipline is put on with the uniform
and taken off with the uniform; it does not go into their soul
and mind; it does not become part of their character—which
is what we want.

7. Then there is the fact that the glamour wears off when they
come to the age to go into the Service. Only ten per cent join
the Army.

8. Then, of course, the system fails to give any idea to the boys
of their duty as citizens.

9. It involves the expenditure of a certain amount of public
money.[17]

Opposed to these nine—by any standard, terminal—reservations,
stand the nine luminous virtues of Scouting: It is nonmilitary; appeals widely to men qualified to act as officers; is applicable to
small centers; provides unceasing moral training and discipline;
teaches boys to be manly and independent; is already widely in use
throughout the empire and so can standardize the training of the
race, if desired; can help boys throughout the dominions communicate with one another; does not cost the taxpayer anything. Above
all, and here Baden-Powell deals in his characteristically evasive
way with Scout militarism, although completely nonmilitary,
Scouting in fact produces more—and better—recruits for the army
than does the Cadet Corps:

> Although our policy is not to make the boys into soldiers, but
> as a first aim to make them good citizens, the results show
> that a large proportion of our boys who have left us have gone
> into the Service, and they join from an idea of serving their
> country, and not, like so many other recruits, from want of
> employment.[18]

Unlike the overmilitarized Cadet recruit, with his undernourished
character, the Scout recruit enters the army already

> thoroughly grounded in discipline and sense of honour and
> duty, as well as in campaigning, scouting, pioneering, and
> signalling, and it only needs the polish of drill to make him
> into a first-rate, all-round soldier. Let anyone ask a com-
> manding officer of a regiment who has tried both, which he
> would prefer to have—a Cadet or a Boy Scout—as a recruit
> and the answer will invariably be that he would prefer the
> Scout.[19]

With his arguments well in hand, Baden-Powell defended his Scout movement from any Cadet incursions with the same tenacity with which he defended Mafeking from the Boers. A 1914 memo for his Scout committee entitled "Scouting versus Cadet Training: Steps Taken So Far Towards Carrying Out the Campaign—by the Chief Scout," suggests the exhaustiveness of his battle plan. It contains three columns—Addresses, Authorities, Press—itemizing under each category the specific efforts he has made. Here we find that he has addressed not only the Council of Hygiene on Scout health training but also four important meetings of people interested in education, as well as educational authorities in Leeds and Liverpool on the purposes of Scout citizenship training; has interviewed the minister of education and the permanent undersecretary, in addition to Professor Michael Sadler, president of the Teachers' Registration Council; and published (or prepared for publication) an interview, an article for the *Windsor* magazine, a letter for the *Times*, and an article for a monthly magazine.[20] In countless articles, letters, and talks he stressed the inadequacy of Cadet training for the vital task of preparing obedient, efficient, disciplined citizens. Had it been able to do the job, "I should not have bothered about evolving the scout scheme."[21] He gently rebuked the archbishop of Canterbury for suggesting that Scouts should become Cadets, and was assured by the duke of Connaught's secretary, in thanking Baden-Powell for the "letter which has been circulated amongst all the Members of the House of Lords," that the duke "shares your views about the advantages of the Boy Scout system over the Cadet system for younger boys."[22]

Whether the Cadet system, if unopposed by Baden-Powell, might have made its way more fully into the mainstream of British culture as part of some national program of youth education is uncertain; it had virtually no chance, however, with Baden-Powell staunchly against it. The various impulses to enlarge the training came to nothing, and it must have given Baden-Powell great satisfaction in 1923 when the financial support that the War Office had annually provided the Cadet force was withdrawn, a result of the need to reduce army expenditure. The savings of public funds—the ninth point of Baden-Powell's original concern—was approximately £10,000.

Despite Baden-Powell's success in contrasting his peace Scouts to the militaristic Cadets, it was always the specter of Scout militarism that generated most of the opposition to his movement. With few exceptions critics of Scouting objected to the constricting military bias of the training, arguing that whatever Scouting might claim, it was in fact dedicated to fostering the military spirit and turning out well-disciplined miniature soldiers at the expense of other human qualities. These concerns not only constituted the ongoing vocal opposition to Scouting, they also were the motivating force behind the formation of several youth groups established to counter what their founders saw as Scouting's pernicious military nature.

The first of these, the Order of Woodcraft Chivalry, grew out of the dissatisfaction in 1914-15 of several prominent Scout workers in the Cambridge area. Looking for something more sustaining than what they took, in the words of I. O. Evans, author of *Woodcraft and World Service*, to be the "fierce patriotism of a militant nation,"[23] they attracted the attention of Ernest Westlake, a Quaker scientist with a strong interest in G. Stanley Hall's recapitulation theories. In 1916, together with his son Aubrey, Westlake founded the Order of Woodcraft Chivalry, designed to remedy some of the deficiencies in Scout training, which, while admiring it in many ways, the order found "unduly prosaic, civilised, and military."[24] It attempted explicitly to amalgamate the best woodcraft principles of Ernest Thompson Seton's Woodcraft Indians with "the many good points of the Boy Scout movement"[25] to shape an educational experience that would better enable the child to realize the full richness of his nature, as well as to "seek to foster and develop all these faculties, instincts, and inclinations, which find their highest expression in service."[26]

The "special points" of the new movement, particularly in contrast to the Scouts, were defined as follows:

1. That it admits of being run co-educationally;
2. That its constitution, scheme of self government, activities, and tests make it applicable and suitable to schools, secondary schools in particular;
3. That it endeavours to cater for the youth by means of a senior division called "The Company of Pathfinders";
4. That it introduces the spirit and practice of Woodcraft; by which is meant, not only the lore of the woodman, but also that simple life in Nature which is the heritage, material, mental, and spiritual, of man in common with all living creatures;
5. That it carries on the movement and its ideals into adult life.[27]

The combination of Seton and Baden-Powell produced a curious blend of Scout character-training apparatus embedded in the rhetoric, idealism, and to some extent, organization of the Woodcraft movement. Thus there is a motto—"Blue Sky"—analogous to

Baden-Powell's "Be Prepared"; a Woodcraft oath, corresponding to the Scout oath; and even a Lodge Law, taken directly from the English and American Scout law, with appropriate modifications for Woodcraft principles.[28] At the same time there is a Grand Lodge, colorful ceremonials, a celebration of the primitive, and official positions like those of the Gleeman, the Keeper of the Purse, the Keeper of the Fire, and the like, which derived from Seton's Woodcraft Indians. The opening paragraph of *Woodcraft Chivalry* gives the best sense of the movement's flavor:

> As the Keeper of the Log called the roll, there softly came, first from one place and then from another, in different intonations the answer, "Blue Sky": and from above us was the blue expanse in all its loveliness. Then there was silence, and nought was heard save the wind in the trees, the subdued hum of insects and the occasional note of a bird.
>
> In such an atmosphere, and in such surroundings were enrolled the first members of the Order of Woodcraft Chivalry. With the watchword, "Blue Sky," still in their thoughts, and Nature as their witness, they promised to the best of their ability—
>
> To obey the Lodge Law;
>
> To help others at all times;
>
> To keep themselves physically fit, mentally awake and morally straight.
>
> I think the above extract, taken from an account of the first Common Council of the first Lodge to be started, forms a fitting introduction to our subject, as therein the spirit, aims and general setting of the scheme are concisely stated.[29]

The insistence on nature as the great educator, accounting for the stress on woodcraft activities, was rooted in the scientific theory that individual growth recapitulates the entire history of the living organism; and that just as the human race has evolved from the simple to the increasingly complex, so the ideal form of education for the child is to immerse him at the start in the simple and primitive processes of nature. Once we recognize that our mental and spiritual faculties develop through the same evolutionary stages as the human race,

> then to attain self-realisation—the complete development of all our faculties—it is essential that the child, the summation

of the whole evolutionary process, should receive an education recapitulating the ancestral and racial experience, by actually and practically passing through the various stages through which mankind has evolved. This means that Woodcraft is not only necessary, as representing the primitive and simple side of life, but is in tune with the nature of every man, to which, as fostering growth, it appeals instinctively; for Woodcraft, the adventurous open-air life, has ever been the school of manliness, and of social and political freedom.[30]

With its arcane theoretical underpinnings, diffident, unworldly leadership, and poetic nature, the Order of Woodcraft Chivalry was never destined for national popularity. It remained a primarily elitist, Quaker movement, with a basically middle-class membership ranging from two hundred to three hundred. Despite its size, however, it retains its interest for us today as the first genuine woodcraft alternative to Scouting.

There was nothing diffident about the leadership of the Kibbo Kift Kindred, established in 1920 by John Hargrave, Scouting's first commissioner for camping and woodcraft. A powerful personality of commanding presence and energy, an illustrator of some talent, and an accomplished woodsman, Hargrave was thought by many to be on his way to becoming Baden-Powell's successor as Chief Scout. He certainly shared some temperamental affinities with the Chief Scout—too many, no doubt, for either of their liking. In *The Great War Brings It Home*, a book published in 1919 but actually written some years earlier, before he volunteered as an ambulance driver in the war, Hargrave went well beyond Baden-Powell in denouncing the failure of British civilization in general and its school system in particular to train people in proper values and prepare them for a productive life:

> The Great War brings home the fact that our great disorganised civilisation has failed, that our disorganised system of religion has failed. Our disorganised charities, our disorganised grab, our disorganised lust and greed, our disorganised teaching, and disorganised government, all these things have failed to prevent the outbreak of such a hell upon earth as makes the devil acknowledge himself out-devilled.[31]

Everything has failed because it has grown away from nature and the natural; what is required, as the book's subtitle—*The Natural*

Reconstruction of an Unnatural Existence—suggests, is the creation of a
new healthy environment in touch with nature. Only in this way
can the evils of industrial civilization and the terrible national
deterioration everywhere apparent be remedied. Hargrave desired
to move forward "to a simpler and more natural life ... keeping
knowledge and physical training hand in hand and try to breed a
race of Intellectual Savages."[32] His means of achieving this—and
we see the appeal that Scouting seemed to hold out to him—was
through a definite scheme of training involving outdoor education
and open-air camps. Advocating national training camps, Hargrave was convinced that the culture's salvation could only be
achieved through "Outdoor Reconstruction, in order to counteract
all the complaints engendered by indoor existence and the millions
of germs which are harboured in the dust of the schoolrooms and
factories."[33]

It is easy to understand both why Hargrave would be attracted
to Scouting and why, at the same time, it would ultimately prove
an inappropriate organization for him. For while the diagnosis of
the failure of the school system, the anxiety over national deterioration, and the value attached to outdoor education appeared to be
shared by Baden-Powell and Hargrave, they were in fact each
moving in entirely different directions. Hargrave's "intellectual savage" could not be further from the efficient, unquestioning citizen
Baden-Powell had in mind, and if there were superficial resemblances between their common endorsement of the importance of
outdoor living, the profound significance Hargrave attached to it
had very little to do with the role Baden-Powell assigned it as a
useful adjunct to proper character training. In addition, no organization could possibly have been big enough to contain two egos of
the size and wilfullness of Baden-Powell's and Hargrave's. But more
unlikely marriages have no doubt succeeded, and in 1916, after he
was invalided out of the war as an ambulance driver, Hargrave
was appointed commissioner for camping and woodcraft. It did not
take him long to realize that Scouting was not the agency for the
national reconstruction he sought. He became increasingly dissatisfied with its militarism and imperialism, which he felt were betray-
ing the commitment to the notion of woodcraft idealism he had
always thought (not altogether accurately) it was intended to pursue.

Writing as "White Fox" in *The Trail*, the independent magazine
of the London Scout Council, Hargrave began in 1919 to criticize
Scout policy's desertion of the true woodcraft way and the proper
concern for world brotherhood. Initially raising the question in
November 1919, as we have seen, of precisely what sort of character

Scout character training was after—the Nelsons and Drakes, who defended the empire by force, or men who stood up for their principles even if it meant defying established authority?—Hargrave turned one year later to a scathing indictment of how Scouting's ideals had degenerated into a narrow, self-serving imperialism. For Hargrave, Scouting's dilemma was that it tried to straddle two stools, "one labelled 'World Brotherhood,' the other labelled 'Our Empire First.' "[34] Such a position was untenable, demonstrating the movement's confusion. To illustrate how this confusion permeated Scouting, Hargrave went to the text of *Scouting for Boys* itself, analyzing what he considered the essentially irreconciliable jumble of two sets of ideas:

1. Woodcraft Nature lore and World Friendship.
2. Patriotic "Jingoism" based upon Force.[35]

He engages in some compelling textual criticism, juxtaposing Scouting's assertions that it is without military implications against the exhortations to learn to be good shots; notions that the empire is spreading its blessings of peace and justice against the fact that "By hard fighting (of other nations and tribes) we learned to respect one another, and are therefore all the firmer today in our mutual friendship."[36] He laments that the book advocates the " 'Trade War after the War' as an ideal of the Scout movement,"[37] and that senior Scouts ought to see themselves as trade Scouts for the commercial war Britain must now wage against Germany.

The two ideals, Hargrave emphasized, were strictly opposed to one another; if Scouting were to stand consistently for world brotherhood, "a drastic revision of the official handbook is urgently needed and many modifications and alterations in the Royal Charter, and the rules, and in the administration of the whole organisation."[38]

Hargrave then calls for new ideas to lead Scouting out of the doldrums of its outmoded ways into a productive future, including a restructuring of the movement along woodcraft lines; the fostering of social conditions among woodcraft initiates so as to encourage marriages and the creation of children imbued with the woodcraft message; the advocacy of a new method of teaching world history to bring about, among other things, an international educational policy; an international currency system; and the abolition of secret treaties. Since any effort to work toward a world federation necessarily involves genuine political issues, Hargrave acknowledges that this involvement runs counter to the official Scout position that it is nonpolitical. But he distinguishes between the inescapable political reality of living in a human community and the activity of party politics, "which means the wangling of various groups."[39] One is part of living, the other is to be avoided. But then he assaults basic Scout dogma by pointing out that

> Unfortunately, it would appear that the Boy Scout movement is political on party lines. It is very strongly political on the Imperial side. It looks for its backing to those who have the power (i.e. money), and most of these people are naturally anxious to keep the Scout movement very distinctly imperialistic in its methods of training British boys. So you see you *are* political anyhow.[40]

Anticipating the very criticism that Baden-Powell and others were shortly to levy against him—that his position was sheer bolshevism—Hargrave equates bolshevism with imperialism, arguing that Scouting must reject both:

> Red armies and White armies may rise and fall, fight and grab, but the Scout movement should hold aloof from all Bolshevism (i.e., force), and all imperialism (i.e. force). They both try to impose their will by force of arms, therefore they are both out of line with the teaching of Christ.[41]

If Scouting is to pull itself together and get back on the "World Trail"[42] from which it has deviated, Hargrave recognizes, it will have to do something about its royal charter and its endowment fund, the first of which commits the movement to maintain the goals and methods it has already established, the second of which requires that it remain popular and satisfy the monied classes that support it. And just to make sure he hasn't left anything out, Hargrave ends his list of constructive suggestions by calling for a new system of democratic governance for Scouting in which the members of the governing council are elected by the movement as a whole instead of being appointed by the Chief Scout.

Scouting's response to this horrendous public exhibition of disloyalty—Baden-Powell was never much on grousing, we recall—was swift and inevitable. Several months later the London Council voted him out of his position on the council and passed a resolution forbidding him from speaking at any Scout meeting in London or ever writing in *The Trail* or any other Scout magazine. Hargrave's Scouting days were over.

Such an event, of course, came as no surprise. One didn't publicly criticize the founder and the assumptions of the Scouting movement without understanding that such an act effectively constituted one's resignation. In addition, Hargrave had already launched his Kibbo Kift Kindred movement in August 1920, discussing his ideas, among other places, in *The Trail*, so that his official severance from Scouting was not a serious blow to him. An interesting sidelight to the episode of Hargrave's use of *The Trail* to criticize the Scouts and convey his own woodcraft ideas was the decision of the Scout leadership to incorporate the magazine, since 1918 simply an independent publication of the London Scout Council, as an official part of the Scout movement. Only in this way, Baden-Powell argued, could they be confident that the magazine and its editor, Alfred G. Barralet, would be responsible to Scouting's needs and eschew all perverse efforts at bolshie indoctrination:

> In explanation of my urging the "political" value of Headquarters taking over *The Trail* and Barralet, I may say that the Kibbo Kift organisation is now apparently a political one with Bolshevist tendencies and is pushing its propaganda insidiously through our Movement. . . .
>
> To what extent Barralet realises this or is in collusion with this I don't know . . .
>
> Thus if we take over *The Trail* we get its followers or such of them as care to stick to it, and the Bolshies could then have to start fresh with a paper which would have no footing in the Movement.
>
> In Barralet we should have a popular and able adventurer under our hand, who otherwise, as a free lance, would be at the least a nuisance.
>
> By taking his paper we disarm him, and the Bolshies.[43]

Meaning, according to Hargrave, "strength" or "proof of great strength" in Old English, the Kibbo Kift which he unleashed to redeem Britain from its fallen ways was at once a simple woodcraft movement for children, organizing boys and girls in small tribes to teach them woodcraft skills and indoctrinate them in the ideals of world peace, and at the same time a fantastic farrago of eclectic ideas about human nature, economics, and politics, all shrouded in obscure rhetoric and rooted in quaint ritual. Its coherence (if any) was to be found less in the movement's philosophy than in the charismatic personality of its Head Man, as Hargrave chose to be called, who clearly had something wonderful in mind, even if he had difficulty explaining it to the outside world. The unpretentious, practical side of the movement can be seen in the declaration that all Kin children were asked to sign upon joining:

> I wish to be a Kibbo Kift and to
> 1. Camp out and keep fit,
> 2. Help others,
> 3. Learn how to make things, and
> 4. Work for world peace and brotherhood.[44]

But the reasonable program of woodcraft training it offered was in the long run overwhelmed by the burdens of its muddled philosophic and social ambition, and by the erratic and autocratic behavior of its leader. As Hargrave eschewed the conventional handbook outlining the aims of his new organization—"A movement, says the Kindred, born of a handbook is strangulated at birth"[45]— it was not until the publication in 1927 of the *Confession of the Kibbo Kift* that we have a full discussion of what the Kindred are about. Ranging widely, if murkily, over a broad array of subjects, the book is a combination of the radical and the reactionary. Thus, while Hargrave wishes to break free from the sterile constraints of an outmoded civilization

> —The Kin is always experimenting with new ideas because it considers this civilisation to be past its zenith and on the decline. It has focus, uniformity and obligation because it has to resist and overcome the inertia of the reactionary, conservative mind, and the shifting nebulosity of the anarchic mind; both negative. The first reflects the rigid inertia of the Few, the second reflects the chaotic flux of the Many—[46]

he comes out strongly against homosexuality, concern for women's rights, and any notion of sexual equality, which he sees as "a form of body contempt [belonging] to a dysgenic phase of democratic enfeeblement."[47]

But if the new ideas do not involve any recognition of "the masculine type of woman or the effeminate type of man,"[48] they do include all manner of speculation about the need to undo the muscle-bound nature of man's brain and let his body-impulses back into fruitful contact with the earth; to facilitate self-realization by freeing the individual from the pressures of the crowd "in which the individual has been altogether pulped";[49] to disseminate Kindred ideas by penetrating to the major "points of direction"— banking and finance, the cinema, the wireless, schools and universities, industry—which control the channels of mass suggestion; and above all, to guarantee the economic security of everybody in the country by changing the method of industrial cost accounting, which usually operates so that the money paid to those in industry will not pay for the products they manufacture, in such a way that it will hereafter "be based on the proper recognition of the Just Price."[50]

By turns Lawrentian, Wellsian, Nietzschean, with smatterings of Carlyle and Blake and a good deal of G. Stanley Hall's recapitulation theory (*The New Age*, in reviewing it positively, praised it for having drawn "something useful from St. Paul, Mme. Blavatsky, Charlie Chaplin, Cromwell, Lao Tze, Nietzsche, Noah and Tolstoy"[51]), the *Confessions of the Kibbo Kift* was a heady brew for anyone to attempt. In fact, despite his avowed aim of national regeneration, Hargrave was very much an elitist, seeing the initiates into the Kibbo Kift mysteries as comprising a specially privileged group:

> Those who share this view are entitled to cut themselves off from the crowd by the use of a slang, cant, or jargon of their own, as well as the use of special signs and possibly insignia to preserve themselves from the pressure of the crowd.[52]

The difference from the crowd was further emphasized by the deliberately odd costumes Hargrave prescribed for his members: shorts, jerkin and cowl, rough ash staff, and rucksack for his men; a one-piece dress to the knee with leather belt and headdress for the women. Understanding, with Carlyle, the expressive nature of clothing, Hargrave notes that "The costume of the Kin releases efficiency, calls forth conscious unity of purpose, and proclaims a dynamic difference in impressive silence."[53] Together, "What may now appear to be the unnecessary frills and trimming of quaint terminology and outlandish costume will, once the central teaching is recognized, be seen as vital details of a particular body of people suited to the special activities of such a group."[54]

Given the movement's peculiarities, the number of people willing to be so identified remained exceedingly small; according to one estimate, the attendance at the annual camp during the peak year of 1924 was 236. Hargrave gradually turned increasingly to economic and financial questions and further away from woodcraft ideas. By the late 1920s he had become an enthusiastic proponent of Major Douglas's Social Credit theory, eventually, in the early 1930s, affiliating the Kibbo Kift with the Social Credit movement. By 1933, having joined up with the Legion of the Unemployed, the

Kibbo Kift changed its name to that of the Green Shirt movement for Social Credit, based on the green shirts worn by the Legion. In 1935, it became the Social Credit Party of Great Britain.

Long before the Kibbo Kift deserted woodcraft for economics and monetary reform, its eccentricities—particularly the authoritarian style of its Head Man, who frequently chose to put an end to debate with the portentous "I have spoken"—had driven away a number of early adherents. In 1924, some members of the Royal Arsenal Co-operative Society who had supported several Kindred tribes in south London left the movement over the issue of its undemocratic nature. In 1925, they founded instead a purely cooperative organization called the Woodcraft Folk, or Federation of Co-operative Woodcraft Fellowship, appointing Leslie Paul, an enthusiastic twenty-year-old woodcrafter and journalist, as its president. Drawing heavily upon Seton's woodcraft practices, Hall's (by now standard) recapitulation theory, and stressing tribal organization, ceremony, song and dance, the teaching of world history, and the study of arts and crafts, the Woodcraft Folk sought to provide a genuine labor alternative to the traditional youth organization with its "distinct imperialist bias."[55] The Woodcraft Folk charter defines the movement's ideals:

We declare that it is our desire:

1. To develop in ourselves, for the service of the people, mental and physical health, and communal responsibility, by camping out and living in close contact with nature, and by using the creative faculty both of our minds and our hands, and by sincerity in all our dealings with our neighbours.

2. To make ourselves familiar with the history of the world and the development of Man in the slow march of evolution, that we may understand and revere the Great Spirit that urges all things to perfect themselves.

3. We further declare that the welfare of the community can be assured only when the instruments of production are owed by the community, and all things necessary for the good of the race are produced by common service for the common use:

When the production of all things that directly or indirectly destroy life ceases to be;

And when man shall turn his labour from private greed to increase the happiness of mankind, and when nations shall cease to suckle tribal enmities and unite in common fellowship.[56]

With its sensible leadership and a sound program that avoided the rhetoric, excesses, and elitism of the earlier woodcraft movements, the Woodcraft Folk proved to be the most substantial and enduring of these efforts, listing a membership in the mid-1930s of approximately three thousand. A minuscule number, of course, when compared with the Scouts and Boys' Brigades, but extraordinary in the context of what the Order of Woodcraft Chivalry and the Kibbo Kift Kindred managed to achieve.

But even with its relative success, the enormous discrepancy between its enrollment and that of the national mainstream movements points up the failure of the British working-class movement ever to devise a serious alternative to that indoctrination into patriotism and obedience purveyed by organizations like the Scouts and the Boys' Brigade. As noted in the preface to Leslie Paul's *Republic of Children.*

> It is a strange and perturbing thought that the working-class movement of this country, with its genius for organization, should have shown an almost complete disregard of the importance of organising the children and young people from its own homes. It is as if we had swallowed whole the capitalist bait: that political education is a dangerous occupation for the young. In the meantime we allow the imperialists, the militarists, the churches, and the social workers to have a free hand with them. Why?[57]

The answer has to do both with the appeal of the Brigades and Scouts, the allure connected to their "manly" activities as opposed to the slightly rarefied and spiritualized attractions offered by the more visionary woodcraft movements, as well as with the more or less total inability of the politically left woodcraft movements to sell themselves to the adult establishment, whose support—financial and otherwise—they would need if they were ever to flourish. Traduced in part by an ingenuous enthusiasm for their systems that made them think that the purity of their goals and the pleasures of their training were sufficient, they were never interested in forging those links with money and power, in negotiating in that imperfect world of political reality that any mass movement requires. In their uncompromised idealism they managed to leave the business of youth training essentially where they found it—in the hands of those same Brigades and Scouts whose ideology and authority they had wished to challenge in the first place.

9

"SCOUTS,
WHITE MEN AND
CHRISTIANS"

Scouting was never reluctant to proclaim itself a worldwide brotherhood in which race, class, religion, and color were irrelevant to an appreciation of an individual's worth. Arguing for the equality of all people and extending to everybody who wanted it the opportunity to participate in the great game of Scouting, Baden-Powell invested the movement with a set of ideals at once unobjectionable and all-embracing. But the simple human appeal of Scouting's program was rather more complicated in practice than its admirable principles would suggest. For Baden-Powell was far from blind to matters of race or class or religion or color, and the movement he created was necessarily informed by the values and judgments of its founder.

It might be objected, I realize, that in moving back and forth between Baden-Powell's thought and Scout policy I am attributing to the Scouts what is a set of personal values held by Baden-Powell. To this I must reply that Baden-Powell's complete public identification with the organization he created effectively denied him the luxury of speaking only for himself. His judgments are not private but rather part of the central educational role he claimed for himself as founder of the Scouts. The Chief Scout's musings on life, death, and sex are an essential piece of the total discourse of Scouting, as legitimate a feature of Scouting history as the specific regulations agreed upon by the Scout council. To link the values of the man with those of the movement is not only methodologically defensible but necessary.

Given Scouting's ostensible commitment to equality, brotherhood, and other respectable pieties concerning the oneness of mankind, it is at first glance astonishing to find Baden-Powell's thought laced with a full range of racist stereotypes. Starting with blacks and moving without self-consciousness through diverse racial and ethnic groups, Baden-Powell exhibits a virtuosity of contempt for other breeds that is rather startling in its purity. Cautioning us, in his account of *The Matebele Campaign*, not to infer from his anger against the "laughing black fiends"[1] that "I am a regular nigger-hater, for I am not,"[2] Baden-Powell nevertheless ascribes to the Africans—as well as to Aborigines, Filipinos, Indians, and Chinese, to name a few—every imaginable canard about their intelligence, loyalty, character, will power, and honesty. The rhetoric with which he engages human diversity (except, of course, in his official Scout pronouncements) is not substantially different from the crude caricatures of all foreign types employed by G. A. Henty, John Buchan, and Sapper, popular novelists who helped inculcate in generations of boys the smug satisfaction of being white and British. The effortless superiority of Sapper's Bulldog Drummond, regarding with patronizing good nature those unfortunate enough to be born non-British, is very much the vantage point from which Baden-Powell scrutinized the world.

Before going on to examine in detail some of these views, it is important to try to comprehend how they could characterize the thinking of a man who launched a movement dedicated to world understanding. The reason has to do with the basic imperialist ideology underlying Scouting. For we must remember that despite the internationalist stance that Scouting assumed after World War I, it grew out of the conventional imperial concern with the health of the far-flung British empire and the capacity of the nation to sustain it. Baden-Powell's impulses in forming the Scouts were less abstractly ideal than narrowly practical: He wanted an efficient citizenry that would avoid sedition at home so that it might better shore up the empire abroad. In this way he shared the anxieties and the vision of the turn-of-the-century Social Imperialists, whose worry about the state of the empire led them to be worried about the usefulness of the people at home as well. The Scouts simply

represented Baden-Powell's contribution to the solution of a problem that occupied many people.

An essential, if sometimes unacknowledged, piece of imperial
ideology is the necessary belief in the inferiority of the people whose
lands are being appropriated. Imperial conquest, as Joseph Conrad
noted, is always redeemed by the idea,[3] and the idea is made viable
only by the conviction that the people upon whom civilization is
being conferred desperately need help, having nothing of their own.
Imperialism brings with it the insistence on the nothingness of "the
other," and its need to be shaped into something humanly significant not only for its own sake but for the sake of the world at large.
Any conception of equality among people, particularly between the
subject people and those whose divine mission it is to rule, would
obviously undercut the philosophic justification of imperialism.
Such a notion, therefore, is literally unthinkable, and to assume
that Baden-Powell, as a well-adjusted imperialist, might entertain
such a profoundly disturbing view would be to misunderstand both
him and the imperial ethos in which he lived.

The attitudes we are about to investigate, then, while not admirable, are at least explicable, forming part of a coherent ideology
in which the founder of Scouting could cheerfully combine the most
pernicious kind of racism with sincere aspirations for world harmony. The earliest work we have embodying Baden-Powell's judgments of the African are his accounts of two military expeditions
he made against them in the 1890s. Antedating Scouting by
roughly ten years, *The Downfall of Prempeh* (1896) and *The Matebele
Campaign* (1897) nevertheless reveal a set of assumptions about native behavior that Baden-Powell, even as Chief Scout, never repu-
diated. The common thread uniting both accounts is the testimony
about the savagery, stupidity, and the indolence of the natives.
When Prempeh, king of the Ashanti, wanted to darken the red
stucco of his palace walls, Baden-Powell dutifully reports, "the
blood of four hundred virgins was used."[4] Nothing much better
could be expected of such a man, of course, with "his flabby yellow
face glistening with oil, and his somewhat stupid expression rendered even more idiotic by his sucking a large nut like a fat cigar".[5]
Prempeh's flaccid stupidity is emblematic of a country that seems
to lack intelligence and wit of any sort. Attempting to put together
a native levy to assist in the march to Prempeh's village, Baden-
Powell laments his inability to find natives capable of working:

> The native was apparently incapable of grasping any idea
> of punctuality; lying was the natural form of every statement

or promise he made; lying was the natural attitude assumed by his body, especially when any work was to be done.

Moreover, in the present instance, the trade gin of the metropolis had come sweet to the lips of the countryman just called up from his village, and his natural stupidity was thereby rendered doubly dense. One good point about these warriors was their cowardice; the least hint of an intention of backing up an order with force ensured its prompt obedience....[6]

Assembled finally by the threat of beatings, the natives, in all of their dullness (demonstrated, apparently, by their lack of enthusiasm for helping the white man punish a native king), resemble something not quite human:

> Then it is a sight for the gods to see.... The stupid inertness of the puzzled negro is duller than that of an ox; a dog would grasp your meaning in one-half the time. Men and brothers! They may be brothers, but they certainly are not men.[7]

In the midst of detailing his preparations for the march to Prempeh's stronghold, Baden-Powell even has time for some philosophic meditation on why slavery is not so repugnant for the native of limited ambition and talent:

> Wherever there is a good market for them, it is to the interest of the owner to keep them well fed and in good condition. In those parts where domestic slavery prevails, there is often little or no hardship. An occasional lick from a whip is, to an unintelligent savage, but a small matter where in the opposite scale he has the very substantial compensation of protection, food, and home—advantages which are not always shared by his white brother when fate has frowned and has turned him into the cold to work out his living among the unemployed.
>
> The worst part of slavery is, as a rule, the hardships entailed in the slave-caravan marches, which have to be conducted at a forced pace over desert and devious routes, in order to avoid the good intentions of the European anti-slavery forces.[8]

Prempeh is subdued without any fighting—a source of some regret to Baden-Powell, who notes that "The ammunition is ready and we really hope that now at least a brush will be our reward."[9]

As battles with the poorly armed natives tended to be more like sport than anything else, Baden-Powell was forced to suffer through the humiliation and imprisonment of Prempeh without any of the compensatory pleasure of the hunt:

> The longest march seems short when one is hunting game. Your whole attention is fixed at the same time on "distant views," and on the spoor beneath your nose. Your gun is ready, and every sense is on the alert to see the game. Lion or leopard, boar or buck, nigger or nothing, you never know what is going to turn up.[10]

(The dehumanizing of the native, a technique fundamental to the imperial sensibility everywhere, is powerfully articulated in this passage that defines him as just another animal exciting to hunt.)

Baden-Powell professes no particular animus against the black man; it is simply that he must be treated in a special way, with a harshness that would not be appropriate for a white man:

> But, however good they may be, they must as a people, be ruled with a hand of iron in a velvet glove; and if they writhe under it, and don't understand the force of it, it is no use to add more padding—you must take off the glove for a moment and show them the hand. They will then understand and obey.[11]

Presenting the native as an animal to be hunted and a recalcitrant child to be disciplined, Baden-Powell employs one of the effective rhetorical strategies of imperialism to deny him that fully independent adult status that would be morally distressing to the imperial mission. There are, to be sure, isolated instances of good natives, though even here the rhetoric of imperialism finds a peculiarly trenchant way of dealing with such an anomaly. Discussing the virtues of a loyal native scout, Jan Grootboom, who served him well, Baden-Powell cites the testimony of an approving white scout:

> As one of Grey's Scouts—and one who loathed the ordinary Kaffir—said of him: "He is not a proper nigger; his skin is black, but he has a white man's heart. I will shake hands with him."[12]

Baden-Powell was sufficiently taken with this evaluation to use it as his own in several places when demonstrating the possibility

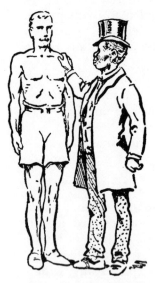

A WHITE MAN AND A MAN.

of finding competent, courageous natives: " 'Yes'—Jan had proved himself a white man—if in black skin."[13] White and black, then, embody sharply opposed moral aggregates; the only way to account for the admirable native, in such a system, is to assume that within the black skin lurks a white heart or head or guts. To be a "white man" constitutes for Baden-Powell a potent shorthand for describing what is best in people: "By gentleman I don't mean a toff with white spats and eye-glass and money, but a 'white man,' a fellow whose honour you can rely upon through thick and thin to deal straight, to be chivalrous and to be helpful."[14]

The view of the black man as at best ineffectual and childlike, at worst savage, rupt, and indolent remained constant throughout Baden-Powell's life. His position as Chief Scout and his experiences as a world traveler did nothing to alter his sharply honed sense of the vast difference between white and black, a difference that he suggested even animals appreciated. In *Indian Memories*, Baden-Powell reminisces about the young wild boar who lived in his compound and would come out when food was brought:

> I think he knew the difference between a white man and a black, for when I offered it to him he would approach very suspiciously and make snaps at the food and dart away again. When, however, my native servant took the food out, the little brute went straight for him, cutting at his legs with his diminutive tusks....[15]

The young boar was apparently as capable of the same keen discrimination as the dog in Africa who, finding himself thirsty and without his master, "took his bowl in his mouth and made his way to the magistrate's office in the town, where he knew there would be a white man therefore a friend to animals."[16]

The message he always conveyed to the Scout readers of his books is how inferior and primitive the black is wherever he is to be found. In *Boy Scouts Beyond the Seas* (1913), he points out that in

Australia the current blacks, who replaced a "cowardly, murderous lot who fell back before the whites,"

> are not quite like other negroes, and they have a great deal of hair, and their foreheads are low and come very forward over the eyes, so that they are even plainer than the African nigger, and he is no beauty. . . .
>
> Like the Bushmen, the lowest type of native in Africa, some of them live in a sort of nest without having the sense to build themselves huts—they are almost like monkeys, and yet in both countries they draw very good pictures on the rocks with coloured chalks and charcoal.[17]

The Australian Negroes, living "almost like monkeys," are not terribly different from the aborigines who inhabit a group of gulf islands, "an absolutely wild, uneducated people who know nothing about law or civilization, living almost like animals, but not quite. They have rules and customs of their own. They have not proper religion, but they believe that they have 'a little body inside their body.'"[18] Both these can be contrasted with the Filipino natives, "a dark but civilised race, nice, but inclined to be rather lazy, so they don't make as much out of their country as the more energetic white men do."[19]

Occasionally, "cheerful-looking blackies" are invoked to help encourage British youth in some healthy practice, as for example those of an African tribe with "great grinning mouths, showing their white, even teeth,"[20] which they keep clean: "I hope that Wolf Cubs, at any rate, will not be beaten by a blackie at his, and that you will clean your teeth, as they do, every morning and every evening."[21]

Nowhere in Baden-Powell's extensive writings do we find any indication that nonwhite cultures might possess their own integrity and form or that blacks could seriously maintain any claim to equality with whites. Charming in their innocence, and at times even capable, with strict tutelage, of proper obedience, blacks primarily testify by contrast to the glories of white European civilization, as well as to the immense challenge that civilization faces in bringing them up to scratch by teaching them to be bricks and play the game as any proper white sportsman would. And even when they do learn the rules, blacks still cannot quite be expected to perform the way the white sportsman can. Arguing for the importance of self-control in making a gentleman, Baden-Powell points out, in *Rovering to Success*,

> I used to play polo against a certain team who had a very good black player; but he had his weak spot, he was not a gentleman, he had a bad temper.
>
> So one only had to bump into him once or catch his stick just as he was about to hit the ball [both allowable in the game] and he lost his temper, and with it his head, for the rest of the game, and was perfectly useless to his side.[22]

Presumably one of the best ways to train blacks properly would be to enroll the rising generation of them in the Scout movement, and this brings us to a fascinating episode in Scout history concerning the role of the black Scout in the South African movement. The problem Baden-Powell faced in this racially segregated country is what should an organization that insists it "overlooks all differences of creed, colour, country, caste and class"[23] do about the desire of blacks to join the Scout brotherhood? The issue put squarely on the line the matter of Scout principle and the absolute moral imperatives Scouting claimed to represent. Its resolution made abundantly clear that when arrayed against the forces of social prudence and expediency, principles turn out to be thoroughly negotiable.

The principles, of course, were unambiguous: As Baden-Powell writes to the duke of Connaught in 1936, explaining the difficulties of his position, the movement was intended to be "open to all, irrespective of class, colour, creed or country."[24] The risks were equally clear: The potential loss of white membership if blacks were permitted to join. "White parents would never allow their children to consort with black. Any attempt on the part of the Scout Movement to bring this about would mean its boycott by the whites."[25]

From the start, Baden-Powell sided with the risks. "I am inclined to agree with Major Edwards," he writes in 1916, "regarding the exclusion of coloured boys from the Scout movement in the Cape, at any rate for the present,"[26] a position he endorses a year later, when he advises H. W. Soutter in Johannesburg that "the course you are taking is the right one, namely to let the natives use some of our ideas but not to admit them directly into the Brotherhood."[27] Baden-Powell hoped the pressure would be taken off by the establishment in the early 1920s of a distinct movement for the natives, known as the Pathfinders, to be run under the supervision of the Boy Scout Association, but separately administered, and calling for separate uniforms. The Pathfinders, Baden-Powell stressed, anxious that some might misunderstand, were definitely not part of Scouting, but a separate organization, run on parallel lines, with "similar ideals adapted to the mentality of the native."[28] Although Baden-Powell claimed the experiment was moderately successful, with some 4,000 blacks enrolled, in fact it did not in the least solve the problem. Blacks continued to want to join the Scouts proper, and Baden-Powell continued to want to make the issue go away. When confronted by a group of blacks who confessed their puzzlement that they were not admitted to a movement that explicitly stated that there was no color bar. Baden-Powell took dazzlingly evasive action:

> In replying to the deputation I expressed my hearty sympathy wth them, having seen their good work at service esp. in Matabeleland and Mafeking. I fully appreciated their tribute to the Scout and Guide movement.... But I pointed out that the movement is scarcely as yet on its right footing in South Africa which is the reason for my present visit here. Nor am I in a position to give orders on this point. Undoubtedly there were prejudices of long standing and wide prevalence.

I shall study the question closely in the different parts of the country to see whether a way out of the difficulty can be devised... There are many sides to the question which need study and consideration—and I want to cut fairly to all. If the coloured people are in a hurry for immediate action they might send their boys to the B.B. [Boys' Brigade] or CLB [Church Lads' Brigade] which have their coloured battalions.[29]

The dilemma was real, complicated by Baden-Powell's recognition that as the blacks grew in number and self-awareness, a certain element of white self-interest would argue for including them in the Scout system of character training. Beyond the issue, that is, of what "As Scouts, as white men and as Christians,"[30] constituted proper behavior towards the blacks, Baden-Powell saw a rather less exalted political situation developing, with blacks "now becoming educated and therefore class conscious. It seems up to us to inculcate in them a feeling of good-will and a sense of having been fairly treated rather than to let them grow up dissatisfied and disgruntled, and therefore ready dupes to communists and agitators."[31]

After years of anxiety and debate about how to proceed, the issue was finally resolved in 1936 with a master stroke of political expediency that managed to avoid the real issue of Scout policy entirely. The solution, hammered out over a two-day meeting in February of the South African Scout Council, called for the creation of three independent parallel organizations federated under the direct supervision of the parent Scout Council. The three organizations, each of which would have its own administrative apparatus and remain entirely separate from one another and the actual South African Boy Scouts, more or less covered the full range of ethnic variety offered by the country: The Pathfinder Boy Scouts, for the blacks; the Indian Boy Scouts, for the considerable number of Hindus and Moslems in South Africa; and the Coloured Boy Scouts, for the half-castes. All came under the rules and regulations of the European Scout Council, all had representation on that council, all had the authority to wear appropriate Scout uniforms with one exception: Any of the non-European sections wishing to wear the distinctive Baden-Powell hat could only do so if "it is worn with a pugaree or some other distinctive and visible dressing, their junior sections using a head-dress of different colour to that of the Wolf Cubs."[32] Insisting on the differentiation of uniform underlined the council's central concern that no one confuse the three federated sections with the original one:

The Scout Council desires to make it clear that these proposals do not mean amalgamation, affiliation or any form of
closer union between the European and non-European sections
of the community. Each of the sections will be self-contained,
self-governing and entirely separate from the others. . . .

The Scout Council would emphasize that it is not intended
that there shall be any joint scout activities, but that each section shall pursue its separate path along its own racial lines.[33]

In short, a way of extending Scout privileges and training to the
natives without compromising the racial purity of the "European
section" and arousing the antagonism of the white community.
Baden-Powell rejoiced in this imaginative solution, assuring the
duke of Connaught that "this Federation can, and will do a very
valuable work in promoting loyalty and the ethics of good citizenship among the uncultured races who are only now emerging from
primitive savagery into civilization."[34] It prevented the South African council from amending its constitution—which it was on the
verge of doing—to state that the movement was only for white boys
and yet managed to include natives and blacks in a way that guaranteed that the white Scouts would in fact not be contaminated by
contact with these lesser races.[35] Baden-Powell applauded the moral
force of the decision, seeing it as "a step that puts the movement
on to a higher status with wider responsibilities throughout the
union. . . . We may be criticized but the Scoutlike way is to go on
with the right and to do justice to the Non-Europeans and to give
them equal chance of becoming good citizens."[36]

The lamentable part of this whole episode was not simply the
failure of the movement to deal directly with the principled question
of what its policy of being open to all actually meant, but the
swaddling of its failure in self-righteous rhetoric. Conferring on this
manipulation of the native the sanction of a courageous moral
stand of which Scouting could be proud only emphasized the
cynicism of its position. Scouting's decision to finesse rather than
speak out on the color issue certainly comprises one of the less
edifying chapters in its history.

The Indian represented a different sort of problem from the
black for Baden-Powell. While the defects of the black were seen to
be those stemming from their primitive, childlike state—savagery,
petulance, indolence, stupidity—requiring the careful nurture of
British civilization to bring them to a state of cultural maturity,

Baden-Powell viewed the Indian as a rather more sophisticated people with an arrogance and pretension to superiority—or just as bad, equality—that needed to be chastened. In addition, the seething Indian political self-consciousness posed a threat to the stability of the empire that no one concerned with imperial strength could overlook. Baden-Powell's emphasis is accordingly on the need to keep them under control, justified by the fact that they don't yet possess sufficient character and honesty to permit them to function on their own. The British role is to protect them from themselves—and incidentally to preserve British control of the country.

An exemplary instance of how to deal with the Indian is given in *Yarns for Boy Scouts* (1909), in which Baden-Powell recounts how his uncle William Cotton Oswell, meeting a surly native who refused to show proper deference by stepping aside on a path, taught him a lesson by throwing him bodily into a rice paddy. Baden-Powell's commentary is instructive:

> This reads to a Scout, perhaps, as rather a bad tempered thing to do; but you must remember that some of these natives are not possessed of the same ideas and minds as white men; they have no idea of chivalry themselves, and are full of conceit and self-importance, and if this is allowed to grow without check they are apt to become insolent and mutinous, which is a very dangerous thing in a country like Africa, where millions of natives are ruled by a very small handful of whites.
>
> It is therefore necessary to remind them now and then to respect British rulers, and nothing commands respect more than a show of bodily strength and pluck when their conduct deserves it. But it should never by any chance be carried to the extent of bullying.
>
> With reference to the story of Oswell's treatment of the uncivil Indian, you need not suppose that he was so bad a scout as to use natives badly as a rule; on the contrary, he fully recognized and valued their good points—when they had any.[37]

The unwarranted—and thoroughly unattractive—assertiveness of the native can further be seen by contrast to a previous, but no less unappealing, servility. Recalling how, when he first arrived in India, he wrote that "the niggers seem to me cringing villains.... If you meet a man in the road and tell him to dust your boots, he does it," he notes in *Indian Memories* (1915) that everything has changed:

It is very different nowadays, when the natives are put on a higher standing with the Europeans. In some quarters it is complained that they are allowed to become too familiar: in a native state under native rule they still carry out the practice of saluting their own rajahs and any white man who comes there, but in British India they now treat a white man merely as an equal. Theoretically this is as it should be, but practically, until they are fit to govern themselves, it is a danger— to themselves.

It is generally acknowledged that to be able to rule a man must first have learnt how to obey. In the training of the average Indian boy there is not as yet any discipline nor any attempt to inculcate in him a sense of honour, of fair play, of honesty, truth, and self-discipline and other attributes which go to make a reliable man of character.[38]

And we remember the outrage of General Nicholson, in the tableau from the first edition of *Scouting for Boys*, where Mehtab Singh refused to take off his shoes in Nicholson's presense: "But you forget that you are dealing with a Briton—one of that band who never brooks an insult even from an equal, much less from a native of this land."

The need to keep the Indians in check politically caused the Scouting authorities to be wary about extending Scouting membership to natives. Although proper training in loyalty might be precisely what they needed, organizing them in any way was potentially dangerous, opening up the possibility of infiltration by revolutionary elements. Baden-Powell was eager to enroll native boys into the movement (in their own troops of course), but was sympathetic to the concern of government officials about the threat of sedition. There is always the danger of moving too quickly with natives who lack the foundation of sound character:

I am fully persuaded that half the trouble brought about by the natives imbibing Western ideas is due to the fact that they are not grounded in the very essential quality of Character as the first step to their education. They are singularly without character by nature and are then merely crammed up with knowledge and visionary ideas till their heads become too big for their hats; then they seek for an outlet through revolutionary societies, etc.[39]

Despite the governmental concern that "in the present condition of Indian politics any such organisation among Indian boys would be exposed to evil influences,"[40] Scouting finally decided to address the deficiencies in the native character by opening itself to separate Indian troops in 1921.

Ironically, it was Baden-Powell's very concern with character and his conviction of the difficulties of conveying the proper ideals to Indian lads that led to the Indian Scout movement severing all relationship with the Boy Scout Association in 1937 and setting up its own independent organization. The difficulties centred on the notion of honor that Baden-Powell pointed out was "the keystone to character."[41] The Hindustani language, Baden-Powell claimed, had no word that carried the full weight of the Scout conception of "honor," a problem that made the task of shaping Indian character along proper lines far more complicated than it would otherwise have been. Immediately a deluge of protest broke out from Indian Scout officials throughout the country who argued, not implausibly, that Baden-Powell was implying that the Indians had no sense of honor. This tactless comment called for repudiation, but Baden-Powell refused to acknowledge that he was guilty of at least an impropriety. He steadfastly defended his position on linguistic grounds. In response to a request from a British Scoutmaster in India who begged Baden-Powell to help him (and other Scouts) withstand the crisis that was developing, Baden-Powell clung to his semantic guns:

> When in India I asked one or two Scouters what word they used for "Honour" in teaching their boys character and they said, "Izzut." I asked 2 or 3 other men what was the Hindustani for "Honour" and they could only suggest "Izzut." But Izzut does not convey the idea of Honour. I allow we have not the exact equivalent in English for Izzut and have to borrow from the French—"Prestige."[42]

Claiming that he was sorry to have caused such a fuss, he nevertheless would not apologize—or admit that the comment might have legitimately caused offense. Should Indians desert the movement because of his statement, even that might not be bad:

> But the very rapid increase of Scout numbers in India last year led one to fear a mushroom growth and if, as a result of this agitation, there is an equally big slump in numbers, I think it will be all to the good for the soundness of the Movement and its future success.[43]

On 6 July the Bombay Provincial Scout Council passed a resolution pointing out that there were a number of words that effectively caught the sense of honor, words that were already being used with the Scout Promise in India, and asking for the Chief Scout to rectify the misunderstanding.[44] But Baden-Powell would have none of it and would not answer. On 11 August the council met again. Regretting that no action had been taken on their earlier resolution, they called upon general headquarters to respond before 30 September on threat of "the immediate severance of the Boy Scout Association of India from the control of Imperial Hqrs., and the establishment of an independent federation for India composed of representatives from autonomous Province and State Associations."[45] Such were the consequences of Baden-Powell's decision to cling unyieldingly to his principles. He could, after all, be tenacious when it mattered.

Both in its conscious articulation of values, attitudes, and even policy, as well as in its configuration of unquestioned racial assumptions, there was little that was actually color-blind about Scouting. The huge number of nonwhites constituting the British empire made it impossible that Scouting's professed indifference to color could be real, any more than its professed indifference to class was real. Both the poor whites of Britain and the natives of the empire in fact represented similar objects of concern.[46] In their moral and intellectual weakness, and their inability to comprehend the salutary nature of obedience and selfless service, the working-class lads of London, like the blacks of South Africa, required the shaping influence of Scout ideals to enable them to participate fully in the responsibilities and privileges of the empire. Scouting pursued its colonizing mission with a detailed set of preconceived ideas about the inhabitants to be found in the exotic lands of Africa and in the equally exotic slums of London.

Like class and color, religion was another area in which purported Scout indifference proves rather more complicated upon analysis. Certainly there was no issue at all on the level of policy. Baden-Powell's main concern about Scouting's religious position was that it not limit the potential popularity of the movement by insisting on a strict religious affiliation of the sort required by the Boys' Brigade, and that it not alienate the country's religious and moral establishment by paying too little attention to religion. The solution was fashioned at a Scout conference in 1909, with the clever formulation that every Scout was *expected* to "belong to some religious denomination and attend its services."[47] This succeeded in satisfying the

Church authorities that religion was an appropriate part of the movement, while at the same time leaving the question of observance or even belief entirely up to the Scout. If it was expected that there would be some form of belief, nevertheless nobody was excluded who had none. The "expected" became an effective escape clause that permitted boys to join who had no notion of religion whatever.

Although as a matter of policy Baden-Powell and his organization did remain happily indifferent to religious preferences of any kind, both were concerned about the behavior and values of the Jew, whom they viewed largely through the prism of a traditional anti-Semitic stereotype. I am not suggesting that either the movement as a whole or Baden-Powell in particular was guilty of anything akin to programmatic anti-Semitism—they were not—but it remains the case that woven into the strands of both are conceptions of Jewish character that are unacceptable for anybody to hold, particularly those associated with a movement professing Scouting's ideals.

Perhaps the ugliest item on the record is the report that Captain Walker, one of Baden-Powell's early Scout traveling commissioners, submitted about his trip to Russia in 1920. Depicting the Jews as manipulating the Russian Revolution for their own ends, it teems with a genuine—and virulent—anti-Semitism:

> Before long Europe will wake up and find with surprise how greatly she is in the power of the Jews. In England, for example, we have our Samuels, our Isaacs, and Lawsons, and scores of the men who control the Empire who are not British but Jews, and who will put Jewish interests before British interests. Then there are the international Jew Financiers, Rothschilds, and others as clever but less well known. They have no country and no patriotism but only work for themselves and their race. They, to a large extent hold the control of Europe in their hands and use it for their own ends. They have far too much sense to fight themselves; they stir up other people to make wars, make fortunes by war speculation and lend them to the people who are fighting, at a good rate of interest.
>
> A friend of mine, an Englishman, had the pleasure of hanging a Jew a few days ago. A Russian Captain a year ago was caught by the bolsheviks, imprisoned and condemned to death because he kept his nails clean and brushed his clothes. He escaped and a day or two ago while on the station platform ran into the Jewish Commissar who had condemned him to

death. The Jew was searched and they found papers on him proving his identity and that he was here to raise the Crimea in favour of the bolshevik. When they took him under a handy lamp-post the Russians began to have an argument as to who was to have the pleasure of doing the deed "so just to save any unpleasantness among my friends" said the Englishman "I just stepped along and yanked him up myself."[48]

Walker even recommends that Baden-Powell obtain a copy of the *Protocols of the Elders of Zion*, an insidious, bogus treatise much beloved by anti-Semites that claims to reveal the plans for world domination hatched by the scheming Jewish leaders. Baden-Powell received the report with equanimity, apparently finding nothing in it objectionable.

While Baden-Powell is guilty of none of Walker's excesses, it is clear from a variety of comments that Walker's vision was not essentially different from his own. In a letter to Sir Alfred Pickford about a Mr. Weinthal, an editor and old South African acquaintance of his, for example, Baden-Powell echoes the anti-Semitic allegation, found in Walker's report, about Jews being out only for their own ends. Weinthal, he points out, is not that kind of Jew: "He is a Jew by descent but not in practise and I think he is wholeheartedly out for the good of the show and not for himself."[49]

When asked for his advice regarding a Jewish officer assigned to a regiment whose subalterns told him he was not wanted, Baden-Powell expressed a similar concern:

> For my part, looking at the general question we have to recognise the fact that there is a prejudice against Jews not only among the officers but also among the NCOs and men, which is a very important point in discipline.
>
> The senior officers can possibly get over their prejudice but with the younger officers who have to live with [him] and be comrades it is a different thing—and they cannot help feeling that the average Jew who comes into the service does not do so for love of soldiering so much as to gain position in society (Jews without money do not join the army), using them, the Regt., as his introduction. He is as a rule not an English gentleman and very often not even an English public school man—so he cannot well amalgamate.[50]

Inveterate Jewish vulgarity, of the kind that keeps the male Jew from being an English gentleman, is most memorably reflected in

Baden-Powell's own illustration, in *Life's Snags and How to Meet Them* (1927), of the socially pretentious nouveau riche woman displaying her jewels. The caricatured features are precisely those one finds in the German anti-Semitic publications of the 1930s.[51] Less dramatic but expressing the same reservation about Jewish character is the passing comment he makes in his 1935 diary on a visit to Tanganyika about the chances of "Mrs Abrahams wife of Chief Justice ... being next in rank [who] wishes to become Chief Commissioner—but the Chief Justice is unpopular since he is a Jew and boasts unfailingly in season and out."[52]

YET THERE'S 5 PER CENT OF GOOD IN EVEN THAT—SOMEWHERE

Baden-Powell seems also to share the notion, dear to the heart of the early twentieth-century anti-Semite, that socialist agitation generally and the Russian Revolution in particular were part of a Jewish conspiracy. Given Baden-Powell's anxieties about socialist sedition undermining the imperial wall of harmonious bricks, such a conviction was serious indeed, requiring little else to condemn the Jewish character.[53] In a 1924 issue of the *Scouter*, Baden-Powell argues that,

> I am not touching on party politics when I say that Moscow, under its German–Jew direction, is working hard to

make its own use of the after war confusion, and to spread its blighting influence everywhere, even over its own people.[54]

When a Mr. Yellin of the Jewish Boy Scouts in Palestine objected to this comment, Baden-Powell wrote to him,

> I am very glad that you have warned me through the editor of the *Scouter* that a misconstruction has been placed on my remarks to the Scouters of January 1st in regard to the Jews.
>
> I promise therefore to apologise and to explain the matter in the next available issue of the *Scouter* in the terms enclosed.
>
> I sincerely hope that this will show you that in speaking of this individual I had no idea of making any allegation against Jews in general.
>
> I shall be very grateful if you will make known to your friends my great regret at having unwittingly caused this misapprehension to arise.[55]

But Baden-Powell didn't just publish an apology. Before responding to Yellin, he sent a note to a staff member asking if it could be determined from the secretary of the Empire League whether or not he was right in describing the head of the Moscow Soviet as a German Jew. A memo came back as follows:

> Mr. Wilson of the British Empire Union says that the Lenin revolution was kept going by the German banks, but that Lenin himself (whose real name was Ulianoss) was a *Russian*. The other leaders were mostly aliens. Trotski (whose real name was Braunstein) was a German Jew, also Kameneff and Litvinoff, and there is no doubt that the German Jews were behind the movement—in fact engineered it, though it is difficult to state proofs.[56]

Armed with this information, Baden-Powell then published his "apology" in the July issue of *Scouter:*

> In my outlook for January last I said—"I am not touching on party politics when I say that Moscow, under its German-Jew direction. . . ."
>
> I have received a protest from an officer of the Jewish Boy Scouts in Palestine who evidently feels that this is an allegation against Jews generally and also against Germans. Such an idea never occurred to me.

As a matter of fact the Bolshevist of whom I am writing has
been described to me as a German by birth and Jew by religion.

I am glad to learn that the Zionists of Palestine resent his
being described as a Jew, because as they inform me—"as far
as our knowledge goes those of the Soviet leaders who are of
Jewish origin have most if not all of them renounced the faith
of their forefathers."

I am so very sorry if my remarks about an individual should
have been taken to imply, even indirectly, an attack on Jews
generally, for I have on the contrary the greatest admiration
for the race. My article had no political or sectarian intention
whatever.[57]

Seemingly oblivious as to why people might have found his initial
remark offensive, Baden-Powell responds as if the issue were all the
time a question of fact as to whether or not "Trotski" could be
considered a Jew. In its willful failure to acknowledge the full social
implications behind his statement, his answer is even more disturbing than his original comment. It is, altogether, an episode that tells
us more about Baden-Powell's attitudes toward Jews than even he
was probably aware.[58] Baden-Powell's feelings about Jews were
sufficiently strong that when he was asked in 1933 by the League
to Combat Anti-Semitism to contribute a statement protesting the
Nazi persecution of the Jews, he responded that "I am afraid I
have not the time to write more than a very brief message that
would be as follows: Nationalism carried too far is no longer true
patriotism but is a vice which leads to war."[59] Managing to avoid
any mention of Nazis, Jews, or the rights of individuals to live their
lives in peace under protection of the law, it was not a statement
that expressed much outrage at what was happening.

With or without Jewish leadership, Bolshevist agitators out to
capture the minds of the young constitued the postwar peril that
Baden-Powell invoked in advertising the importance of the Scouts.
Unlike his prewar German peril of invasion, which involved preparing the youth of the country, both physically and morally, for
selfless and disciplined service on the battlefield, the Bolshevist invasion required preparing youth to resist the slippery arguments of
agitators who would try to lay claim to their minds. The urgency
with which Baden-Powell touted the Scout crusade after the war
thus had a rather more narrowly defined educational character than
it did previously. Britain's rising generations had to be able to reject
the blandishments of the Bolshies, and no institution better

equipped them to do so than the Scouts: "We are out to develop efficient citizenship and to prevent bolshevism. Bolshevism is the result of ignorance led by half-baked intelligence. To this end we want to put into the *mass* of boys what is at present only got by the few."[60] A properly trained Scout was to be Britain's best antidote to Communist lies. Unlike the Scouts, who can't be taken in,

> These thieves ... know that a very large number of lads *are* fools.
>
> That is how Bolshevism succeeded so well in countries where the young men were largely fools or funks—and the two generally go together.
>
> A man comes along and makes a speech, or hands out a paper telling them what a splendid thing it would be to be free, to be bound by no laws, to work or not when they pleased, to get lots of money and have the use of other people's property as their right.
>
> But he did not explain how it was to be done—that you had to murder the other people to get their property, and let the country become ruined and bankrupt because nobody wanted to do any work.[61]

Baden-Powell never renounced his official insistence that Scouting had no political bias, but he does at least acknowledge the educational contribution Scouting can make in establishing a healthy political climate that will be free of socialism's noxious vapors:

> Wrong ideas and fallacies are actually and deliberately taught to children in Socialist schools. False doctrine, heresy, and schism are definitely preached to workers by means of leaflets and addresses so that antagonism is the prevailing spirit. It is all based on wrong grounds. We don't, in the Scouts, want to join in the politics which somehow get mixed up with the economic question, but we do want to educate the coming man as to where his best interests lie and how, in serving his country's commercial interests, he is also serving his own.[62]

Baden-Powell's aspirations for a Scouting movement that would be totally absorbed into the educational system of the country, affording character training and proper political indoctrination to

every member of the rising generation, led him, in the 1930s, to an
immense admiration for the Balilla, the fascist youth organization
Mussolini had established in Italy for similar purposes. His enthusiasm for the methods, aims and spirit of the organization was
matched by his delight in Mussolini himself and his vision of the
role appropriately educated youth would play in the future of Italy.
In an article following an interview with Mussolini in 1933,[63]
Baden-Powell noted,

> The Duce realises that if his Fascist revolution is to live its
> permanence will largely depend on the moulding of the men
> of tomorrow.
> As he remarked to me, "Our future is in the hands of the
> boys."
> He is himself a "boy-man," with sons of his own and fond
> of boys; but apart from this he recognizes their future impor-
> tance to the state, and also he recognizes the omission in the
> normal system of education of any adequate steps for training
> them to meet that responsibility. So he had added a new
> branch to the national education which aims to produce, by
> progressive development, men strong in body, disciplined in
> character, capable as craftsmen, and united in patriotism for
> the defence of their country.
> The B.S.M. had been widely established in Italy many
> years before Mussolini's advent, and when his scheme came
> to be adopted for all boys the Scouts were naturally absorbed
> into it.
> But to them the change was not a great one, since the new
> organisation was formed on the lines of the Scout movement.[64]

Baden-Powell thought it a brilliantly successful "experiment in
applying Scout training to the national education."[65] He was impressed not only by the principles of the training—many of which,
he proudly pointed out, were in any case taken from the Scouts—
but by the resources, both material and human, committed to it.
The extraordinary facilities of a Provincial Headquarters, with its
modern health clinic, its workshops, electrical and wireless equipment, cinema and dormitories overwhelmed him, as did the sight
of the enthusiastic instructors readying themselves for their educational task: "It was a joy to see these splendid types of young
manhood earnestly preparing themselves for the best service for
their country, namely for building up, wholesale, a new manly and
united nation."[66] Above all, there was the intense pleasure the boys

themselves took in being part of this disciplined effort to create a new Italy—telling proof of the rightness of Mussolini's vision:

> I found that there was undoubted keenness on the part of the boys; one could see it. I asked, for instance, what punishment they had for non-attendance. None; the boys came eagerly, proud of themselves and full of enthusiasm.
>
> When in company with the Provincial Commissioner I visited the gymnasium I noted one little straw which suggested how the wind blew.
>
> A squad of boys was at voluntary fencing practice. When the Chief came in all work stopped, every lad sprang to attention and gave the Fascist salute.
>
> Till the Commissioner had returned it and had told them to carry on, all stood still as graven images. Once released, however, they were cheery and friendly, laughing and chattering with the Commissioner, and I realized that though there was strict discipline a strong human touch underlay it.[67]

In comparing the Scouts with the Balilla, Baden-Powell points out two essential differences. First the Balilla sought "to develop a strong nationalistic spirit coupled with efficiency for military service,"[68] (Baden-Powell's position notwithstanding, the difference between the two on this issue is not so great); second, the Balilla was an official organization of the government, not a private, voluntary movement like the Scouts. Despite its official status, however, the Balilla retained a certain voluntary feature in that all members had first to obtain the consent of their parents. Given the fact that "it is not obligatory on the youngsters,"[69] Baden-Powell expressed some astonishment that so many seemed to be taking it up:

> I asked Signor Mussolini how this was brought about, and with very appropriate gesture he said, "Simply by moral force." The fact that moral force is already exercising so strong an effect on this young experiment augurs well for the future of Italy.[70]

Ending his account of the Balilla and his discussion with Mussolini with an evocation of the moral force sweeping through Italy, Baden-Powell finds nothing objectionable about either. Mussolini's commitment to preparing Italian youth "for those very things that are needed for a modern nation, namely an improved general standard in strength of character, of body, mind and spirit,"[71] was Baden-Powell's own, and he viewed its success with considerable pleasure and respect.

By 1940, however, admiration for the vision and achievements of Italian fascism was not something one was happy to acknowledge, and it is fascinating to watch Baden-Powell, a year before his death, try to repair the evidence of his earlier misplaced enthusiasm. Sending Percy Everett some notes on youth-training schemes, Baden-Powell presents his 1933 interview with Mussolini in a somewhat different light. Here he indicates he criticized the Balilla on four grounds: It was obligatory instead of voluntary; it aimed for a narrow nationalism; it was purely physical, lacking any spiritual dimension; it encouraged mass cohesion instead of stimulating individual character growth. In addition to the fact that none of these objections figured in his initial response to Mussolini's scheme, the way in which he now portrays Mussolini's discussion of the degree to which the movement can be thought of as voluntary is particularly interesting:

> Mussolini objected that every boy had to consult his parents about joining the Balilla. With the parents the force of moral suasion prevailed, which in Italian fashion he illustrated by placing his finger across his nose and above it with his eyes he gave a cruel malevolent leer, then squeezing the palms of his hands together he said, "Of course for the *parents* it is different. They feel the moral obligation for their sons to join the Balilla."
>
> Then he added with a grin, which implied if they didn't feel it they would be likely to feel a knife in their gizzard, that he did not recognize the importance of the boys' own initiative in the matter from [*sic*] desire to become a useful citizen.[72]

So much for the moral force that Baden-Powell had found so exhilarating seven years earlier. The movement's vast regenerative potential had in practice produced only "results ... which were mainly eyewash of smart military uniforms, without inner discipline."[73] But Baden-Powell's retroactive displeasure with the Balilla does not obscure the fact that in the group of young boys snapping to attention to give the Fascist salute he found an appealing model of a disciplined, efficient patriotism that any country would be proud to generate. Salesmen of socialist perfidy, Baden-Powell realized, would not fare well in their midst.

Nor would they in Germany, whose efforts to fashion a loyal citizenry Baden-Powell also found laudable in the 1930s. Sharing

Mussolini's concerns, "Hitler has apparently adopted a similar course. Both leaders realize that to be strong the nation must be united in patriotism. And this uniform patriotism must be impressed upon the young while still impressionable."[74] Irresistibly drawn to any system of youth training that sought, as Scouting did, to encourage strong patriotism in its young men and women, as well as to powerful leaders who could transcend the petty squabbles of politics to make things happen, Baden-Powell was blind to the full reality of Germany:

> Dictators in Germany and Italy have done wonders in resuscitating their people to stand as nations. They have recognized that mere scholastic education is not enough for building up a manhood at once efficient, healthy and patriotic—i.e., a *strong nation*. Mussolini told me he had found Italians a divided people and that the only way to make them a united whole was to get hold of the youth, from 8 years old to 22, and train them up to a common ideal of manliness and patriotism for defence of their country. He had seen the Boy Scout movement and considered it good as far as it went in Italy with those that adapted it, but it needed enforcement to make it apply to the whole of the country's youth. Thus the Balilla organisation and training was founded on that of the Boy Scouts.
>
> So, too, Germany has amalgamated its various youth societies into one general scheme of training.
>
> Though we see these nations definitely training their oncoming citizenhood, we in Britain are doing nothing beyond a call to voluntary athletic training.
>
> Yet, in these dangerous and unrestful times it is more than ever necessary for our country to train its youth to a better standard of efficiency.[75]

Despite the advice of his International Bureau, particularly Hubert Martin, its director, he was eager for the Scouts to establish official relations with the Hitler Jugend as late as 1937.[76] In response to a statement of Martin's that a certain Herr Riecke, a German youth leader who wanted to form a genuine Scout Association to offer alternatives to the Hitler Jugend, had been sent to a concentration camp for his efforts, Baden-Powell rallied to the defense of the government by telling Martin that "The man whom you quoted as sent to prison, Rieke [*sic*], was sent there, not for international tendencies, but for homosexual tendencies!"[77]

The International Committee's position, clearly articulated in 1935, that the Scouts "have nothing in common with Hitler Jugend and that any contact between Scouts and Hitler Jugend is undesirable,"[78] never ceased to trouble Baden-Powell, who continued to push for cooperation between them. Giving up the possibility of extending Scouting's connections to another youth movement, particularly one that shared so many of Scouting's ideals, was not something Baden-Powell took lightly. As long as there was no serious threat that the Jugend could create Nazis out of decent British Scouts, Baden-Powell could see no reason why he shouldn't deal with them.[79] Baden-Powell lost on this one. Scout leadership refused to recognize the Jugend, but the issue was yet another instance of what we have seen throughout this chapter, that the worldwide brotherhood of Scouting as envisioned by Baden-Powell was far more problematic than it appeared, as interesting for those it sought to include as for those it felt comfortable keeping out.

THE EMPEROR

OF YOUTH

In emphasizing the national anxieties that the Scouts at once called attention to and promised to help assuage, I do not wish to suggest that all of Edwardian England was writhing in the coils of self-doubt. Quite the contrary. The short-lived Edwardian era (which we can date from 1901 to the outbreak of war in 1914, despite Edward's death in 1910) was as dense and as filled with antithetical social tendencies as its lengthy Victorian predecessor. Conservative lament coexisted with liberal reform, complacency with a gnawing sense that all was about to end. If Lord Meath and his colleagues inveighed against the fecklessness of the poor, in 1906 the Liberals won a landslide election, and the period saw the establishment of important social legislation like the Old Age Pensions Act, the National Insurance Act, and other vital pieces of the modern welfare state. But though the complexities of early twentieth-century Britain properly prohibit simple reductiveness, it is nevertheless clear that the Scouts, in their concern with deterioration and the role of the rising generation in combating it, embodied one significant strain in the culture.

At a time when the verities of a traditional class structure were coming under increasing attack, Scouting offered the nation the comforting prospect of social regeneration without any attendant social change. It was not the inequities of economic and educational opportunity maintained by a rigid class system that were the issue, Scouting argued, but rather the moral makeup of those young people effectively closed out of its advantages. By proposing to teach them to understand their humble role in the society, Scouting earned the esteem of those worried about the potential for unrest that rose as the working class exercised its political power. The Scouts' message that attitude, not patterns of unevenly distributed affluence, had to change, provided the answer the upper classes wanted to hear. The enthusiasm with which they affirmed Scouting helped account for its extraordinary success.

Presenting itself as a socially progressive force, Scouting in fact was profoundly conservative, locating the root of most social problems in the character structure of the individual. Its efforts to counter the effects of urban pestilence through training in discipline and the therapeutic summer camping experience did little to alter or resist the conditions that led to the genuinely dehumanizing consequences of urban poverty. Allegedly an experiment in classlessness, Scouting built on, rather than sought to erase, the divisions of a highly stratified society. Baden-Powell's response to the social pathologies of postindustrial Britain was to return to the mythical world of heroic chivalry and those virtues of loyalty and discipline he felt would best guarantee national harmony. In this his voice was but one among the many we have heard speaking out for the socially healing powers of obedience.

Following its British birth, the brotherhood of Scouting rapidly expanded around the world. The pleasure that boys of all nationalities took in the company of their peers, in the satisfaction afforded by uniforms, badges, and bracing masculine activities, made it a natural product for global export. As important as the excitement it generated among the boys themselves was the social utility it offered the adults who adapted it into their different cultures. A system that undertook to train the rising generation to be obedient, dutiful citizens was hard to quarrel with, and the international growth of Scouting suggested that in fact few countries found reasons to resist. The Czar's response to the Scouts, as reported by Baden-Powell after a 1910 interview with him in Russia, that he was "much impressed by the possibilities which lie in the movement for developing discipline, patriotism and loyalty to the throne,"[1] underlines that principle of self-interest that established political

authority of every sort found in Scouting. In 1920, in addition to
the British dominions and colonies overseas, twenty-one countries
sent representatives to the first World Jamboree in London. And
that number continued to grow. For the second Jamboree in Den-
mark in 1924, twenty-four nations were represented; at the third
World Jamboree in 1929, Scouts from forty-two nations assembled
outside of Birkenhead in England.

Scouting's vast and enduring success defines a major irony in its
history, namely that the institution Baden-Powell designed to shore
up an empire in peril went on to flourish well beyond the crumbling
of that empire. Scout loyalty could do nothing to keep Britain
great, or to withstand those currents of nationalism that gradually
effaced all major traces of British world domination. Indeed,
insofar as they encouraged, in World War I trenches, the willing
acquiescence in their own slaughter of a generation of Britain's
future leaders, Scout ideals might be said to have contributed to,
rather than countered, the weakness Baden-Powell set out to cure.

In another sense, its enormous popularity notwithstanding,
Scouting must be judged a failure. For despite Baden-Powell's
claims of seeking to rescue the hooligan and street lads from the
dismal futures awaiting them, Scouting never seriously pursued the
intractable wastrels "drifting, owing to their environments, to evil."[2]
Such types would rarely, to begin with, volunteer to give themselves
over to Scouting's structured program, nor be inclined to take
kindly to the discipline and obedience enjoined on them by the
Scout Law. The ordered life of the clubhouse was not for them.
Furthermore, as Baden-Powell well knew, the legitimate street
urchin hardly constituted the kind of company that respectable
families would choose for their sons. At the same time that Baden-
Powell's rhetoric sold the country on Scouting's critical mission to
redeem Britain's lost youth, his more prudent recruiting policy
eschewed the desperate cases, opting instead for the more docile
sons of middle-class and proper working-class households. Content
to enlist the large number of boys who were attracted to it wherever
they were found, Scouting never managed to implement that full-
scale moral rehabilitation it announced as its mission. It is fair to say
that in the three-quarters of a century of its existence Scouting has
sustained itself less through the efficacy of its ideology in dealing
with national problems than through its ability to interest the
young—as well as their elders—in its activities. Whatever its real
social aims, it works finally because adolescents continue to find it
attractive.

*   *   *

As the founder of the world's largest, most enduring youth organization, Baden-Powell distinguished himself from his fellow youth
leaders not simply by the popularity of his movement but also by the
scope of his ambition. Desiring to colonize all (or almost all) of
Britain's youth for service to the empire, he sought to lay claim to
their hearts and minds as no one had attempted before. The total
institution he envisioned, providing a framework that would nurture a recruit from youthful Cub Scout to mature Scoutmaster,
required from Baden-Powell the capacity to equip it with its sustaining ideology. With the Scout handbook, his articles in *The Scout*
magazine, and his many books of popular wisdom, such as *Rovering
to Success, Life's Snags and How to Meet Them, Paddle Your Own Canoe*,
and *Adventuring to Manhood*, among others, Baden-Powell was equal
to the task. He fashioned for himself the role of universal teacher,
supplying his Scouts with sufficient moral and intellectual direction
to free them from the need of other sources of instruction. His
attempt to create a self-contained discourse for Scouting even led
him to experiment, in the fall of 1913, with digesting the news of
the day in the pages of *The Scout* so that his young readers would
be able to learn about world events in a palatable Scout way
without having to go outside the magazine. He continued the effort
until late January, and while it never amounted to very much more
than a cursory summation of various events, the impulse behind it
suggests the extent to which he sought to shape the moral imaginations of his Scouts.

Although Piers Brendon badly caricatures Baden-Powell by insisting on seeing him as the incorrigible boy–man, always "inspired by
spontaneous juvenility not by calculating maturity,"[3] he is surely
right to treat him as an eminent Edwardian, revealing aspects of
his age much as Lytton Strachey's four *Eminent Victorians* illuminate
theirs. Indeed, in his vision, his love of power masquerading under
the banner of self-denial, his skill at manipulation, his "intoxicated
heart"[4] always seeking the widest possible field of recognition,
Baden-Powell is in many ways like the four representative figures—
Cardinal Manning, Florence Nightingale, Thomas Arnold, and
General Gordon—through whom Strachey pursues the truth of an
era. Sharing characteristics of the ecclesiastic, the woman of action,
and the educator, Baden-Powell perhaps most closely resembles his
fellow soldier, Charles George Gordon, the possessed soul who
found his fulfillment in Khartoum in 1884, transfixed by the spear
of one of the Mahdi's followers. Strachey's analysis of Gordon's
needs provides an appropriate assessment of Baden-Powell's as
well:

The grosser temptations of the world—money and the vulgar attributes of power—had, indeed, no charms for him; but there were subtler and more insinuating allurements which it was not easy to resist. More than one observer declared that ambition was, in reality, the essential motive in his life—ambition, neither for wealth nor titles, but for fame and influence, for the swaying of multitudes, and for that kind of enlarged and intensified existence "where breath breathes most—even in the mouths of men." Was it so? In the depths of Gordon's soul there were intertwining contradictions—intricate recesses where egoism and renunciation melted into one another, where the flesh lost itself in the spirit, and the spirit in the flesh.[5]

In all of his uniqueness Baden-Powell nevertheless remains, as Gordon does for Strachey, a "characteristic specimen"[6] who helps define the nature of his age even as he imposed himself upon it. To encounter Baden-Powell is to discover at once an original, compelling personality who gave the world its most distinctive youth organization, as well as a thoroughly indoctrinated exponent of imperial ideology who articulated the prejudices and ideals of an incipiently crumbling empire. However negligible a role the Scouts played in stemming the decay, they testify both to the creative genius and to the limitations of their founder. Building his obedience-engendering scheme into a movement endorsed throughout the world was an enormous, in many ways troubling, achievement that has earned him a permanent place in its history. Seldom has the doctrine of selflessness, which Baden-Powell propagated to such effect, served its creator so well. The writer of the lead article in the *Morning Post* of 10 September 1913 seems to have understood accurately the depth of Baden-Powell's ambition and the nature of his triumph, when he commented,

The world is to the young, and whoso captures the imagination and the allegiance of the young achieves a conquest wider than any of Caesar or Napoleon. That is what Sir Robert Baden-Powell has done. As Chief Scout today his dominion is one that Emperors might envy, and it is one not merely of the day but of enduring and extending power . . . .

NOTES

THE IMPERILED ISLAND

1. J. A. Hobson, *Imperialism: A Study* (London: James Nisbet, 1902), p. 23.
2. *Headquarters Gazette* 5 (November 1911): 2. Baden-Powell employed the metaphor on various occasions. See his use of it in 1915:

> One of the great sewing machine factories has, during the past few months, added to its peaceful occupation the manufacture of ammunition for war. . . .
> I know another factory—one which in normal times makes citizens for the state. It is now in addition to this work helping some of its members to become capable men for the defence of their homes against aggression, of their nation against militarism, and of their principles of Honour and Justice against destruction. (*Headquarters Gazette* 9 [February 1915]: p. 90)

And again in 1917, in an internal memo dealing with the need to resolve any potential conflict between Scouts and Cadets:

> If we all work together on this understanding I feel convinced that between us, by a combine of energy, it is possible to bring into being a vast citizen-making factory, which may give results of untold value in preparing our citizens for the great work which lies before them in the next generation in making good the havoc of the present war. (American Scout Archives)

3. Reginald A. Bray, *Boy Labour and Apprenticeship* (London: Constable, 1911), p. 90.
4. H. S. Pelham, *The Training of a Working Boy* (London: Macmillan, 1914), p. 9.
5. One of Baden-Powell's maxims (British Scout Archives, book 6, p. 55).
6. Arnold Freeman, *Boy Life and Labour* (London: P. S. King, 1914), p. 53.
7. Charles Russell, *Manchester Boys: Sketches of Manchester Lads at Work and at Play* (Manchester: University Press, 1905), p. 8.
8. Finding people designated by nature for certain kinds of jobs was not limited to youth workers. It was also part of the scientific, socially efficient view of Eugenicists, Fabians, and others. Consider, for example, the position of Cyril

Burt, the influential British psychologist, who wrote in 1920 that it was "the duty of the state, through its school service, first, to find out to what order of intelligence each child belongs, then to give him the education most appropriate to his powers and finally, before it leaves him, to place him in the particular type of occupation for which nature has marked him out." Cited in L. S. Hernshaw, *Cyril Burt, Psychologist* (Ithaca: Cornell University Press, 1979), p. 88.

9. Baden-Powell, *Yarns for Boy Scouts* (London: C. Arthur Pearson, 1909), p. 182. References to these exemplary bricks litter his writings. Here is his exhortation to the Girl Guides:

> If you are divided among yourselves, you are doing harm to your country. You must sink your differences.
>
> If you despise other girls because they belong to a poorer class than yourself, you are a snob; if you hate other girls because they happen to be born richer and belong to higher class schools than yourself, you are a fool. We have got, each one of us, to take our place as we find it in this world, and make the best of it, and pull together with the others around us.
>
> We are very like bricks in a wall; we have each our place, though it may seem a small one in so big a wall. But if one brick gets rotten, or slips out of place, it begins to throw an undue strain on others, cracks appear, and the wall totters. (*Handbook for Girl Guides* [London: Thomas Nelson, 1912], p. 418)

10. Baden-Powell's phrase in *Aids to Scoutmastership* (London: Herbert Jenkins, 1919), p. 12.
11. *Scouting for Boys* (London: Horace Cox, 1908), p. 264.
12. *Headquarters Gazette* 9 (January 1915): 23
13. Leading article from the *Morning Post* of 10 September 1913. Clipping in British Scout Archives.
14. Fifth Annual Scout Report, 1914, p. 24.
15. For the most sustained presentation of this view of Baden-Powell, written in this case by a non-Scout, see Piers Brendon, *Eminent Edwardians* (Boston: Houghton Mifflin Co., 1980). The following description of Baden-Powell suggests Brendon's approach to his subject:

> For the whole of his "extraordinarily happy life" he was, indeed, a perennial singing school-boy, a permanent whistling adolescent, a case of arrested development *con brio*. He was unabashedly a "boy-man" and he recommended the condition as one to which his Scoutmasters should aspire. Only thus would they be filled with "that bright, cheery spirit of adventure" which was the "life-blood" of their work. Or rather play, for Baden-Powell always insisted that Scouting was essentially a matter of "fun and jollity," a game. Life itself, he said, should be looked on "as a game, and the world as playground," and happiness as the goal. (pp. 201–202)

16. William Hillcourt, *Baden-Powell: The Two Lives of a Hero* (London: Heinemann, 1964), p. ix.

I : THE CHIEF SCOUT

1. Eileen K. Wade, *The Piper of Pax: The Life Story of Sir Robert Baden-Powell* (London: C. Arthur Pearson, 1924), p. 13.
2. *Headquarteers Gazette* 8 (November 1914): 318.
3. *Lessons from the 'Varsity of Life*, p. 32.
4. Ibid., p. 43.
5. Ibid., p. 24.
6. Ibid., p. 273.
7. The following four letters are from the American Scout Archives.
8. *'Varsity of Life*, p. 315. See for example, his 1918 letter to Duke Don Pedro de Galantina, president of the Spanish Boy Scouts, explaining the way the British Scouting organization works:

> With a view to progressing with the social evolution of the times, we admit on our Advisory Council men representing all parties of religion and politics and we consult the leaders of Labour with a view to meeting their ideas as far as possible. As a polo player I learned in order to obtain possession of the ball it is not wise to charge an opponent who is also trying to direct it—you may yourself come to grief: it is better to ride along-side him and gradually to edge him off so that you have your way. It is no use to put Scouting up as a target for attack but to make it acceptable to all as far as possible. (British Scout Archives)

9. The following five letters are all in possession of the American Scout Archives.
10. These four letters dealing with the desire for active service are in possession of the American Scout Archives.
11. *The Downfall of Prempeh* (London: Methuen, 1896), p. 161.
12. Baden-Powell to his mother, 11 February 1906 (American Scout Archives).
13. *The Matabele Campaign, 1896* (London: Methuen, 1897), p. 63.
14. Baden-Powell to his mother, 7 June 1896 (American Scout Archives).
15. *The Matabele Campaign*, p. 299.
16. Baden-Powell to his mother, 7 March 1897 (American Scout Archives).
17. The book was actually published once the Mafeking siege had begun. While mail regularly flowed to and from Mafeking throughout the siege—the Boer "lines" hardly constituting a tight cordon around the town—Baden-Powell heightened the book's drama by having printed across the table of contents in dark type the titillating (if rather misleading) note that, "The Corrected Proofs of this Book accompanied the last Dispatches that got through the Boer lines"—another tribute to Henrietta's insistence on "grouping."
18. Baden-Powell to his mother, 8 July 1899 (American Scout Archives).
19. Cf. William Hillcourt, p. 175.
20. To *maffick*, according to *Webster*, is "to celebrate with boisterous rejoicing and hilarious behavior." It comes from "Mafeking night, English celebration of the lifting of the siege of Mafeking."
21. The National Army Museum in London has a collection of nineteen musical pieces, and there are no doubt countless others. Some representative titles: "The Baden-Powell Schottische," "The Baden-Powell Galop," "The Hero of Mafeking Valse," "Our Hero, 'Baden-Powell,'" "Major General British Pluck," "Baden-Powell March," "Mafeking Hero," "Baden-Powell Mafeking Marches."

22. Report to Lord Roberts, 18 May 1900 (Public Records Office, London).
23. The following entries with dates are taken from Baden-Powell's Mafeking staff diaries (American Scout Archives).
24. *'Varsity of Life*, p. 202.
25. Report to Roberts, op. cit.
26. Brian Gardner, *Mafeking: A Victorian Legend* (New York: Harcourt, Brace and World, 1967), p. 42.
27. Royal Commission on the War in South Africa (1903), p. 423. Baden-Powell testified on 19 March 1902.
28. *'Varsity of Life*, p. 200.
29. Angus Hamilton, *The Siege of Mafeking* (London: Methuen, 1900), pp. 120-21.
30. Baden-Powell to J. Hanbury Williams, 28 April 1900 (American Scout Archives).
31. Draft of 1933 article, "My Most Interesting Experience", for the *News of the World* (British Scout Archives, FF 21).
32. Both letters to his mother are from the American Scout Archives.
33. Hamilton, p. 192.
34. Ibid., p. 193.
35. In an interview late in April 1900 with Vere Stent, one of the correspondents in Mafeking, Benjamin Weil summarized the firm's supplies at the start of the siege as follows:

> I had in my possession independent of flour, meal, and grain, four hundred and ninety-nine tons of food stuff; of produce such as forage, bran, mealies, oats, flour and meal I had in store no less an amount than two million four-hundred and twenty-six colonial tons. Of fuel, an equally important matter, I had lain down ninety-three tons. Spirits and beer are of course measured by the gallon, and of these we had in stock seventeen thousand three hundred and two gallons. (Weil papers, 259/60, British Library)

This was in addition to the vegetables grown in town as well as the substantial amounts of livestock and tinned meats available.

36. I don't mean to suggest by this that Baden-Powell did nothing at all to provide sustenance for the natives. For those who could afford it, the fare offered by the soup kitchens was better than nothing. Baden-Powell's general orders of 17 February testify to his awareness that the natives had to ingest something:

> It is requested that, in future, all scraps of food be carefully collected in all kitchens and cooking places, with a view to starting a central soup-kitchen for feeding natives.
> If all hands help in this matter it may be the means of saving numbers from starvation.
> Pans will be supplied to all cooks, and the latter are desired to put into them scraps and remnants of food-stuff of every description. A cart will go round daily and call for them.
> "Scraps" will include bones, offal, vegetable-parings, coffee grounds, scrapings from cooking pots and plates, etc., etc. (American Scout Archives)

37. Emerson Neilly, *Besieged with B-P* (London: C. Arthur Pearson, 1900), pp. 227-28.

38. Ibid., p. 229.

39. Hamilton, p. 249.

40. Baden-Powell staff diary, 20 April 1900 (American Scout Archives).

41. Appendix B of Baden-Powell's report to Lord Roberts on the siege, National Army Museum. On 23 April, in his staff diary, Baden-Powell estimated that he had breadstuffs enough for fifty-two days, sowen for a minimum of fifty-eight days (at a rate of three thousand quarts a day), ninety days' worth of fresh and tinned meats, plus an additional sixty days' worth of horse for the soup kitchens. He was clearly not planning to run out of food for the whites; just as clearly, he could have distributed food more equitably so that without imperiling the lives of the British he could have prevented some of the horrors of starvation for the blacks.

In spite of the evidence of his own diary entry suggesting the considerable resources at his disposal, as late as 23 April Baden-Powell maintained the public posture after the siege that he had barely enough food to survive. Testifying at the Royal Commission on the War in South Africa in 1902, he told the commission, in response to Lord Elgin's question about the extent of his supplies, that

> the facts have been rather misrepresented about the supplies that we had there because we supplied Bulawayo the moment we were relieved. That looks as if we had a lot of supplies there. As a matter of fact, we had about 10 days' supplies left at our then ration, which was very small; and I doubt if the men would have had much strength after another 10 days, so that we could not very well have reduced on that ration. The ration was three-quarters of a pound of meat (generally horse sausage), six ounces of oatcake that was made out of the horses' oats, three pints of sowens, a sort of porridge made of these oats also—the same oats had to go through both operations—and half an ounce of tea. That just kept the men fit; it did not leave much strength in them, and if we had reduced it I think the men would have so broken down that they could not have got out at all. (Minutes of evidence of the Royal Commission on the War in South Africe, p. 428)

It is hard to reconcile the disparity between the ten days of his commission testimony and the provisions for several months noted in his diary.

42. The following letters are from vol. 4 in the Roberts Letter Books collection of the National Army Museum.

43. Roberts to Lord Lansdowne, Home and Overseas Correspondence, vol. 2, National Army Museum.

44. Ibid.

45. Cf., Roberts's letter to Lansdowne of 19 June 1900 (Roberts Correspondence, 5 June–5 September) singling out Baden-Powell with the letter of 4 July to Milner (Roberts Letter Book, 19 June–17 July, 1900) naming Kitchener, Hamilton, and Lyttelton, in that order.

46. Milner letter, op. cit.

47. Roberts to Kitchener, 20 July 1901, Roberts Letter Books, vol. 1.

48. The Kitchener/Roberts correspondence is all in the National Army Museum. While Roberts was distressed at these reports, he did not seem altogether surprised. He replied to Kitchener on 4 May,

> It is curious that Baden-Powell should not be acting with more vigour. He certainly showed himself to have resource while defending Mafeking,

but he disappointed me afterwards, and I gather that those who were with him at Mafeking do not look upon him as a great commander. So much stir was made in this country about the defence of Mafeking that some people thought that Baden-Powell should have been knighted, but promotion to Maj. General's rank and the C.B. seem to me quite a sufficient reward. (Letter Book, vol 1, 5 January 1901-6 August 1901)

49. *Rovering to Success* (London: Herbert Jenkins, 1922), p. 106.
50. Baden-Powell to his mother, 14 September 1912 (American Scout Archives).
51. Baden-Powell to his mother, 8 February 1913 (American Scout Archives).
52. *'Varsity of Life*, p. 138.
53. Cf. letter to his aunt explaining that he has been appointed inspector general of cavalry: "I don't know where all my good luck comes from, but it has been a tremendous surprise to me—and it lands me on the top of *my* tree at one bound" (British Scout Archives, "Pre-1907" folder).
54. Cited in Hillcourt, p. 417.

2: FORTIFYING THE WALL OF EMPIRE

1. Baden-Powell Papers, Add. Mss. 50255, British Library.
2. Hillcourt, p. 252. There are dozens of books on Baden-Powell and Scouting, but the standard "official" Scout histories in addition to Hillcourt's, all of which share the accepted chronology, are as follows: Henry Collis, Fred Hurll, and Rex Hazlewood, *Baden-Powell's Scouts: An Official History of the Boy Scouts Association* (London: Collins, 1961); E. E. Reynolds, *Baden-Powell: A Biography of Lord Baden-Powell of Gilwell* (London: Oxford University Press, 1957; originally written in 1941) and *The Scout Movement* (London; Oxford University Press, 1950); Eileen K. Wade, *The Piper of Pax: The Life Story of Sir Robert Baden-Powell* (London: C. Arthur Pearson, 1924) and *The Story of Scouting* (London: C. Arthur Pearson, 1935; originally published as *Twenty-one Years of Scouting* in 1929); Cf. Michael Rosenthal, "Knights and Retainers: The Earliest Version of Baden-Powell's Boy Scout Scheme," *Journal of Contemporary History* 15 (October 1980): 603-17.
3. Eton College *Chronicle* (22 December, 1904), p. 600.
4. Alfred Stead, *Great Japan: A Study of National Efficiency* (London: John Lane, The Bodley Head, 1905), pp. 449-50.
5. Although not decisive, one small detail of the manuscript of *Scouting for Boys* is interesting in this regard. In the original version of the sentence that reads, in the 1908 edition (p. 22), "It is not intended that boy scouts should necessarily form a new corps separate from all others," the word *necessarily* has been inserted by caret, presumably as an afterthought, between *should* and *form*. A minor change, to be sure, but one that would seem to suggest that Baden-Powell was deliberately trying to leave open the possibility of a separate body, which the initial manuscript formulation would rule out.
6. In addition to the points I have discussed, there are other particular ways in which the Eton proposal anticipates Scouting, such as the suggestion about wearing the distinguishing hat, belt, or crest, and the method of inculcating an idealized version of English history through the reading of exemplary texts such as Conan Doyle, Fitchett and the rest. And it is perhaps not too

farfetched to see in the monthly assessment each boy is asked to make of his contribution to the good of the country a rather less taxing forerunner of the daily good deed of the Scout.

7. *Boys' Brigade Gazette* (June 1906): 150.
8. Ibid.
9. Ibid.
10. See, for example, page three of his deposition, taken on 17 December 1924 for the Supreme Court of New York County, concerning the origins of Scouting (British Scout Archives).
11. Typed copy of essay by Seton entitled "History of the Boy Scouts," p. 10. This essay is in the possession of Mrs. Dee Seton Barber, Seton's daughter, in Santa Fe, New Mexico. Referred to henceforth as Barber Collection.
12. Ibid., p. 3.
13. Ibid., p. 17.
14. *Ladies' Home Journal* (June 1915): 15.
15. Ibid., p. 7.
16. Ernest Thompson Seton, *How to Play Indian* (Philadelphia: Curtis, 1903), p. 3.
17. Ibid., p. 5.
18. Ibid.
19. *The Red Book or How to Play Indian* (1904), p. 5.
20. Seton's schedule, according to his own testimony, was as follows:

> The second lecture on the same subject, was at Tyne Theater, Newcastle, November 20th, besides which, that same autumn, I gave informal talks to the Masters, urging the plan at many schools, including Rossall, October 11th, Haileybury, October 15th, Ealing Manse, October 17th, Aysgarth, October 19th, Dover College, October 22nd, Uppingham, October 29th, Cheltenham, November 2nd, Felsted, November 4th, Bradfield College, November 9th, Aldenham, November 11th, Fettes College, November 30th, Loretto, December 1st, and Harrow, December 3rd, 1904, and later before the P. N. E. Union, when at Brighton and Hampstead. (Typed copy of Seton letter to Baden-Powell, 24 June 1910 [Barber Collection]).

21. Letter from Baden-Powell to E. T. Seton, 1 August 1906 (Barber Collection).
22. Baden-Powell Diary (American Scout Archives).
23. Baden-Powell to E. T. Seton (Barber Collection).
24. Typed copy of letter from E. T. Seton to Baden-Powell, 30 Sept. 1909 (Barber Collection).
25. Typed copy of letter from E. T. Seton to Baden-Powell, 24 April 1910 (Barber Collection).
26. The "Boy Patrols" was finished on 15 February 1907. In defining the movement's rationale as the need to develop good citizenship in the rising generation, as well as in the scouting method it proposes to achieve that end, the paper clearly indicates that Baden-Powell had put the different parts of his idea together into a workable form. It also mentions the subjects (tracking, deduction, woodcraft, and the like) that will be taught, the fact that games and competitions will be used, and the organization of patrols, patrol leaders, and scoutmasters that will structure the scheme. It points out that a handbook giving all details is in the process of being prepared.
27. Ernest Thompson Seton, *The Birch-bark Roll of the Woodcraft Indians* (New York: Doubleday, Page, 1906), p. 5.

28. Ibid., p. 1.
29. Ibid., p. 3.
30. Ibid.
31. Ibid., p. 4.
32. Ibid.
33. Ibid., p. 45.
34. Ibid., p. 20.
35. *Scouting for Boys*, p. 24.
36. Ibid., p. 25.
37. *Birch-bark Roll*, p. 21.
38. Ibid.
39. Ibid., p. 47.
40. *Scouting for Boys*, p. 25.
41. *Birch-bark Roll*, p. 5.
42. Ibid.
43. *Scouting for Boys*, p. 30.
44. Ibid., p. 32.
45. Copy of letter from E. T. Seton to Baden-Powell (Barber Collection).
46. *Scouting for Boys*, p. 25.
47. Copy of letter from E. T. Seton to Baden-Powell, 24 April 1910 (Barber Collection).
48. Baden-Powell to E. T. Seton, 14 March 1908 (Barber Collection).
49. *Scouting for Boys*, p. 1.
50. Copy of letter from E. T. Seton to Baden-Powell, 24 April 1910 (Barber Collection).
51. *Scouting for Boys*, p. 134.
52. *Birch-bark Roll*, p. 40.
53. *Scouting for Boys*, p. 154.
54. *Birch-bark Roll*, pp. 43–44.
55. *Scouting for Boys*, p. 161.
56. Copy of letter from E. T. Seton to Baden-Powell, 24 April 1910 (Barber Collection).
57. Baden-Powell to E. T. Seton (Barber Collection).
58. "A History of the Boy Scouts," p. 41 (Barber Collection).
59. Baden-Powell to E. T. Seton, 13 February 1908 (Barber Collection).
60. Copy of letter in Barber Collection.
61. Copy of letter from E. T. Seton to Baden-Powell, 24 June 1910 (Barber Collection).
62. Sidney Dark, *The Life of Sir Arthur Pearson* (London: 1922), p. 144.
63. Percy W. Everett, *The First Ten Years* (Ipswich: The East Anglican Daily Times, 1948), p. 8.
64. Letter in collection of American Scout Archives.
65. Back cover of *The Scout*, 18 April 1908.
66. *Headquarters Gazette* 1 (August 1909): p. 4.
67. Brownsea Island report (British Scout Archives).
68. Ibid. Despite these claims, Arthur Primmer, one of the Brownsea Scouts from the Boys' Brigade, told me that the public school boys and the others did not actually have much to do with one another, even though the relationship between them was perfectly cordial.
69. Ibid.
70. Ibid.

3 : WORKING-CLASS LADS AND PUBLIC-SCHOOL IDEALS

1. Some representative titles: *The Town Child* (R. A. Bray); *Boy Life and Labour: The Manufacture of Inefficiency* (Arnold Freeman); *The Boy and His Work* (S. J. Gibb); *The Training of a Working Boy* (H. S. Pelham); *Manchester Boys: Sketches of Manchester Lads at Work and at Play* (Charles Russell); *The Children of the Slums* (James Samuelson); *Problems of Boy Life* (J. H. Whitehouse, ed.).

2. Cf. Edward Said's *Orientalism* (New York: Pantheon, 1978). The "Boy Expert" studies, fixes, and represents the poor to the rest of the world in much the same way as the Orientalist defines "the truth" of the Orient.

3. H. S. Pelham, *The Training of a Working Boy* (London: Macmillan, 1914), p. 1.

4. Charles Russell, *Manchester Lads: Sketches of Manchester Lads at Work and at Play* (Manchester: University Press, 1905), p. 8.

5. E. Wingfield-Stratford, quoted in T. C. Worsley, *Barbarians and Philistines: Democracy and the Public Schools* (London: Robert Hale, 1940), p. 17.

6. British Scout Archives, Box D., Cadets, 1910–16. Article on Cadets and Cadet Training, dated 1916.

7. British Scout Archives, Box B, Scouting in Schools, 1910–24. Summary of address given at London University and included in draft of essay entitled "Harry Lauder's Political Creed."

8. Phrase used by Baden-Powell in letter concerning public schools and Scouting, dated 1 July 1920 (British Scout Archives, Box B, Scouting and Schools, 1910–16).

9. H. Bompas Smith, "Methods of Moral Instruction and Training in English Public Schools and Other Secondary Schools for Boys," in Michael Sadler (ed.), *Moral Instruction and Training in Schools: Report of an International Inquiry* (London: Longmans, Green, 1908).

10. Rupert Wilkinson, *The Prefects: British Leadership and the Public School Tradition* (London: Oxford University Press, 1964), p. 83.

11. Worsley, p. 189.

12. Typewritten memo from Baden-Powell to staff of S. A. C., 15 February 1903 (Baden-Powell Papers, National Army Museum).

13. American Scout Archives.

14. Worsley, p. 8.

15. Sadler, p. xxxviii.

16. H. Bompas Smith in Sadler, p. 106.

17. Paul Jones, *War Letters of a Public School Boy* (London: Cassell, 1918), p. 219.

18. Baden-Powell, *Lessons from the 'Varsity of Life* p. 101.

19. Cyril Norwood, *The English Tradition of Education* (London: John Murray, 1929), p. 101.

20. Thomas Seccombe in his preface to Alex Waugh, *The Loom of Youth* (London: Grant Richards, 1917).

21. H. B. Gray, *The Public Schools and the Empire* (London: Williams and Norgate, 1913), p. 165.

22. According to one observer, "Imperialism, militarism, and athleticism in the last quarter of the nineteenth century became a revered secular trinity of the upper-middle class school" (J. A. Mangan, "Athleticism: A Case Study of the Evolution of an Educational Ideology," in Brian Simon and Ian Bradley, eds., *The Victorian Public School* [Dublin: Gill and Macmillan, 1975], p. 157).

23. By the end of the century it was not the public school system in general but the playing fields in particular that were associated with the imperial battle-

fields. There was no confusion about this. J. G. C. Minchin wrote in 1901, "If we asked what our muscular Christianity has done, we point to the British Empire. Our Empire would never have been built up by a nation of idealists and logicians." Quoted in P. C. McIntosh, *Physical Education in England since 1800* (London: George Bell, 1968), p. 68.

24. "Modern Warfare, or How Soldiers Fight," quoted in I. F. Clarke, *Voices Prophesying War, 1763–1984* (London: Oxford University Press, 1966), p. 132. See Baden-Powell's own explanation of the way the army works:

> In battle, each unit—that is each company or battalion—is like a player in the game, so he has to be trained to it—to be able to run and dodge, dribble and kick, and to play according to the rules. In the same way, a soldier has to learn to shoot and to drill and to fight according to his orders. Then each unit has its place in the battlefield, just as each player has his place on the football field. (*Marksmanship for Boys: The Red Feather and How to Win It.* [London: C. Arthur Pearson, 1915], p. 39)

25. Baden-Powell's enthusiasm for the poem led him to include it in *Scouting for Boys* under the title, "Play the Game." He turns it, in fact, into a dramatic performance, establishing a different scene for each stanza. The recitation of the third stanza, for example, takes place in the context of "A procession of all kinds of men, old ones at the head, middle-aged in the centre, young ones behind—soldiers, sailors, lawyers, workmen, footballers, etc. etc.—Scotch, Irish, English, Colonial—all linked hand in hand" (p. 251). Stage directions then require, following the articulation of the last line, that the "one in the centre then calls back to the juniors: 'Play up! Play up! And Play the game!' The smallest of the juniors steps forward and cries to the audience—'PLAY UP! PLAY UP! AND PLAY THE GAME!' (p. 252). For another Henry Newbolt poem that brings together school, playing field, and sacrifice for the empire, see "Clifton Chapel." It is also worth noting a letter Baden-Powell included in the match program at the Tottenham Hotspur Football Ground following his opening an adjoining rifle range in October 1914:

> As an old Carthusian footballer I need scarcely say how much I love the game.
> But as one who loves his country and his fellow-countrymen, I see in football something more than a mere game. It is a school for teaching men those things which are best for every true Briton to practise.
> It teaches him to "play the game" with pluck, good temper, and no shirking; it teaches obedience to the rules, obedience to your captain, it teaches a man to play in his place, to back up and to play hard, not for his own glorification, but wholly and solely that his side may win.
> The war is showing day by day the effect of this teaching. Our gallant fellows at the front are carrying their football training into practice on the battlefield. They are "playing the game" in all conscience! Not much shirking there! They are playing in their places and playing hard—not for their honour and glory but that their side may win. (*Headquarters Gazette* 8 [November 1914]: 336)

26. Pelham, p. 128.
27. Eustace Miles, *Let's Play the Game, or the Anglo-Saxon Sportsmanlike Spirit* (London: Guilbert Pitman, 1904), pp. 4–5.

28. Ibid., pp. viii–ix.
29. Ibid., p. 10.
30. Ibid., pp. 47–48.
31. Ibid., pp. 34–35.
32. Ibid., p. 63.
33. Ibid., p. 94.
34. Jones, *War Letters of a Public School Boy*. Comment appearing on the title page.
35. Ibid., father's introduction, p. 2.
36. Ibid., pp. 49–50.
37. Ibid., pp. 50–51.
38. Ibid., p. 218.
39. Ibid., p. 224.
40. Ibid., p. 156.
41. Ibid., p. 172.
42. Ibid., pp. 3–4.
43. Ibid., p. 199.
44. Worsley, pp. 9–10.
45. Consider, for example, Baden-Powell's own sense of the importance of playing the game in his comparison of German rigidity and English spirit:

> It is just the opposite to the free spirit where a man is trusted on his honour to play the game, and which is known amongst us as "good form." This spirit of playing the game is, I hope, more characteristic of the British nation than of any other, and it is the highest form of national discipline.... But it is too valuable a quality to be played with or neglected. It ought to be definitely and fully recognized as part of the education of our children. That is the main reason for the existence of the Boy Scout Movement. We want to make our nation entirely one of gentlemen, men who have a strong sense of honour, of chivalry towards others, of playing the game bravely and unselfishly for their side, and to play it with a sense of fair play and of happiness for all. (Baden-Powell, *Headquarters Gazette* 8 [November 1914]: 319)

46. Wilkinson, pp. 39–40.
47. Character training schemes in general, whether Scouting or any of the more recent ones, such as the Outward Bound Program, for example, do not seem to have any demonstrable long-term effects on the participants. See Kenneth Roberts, Graham White, and Howard Parker, *The Character Training Industry: Adventure Training Schemes in Britain* (London: David and Charles, 1974).
48. Worsley, pp. 160–61.
49. *'Varsity of Life*, p. 278.

4: THE SCOUT LAW

1. Draft of essay entitled "The Scout Promise and Law," in British Scout Archives, Box K, Scout Law.
2. The shift from oath to promise was made by Baden-Powell because he thought an "oath to God" was "too big a thing for any boy to undertake." Ibid.
3. Ibid.

4. *Scouting for Boys*, 2nd ed., p. 24. See also my discussion in chapter six on the criteria for awarding proficiency badges as another instance of Baden-Powell's concern that standards not diminish the number of possible recruits to Scouting.

5. *Scouting for Boys*, 1st ed., p. 24.

6. Memo labeled Circulated to All Members of Executive Committee: "Proposed Alteration to the Second Scout Law, July, 15, 1930" (British Scout Archives, Box K, Scout Law).

7. Ibid.

8. *Scouting for Boys* (1908), p. 264.

9. *Pigsticking or Hoghunting* (London: Harrison, 1889), preface.

10. Ibid., p. 208.

11. *Indian Memories* (London: Herbert Jenkins, 1915), p. 38.

12. *Yarns for Boy Scouts* (London: C. Arthur Pearson, 1909), p. 53.

13. *Lessons from the 'Varsity of Life* p. 86.

14. *Indian Memories*, p. 38.

15. *Yarns for Boy Scouts*, p. 53.

16. *Pigsticking or Hoghunting*, p. 4. I do not want to suggest that Baden-Powell was in any way unique in his embracing of pigsticking as a crucially important sport for the men who went forth to maintain the empire. Like so much else about Baden-Powell's thought, he was thoroughly representative in the ecstatic claims he made for the life-giving joys of pigsticking. As Philip Woodruff makes clear,

> The game of games, easily first in the estimation of all who practised it was pigsticking. It was generally encouraged and, though it would not be true that a man had to hunt pig to be thought well of, there is no doubt that he had a better chance if he did. To be good after a pig a man must be a horseman, which was in any case a great asset to a district officer. And he must also have the same qualities—the power of quick but cool judgment, a stout heart, a controlled but fiery ardour and a determination not to be beaten—that are needed at the crisis of a riot, or for that matter of a battle. The kind of man who has those qualities needs to exercise them.... Ugly lusts for power and revenge melted away and even the lust for women assumed—so it was said—reasonable proportions after a day in pursuit of pig. (Philip Woodruff, *The Men Who Ruled India: The Guardians* [London: Jonathan Cape, 1954], p. 180)

17. *Scouting for Boys*, p. 190. It is interesting to see how he adjusts the code to meet the demands of the Girl Guides' less violent female sensibility. In the *Handbook for Girl Guides*, the knightly code omits all reference to things that speak explicitly of fighting, so that the laws included here are the following:

Be always prepared to—

Defend the poor and help them that cannot defend themselves.

Do nothing to hurt or offend anyone else.

At whatever you are working try and win honour and a name for honesty.

Never break your promise.

Rather die honest than live shamelessly.

Perform humble offices with *cheerfulness* and grace, and do good unto others (pp. 356-57).

18. *Aids to Scoutmastership* p. 105.
19. *Yarns for Boy Scouts*, p. 117.
20. Ibid., p. 119. While it is difficult to track down all of Baden-Powell's sources for his Roundtable codes of behavior, this one quite clearly is taken from the oath King Arthur demands of his knights in Book III, chapter 15, of Malory's *Le Morte d'Arthur*. In addition to the various chivalric tenets that he made up altogether and attributed to Arthur, Baden-Powell also reveals himself to be a sloppy reader. Book III ends with the statement, "Explicit the wedding of King Arthur." This does not mean that the wedding occurred in the last chapter of Book III when the knights swear their oath. The actual wedding takes place in chapter 5, and many days elapse between that and the events of the last chapter. To see precisely what Baden-Powell invented for his knights' code in order to make them proper ancestors of the Scouts, it is instructive to see what Arthur—as opposed to his modern interpreter—does indeed ask of his knights:

> He gave them lands, and charged them never to do outrageousity nor murder, and always to flee treason; also, by no means to be cruel, but to give mercy unto him that asketh mercy, upon pain of forfeiture of their worship and lordship of King Arthur for evermore; and always to do ladies, damosels, and gentlewomen succour, upon pain of death. Also, that no man take no battles in a wrongful quarrel for no law, ne for no world's goods. Unto this were all the knights sworn of the Table Round, both old and young. (*Le Morte D'Arthur*, ed. Janet Cowen, vol. 1 [Baltimore: Penguin Books, 1978], pp. 115-16)

21. *Yarns for Boy Scouts*, pp. 119-20.
22. Ibid., p. 120.
23. Ibid., p. 143.
24. Ibid., p. 144.
25. Typewritten memo from Baden-Powell to staff of South African Constabulary, 15 February 1903 (Baden-Powell Papers, National Army Museum).
26. *Young Knights of the Empire: Their Code and Further Scout Yarns* (London: C. Arthur Pearson, 1916), p. 163.
27. *Headquarters Gazette* 8 (February 1914): 37.
28. First issued in 1886. By 1898 there were over 300,000 in print.
29. *The Citizen Reader* (London: Cassell, new and rev. ed., 1904), introduction.
30. *Scouting for Boys*, pp. 199-200.
31. *From Conquest to Collapse, European Empires from 1815 to 1960* (New York: Pantheon, 1982), p. 169.
32. *Boy Scouts Beyond the Seas*, "My World Tour" (London: C. Arthur Pearson, 1913), p. 99.
33. Ibid., p. 93.
34. Ibid., p. 100.
35. *Yarns for Boy Scouts*, p. 188.
36. *Scouting for Boys*, p. 191.
37. Ibid., p. 199.

38. Ibid., p. 3. The fortnightly edition of *Scouting for Boys* makes Baden-Powell's contempt for such a type even stronger. Not only is he no better "than an old woman," but "merely gets killed like a squealing rabbit, being unable to defend himself" (First fortnightly part, p. 10).
39. *Scouting for Boys*, p. 5.
40. *The Trail* 2 (November 1919): 254.

5: THE SPECTER OF DETERIORATION

1. *Scouting for Boys*, p. 276.
2. *The Nation in Arms*, 4 (June 1909): 225.
3. Colonel G. Malcolm Fox, *National Physical Training* (London: Reformatory and Refuge Union, 1905), p. 4.
4. C. F. G. Masterman in *The Heart of the Empire* (London: T. Fisher Unwin, 1901), p. 8.
5. Lord Beresford in J. B. Atkins, ed., *National Physical Training: An Open Debate* (London: Isbister, 1904), p. 34.
6. I don't mean to suggest that the stunted, town-bred lad was entirely new to Britain. He had certainly been evoked before as irrefutable proof of urban deterioration. But even if by the 1880s he was fairly well established, the anxieties triggered by the Boer War intensified the frequency of allusions to him. For an interesting discussion of the theory of urban degeneration, see Gareth Stedman Jones, *Outcast London* (New York: Pantheon, 1984), especially chapter 6.
7. "People say that we have no patriotism nowadays, and that therefore our Empire will fall to pieces like the great Roman empire did, because its citizens became selfish and lazy, and only cared for amusements", Baden-Powell cautions in *Scouting for Boys*, p. 18. But it need not be that way: "Don't be content, like the Romans were, and some people now are, to pay other people to play your football or to fight your battles for you. Do something yourself to help in keeping the flag flying" (p. 18). The manuscript version of *Scouting for Boys* comparing the two empires cites a broader array of symptoms than those Baden-Powell chooses to include in the published text:

> The first signs of decay in Rome was the disappearance of the Roman farmer: so in England the country people are taking to town and town life.
> The cost of living and the growth of luxury, over population, and want of thrift produced masses of unemployed in Rome before its fall, as they are doing today, where we have the additional elements of decay in excessive drinking, smoking, use of patent medicines, and impure milk, etc. (p. 176)

Baden-Powell notes the loss of preeminence in games as indicative of England's decline:

> In games which we used to regard as essentially our own, foreigners of all nations seem to be approaching us; French at golf; Americans at running, jumping and yacht sailing; Belgians at rowing; Colonials at football and cricket; Germans at swimming, and so on." (p. 176)

Following the analysis of Elliot Mills (see below), Baden-Powell also mentions the erosion of religion, as well as municipal extravagance, excessive taxation, and the transfiguration of true statesmen into self-serving party politicians as additional signs of England's emulation of Roman decay.

8. *Scouting for Boys*, p. 261.
9. Elliot Mills, *The Decline and Fall of the British Empire* (London: Simpkin, Marshall, Hamilton, Kent, 1905), p. 40.
10. Ibid., p. 47.
11. Original terms of reference to the Inter-Departmental Committee on Physical Deterioration, which submitted its report on 20 July 1904.
12. Speech in the House of Lords. Hansard, vol. 150 (6 July 1903) col. 1324.
13. Ibid., col. 1327.
14. Ibid., cols. 1336–37.
15. Sir Frederick Maurice, "Where to Get Men," *Contemporary Review* 81 (January 1902): 79.
16. Ibid., p. 78.
17. Ibid.
18. Ibid., p. 79.
19. The statistical table provided by the Medical Service shows that of the men passed into the army as fit during the period from 1893 to 1902, only 3 percent, as opposed to the 15 claimed by Maurice, had to be discharged within two years. And the figures of 1900 in particular show that only 2.6 percent had to be released within two years for medical reasons.
20. Maurice, p. 86.
21. Report of the Inter-Departmental Committee on Physical Deterioration, p. 92.
22. Ibid., p. 75.
23. Ibid., p. 380.
24. Pethick Lawrence in *The Heart of the Empire* (London: T. Fisher Unwin, 1901), p. 72.
25. Inter-Departmental Committee on Physical Deterioration, p. 87.
26. A. Watt Smyth, *Physical Deterioration: Its Causes and the Cure* (London: John Murray, 1904), pp. 62–63.
27. Ibid., p. 26.
28. Reginald Bray, "The Children of the Town," in *The Heart of the Empire*, p. 126. See also Mary Barnett's discussion of the consequences of city living:

> Recent developments have clearly shown that not only does juvenile delinquency increase in direct proportion to population, but it has also shown that the further a growing child is removed from the health-giving influences of the country, the more frequent are his lapses into mischief and crime. One of the most apparent effects of town life upon the character of a child is seen in a lack of reverence. Country dwellers, from an early age, are witnesses of the works of Nature, and therefore their subconscious mind is imbued with a spirit of reverence. ... It is largely owing to the fact that the world is beginning to say "he has no fear of God or man." (Mary G. Barnett, *Young Delinquents: A Study of Reformatory and Industrial Schools* [London: Methuen, 1913], pp. 1–2)

On the theme of city versus country generally, see Raymond Williams, *The Country and the City* (New York: Oxford University Press, 1973).
29. Davies and Gibson, p. 41.
30. Lawrence in *The Heart of the Empire*, p. 56.

31. James Cantlie, *Physical Efficiency* (London: G. P. Putnam's Sons, 1906), pp. 110–11.

32. Ibid., p. 112.

33. Thomas Oliver, *Maladies Caused by the Air We Breathe Inside and Outside the Home* (London: Baillière, Tindall and Cox, 1906), p. 7.

34. Cantlie, p. 62.

35. Eugen Sandow, *The Construction and Reconstruction of the Human Body* (London: John Bale and Davidson, 1907), p. 29.

36. Arthur Conan Doyle, preface to *The Construction and Reconstruction of the Human Body*, p. x.

37. Ibid., p. xi.

38. Bernard Gainer, *The Alien Invasion: The Origins of the Aliens Act of 1905* (London: Heinemann Educational Books, 1972), p. 3.

39. The British Brothers League was founded by William Shaw in 1900 to bring together "all those who already shared his belief that the alien snatched the Englishman's bread from his lips, in order to agitate for a measure of restriction" (Gainer, p. 68). The basis of the league was the East End working man. Membership was achieved simply by signing one's name to the lists, there being no dues, oaths, or responsibilities. The League in a sense replaced an earlier organization, the Society for the Suppression of the Immigration of Destitute Aliens, which was founded in 1886 and financed by Arnold White and the earl of Dunraven. The earl of Meath (then Lord Brabazon) and Lord Beresford were ardent supporters of its goals.

40. Gainer, p. 3. and passim.

41. Report of the Royal Commission on Alien Immigration, 1903, p. 38.

43. National Council of Public Morals, *To Save the British Race* (London, 1921), p. 39.

43. Ibid., p. 8.

44. Ibid., p. 9.

45. Ibid., p. 10.

46. *Youth and the Race* (London: Chapman and Hall, 1922), p. 208.

47. Reports issued by the commissions included *The Declining Birth Rate* (1916), *The Cinema: Its Present Position and Future Possibilities* (1917); *Problems of Population and Parenthood* (1920); *Youth and the Race* (1922).

48. *To Save the British Race*, p. 41.

49. Entitled simply "The Decline in the Birth Rate," the essay had originally appeared in the London *Times* under the racier title, "Physical Degeneracy or Race Suicide."

50. Webb, pp. 16–17.

51. Ibid. p. 19.

52. Ibid.

53. Quoted in *Campaigns of Peace*, a booklet issued by the National Council of Public Morals (London, 1919), pp. 18–19.

54. *The Declining Birth Rate* (London: Chapman and Hall, 1916), p. 37.

55. Ibid., p. 43.

56. Ibid., p. 71.

57. Ibid.

58. Ibid., pp. 74–75.

59. *To Save the British Race*, p. 10.

60. Sir Francis Galton, "Eugenics: Its Definition, Scope and Aim," *Nature* 70 (1904): 82.

61. Ibid.

62. G. R. Searle, *Eugenics and Politics in Britain, 1900-1914* (Leyden: Noordhoff International, 1976), p. 9.
63. Galton, p. 82.
64. Ibid.
65. Galton was eighty-two when he delivered his lecture before the Sociological Society in 1904, hardly the age to lead a crusade. He died in 1911. The will he left created a Galton Professorship of Eugenics at the University of London, specifying Karl Pearson as the first occupant of the chair.
66. Karl Pearson, *Social Problems: Their Treatment, Past, Present, and Future* (London: Dulan, 1912), p. 13. Originally delivered as a lecture at the Galton Laboratory on 12 March 1910.
67. Karl Pearson, *Nature and Nurture: The Problem of the Future* (London: Dulan, 1910), p. 12.
68. Karl Pearson (with Ethel Elderton, Amy Barrington, H. Gertrude Jones, Edith M. M. de G. Lamotte, and H. J. Laski), *On the Correlation of Fertility with Social Value* (London: Dulan, 1909), p. 25.
69. Ibid., p. 45.
70. Karl Pearson, *On the Scope and Importance to the State of the Science of National Eugenics* (London: Dulan, 1909), p. 25. Originally delivered as a lecture at Oxford University on 17 May 1907.
71. Ibid., p. 37.
72. Karl Pearson, *Darwinism, Medical Progress, and Eugenics* (London: Dulan, 1912), p. 27. The Cavendish lecture of 1912.
73. Ibid., pp. 28-29.
74. Pearson, *Science of National Eugenics*, p. 51.
75. Karl Pearson in *Annals of Eugenics* 1 (1925-26): 3.
76. William Bateson, *Biological Fact and the Structure of Society* (Oxford: Clarendon Press, 1912), p. 31. The Herbert Spencer Lecture of 1912.
77. Ibid., p. 32.
78. Karl Pearson, *Social Problems*, p. 8. For a fascinating study and thorough debunking of theories that correlated cranial capacity with intelligence, see Stephen Jay Gould's *The Mismeasure of Man* (New York: W. W. Norton, 1981).
79. Karl Pearson, *National Life from the Standpoint of Science* (London: Adam and Charles Black, 1905), p. 21.
80. Ibid., p. 22.
81. Ibid., p. 23.
82. Ibid., p. 46.
83. Ibid., p. 38.
84. C. W. Saleeby, *The Progress of Eugenics* (London: Cassell, 1914), p. 24. Commenting on the 1904 definition of eugenics Galton delivered to the Sociological Society, Saleeby notes that Galton included not only the influences that worked upon the inborn qualities of the race, but also those that helped develop those qualities—or the forces of nurture. Saleeby goes on:

> I am aware that, under the pressure brought to bear upon his extreme old age, Galton later adopted a definition which omitted any reference to nurture, but I prefer that which he offered ten years ago, and for which a logical and biological warrent exists. (p. 56)

85. Ibid., p. 19.
86. Ibid., p. 84.
87. Ibid.

88. Ibid., p. 85.
89. Ibid., p. 88.
90. R. F. Horton, *National Ideals and Race Regeneration* (London: Cassell, 1912), p. 38.
91. Arnold White, "Eugenics and National Efficiency," *The Eugenics Review*, 1 (July 1909): 111.
92. Robert Scally, in *The Origins of the Lloyd George Coalition* (Princeton: Princeton University Press, 1975), p. 13, refers to these qualities as "useful mainly to employers, sergeant majors, and conservative politicians."

6 : SCOUTING FOR BOYS

1. Regarding it primarily as a useful guide to outdoor living is by no means just a contemporary mistake. Reviewing the first five parts under the title, "Scouting as a Sport", the London *Times* reviewer of 17 March 1908, commended it to grown-up sportsmen and all those interested in outdoor living: "His little books form an encyclopaedia of the practical information required by boys who wish to follow the example of the true frontiersman."
2. *Scouting for Boys*, p. 3. The page references for all citations from the first edition of *Scouting for Boys* in this chapter will be indicated in parenthesis at the end of the quotation.
3. The opening sentence of the typescript, in fact, makes this point too emphatically for comfort: "We had an example of what Boys Scouts can do *not merely as peace scouts* but on active service ..." (British Scout Archives). Since Baden-Powell always insisted that his scheme was entirely for peace Scouting, the *not merely*, which clearly tends to diminish the value of peace Scouting when compared with the real business of active service, was making precisely the wrong kind of point and was dropped from the published text.
4. This appears on page 48 of the first issue of the fortnightly edition. The earlier reference is on page 37, in which he writes, "The motto in it is the Scout's motto of BE PREPARED (B-P my initials)."
5. The original Roosevelt quotation appears on page 164 of the manuscript copy of *Scouting for Boys* in the British Scout Archives.
6. See the next chapter for a fuller discussion of the importance of rifle shooting to the Scout movement.
7. As I have indicated earlier, the exhortation to "be a brick" in the wall of country and empire is Baden-Powell's frequently repeated statement of this obligation to serve. It is interesting to compare it with another form of the idea that he dispensed in 1900 while in the Transvaal, in response to the news that he had been elected patron of the Baden-Powell League of Health and Manliness, an antismoking organization whose members, most of whom were former or current choirboys, pledged not to smoke before they were twenty-one. Thanking them for the honor, Baden-Powell praises them for trying to do their proper duty to themselves:

> You who are Choir-boys, or past Choir-boys—will recognize that if each sings his part in the harmony under the direction of the leader— that is, if each one does his duty—the result is a pleasing anthem— whereas if each sang what he likes best there would be a fair old cats' chorus. So it is in life—if each does his duty in his proper line or profession the whole community moves prosperously and successfully. (British Scout Archives, vol. 43: "Pre-1907")

8. The lunacy of objecting to Scouting and its values is also conveyed in an incident Baden-Powell recounts from his own experience. Discussing in an early issue of *Headquarters Gazette* the marvelous response that greeted him as he went around the country talking about Scouting, Baden-Powell notes that "only at one place did I hear of an objector, a school master of considerable experience and standing.... I made a particular request that I might be introduced to him ... in order to hear his objections ... but alas! on my arrival I found that he was not to be seen, being now the inmate of a lunatic asylum" (7 [April 1910]: 1).

9. On the revival of knighthood generally in late nineteenth- and early twentieth-century England, see Mark Girouard, *The Return to Camelot* (New Haven: Yale University Press, 1981).

10. A passage from the typescript of *Scouting for Boys* that did not find its way into the published edition further elaborates on Baden-Powell's prewar admiration for the Germans. Arguing for the need for practical training in good citizenship, Baden-Powell points out.

> In Germany this thought is ever present. A wise and patriotic government are taking methodical steps to insure good practical citizenship by means of discipline and knowledge throughout the nation.
>
> If they thus qualify themselves to become the best nation they will deserve to take their place as rulers of the world; but there is no reason why, placed as we are, we Britons should not keep our ancient character and with it maintain our Empire.

11. Christopher Hibbert, *The Great Mutiny: India 1857* (London: Allen Lane, 1978), pp. 292–93.

12. Ibid., p. 293.

13. Letter to Herbert Edwardes, Ibid., p. 293.

14. Ibid., p. 293.

15. The actual incident was witnessed by Lord Roberts, at the time a young officer, and it is instructive to compare the two versions. According to Roberts, at the end of a meeting between Nicholson and some native officers,

> Mehtab Sing, a general officer in the Kapurthala Army, took his leave, and, as the senior in rank at the durbar, was walking out of the room first, when I observed Nicholson stalk to the door, put himself in front of Mehtab Sing and, waving him back with an authoritative air, prevent him from leaving the room. The rest of the company then passed, and when they had gone, Nicholson said to Lake [a British major]: "Do you see that General Mehtab Sing has his shoes on?" Lake replied that he had noticed the fact but tried to excuse it. Nicholson, however, speaking in Hindustani, said, "There is no possible excuse for such an act of gross impertinence. Mehtab Sing knows perfectly well that he would not venture to step on his father's carpet save barefooted, and he had only committed this breach of etiquette to-day because he thinks we're not in a position to resent the insult, and that he can treat us as he would not have dared to do a month ago." Mehtab Sing looked extremely foolish, and stammered some kind of apology; but Nicholson was not to be appeased, and continued: "If I were the last Englishman left in Jullundur, you (addressing Mehtab Sing) should not come into my room with your shoes on"; then, politely turning to Lake, he added, "I hope the

Commissioner will now allow me to order you to take your shoes off and
carry them out in your hands, so that your followers may witness your
discomfiture." Mehtab Sing, completely cowed, meekly did as he was
told. (Lord Roberts, *Forty-one Years in India* [London: Macmillan, 1905],
p. 75)

It is interesting to see the way Baden-Powell emphasizes the inferiority of
the native and the contempt the superior Englishman feels for him. Although
these features are obviously implicit in the actual event, Baden-Powell not
only makes them explicit but revels in them as well, striking a curious note in
a movement presumably committed to a different set of ideals. This minor
triumph of empire is also honored in a poem by Henry Newbolt, whose "Vitai
Lampada" figures prominently in *Scouting for Boys*. Newbolt's rendering of the
situation is as follows:

A BALLAD OF JOHN NICHOLSON

It fell in the year of Mutiny
　　At darkest of the night,
John Nicholson by Jalándhar came,
　　On his way to Delhi fight.

And as he by Jalándhar came
　　He thought what he must do,
And he sent to the Rajah fair greeting,
　　To try if he were true.

"God grant your Highness length of days,
　　And friends when need shall be;
And I pray you send you Captains hither,
　　That they may speak with me."

On the morrow through Jalándhar town
　　The Captains rode in state;
They came to the house of John Nicholson
　　And stood before the gate.

The chief of them was Mehtab Singh,
　　He was both proud and sly;
His turban gleamed with rubies red,
　　He held his chin full high.

He marked his fellows how they put
　　Their shoes from off their feet;
"Now wherefore make ye such ado
　　These fallen lords to greet?

"They have ruled us for a hundred years,
　　In truth I know not how,
But though they be fain of mastery,
　　They dare not claim it now."

Right haughtily before them all
  The durbar hall he trod,
With rubies red his turban gleamed,
  His feet with pride were shod.

They had not been an hour together,
  A scanty hour or so,
When Mehtab Singh rose in his place
  And turned about to go.

Then swiftly came John Nicholson
  Between the door and him,
With anger smouldering in his eyes
  That made the rubies dim.

"You are overhasty, Mehtab Singh,"—
  Oh, but his voice was low!
He held his wrath with a curb of iron,
  That furrowed cheek and brow.

"You are overhasty, Mehtab Singh,
  When that the rest are gone,
I have a word that may not wait
  To speak with you alone."

The Captains passed in silence forth
  And stood the door behind;
To go before the game was played
  Be sure they had no mind.

But there within John Nicholson
  Turned him on Mehtab Singh,
"So long as the soul is in my body
  You shall not do this thing.

"Have ye served us for a hundred years
  And yet ye know not why?
We brook no doubt of our mastery,
  We rule until we die.

"Where I the one last Englishman
  Drawing the breath of life,
And you the master-rebel of all
  That stir this land to strife—

"Were I," he said, "but a Corporal,
  And you a Rajput King,
So long as the soul was in my body
  You should not do this thing.

"Take off, take off those shoes of pride,
  Carry them whence they came;
Your Captains saw your insolence
  And they shall see your shame."

When Mehtab Singh came to the door
  His shoes they burned his hand
For there in long and silent lines
  He saw the Captains stand.

When Mehtab Singh rode from the gate
  His chin was on his breast:
The captains said, "When the strong command
  Obedience is best."

(Henry Newbolt, *Poems: New and Old* [London: John Murray, 1912], p. 61)

16. The *Spectator* review of *Scouting for Boys* 25 September 1909, pp. 463–64) was especially pleased with the simple, nonsectarian politics of the book and with the clear diagnosis of the causes of poverty:

> The boys are instructed in the story of the Empire and the duties and privileges which its possession entails. They are made to feel the responsibilities of citizenship and the bond of a common race; and if any party politician objects to this teaching, so much the worse for that party politician. They are taught the fundamental truth that unemployment and kindred evils are not the outcome of private ownership of capital, but of unfitness and deterioration in one class of citizens. Boy Scouts when they grow up will not be sentimentalists and doctrinaires. ... The Boy Scout will grow up a sound Imperialist, and, what is more important, a good citizen.

17. See William Beveridge, *Unemployment: A Problem of Industry* (London: Longmans, 1907), and B. Seebohm Rowntree, *Poverty: A Study of Town Life* (London: Macmillan, 1901).
18. The six-pence requirement represented a toning down of Baden-Powell's aspirations for the thrift of the first-class Scout; the original manuscript stipulation called for a shilling.
19. *Scouting for Boys*, 3rd edition, 1910, p. 286. The movement from the initial manuscript formulation to deletion in the third edition constitutes a coherent and gradual repudiation of anything to do with socialism. The manuscript version has a much stronger personal flavor than what Baden-Powell permitted in the published edition:

> I should have liked to be a Socialist at one time to get money more evenly distributed so that there would be no millionaires and no paupers, but everyone pretty well off. When I looked it up in History it proved to be a very old story and one which didn't work. It needs such tremendous discipline that it would be something like slavery to everybody. (Ms. p. 173, British Scout Archives)

20. Ibid., p. 7.
21. Ibid., p. 33.
22. Letter from Baden-Powell to Percy Everett, 9 September 1908. Everett Papers (British Scout Archives).

23. The old phrase, post coitus triste, is illustrated in excess of all forms, and especially in self-abuse. Weakness always brings more or less depression, and in some cases the physical exhaustion of muscles and nerves, if intensified by excess, brings pain and traces of convulsion, epilepsy, palpitation, and photophobia, differing according to individual predispositions and powers of resistance. Neurasthenia, cerebrasthenia, spinal neurasthenia, and psychic impotence generally result not more in the loss of fluid than from expenditure of physical force and often by tissues connected with the sympathetic system. Subjective light sensations, optical cramps, perhaps Basedow's disease, intensification of the patellar reflex, weak sluggishness of heart action and circulation seen in cold extremities, purple and dry skin, lassitude with flaccidity, clammy hands, anemic complexion, dry cough, and many digestive perversions can often be directly traced to this scourge of the human race. The onanistic psychosis seems especially to predispose to convulsive disorders like epilepsy, to which it is so akin, but weakness of memory and attention, paranoia, agitation, cachexia, various neuroses of the stomach which Preyer and Fournier have studied, dwarfing or hypertrophy of the organs themselves, and many of the lighter and transitory forms of psychic alienations, are also produced. (G. Stanley Hall, *Adolescence* [New York: D. Appleton, 1911], pp. 442–43)

24. Baden-Powell to Peter Keary, 6 March 1908, in Paul Richards, ed., *The Founding of the Boy Scouts as Seen Through the Letters of Lord Baden-Powell, October 1907–October 1908* (East Bridgewater, Mass.: The Standish Museum and Unitarian Church, 1973).

25. Ibid., 12 March 1908.

26. Ibid., 17 March 1908.

27. The comment sounds very much like the suicide note Father Time leaves behind in Hardy's *Jude the Obscure* to explain his killing Jude's two children and himself: "Done because we are too menny." I should point out that the criticism of lower-class lack of restraint is not entirely eliminated from *Scouting for Boys*, even if it is not explicitly linked to the problem of unemployment. In lamenting the vast amount of preventable deterioration creeping in among the rising generation, Baden-Powell mentions, along with the facts of self-abuse, venereal disease, and drink, "Also much pauper over-population due to want of self-restraint on the part of men and women" (p. 164).

7: "THE PEACE SCOUTS" AND EDWARDIAN MILITARISM

1. Baden-Powell, "'Boy Scouts' in Connection with National Training and National Service," *Journal of the Royal United Service Institute* 55 (May 1911): 592.

2. Everett Papers British Scout Archives. Letter is dated 26 May 1909. This necessity for a strictly nonmilitary image was made clear on numerous occasions. Consider, for example, this letter written from Scout Headquarters to Lord Meath, an active campaigner for military training for all boys, in 1910:

I understand from the clerk at the Headquarters of the Boy Scouts that you called yesterday, but unfortunately found the establishment dispersed for the holidays.
I gather that your wish was to find out whether we were Military or Peace Scouts. I may say for your Lordship's information that we are a

Peace Organization, at the preesent time, the main reason being that a very large number of people will allow their boys to join the Boy Scouts, who are not in favour of the general military service. (Scout Archives, Box Q, Letters of Interest)

The letter was written by a member of Baden-Powell's staff, not Baden-Powell, but clearly speaks to Scout policy.

3. G. R. Searle, *The Quest for National Efficiency* (Berkeley: University of California Press, 1971), p. 96. Compare Baden-Powell's analysis of the virtues of World War I:

The Damocletian sword of war ever hanging over a country is not without its merits in keeping up the manliness of a people, in developing self-sacrificing heroism in its soldiers. in uniting classes, creeds, and parties, and in showing the pettiness of party-politics in its true proportion.

In any case this war will have proved how essential to the safety of the nation it is to be prepared, in season and out, not merely for what may be probable, but for what may even be possible. (British Scout Archives, Loose Leaf Notebook labeled "Miscellaneous")

4. Cf. V. G. Kiernan's discussion of this point in *The Lords of Human Kind: European Attitudes Towards the Outside World in the Imperial Age* (London: Weidenfeld and Nicholson, 1969), p. 314: "A rough and ready but tenacious habit grew up of classifying peoples, not in India alone, as 'martial' or 'non-martial,' and of paying more respect (or less disrespect) to the first."

5. Baden-Powell's lecture on Scout Militarism, p. 6, in Scoutmasters' Training course, 1911 (Scout Archives, Book 2).

6. Baden-Powell to Capt. MacIlwain, 9 December 1909 (American Scout Archives). See also the letter from Scout headquarters to Lord Meath, op. cit., which goes on to say "In regard to military drill, it is our policy to have military drill if the Scoutmaster desires it. Personally, I should like to see all Boy Scouts drilled. I look upon the Movement as a further saving of the situation for the nation in the future, and that it will pave the way directly for its national service."

7. *Headquarters Gazette* 1 (December 1909): 9.

8. London *Times*, 6 May 1903. Accounts from the other newspapers were almost identical.

9. The role of military drill is officially announced in the third clause of the Brigade's constitution, which was adopted in 1885: "Military organization and drill shall be used as a means of securing the interests of the boys, banding them together in the work of the Brigade, and promoting among them such habits as the Brigade is designed to form. Strict discipline and obedience shall be enforced by all officers."

10. Olive Anderson, "The Growth of Christian Militarism in Mid-Victorian Britain," *English Historical Review* 86 (January 1971): 46-72.

11. Maurice's two influential papers were both published in the *Contemporary Review*: "Where to Get Men," 81 (January 1902): 79-86; and "National Health: A Soldier's Study," 83 (January 1903): 41-56.

12. See my discussion of Maurice's method in chapter 6.

13. On the theme of national efficiency see G. R. Searle, *The Quest for National Efficiency*; Bernard Semmel, *Imperialism and Social Reform* (New York: Doubleday, Anchor, 1968); and Robert J. Scally, *The Origins of the Lloyd George*

Coalition: The Politics of Social Imperialism, 1900–1918 (Princeton: Princeton University Press, 1975).

14. Ian Hamilton, "National Life and National Training." Address delivered in the Central Hall, Birmingham, on 24 September 1912, to the Birmingham and Midland Institute, p. 12.

15. Ibid., p. 15.

16. Ibid., p. 7.

17. Eric George, *National Service and National Education* (London: P. S. King, 1913), pp. 28–29.

18. Ibid., pp. 19–20.

19. *The Nation in Arms* 4 (1909): 170.

20. Newcastle *Journal*, 23 September 1909, in Jewish Lads' Brigade cutting book, item AJ 34, in the collection of the Mocatta Library, University College, London.

21. Letter dated 31 July 1908 (Barber Collection).

22. Comment by Sir George Taubman-Goldie following a paper read by Baden-Powell at a meeting of the National Defence Association, *National Defence* 4 (August 1910): 440.

23. Baden-Powell, "The Training of the Territorial Army," *National Defence* 2 (January 1909): 300.

24. Baden-Powell, paper read before the National Defence Association, 6 May 1910, published in *National Defence* 4 (August 1910): 438.

25. Baden-Powell, "'Boy Scouts' in Connection with National Training and National Service," *Journal of the Royal United Service Institute* 55 (May 1911): 593.

26. Early members included L. S. Amery, Rudyard Kipling, the earl of Derby, Admiral Beresford, the earl of Malmesbury, the duke of Argyll, the duke of Westminster, Leo Maxse, and the bishop of Chester, among others.

27. *The Briton's First Duty: The Case for Conscription* (London: Grant Richards, 1901), p. 9.

28. Ibid., p. 26.

29. Ibid., p. 86.

30. Ibid., p. 87.

31. Ibid., pp. 194–95.

32. Ibid., pp. 199–200.

33. Lord Roberts, *Facts and Fallacies* (London: John Murray, 1911), p. 12.

34. Lord Roberts's *Message to the Nation* (London: John Murray, 1912), pp. 4–5.

35. Ibid., p. 6.

36. Ibid., pp. 6–7. Caroline Playne, an acute critic of British prewar militarism, gives another example of British admiration for German's devotion to the business of war. She cites from Lord Fisher's *Memories* the following incident: "Fulminating against the British government's refusal to build more warships, Fisher looked enviously at what the Germans had achieved: 'Owing to our apathy during the last two years they are ahead with internal combustion engines! *They have killed fifteen men in experiments with oil engines, and we have not killed one*! And a d———d fool of an English politician told me the other day that he thinks this creditable to us!'" (Caroline E. Playne, *The Pre-War Mind in Britain* [London: George Allen and Unwin, 1928]), p. 136.

37. Roberts, p. 9.

38. Ibid., p. 11. Although the sacred mission of convincing people of the impending German invasion was more properly Lord Roberts's than Baden-Powell's, Baden-Powell did not himself hesitate to foster whatever anxiety about the German menace might be useful in helping promote the need for a disciplined

British youth. He caused a minor parliamentary stir when, in an address to officers of the Territorial forces in Newcastle in 1908, he referred to Germany as "the natural enemy of this country."

39. J. O. Springhall, *Youth, Empire and Society: British Youth Movements, 1883-1940* (London: Croom Helm, 1977), p. 128, note 24.

40. Francis Fletcher Vane, *The Boy Knight* (London: Council of National Peace Scouts, 1910), p. 7.

41. Ibid., pp. 14-15.

42. Quoted in J. O. Springhall, "The Boy Scouts, Class, and Militarism in Relation to British Youth Movements, 1908-1930," *International Review of Social History* 16 (1971): 137.

43. The twelfth earl of Meath sat on the Scout Council and was Scout commissioner of Ireland from 1911-1928. In addition to founding the Lads' Drill Association in 1899, he was one of the founders of the Duty and Discipline Movement (1910). He was a member of the executive council of the National Service League and the general council of the Legion of Frontiersmen. He also originated the Empire Day Movement, which he ran from 1903 to 1913. He was a vice-president of the Navy League (1909) and a president of the British Girls' Patriotic League (1911) as well as the League of Empire. See J. O. Springhall, "Lord Meath, Youth, and Empire," *Journal of Contemporary History* 5 (1970): 97-111.

44. Meath, Introduction to the Association's annual report of 1904, quoted in Michael Sadler, ed., *Continuation Schools in England and Elsewhere* (Manchester: University Press, 1907), pp. 87-88.

45. *The Frontiersman*, January 1910, p. 10.

46. A. J. Dawson, *The Frontiersman's Pocket Book* (n.d.), pp. 379-80.

47. William Sergeant, *The Frontiersman*, June 1910, p. 86.

48. *The Frontiersman*, January 1910, p. 16.

49. *The Frontiersman*, June 1910, p. 86.

50. Ibid.

51. *Essays on Duty and Discipline* (London: Cassell, 1911), p. vii.

52. Ibid., p. 14.

53. Ibid., p. 265.

54. Ibid., p. 264.

55. Ibid., pp. 269-70.

56. Ibid., p. 124.

57. Ibid., p. 197.

58. Ibid., p. 215.

59. Introduction to lecture by Baden-Powell, "'Boy Scouts' in Connection with National Training and National Service," *Journal of the Royal United Service Institute* 55 (May 1911): 586.

60. F. W. Hirst, *The Six Panics and Other Essays* (London: Methuen, Ltd., 1913).

61. George Chesney, *The Battle of Dorking* (London: Blackwood's Magazine, 1871), pp. 63-64.

62. For a full discussion of the subject, see I. F. Clarke, *Voices Prophesying War, 1763-1984* (London: Oxford University Press, 1966). See also Samuel Hynes, *The Edwardian Turn of Mind* (Princeton: Princeton University Press, 1968).

63. William LeQueux, *The Invasion of 1910* (London: George Newnes, 1906), p. 1.

64. Ibid., p. 2.

65. Ibid., p. 80.

66. Ibid., p. 166.

67. Ibid., p. 242.

68. *Spectator* 102 (6 February 1909): 208–209.
69. *The Nation in Arms*, 4 (October 1909): 406.
70. *The Nation in Arms* 4 (December 1909): 477–78.
71. W. Douglas Newton, *War* (New York: Dodd, Mead, 1914), p. 58.
72. Ibid., pp. 58–59.
73. Ibid., p. 236.
74. P. G. Wodehouse, "The Swoop! or How Clarence Saved England: A Tale of the Great Invasion," in *The Swoop! and Other Stories* (New York: Seabury Press, 1979), pp. 10–11. The story was first published in 1909.
75. Ibid., p. 12.
76. Ibid., p. 13.
77. Ibid.
78. Ibid., p. 4.
79. Ibid.
80. *The Novels and Plays of Saki* (New York: Carroll and Graf, 1984), p. 169. Future page references will appear in parentheses. The novel was first published in 1913.
81. Quoted in Dennis Hayes, *Conscription Conflict* (London: Sheppard Press, 1949), p. 56.
82. Consider, for example, the far-reaching—and typical—claims made by the National Service League for the efficacy of military training:

> We have frequently pointed out that National Service, besides giving us national safety, provides the key to the solution of nearly all the great social problems with which our industrial civilisation is confronted. Doctors, schoolmasters, philanthropists, ministers of religion: all are brought face to face with compulsory military training as one of the chief remedial or preventive measures for the various evils which they are respectively called upon to investigate. (*The Nation in Arms* 4 [March 1909]: 81)

83. *The Nation in Arms* 1 (May 1906): 1.
84. James Anson Farrar, *Liberalism and the National Service League* (London: T. Fisher Unwin, 1909), p. 17.
85. Ibid., pp. 18–19.
86. J. Bruce Glasier, *The Peril of Conscription* (London: I.L.P., 1915), p. 17.
87. Ibid., p. 18.
88. Playne, p. 147.
89. Roberts's speech to the inhabitants of Manchester, 30 January 1906, *The Nation in Arms*, 1 (January 1906): 119–20. The salutary moral effects claimed for military training by league adherents were as absurdly extreme as Farrar's description suggests:

> Four months training in the infantry or in the cavalry have suddenly been discovered to possess a moral and educational value of unsuspected superiority to anything yet known to human experience. The idea of a dose of military discipline as the only chance for the salvation of the working classes has become the common possession and mark of every cultivated mind.... The petty tyranny of the military martinet is to raise the next generation to higher things. Camp life, and sleeping eight in a tent, is to redeem us from the pleasant vices of the past, and the Golden Age is to come with the ability of every ploughboy to handle a rifle.

(Farrar, *Invasion and Conscription* [London: T. Fisher Unwin, 1909], pp. 55-56)

90. T. C. Horsfall, *The Influence on National Life of Military Training in Schools* (London: J & A Churchill, 1906), p. 8.
91. Blatchford in *The Nation in Arms* 4 (June 1909): 238.
92. *The Nation in Arms* 3 (March 1908): 56.
93. *National Service Journal* 1 (December 1906): 97.
94. Lord Roberts, *Defence of the Empire* (London: Spottiswoode, 1905), p. 13.
95. Ibid., p. 14.
96. *Scouting for Boys*, p. 3.
97. Ibid., p. 246.
98. Ibid., p. 266.
99. Baden-Powell, *Aids to Scoutmastership*, p. 100.
100. Ibid., p. 68.
101. Baden-Powell message to Scouts in Connection with Imperial Challenge Shield Competition, November 1927 (British Scout Archives).
102. *Scouting for Boys*, p. 249.
103. *Aids to Scoutmastership*, p. 124.
104. *Lessons from the 'Varsity of Life*, pp. 196-97.
105. Sixth Annual Report (British Scout Archives).
106. Flyer on Scouts Defence Corps (British Scout Archives).
107. *Headquarters Gazette* 9 (January 1915): 4-5.
108. Baden-Powell, *What Scouts Can Do: More Yarns* (London: C. Arthur Pearson, 1921), pp. 108-109.

8: PREDECESSORS AND SUCCESSORS

1. In *Youth, Empire and Society*, J. O. Springhall defines a youth movement "by its willingness to admit unlimited numbers of children, adolescents, and young adults, with the aim of propagating some sort of code of living. It should also encourage the participation of its youthful members as leaders and organizers, allow for the possibility of competing for awards and badges, and provide them with a specific identity or status in the form of a uniform" (Springhall, p. 13).
2. Springhall points out that some historians of the Brigade claim that the initial inspiration for the Brigade training method came not from Smith himself but either a business associate, James Findlay, or the Reverend George Reith.
3. Obedience is obviously implied in all this, but it was explicitly added to the Brigade's official definition in 1893.
4. *Boys' Brigade Handbook*, p. 4.
5. Ibid.
6. Smith, excerpt from an address to World Sunday School convention in 1889 (Boys' Brigade Archives).
7. Henty, *Boys' Brigade Gazette* 5 (June 1895): 255.
8. A dispute between Gee and important Anglican churchmen on the issue of temperance resulted, in the early 1890s, in the creation of a separate brigade— the London Diocesan Church Lads' Brigade—which maintained its distinct existence until 1919.
9. Jewish Lads' Brigade pocket book (Mocatta Library, University of London).
10. *Jewish Chronicle*, 26 June 1908 (Mocatta Library, University of London).

11. Cf. Springhall, note 24, on p. 49.
12. While these were the major brigades, there were numerous smaller ones as well. Springhall mentions, among others, the Boys' Naval Brigade, the London Newsboys' Brigade, the Imperial Lads' Brigade, and a Good Lads' Brigade. Cf. Springhall, p. 45.
13. Boys' Brigade Archives.
14. William A. Smith to Baden-Powell, 28 December (Boys' Brigade Archives).
15. Ian Hamilton, "National Life and National Training." Address delivered to the Birmingham Midland Institute, 24 September 1912, p. 19.
16. *Headquarters Gazette* 5 (October 1911): 4.
17. Ibid., pp. 10–11.
18. Ibid., p. 11.
19. Ibid.
20. British Scout Archives, File D, Cadets, 1910–1916.
21. Baden-Powell, *Aids to Scoutmastership*, p. 17. This sentence was also part of a letter appearing in the London *Times* of 14 July 1918.
22. Letter to Baden-Powell, 1 August 1918 (British Scout Archives, File D, Cadets).
23. I. O. Evans, *Woodcraft and World Service* (London: Noel Douglas, 1930), p. 47.
24. Aubrey T. Westlake, *Woodcraft Chivalry* (Weston-Super-Mare, England: Mendip Press, Ltd., 1917), p. 5.
25. Ibid.
26. Ibid., p. 3.
27. Ibid., foreword.
28. The basic ten stipulations of the American model remain, with a significant change in some details. The British insistence on unquestioning obedience is played down and humanized somewhat. The Scout's loyalty, for example, is owed "to all to whom loyalty is due"; while obedience is necessary, the initiate is enjoined to obey, "in no slavish spirit, his parents, his leaders, and all other duly constituted authorities" (*Woodcraft Chivalry*, p. 13).
29. Ibid., p. 3.
30. Ibid., p. 14.
31. John Hargrave, *The Great War Brings it Home* (London: Constable, 1919), p. 51.
32. Ibid., p. 80.
33. Ibid., p. 65.
34. *The Trail* 3 (November 1920): 353.
35. Ibid.
36. Ibid.
37. Ibid.
38. Ibid.
39. Ibid., p. 354.
40. Ibid.
41. Ibid.
42. Ibid., p. 355.
43. Baden-Powell's 1922 memo to General Purpose Committee (British Scout Archives).
44. John Hargrave, *The Confession of the Kibbo Kift* (London: Duckworth, 1927), p. 135.
45. Ibid., p. 99.
46. Ibid., p. 120.
47. Ibid., p. 86.

48. Ibid., p. 84.
49. Ibid., p. 101.
50. Ibid., p. 173.
51. Cited in J. L. Finlay, "John Hargrave, The Green Shirts and Social Credit," *Journal of Contemporary History* 5 (1970): 61.
52. Hargrave, *The Confession of the Kibbo Kift*, p. 102.
53. Ibid., p. 100.
54. Ibid., p. 106.
55. Leslie Paul, *The Folk Trail* (London: Noel Douglas, 1929), p. 15.
56. Ibid., pp. 30-31.
57. Leah Manning, preface to Leslie Paul, *The Republic of Children* (London: George Allen and Unwin, 1938).

9: "SCOUTS, WHITE MEN AND CHRISTIANS"

1. Baden-Powell, *The Matebele Campaign* (London: Methuen, 1897), p. 64.
2. Ibid.
3. If Conrad's "idea which redeems" is the most succinct analysis of how imperialism explains itself, J. A. Cramb's effusiveness must also be heard:

> Imperialism, I should say, is patriotism transfigured by a light from the aspirations of universal humanity, it is the passion of Marathon, of Flodden or Trafalgar, the ardour of a de Montfort or a Grenville, intensified to a serener flame by the ideals of a Condorcet, a Shelley or a Fichte. This is the ideal, and in the resolution deliberate and conscious to realise this ideal throughout its dominions, from bound to bound, in the voluntary submission to this as to the primal law of its being, lies what may be named the destiny of Imperial Britain. (J. A. Cramb, *Reflections on the Origins and Destiny of Imperial Britain* [London: Macmillan, 1900], p. 16)

A more conventional, if no less absolute claim for the moral grandeur of the empire can be found in Lord Wolsley's commitment:

> I have but one great object in this world, and that is to maintain the greatness of our Empire. But apart from my John Bull sentiment upon the point, I firmly believe in doing so I work in the cause of Christianity, of peace, of civilization, and the happiness of the human race generally. (Quoted in Caroline E. Playne, *The Pre-War Mind in Britain* [London: George Allen and Unwin, 1928], p. 127)

4. *The Downfall of Prempeh*, pp. 26-27.
5. Ibid., p. 117.
6. Ibid., p. 165.
7. Ibid., p. 57.
8. Ibid., p. 21.
9. Ibid., p. 136.
10. *The Matebele Campaign*, p. 417.
11. Ibid., p. 64.
12. Ibid., pp. 171-72.
13. *Lessons from the 'Varsity of Life*, p. 141.
14. *Rovering to Success*, p. 84.
15. *Indian Memories*, p. 225.

16. Draft of article on Sixth Scout Law, 1932 (British Scout Archives).
17. *Boy Scouts Beyond the Seas*, p. 199.
18. *Scouting Round the World*, pp. 77-78.
19. *Boy Scouts Beyond the Seas*, p. 119.
20. *An Old Wolf's Favorites: Animals I Have Known* (London: C. Arthur Pearson, 1924), p. 61.
21. Ibid.
22. *Rovering to Success*, p. 87.
23. Report of Baden-Powell's on India for director (British Scout Archives, Box Z).
24. Letter to duke of Connaught dated 7 March 1936 (British Scout Archives, Box B, South Africa, 1931-38).
25. Draft of article written for the *Scouter*, 1936 (British Scout Archives, Ibid.).
26. Baden-Powell to Col. H. S. Browning, 2 December 1916 (British Scout Archives, Box B, South Africa, 1912-30).
27. Baden-Powell to Browning, 13 January 1917, Ibid.
28. Pamphlet on Baden-Powell's South African tour, 1926-27 (British Scout Archives, Ibid.).
29. Diary of South African Tour, 3 October 1926 (British Scout Archives, Founders File 9).
30. Pamphlet on South African Tour (British Scout Archives, Ibid.).
31. Ibid.
32. Memo on the Federation scheme (British Scout Archives, Box B, South Africa, 1931-38).
33. Ibid.
34. Baden-Powell to duke of Connaught, 7 March 1936.
35. The actual risks to the white boys from contact with blacks were in any case minimal. Baden-Powell points out that "The white children have not any real aversion to the coloured natives as such. These are often their caretakers and playmates. The whites may possibly learn from them a certain amount that is undesirable such as lying, laziness, etc: but the actual prejudice against their coloured or native subjects derives itself rather from the views of their parents" (British Scout Archives, Founders File 9, Diary of South African Tour).
36. Report on 1936 visit, 25 February 1936 (British Scout Archives, Box B, South Africa, 1931-38). His entry on 27 February further elaborates the principled rightness of the decision:

> With us it was rather from a sense of justice and fair play to the underdog that we let the natives and Indians come into scouting. They ... have no training in discipline or self-control such as they used to have in their tribal ways, they are becoming race conscious, and sensitive to just or unjust treatment much prompted by educated or politically inclined negroes from America, etc.
> Their ambition, among the youth, is to be Boy Scouts like the white boys—though with no desire for mixing with them.

37. *Yarns for Boy Scouts*, pp. 28-29.
38. *Indian Memories*, p. 17.
39. Letter to General May, acting commissioner for India, 8 May 1916 (British Scout Archives, Box Z, India, 1915-21).
40. Lord Chelmsford to Baden-Powell, 27 November 1916 (British Scout Archives, ibid.).

41. Report of Baden-Powell for directors of public information (British Scout Archives, GG-Z India, 1937-38).
42. Baden-Powell's response to J. S. Wilson, 4 September 1937 (British Scout Archives, Z. India, 1937-38).
43. Baden-Powell to H. W. Hogg, deputy chief commissioner, 7 July 1937 (British Scout Archives, ibid.).
44. The words specifically cited are *Abroo, Iman, Izzat, Sharafat,* and *Chairat.*
45. Resolution of Bombay Provisional Scout Council (British Scout Archives, ibid.).
46. Baden-Powell was himself perfectly aware of the connection. Praising the character-training practices of a headmaster in Kashmir, Baden-Powell notes the possibilities they suggest for redeeming the fallen youth at home:

> Mr. Tyndale-Biscoe has succeeded in the delicate operation of strengthening the moral backbone of large numbers of boys in Kashmir, and in these pages he recounts in a fascinating way how this has been brought about. The book shows how, through Scout methods in capable hands, an effete race may be made manly, healthy, and Christian.
>
> If this can be done in a far land with a foreign people, it gives boundless view of what might be possible and ought to be effected by the same means in our own great slum centres in England. (Foreword to C. E. Tyndale-Biscoe, *Character Building in Kashmir* [London: Church Missionary Society, 1920])

47. Subsequently published in a pamphlet entitled *The Scout Movement and Religious Observances.* The full policy, later incorporated into the official rules, was as follows:

> 1. It is expected that every Scout should belong to some religious denomination and attend its services.
>
> 2. Where a troop is composed of members of one particular form of religion, it is hoped that Scoutmasters will arrange such denominational religious observances and instruction as he, in consultation with the chaplain or other religious authority, may consider best.
>
> 3. Where a troop consists of Scouts of various religions, they should be encouraged to attend the service of their own denominations, and in camp any form of daily prayer and of weekly Divine service should be of the simplest character—attendance being voluntary.

48. Captain Walker's report, 1920 (British Scout Archives, Box A).
49. Baden-Powell to Pickford, 12 September 1927 (British Scout Archives, Box B, South Africa, 1919-30).
50. Baden-Powell Papers, National Army Museum.
51. *Life's Snags and How to Meet Them* (London: C. Arthur Pearson, 1927), p. 70.
52. 17 December 1935 (British Scout Archives, Box C, Tanganyika, 1935).
53. As with so much else of Baden-Powell's thought, Sapper's vision, in his Bulldog Drummond books, of a "Russia ruled by a clique of homicidal alien Jews" is not substantially different from Baden-Powell's own. Sapper, *Bull Dog Drummond: His Four Rounds with Carl Peterson* (London: Hodder & Stoughton, 1959), p. 958.
54. *The Scouter,* 24 January 1924, p. 1.

55. Baden-Powell to Yellin, 5 June 1924 (British Scout Archives, Founders File 22).
56. Memo, 31 May 1924 (British Scout Archives, ibid.).
57. The *Scouter*, July 1924, p. 1.
58. The correspondence, I should add, did not put an end to Baden-Powell's public insistence that the Bolshevik menace was Jewish led. A year later Baden-Powell proposed to put in the *Carthusian* (the Charterhouse magazine) the following notice calling for support for the Scout movement to resist the threat to Britain posed by the communists: "The one hope of safety for our country lies in the whole lot of you pulling together. The Communists in Moscow are clever fellows, many of the leaders being German Jews, and their aim is to upset the present government in all countries." (British Scout Archives, Box A, Scout in Schools, 1925-37).
   Baden-Powell's conviction that Jews and revolutionary unrest went together was further documented during his visit to Hungary in 1928. As he observed in his diary, "The Archduke Josef Franz told my wife and myself of his experiences during the Communist regime in Hungary from March to August 1919. The revolution was run mainly by Jews under Bela Kun (alias Cohen)" (British Scout Archives, Founders File #9 Diary of 1928 trip to Hungary).
59. Baden-Powell to S. M. Salomon, 1 May 1933 (British Scout Archives, Box N, Messages From the Founder, 1933-34).
60. Baden-Powell to a Mr. Helbert, asking for the help of preparatory school masters in regard to Scout training methods (British Scout Archives).
61. *What Scouts Can Do.*, p. 17.
62. *Aids to Scoutmastership*, p. 87. The need to maintain the position that Scouting was free of all political ties, while essential, Baden-Powell realized, for its unencumbered growth, occasionally involved him in some ticklish negotiations. Consider for example his explanations to Reginald Wilson of the conservative British Empire Union as to why the Scouts would not assist in putting on a patriotic play offered under the Union's auspices:

> In reply to your letter of June 15th I would ask you to realize that we are in a very delicate position in the B.S.M. We are gaining successful touch with elements that are near the edge of disloyalty and by winning their confidence we are able to make effective appeal to their rising generation and so to prevent the growth of sedition.
> The British Empire Union, rightly or wrongly, is in some quarters connected with political ideas, and to openly associate ourselves with it in these districts would be to effectually put a stopper to our work.
> Therefore I leave it to the judgement of the Scout Authorities on the spot to say whether they can take part in such activities as that suggested—and I think they must be the most capable of deciding the question locally.
> But I trust you will not suppose that they are therefore out of sympathy with the work of the British Empire Union. I think I may safely say we all admire and favour the line that the Union has taken up and where we can help it without falsifying our own position we are only too willing to do it. (Baden-Powell to Reginald Wilson, 27 June 1922 [British Scout Archives, Founder's File 23])

63. Jotting down some notes for a projected article on "My Most Interesting

Experience" for *News of the World*, Baden-Powell listed his visit with Mussolini along with a visit with King Edward as his two most interesting "incidents," as opposed to the three compelling "episodes" of raising the South African Constabulary, defending Mafeking, and starting the Scout Movement.

64. Collection of Articles, Messages, etc., 1909-33 (British Scout Archives), Founder's File 21).
65. Report by Baden-Powell on Balilla, 1933 (British Scout Archives, Box Z, Italy 1916-37).
66. Article on Balilla (British Scout Archives, Founder's File 21).
67. Ibid.
68. Ibid.
69. Ibid.
70. Ibid.
71. Ibid.
72. Baden-Powell's notes sent to Percy W. Everett on 16 September 1940, Everett Papers (British Scout Archives).
73. Ibid.
74. Statement made at Banquet in Toronto, 16 May 1935 (British Scout Archives, Box N, Broadcasts, 1923-28).
75. Fragment of draft of article, n.d. (probably mid-1930s) (American Scout Archives).
76. Cf. letter to Martin of 8 October 1937, which begins, "In spite of what you have told me about the conclusions of the International Committee, I think the time has come when we, in the British movement at any rate, ought to do something to be friendly with the Hitler Youth" (Somers Papers, British Scout Archives, vol. 1).
77. Ibid.
78. Memo from Martin to Baden-Powell, 22 August 1935 (British Scout Archives, ibid.).
79. Baden-Powell was not worried about the possibility of apostasy. In his view, neither Benneman, the German minister for foreign affairs, nor Ribbentrop, alleged spies, "nor the Hitler Youth could do much to convert our boys to becoming Nazis" (Martin letter, 8 October 1937, British Scout Archives, ibid.).

CONCLUSION

THE EMPEROR OF YOUTH

1. Baden-Powell's Report on Boy Scouts in Russia (British Scout Archives).
2. Baden-Powell, *Scouting for Boys* (London: Horace Cox, 1908), p. 264.
3. Piers Brendon, *Eminent Edwardians* (Boston: Houghton Mifflin, 1980), p. 244.
4. Lytton Strachey, *Eminent Victorians* (London: Chatto and Windus, 1948), p. 274.
5. Ibid., p. 237.
6. Ibid., p. 6.

BIBLIOGRAPHY

BOOKS AND MAJOR PAMPHLETS
AND ADDRESSES BY BADEN-POWELL

Adventures and Accidents. London: Methuen and Co., 1934.
Adventuring to Manhood. London: C. Arthur Pearson, 1936.
African Adventures. London: C. Arthur Pearson, 1937.
Aids to Scouting for N.C.Os and Men. London: Gale and Polden, 1899.
Aids to Scoutmastership. London: Herbert Jenkins, 1919.
An Old Wolf's Favorites: Animals I Have Known. London: C. Arthur Pearson, 1921.
Birds and Beasts of Africa. London: Macmillan, 1938.
Boy Scouts Beyond the Seas. London: C. Arthur Pearson, 1913.
" 'Boy Scouts' in Connection with National Training and National Service." *Royal United Service Institute* 55 (May 1911): 581-99.
'Brownies or Blue Birds.' *A Handbook for Young Girl Scouts.* London: C. Arthur Pearson, 1920.
Cavalry Instruction. London: Morrison and Sons, 1885.
The Cub Book by the Chief Old Wolf. London: C. Arthur Pearson, 1917.
The Downfall of Prempeh. London: Methuen and Co., 1896.
Girl Guiding: A Handbook for Guidelets, Guides, Senior Guides and Guiders. London: C. Arthur Pearson, 1918.
Girl Guides: A Suggestion for Character Training for Girls. London: The Bishopgate Press, 1909.
(With Agnes Baden-Powell). *The Handbook for Girl Guides or How Girls Can Help Build the Empire.* London: Thomas Nelson and Sons, 1912.
Indian Memories. London: Herbert Jenkins, 1915.
Lessons from the 'Varsity of Life. London: C. Arthur Pearson, 1933.
Life's Snags and How to Meet Them: Talks to Young Men. London: C. Arthur Pearson, 1927.
Marksmanship for Boys: The Red Feather and How to Win It. London: C. Arthur Pearson, 1915.
The Matabele Campaign, 1896. London: Methuen and Co., 1897.
More Sketches of Kenya. Macmillan and Co., 1940.
My Adventures as a Spy. London: C. Arthur Pearson, 1915.
On Vedette: An Easy Aide Memoire. London: Gale and Polden, 1893.
Paddle Your Own Canoe or Tips for Boys. London: Macmillan and Co., 1939.
Pigsticking or Hoghunting. London: Harrison and Sons, 1899.
Quick Training for War. London: Herbert Jenkins, 1914.
Reconaissance and Scouting. London: William Clowes and Sons, 1884.

Rovering to Success. London: Herbert Jenkins, 1922.
Scouting and Youth Movements. London: Ernest Benn, 1929.
Scouting for Boys. London: Horace Cox, 1908.
Scouting Games. London: C. Arthur Pearson, 1910.
Scouting Round the World. London: Herbert Jenkins, 1935.
Sketches in Mafeking and East Africa. London: Smith, Elder and Co., 1907.
Sport in War. London: William Heinemann, 1900.
What Scouts Can Do: More Yarns. London: C. Arthur Pearson, 1921.
Young Knights of the Empire: Their Code and Further Scout Yarns. London: C. Arthur Pearson, 1916.
The Wolf Cub's Handbook. London: C. Arthur Pearson, 1916.

OTHER SOURCES

Abrams, Philip. *The Origins of British Sociology: 1834-1914.* Chicago and London: University of Chicago Press, 1968.
Adams, W. S. *Edwardian Heritage.* London: Frederick Muller, 1949.
———. *Edwardian Portraits.* London: Secker and Warburg, 1957.
Adorno, T. W., et al. *The Authoritarian Personality.* New York: Harper, 1950.
Aitken, W. Francis. *Baden-Powell, The Hero of Mafeking.* London: S. W. Partridge and Co., 1900.
Allen, Clifford. *Conscription and Conscience.* London: National Labor Press, 1916.
Amery, L. M. *The Problem of the Army.* London: Edward Arnold, 1903.
Anderson, Olive. "The Growth of Christian Militarism in Mid-Victorian Britain." *English Historical Review* 86 (January 1971): 46-72.
Arnold-Forster, H-O. *The Army in 1906: A Policy and a Vindication.* London: John Murray, 1906.
———. *The Citizen Reader.* London: Cassell and Co., 1904. (First printed in 1886.)
———. *The War Office, the Army, and the Empire.* London: Cassell and Co., Ltd. 1900.
Atkins, J. B., ed. *National Physical Training: An Open Debate.* London: Isbister and Co., 1904.
Baldwin, W. H., and Robson, W. Lessons. *On Character-Building.* London: Thomas Nelson and Sons, 1913.
Balfour, A. J. "Decadence." Cambridge, Eng.: Cambridge University Press, 1908.
Banks, Olive. *Parity and Prestige in English Secondary Education.* London: Routledge and Kegan Paul, 1955.
Barnett, Corelli. *The Collapse of British Power.* London: Eyre Methuen, 1972.
Barnett, Mary G. *Young Delinquents: A Study of Reformatory and Industrial Schools.* London: Methuen and Co., 1913.
Batchelder, W. J., and Balfour, David. *The Life of Baden-Powell.* London: Collins, 1929.
Bateson, William. "Biological Fact and the Structure of Society." Herbert Spencer Lecture. Oxford: The Clarendon Press, 1912.
Beard, Dan. *Hardly a Man Is Now Alive: The Autobiography of Dan Beard.* New York: Doubleday, Doran and Co., 1939.
Beauclerk, C. W. W. de V. *A National Army.* London: King, Sell and Olding, 1907.
Begbie, Harold. *The Story of Baden-Powell.* London: Grant Richards, 1900.
Beveridge, W. H. *Unemployment, a Problem of Industry.* London: Longmans, 1909.
Birch, Austin. *The Story of the Boys' Brigade.* London: Frederick Muller, 1959.
Blacker, C. P. *Eugenics: Galton and After.* London: Gerald Duckworth, 1952.

Blanch, Michael. "Imperialism, Nationalism and Organized Youth." In *Working-Class Culture*, edited by John Clarke, Chas. Critcher, and Richard Johnson. London: Hutchinson, 1979.

Blatchford, Robert. *Britain for the British*. Chicago: Charles H. Kerr, 1902.

———. *Germany and England*. London: Amalgamated Press, 1914.

———. *My Life in the Army*. London: Amalgamated Press, 1910.

Bond, Brian, and Roy, Ian, eds. *War and Society*. London: Croom Helm, 1975.

Bray, Reginald. *Boy Labour and Apprenticeship*. London, Constable & Co., 1911.

———. *The Town Child*. London: T. Fisher Unwin, 1907.

Brendon, Piers. *Eminent Edwardians*. Boston: Houghton Mifflin Co., 1980.

Brew, J. MacAlister. *Youth and Youth Groups*. London: 1968.

Brockington, W. A. *Elements of Military Education*. London: Longmans, Green and Co., 1916.

Bruce, Maurice. *The Coming of the Welfare State*. Rev. ed. New York: Schocken Books, 1966.

Buchan, John. *Francis and Riversdale Glenfell: A Memoir*. London: Thomas Nelson and Sons, Ltd., 1920.

Busk, H. *The Rifle: And How to Use it*. London: G. Routledge and Co., 1859.

Cairns, E.A. *An Absent-Minded War. Being Some Reflections on Our Reverses and the Causes Which Led to Them*. London: John Milne, 1900.

Cantlie, James. *Degeneration Amongst Londoners*. London: Field and Tuer, 1885.

———. *Physical Efficiency*. London: G. P. Putnam's Sons, 1906.

Chesney, George. "Battle of Dorking." *Blackwood's Magazine*, March 1881.

The Cinema: Its Present Position and Future Possibilities. Being the Report of and Chief Evidence Taken by the Cinema Commission of Inquiry Instituted by the National Council of Public Morals. London: Williams and Norgate, 1917.

Clark, Alan. *The Donkeys*. London: Hutchinson, 1961.

Clarke, I. F. *Voices Prophesying War, 1763–1984*. London: Oxford University Press, 1966.

Clouston, T. S. *The Hygiene of Mind*. New York: E. P. Dutton and Co., 1907.

Collis, Henry, with Fred Hurll and Rex Hazlewood. *B-P's Scouts: An Official History of the Boy Scouts Association*. London: Collins, 1961.

Comaroff, John L., ed. *The Boer War Diary of Sol. T. Plaatje*. London: Sphere Books, 1976.

Comfort, Alex. *The Anxiety Makers*. London: Nelson, 1967.

Coulton, G. G. *True Liberalism and Compulsory Service: An Appeal to the British Working Man*. London: J. Miles and Co., 1914.

Cramb, J. A. *Reflections on the Origins and Destiny of Imperial Britain*. London: Macmillan and Co., 1900.

Croall, Jonathan. *Neill of Summerhill: The Permanent Rebel*. New York: Pantheon Books, 1983.

Crum, F. M. *Camp and Character Training*. Glasgow: James Brown and Son, 1922.

———. *With Riflemen, Scouts and Snipers from 1914 to 1919*. Oxford: privately printed, 1921.

Cunningham, Hugh. *The Volunteer Force*. London: Croom Helm, 1975.

Dark, Sidney. *The Life of Sir Arthur Pearson*. London: Hodder & Stoughton, 1922.

Darton, F. J. Harvey. *Children's Books in England: Five Centuries of Social Life*. Cambridge, Eng.: The University Press, 1932.

Davies, Bernard, and Gibson, Alan. *The Social Education of the Adolescent*. London: University of London Press, 1967.

Davin, Anna. "Imperialism and Motherhood." *History Workshop* 5 (Spring 1978): 9–65.

The Declining Birth-Rate: Its Causes and Effects. Being the Report of and Chief Evidence Taken by the National Birth-Rate Commission. London: Chapman and Hall, 1916.

Digby, Kenelm Henry. *Broadstone of Honour (Or the True Sense and Practice of Chivalry)* London: F. C. and J. Rivington, 1822.

Dixon, Norman. *On the Psychology of Military Incompetence.* London: Futura Publications, 1979.

Dodd, J. T. *The Health of the Nation.* London: Simpkin, Marshall, Hamilton, Kent and Co., 1905.

Doyle, Arthur Conan. *White Company.* London: George Newnes, 1901.

Dymond, J. A. G. *Scouting and the Adolescent.* London: Longmans, Green and Co., 1920.

Eagar, W. McG. *Making Men: The History of Boys' Clubs and Related Movements in Great Britain.* London: University of London Press, 1953.

Elderton, Ethel M. *The Relative Strength of Nurture and Nature.* London: Dulan and Co., 1909.

Ellis, F. H. *Character-Forming in School.* London: Longmans, 1909.

Ellis, Havelock. *The Problem of Race Regeneration.* London: Cassell and Co. Ltd., 1911.

Essays on Duty and Discipline. London: Cassell, 1911.

Evans, I. O. *Woodcraft and World Service.* London: Noel Douglas, 1930.

Everett, Percy W. *The First Ten Years.* Ipswich: The East Anglican Daily Times, 1948.

Farrer, James Anson. *Invasion and Conscription.* London: T. Fisher Unwin, 1909.

———. *Liberalism and the National Service League.* London: T. Fisher Unwin, 1911.

———. *Moral Cant About Conscription.* London: International Arbitration and Peace Association, 1907.

Farwell, Byron. *The Great Anglo-Boer War.* New York: Harper and Row, 1976.

Fitchett, W. H. *Deeds That Won the Empire.* London: George Newnes, 1900.

———. *Fights for the Flag.* London: Smith, Elder and Co., 1898.

Fletcher, Ronald. *The Family and Marriage in Britain.* London: Penguin Books, 1966.

Fox, G. Malcolm. *National Physical Training.* London: Reformatory and Refuge Union, 1905.

Freeman, Arnold. *Boy Life and Labour: The Manufacture of Inefficiency.* London: P. S. King and Son, 1914.

French, David. "Spy Fever in Britain, 1900-1915." *Historical Journal* 21 (1978): 355-70.

The Frontiersman's Pocket Book. London: John Murray, 1914.

Gainer, Bernard. *The Alien Invasion: The Origins of the Aliens Act of 1905.* London: Heinemann Educational Books, 1972.

Galton, Francis. "Eugenics: Its Definition, Scope, and Aims." *Nature* 70 (1904).

———. *Probability, the Foundation of Eugenics.* The Annual Herbert Spencer Lecture. Oxford: The Clarendon Press, 1907.

Gardiner, Rolf, and Pocholl, Heinz, eds. *Britain and Germany: A Frank Discussion Instigated by Members of the Younger Generation.* London: Williams and Norgate Ltd., 1928.

Gardner, Brian. *Mafeking: A Victorian Legend.* New York: Harcourt, Brace and World, 1967.

Gathorne-Hardy, Jonathan. *The Public School Phenomenon, 597-1977.* London: Hodder and Stoughton, 1977.

George, Eric. *National Service and National Education.* London: P. S. King and Son, 1913.

Gibb, Spencer J. *The Boy and His Work.* London: A. R. Mowbray and Co., 1911.

——. *The Problem of Boy Work.* London: Wells, Gardner, Darton and Co., 1906.

——. *Starting on the Journey: Advice to Boys on the Choice of Work.* London: A. R. Mowbray and Co., 1912.

Gibbon, F. P. *William A. Smith of the Boys' Brigade.* London: Collins, 1934.

Gibson, H. W. *Boyology, or Boy Analysis.* New York: Associated Press, 1922.

Gillis, John R. "Conformity and Rebellion: Contrasting Styles of English and German Youth, 1900-1933." *History of Education Quarterly* 13 (Fall 1973): 249-60.

——. "The Evolution of Juvenile Delinquency in England, 1880-1914." *Past and Present* 67 (May 1975): 96-126.

——. *Youth and History: Tradition and Change in European Age Relations, 1760 to the Present.* London: Academic Press, 1974.

Girouard, Mark. *The Return to Camelot: Chivalry and the English Gentleman.* New Haven: Yale University Press, 1981.

Glasier, J. Bruce. *Militarism.* London: Independent Labour Party, 1915.

——. *The Peril of Conscription.* London: Independent Labour Party, 1915.

Goffman, Erving. *Asylums.* New York: Penguin, 1970.

Gorst, John. *The Children of the Nation.* London: Methuen and Co., 1906.

——. *Education and Race Regeneration.* London: Cassell and Co., 1913.

Gould, Stephen J. *The Mismeasure of Man.* New York: W. W. Norton and Co., 1981.

Graham, John W. *Conscription and Conscience.* London: George Allen and Unwin, 1922.

Grant, Madison. *The Passing of the Great Race or The Racial Basis of European History.* London: G. Bell and Sons, 1917.

Gray, H. B. *The Public Schools and the Empire.* London: Williams and Norgate, 1913.

Grey, Frank, ed. *B-P's Family in Picture and Story.* London: The Boy Scout Association in Conjunction with Evans Bros., 1938.

Haldane, R. B. *Education and Empire.* London: John Murray, 1902.

Haley, Bruce. *The Healthy Body and Victorian Culture.* Cambridge, Mass.: Harvard University Press, 1978.

Hall, G. Stanley. *Adolescence.* New York: D. Appleton and Co., 1904.

Hamilton, Angus. *The Siege of Mafeking.* London: Methuen and Co., 1900.

Hamilton, Ian. *Compulsory Service: A Study of the Question in the Light of Experience.* London: John Murray, 1911.

——. *National Life and National Training.* London: P. S. King and Son, 1913.

Hargrave, John. *The Confession of the Kibbo Kift.* London: Duckworth, 1927.

——. "The Demilitarisation of the Scout Movement." *Foreign Affairs* (August 1920): 26-27.

——. *The Great War Brings It Home.* London: Constable and Co., 1919.

Harrison, J. F. C. *Learning and Living, 1790-1960.* London: Routledge and Kegan Paul, 1961.

Hayes, Dennis. *Conscription Conflict.* London: Sheppard Press, 1949.

Headley, F. W. *Darwinism and Modern Socialism.* London: Methuen, 1909.

Hearnshaw, L. S. *Cyril Burt, Psychologist.* Ithaca: Cornell University Press, 1979.

The Heart of the Empire: Discussions of Problems of Modern City Life in England. London: T. Fisher Unwin, 1901.

Hecht, Charles E. ed. "Rearing an Imperial Race." *Proceedings of the National Food Reform League Conference on Diet, Cookery, and Hygiene in Schools, London,* 1913.

——. *Our Children's Health at Home and at School.* London: Simpkin, Marshall, Hamilton, Kent and Co., 1913.

Heron, David. *The Influence of Defective Physique and Unfavourable Home Environment on the Intelligence of School Children.* London: Dulon and Co., 1910.

Hibbert, Christopher. *The Great Mutiny: India, 1857.* London: Allen Lane, 1978.

Hilliard, F. H. "The Moral Instruction League, 1899-1919." *The Durham Review* 3 (September 1961): 53-63.

Hirst, F. W. *The Six Panics and Other Essays.* London: Methuen and Co., 1913.

Hobsbawm, Eric, and Ranger, Terence. *The Invention of Tradition.* Cambridge, Eng.: Cambridge University Press, 1983.

Hobson, J. A. *Imperialism: A Study.* London: James Nisbet and Co., 1902.

———. *The Psychology of Jingoism.* London: Grant Richards, 1901.

Holt, Laura. *Blazing the Trail: Being Wise Saws and Modern Instances from the Works of the Chief Scout.* London: C. Arthur Pearson, 1923.

Honey, J. R. de S. *Tom Brown's Universe: The Development of the English Public School in the Nineteenth Century.* New York: The New York Times Book Co., Quadrangle, 1977.

Horsfall, T. C. *The Improvement of Dwellings and Surroundings of the People.* Manchester, Eng.: The University Press, 1904.

———. *The Influence on National Life of Military Training in Schools.* London: J. and A. Churchill, 1906.

———. *National Service and the Welfare of the Community.* London: Simpkin, Marshall, Hamilton, Kent and Co., Ltd. 1906.

Horton, R. F. *National Ideals and Race Regeneration.* London: Cassell and Co., 1912.

Humphrey, A. P., and Fremantle, T. E. *History of the National Rifle Association.* Cambridge, Eng.: Bowes and Bowes 1914.

Hynes, Samuel. *The Edwardian Turn of Mind.* Princeton: Princeton University Press, 1968.

Inglis, Brian, ed. *John Bull's Schooldays.* London: Hutchinson, 1961.

James, C. L. R. *Beyond a Boundary.* London: Stanley Paul and Co., 1963.

James, David. *Lord Roberts.* London: Hollis and Carter, 1954.

Jameson, E. M. *Charterhouse.* London: Blackie, 1937.

Jayne, R. Everett. *The Story of John Pounds.* London: The Epworth Press, 1925.

Jones, E. B. Hugh. "The Moral Aspect of Athletics." *Journal of Education* (June 1900): 352-54.

Jones, Gareth Stedman. *Outcast London: A Study in the Relationship Between Classes in Victorian Society.* Oxford: Clarendon Press, 1971. New York: Pantheon Books, 1984.

Jones, Paul. *War Letters of a Public School Boy.* London: Cassell and Co., 1918.

Keller, Betty. *Black Wolf: The Story of Ernest Thompson Seton.* Vancouver/Toronto: Douglas and McIntyre, 1984.

Kennedy, Paul M. *The Rise of Anglo-German Antagonism, 1860-1914.* London: George Allen and Unwin, 1980.

Kett, Joseph F. *Rites of Passage: Adolescence in America. 1790 to the Present.* New York: Basic Books, 1977.

Kidd, Benjamin. *The Science of Power.* London: Methuen and Co., 1920.

Kiernan, V. G. *From Conquest to Collapse: European Empires from 1815-1960.* New York: Pantheon Books, 1982.

———. *The Lords of Human Kind: European Attitudes Towards the Outside World in the Imperial Age.* London: Weidenfeld and Nicolson, 1969.

Lacy, George. "Some Boer Characteristics." *The North American Review* 170 (January 1900): 43-53.

Langdon-Davies, John. *Militarism in Education.* London: Headley Bros, 1919.

Laquer, Walter Z. *Young Germany: A History of the German Youth Movement.* New York: Basic Books, 1962.

Laski, Harold J. *The Danger of Being a Gentleman and Other Essays.* New York: The Viking Press, 1940.

Leicester, James H., and Farndale, James. *Trends in the Services for Youth*. London: Pergamon Press, 1967.

LeQueux, William. *Britain's Deadly Peril*. London: Stanley Paul and Co., 1915.

———. *German Atrocities*. London: George Newnes, 1914.

———. *The Invasion of 1910*. London: George Newnes, 1906.

———. *Spies of the Kaiser: Plotting the Downfall of England*. London: Hurst and Blackett, 1909.

Lichtheim, George. *Imperialism*. New York: Praeger Publications, 1971.

Long, W. J. *Northern Trails*. Boston and London: Ginn and Co., 1905.

Lowe, Charles. "About German Spies." *Contemporary Review* (January 1910): 42–56.

Lowndes, G. A. N. *The Silent Social Revolution: Public Education in England and Wales, 1895-1935*. London: Oxford University Press, 1937.

Mackenzie, Norman. "Sweating It Out with B-P." *New Statesman* 70 (15 October 1965): 555.

Maclean, A. H. H. *The Public Schools and the War in South Africa*. London: Edward Stanford, 1903.

MacLeod, David I. *Building Character in the American Boy*. Wisconsin: The University of Wisconsin Press, Madison, 1983.

Magnus, L., ed. *National Education: A Symposium*. London: John Murray, 1901.

Mandle, W. F. *Anti-Semitism and the British Union of Fascists*. London: Longmans, Green, and Co., 1968

Marchant, James. *Aids to Purity: Seven Personal Letters*. London: Health and Strength, 1915.

———. *Birth-Rate and Empire*. London: Williams and Norgate, 1917.

Marks, H. *Miniature Rifle Clubs and How to Use Them*. London: Society of Working Men's Rifle Clubs, 1903.

Masterman, C. F. G. *The Condition of England*. London: Methuen and Co., 1909.

Maurice, Frederick. "National Health: A Soldier's Study." *Contemporary Review* 83 (January 1903): 41–56.

———. "Where to Get Men." *Contemporary Review* 81 (January 1902): 79–86.

McBriar, A. M. *Fabian Socialism and English Politics, 1884-1918*. Cambridge, Eng.: Cambridge University Press, 1966.

McIntosh, Peter C. *Physical Education in England Since 1800*. London: G. Bell and Sons, 1952.

Meachem, Standish. "The Sense of an Impending Clash: English Working Class Unrest before the First World War." *American Historical Review* 77 (December 1972): 1343–64.

Meller, H. E. *Leisure and the Changing City, 1870-1914*. London: Routledge and Kegan Paul.

Miles, Eustace. *Let's Play the Game or the Anglo-Saxon Sportsmanlike Spirit*. London: Guilbert Pitman, 1904.

Mills, Elliot. *The Decline and Fall of the British Empire: Appointed for Use in the National Schools of Japan, Tokyo, 2005*. London: Simpkin, Marshall, Hamilton, Kent, and Co., 1905.

Milson, Fred. *Youth in a Changing Society*. London: Routledge and Kegan Paul, 1972.

Minchin, J. G. C. *Our Public Schools: Their Influence on British History*. London: Swan Sonnenschein, 1901.

Morris, Brian. "Ernest Thompson Seton and the Origins of the Woodcraft Movement." *Journal of Contemporary History* 5 (1970): 183–94.

Mosse, George L. *Toward the Final Solution: A History of European Racism*. London: J. M. Dent and Sons, 1978.

Munro, H. H. [Saki]. *When William Came in. The Complete Novels and Plays of Saki.* New York: Carrol & Graf, 1984.

Musgrove, Frank. *Youth and the Social Order.* London: Routledge and Kegan Paul, 1964.

Neilly, J. Emerson. *Besieged with B-P.* London: C. Arthur Pearson, 1900.

Nevill, P. B. *My Scouting Story.* London: Roland House Scout Settlement, 1960.

——. *Scouting in London, 1908–1965.* London: The London Scout Council, 1966.

Newitt, E. F. D. *The Citizen Rifleman.* London: George Newnes, 1906.

Newman, George. *The Health of the State.* London: Headley Brothers, 1907.

——. *Infant Mortality: A Social Problem.* London: Methuen and Co., 1906.

Newsholme, A. *The Declining Birth Rate: Its National and International Significance.* London: Cassell and Co., 1911.

Newsome, David. *Godliness and Goodlearning.* London: John Murray, 1961.

Newton, W. Douglas. *War.* New York: Dodd, Mead and Co., 1914.

Nicholson, Jonathan. *Physical Regeneration.* London: The Health Culture Co., 1904.

Nicolson, Edwin. *Education and the Boy Scout Movement in America.* New York: Columbia University, 1940.

"Noemo, Captain" [psued.]. *The Boy Scout Bubble: A Review of a Great Futility.* London: George Allen and Co., 1912.

Norwood, Cyril. *The English Tradition of Education.* London: John Murray, 1929.

Odell, William. "The Physique of the British Nation." Presidential Address Delivered before the Torquay Natural History Society, 1903.

Oliver, F. S. *Ordeal by Battle.* London: Macmillan and Co., 1915.

Oliver, Thomas, ed. *Dangerous Trades.* London: John Murray, 1902.

——. *Maladies Caused by the Air We Breathe Inside and Outside the Home.* London: Bailliere, Tindall and Cox, 1906.

Pakenham, Thomas. *The Boer War.* New York: Random House, 1979.

Paul, Leslie. *Angry Young Man.* London: Faber and Faber, 1951.

——. *The Folk Trail.* London: Noel Douglas, 1929.

——. *The Republic of Children.* London: George Allen and Unwin, 1938.

Peacock, Roger S. *Pioneer of Boyhood: The Story of Sir William A. Smith, Founder of the Boys' Brigade.* Glasgow: The Boys' Brigade, 1954.

Pear, T. H. *English Social Differences.* London: George Allen and Unwin, 1955.

Pearson, Charles H. *National Life and Character: A Forecast.* London: Macmillan and Co., 1894.

Pearson, Karl. *The Academic Aspect of the Science of National Eugenics.* London: Dulan and Co., 1911.

——. *Darwinism, Medical Progress and Eugenics.* London: Dulan and Co., 1912.

——. *Eugenics and Public Health.* London: Dulan and Co., 1912.

——. *The Groundwork of Eugenics.* London: Dulan and Co., 1909.

——. *National Life from the Standpoint of Science.* London: A. and C. Black, 1905.

——. *Nature and Nurture: The Problem of the Future.* London: Dulan and Co., 1910.

——. *Mendelism and the Problem of Mental Defect.* London: Dulan and Co., 1914.

——, et al. *On the Correlation of Fertility with Social Values.* London: Dulan and Co., 1913.

——. *On the Scope and Importance to the State of the Science of National Eugenics.* London: Dulan and Co., 1909.

——. *Social Problems: Their Treatment, Past, Present and Future.* London: Dulan and Co., 1912.

Pelham, H. S. *The Training of a Working Boy.* London: Macmillan and Co., 1914.

Philipps, R. E. *Letters to a Patrol Leader: The Scout Law.* London: C. Arthur Pearson, 1916.

Philipps, R.E. *Letters to a Patrol Leader: The Tenderfoot and Second Class Tests.* London: C. Arthur Pearson, 1916.

Phillpots, Eden. *The Human Boy and the War.* London: Methuen and Co., 1916.

Pike, E. Royston. *Human Documents of the Lloyd George Era.* London: Allen and Unwin, 1972.

Playne, Caroline E. *The Pre-War Mind in Britain.* London: George Allen and Unwin, 1928.

Price, Richard. *The Imperial War and the British Working Class.* London: Routledge and Kegan Paul, 1972.

"Problems of Population and Parenthood." Being the Second Report of and the Chief Evidence Taken by the National Birth-rate Commission, 1918-1920. London: Chapman and Hall, 1920.

Rae, John. *Conscience and Politics.* London and New York: Oxford University Press, 1970.

Ranger, Terence. "Making Northern Rhodesia Imperial: Variations on a Royal Theme, 1924-1938." *African Affairs* 79 (July 1980): 349-373.

———. *Revolt in Southern Rhodesia, 1896-7.* London: Heinemann, 1967.

Ransford, Oliver. *The Rulers of Rhodesia from Earliest Times to the Referendum.* London: John Murray, 1968.

Raven, Simon. *The English Gentleman.* London: Anthony Blond, 1961.

Reeves, Maud Pember. *Round about a Pound a Week.* London: G. Bell and Sons, 1913.

Reitz, Denys. *Commando* Rev. ed. London: Faber and Faber, 1932.

Rentroul, Robert Reid. *Proposed Sterilization of Certain Mental and Physical Degenerates: An Appeal to Asylum Managers and Others.* London: The Walter Scott Publishing Co., 1903.

———. *Race Culture; or Race Suicide (A Plea for the Unborn).* London: The Walter Scott Publishing Co., 1906.

Reynolds, E. E. *Baden-Powell: A Biography of Lord Baden-Powell of Gilwell.* London: Oxford University Press, 1957 (Originally published in 1941.)

———. *The Scout Movement.* London: Oxford University Press, 1950.

Richards, Paul C. ed. *The Founding of the Boy Scouts as Seen Through the Letters of Lord Baden-Powell.* East Bridgewater, Mass.: The Standish Museums and Unitarian Church, 1973.

Robb, Janet H. *The Primrose League, 1883-1906.* New York: Columbia University Press, 1942.

Roberts, Field-Marshall Frederick. *Defence of the Empire.* London: Spottiswoode and Co., 1905.

———. *Lord Roberts' Message to the Nation.* London: John Murray, 1912.

———. *A Nation in Arms.* London: John Murray, 1907.

Roberts, Kenneth; White, Graham; and Parker, Howard. *The Character Training Industry: Adventure Training Schemes in Britain.* London: David and Charles (Holdings), 1974.

Rowntree, B. Seebohm. *Poverty: A Study of Town Life.* London: Macmillan and Co., 1901.

Russell, Charles, E. B. *The Making of the Criminal.* London: Macmillan and Co., 1906.

———. *Manchester Boys: Sketches of Manchester Lads at Work and Play.* Manchester, Eng.: The University Press, 1905.

———. *The Problem of Juvenile Crime.* London: Humphrey Milford, 1917.

———*Working Lads' Clubs.* London: Macmillan and Co., 1908.

Sadler, Michael. *Continuation Schools in England and Elsewhere.* Manchester, Eng.: The University Press, 1907.

Sadler, Michael. *Moral Instruction and Training in Schools: Report of an International Inquiry.* 2 vols. London: Longmans, Green and Co., 1908.

Saleeby, Caleb W. *The Methods of Race Regeneration.* London: Cassell and Co., 1912.

———. *Parenthood and Race Culture: The Outline of Eugenics.* London: Cassell and Co., 1909.

———. *The Program of Eugenics.* London: Cassell and Co., 1914.

Sandow, Eugen. *Body-Building, or Man in the Making.* London: Gale and Polden, 1905.

———. *The Construction and Reconstruction of the Human Body.* London: John Bale, Sons and Danielson, 1907.

Scalley, Robert J. *The Origins of the Lloyd George Coalition: The Politics of Social Imperialism, 1900-1918.* Princeton: Princeton University Press, 1975.

Scarth, Levenson. *National Ideals.* London: The National Service League, 1910.

Schofield, A. T., and Vaughan-Jackson, Percy. *What a Boy Should Know.* London: Cassell and Co., 1913.

Searle, G. R. *Eugenics and Politics in Britain, 1900-1914.* Leyden: Noordhoof International Publishing, 1976.

———. *The Quest for National Efficiency: A Study in British Politics and Political Thought, 1899-1914.* Berkeley: University of California Press, 1971.

Seeley, J. R. *The Expansion of England.* London: Macmillan and Co., 1883.

Semmel, Bernard. *Imperialism and Social Reform.* Doubleday and Co., 1960.

Seton, Ernest Thompson. *The Birch-bark Roll of Woodcraft.* New York, Doubleday, Page, and Co., 1906.

———. *The Natural History of the Ten Commandments.* New York: Charles Scribner's Sons, 1907.

———. *Trail of an Artist-Naturalist: The Autobiography of Ernest Thompson Seton.* London: Hodder and Stoughton, 1951.

———. *Two Little Savages.* New York: Grosset and Dunlap, 1911. (Originally published in 1903.)

Shadwell, Arthur. *Industrial Efficiency: A Comparative Study of Industrial Life in England, Germany, and America.* 2 vols. London: Longmans, Green and Co., 1906.

Shee, George F. *The Briton's First Duty: The Case for Conscription.* London: Grant Richards, 1901.

———."The Deterioration in the National Physique." *Nineteenth Century* 103 (May 1903): 797-805.

Sherard, Robert H. *Child Slaves in Britain.* London: Hurst and Blackett, 1905.

Simon, Brian. *Education and the Labour Movement, 1870-1920.* London: Lawrence and Wishart, 1965.

———, and Bradley, Ian, eds. *The Victorian Public School.* Dublin: Gill and Macmillan, 1975.

Smyth, A. Watt. *Physical Deterioration: Its Causes and the Cure.* London: John Murray, 1904.

Spargo, John. *The Bitter Cry of the Children.* New York: Macmillan and Co., 1906.

Spender, Stephen. "The English Adolescent." *Harvard Education Review* 18 (1948): 229-40.

Spitz, Rene A. "Authority and Masturbation." *The Psychoanalytic Quarterly* 21 (1952): 490-527.

Springhall, John O. "The Boy Scouts, Class and Militarism in Relation to British Youth Movements, 1908-1930." *International Review of Social History* 16 (1971): 125-58.

———. "The Rise and Fall of Henty's Empire." *Times Literary Supplement,* 3 October 1968, pp. 1105-6.

Springhall, John O. *Youth, Empire and Society: British Youth Movements, 1883-1940.* London: Croom Helm, 1977.

——; Fraser, Brian; and Hoare, Michael. *Sure and Stedfast: A History of the Boys' Brigade, 1885-1983.* London: Collins, 1983.

Stead, Alfred. *Great Japan: A Study of National Efficiency.* London: John Lane, The Bodley Head, 1905.

Stepan, Nancy. *The Idea of Race in Science: Great Britain 1800-1960.* London: Macmillan, 1982.

Stoddard, Lothrop. *The Rising Tide of Color.* London: Chapman and Hall, 1920.

Strachey, John. *The End of Empire.* London: Victor Gollancz, 1959.

Thornton, A. P. *The Imperial Idea and Its Enemies: A Study in British Power.* London: Macmillan, 1970.

Tressell, Robert. *The Ragged Trousered Philanthropists.* London: Granada Publishing, 1965. (Originally published in 1955, the book was actually written around 1906.)

Trevor, Charles T. *Sandow the Magnificent.* London: The Mitre Press, 1946.

Urwick, E. J., ed. *Studies of Boy Life in Our Cities.* London: J. M. Dent and Co., 1904.

Usborne, Richard. *Clubland Heroes.* London: Constable, 1953.

Vachell, Horace A. *The Hill.* London: John Murray, 1905.

Vagts, Alfred. *A History of Militarism.* London: George Allen and Unwin, 1938.

Vane, Francis Fletcher. *'Agin the Government.* London: Sampson, Law, Marston and Co., 1929.

——. *The Boy Knight.* London: Council of National Peace Scouts, 1910.

Wade, E. K. *The Piper of Pax.* London: C. Arthur Pearson, 1924.

——. *The Story of Scouting.* London: C. Arthur Pearson, 1935.

Waldegrave, A. J. *Lessons in Citizenship.* London: Thomas Nelson and Sons, 1912.

——, ed. *A Teacher's Hand-Book of Moral Lessons.* London: Swan Sonnenschein and Co., 1904.

Walvin, James. *Black and White: The Negro and English Society.* London: Allen Lane, 1973.

Warren, Mencil. *Elements of Discipline.* London: Gale and Polden, 1917.

Warwick, Countess of. *A Nation's Youth.* London: Cassell and Co., 1906.

Waugh, Alec. *The Loom of Youth.* London: Grant Richards, 1917.

Webb, Sidney. *The Decline in the Birth Rate.* London: Fabian Tract 131, 1907.

——. *Twentieth-Century Politics: A Policy of National Efficiency.* London: Fabian Tract 108, 1901.

Westlake, Aubrey T. *Woodcraft Chivalry.* Weston-Super-Mare, England: Mendip Press, 1917.

Whetham, W. C. D., and Catherine D. *The Family and the Nation: A Study in Natural Inheritance and Social Responsibility.* London: Longmans, Green and Co., 1909.

——. *Heredity and Society.* London: Longmans, Green and Co., 1912.

White, Arnold. *Efficiency and Empire.* London: Methuen and Co., 1901.

——. "Eugenics and National Efficiency." *The Eugenics Review* 1 (July 1909): 105-111.

——. *The Modern Jew.* New York: Frederick A. Stokes Co., 1879.

Whitehouse, J. H., ed. *Problems of Boy Life.* London: P. S. King and Son, 1912.

Wicksted, J. H. *Conduct and Character.* London: Thomas Nelson and Sons, 1913.

Wilkinson, Paul. "English Youth Movements, 1909-1930." *Journal of Contemporary History* 4 (April 1969): 3-23.

Wilkinson, Rupert. *The Prefects: British Leadership and the Public School Tradition.* London: Oxford University Press, 1964.

Wilkinson, Spenser. *Britain at Bay.* London: Constable and Co., 1909.

Wilkinson, Spenser. *War and Policy*. London: Archibald Constable and Co., 1900.

Winter, J. M. "The Webbs and the Non-White World: A Case of Socialist Racialism." *Journal of Contemporary History* (January 1974): 181–92.

Wodehouse, P. G. "The Swoop! or How Clarence Saved England, A Tale of the Great Invasion." *The Swoop! and Other Stories*. New York: The Seabury Press, 1979. First published in 1909.

Woodruff, Philip. *The Men Who Ruled India: The Guardians*. London: Jonathan Cape, 1954.

Worsley, T. C. *Barbarians and Philistines: Democracy and the Public Schools*. London: Robert Hale, 1940.

Youth and the Race. Fourth Report of and the Chief Evidence Taken by the National Birthrate Commission, 1920–1923. London: Kegan Paul, Trench, Trubuer and Co., 1923.

INDEX

Abraham, Albert, 173
Actual Friends (magazine), 65
Adion, Cyril, 173
Afghanistan, 24
Africa: B-P serves in, 2, 24-8, 30-46, 119;
  Boer War in, 4; *see also* Mafeking
Albert Medal, the, 173
America *see* United States of America
Anderson, Olive, 196
Arnold, Thomas, 280
Arnold-Forster, H.D.: *The Citizen Reader*,
  125; *History of England*, 176
Arthurson, C., 188
Ashanti, the, 24-5; *see also* Prempeh, King
  of the Ashanti
Asquith, H.H., 221

Baden-Powell, Agnes (B-P's sister), 11, 17,
  49
Baden-Powell, Baden (B-P's brother), 17
Baden-Powell, Frank (B-P's brother), 17
Baden-Powell, George (B-P's brother), 17,
  20
Baden-Powell, Henrietta Grace (*née* Smyth;
  B-P's mother): married, 15; widowed,
  16-17; and B-P, 20-21, 50, 284n; B-P
  writes to, 38-9, 48; maintenance, 49
Baden-Powell, Lady Olave (*née* Soames;
  B-P's wife), 47-9, 51
Baden-Powell, Lord Robert Stephenson
  Smyth: biography, 1; growing up, 2, and
  imperialism, 2-3, 170-71; and origins of
  scouting, 4-14, 46, 52-87, 91; on aims
  of scouting, 6-7, 63-4, 91; and class
  system, 9-10, 89-90, 117-18, 156, 183-4;
  influence, 13-14; born, 15-16; and his
  mother, 16-17, 20-21, 50, 284n; at
  Charterhouse, 17-19, 88, 95, 238; joins
  13th Hussars, 20, 88; army career, 20-
  29; in Boer War, 30-46, 93, 285n-286n;
  as head of South African Constabulary,
  44-6, 64, 92-3, 123-4; married, 47-9;
  achievements, 50-51; letter to Eton
  Chronicle, 54-62; and organization of

Scouts, 61-2, 71-6; and Seton, 64-81;
and Pearson, 81-7; experience of youth
work, 88; and war correspondents, 93-4;
and public school ethos, 104-7, 180; and
the "Scout Law," 111-30; and hunting,
119-20; and hara-kiri, 126-7; and British
"decline," 133-5, 137-8, 140-41, 204,
295n-296n; and "race regeneration,"
144, 160; and militarism, 157, 191-5,
197-8, 200-202, 225-6, 299n, 305n;
Pearson on, 158; Saleeby on, 159; on
Scouting for Boys, 161-2; and sexual
continence, 185-90; and National Service
League, 205-6; and Duty and Discipline
movement, 210; and other youth
movements, 237-45; and race, 253-66,
312n-313n; and religion, 266-76; on
Russian response to Scouting, 278-9; use
of metaphor, 282n-283n, 299n;
Adventuring to Manhood, 280; *Aids to
Scouting* (*Cavalry Aids to Scouting*), 29, 53,
121; *African Adventures*, 36; *Boy Scouts
Beyond the Seas*, 126, 258-9; *The Downfall
of Prempeh*, 26, 255-7; *Indian Memories*,
258, 264; *Lessons from the 'Varsity of Life*,
227, 284n; *Life's Snags and How to Meet
Them*, 269, 280; *The Matabele Campaign*,
254-5; *Paddle Your Own Canoe*, 280;
Pigsticking or Hog Hunting, 21-2, 119-20,
293n; *Reconnaissance and Scouting*, 20, 29;
Rovering to Success, 259, 280; *Scouting for
Boys*, 4, 11, 13, 31, 52, 59, 64-5, 70, 75-
9, 81, 83, 85, 108-14, 116, 120-21, 125-
6, 161-91, 193, 226, 236, 246, 287n;
"Scouting for Boys," 63; *Sketches in
Mafeking and East Africa*, 36; *Yarns for Boy
Scouts*, 121-3, 127, 263
Baden-Powell, Warrington (B-P's brother),
  17
Balilla, 272-5
Balliol College, 19-20
Barnett, Mary G., 296n
Barralet, Alfred G., 248
Bateson, Sir William, 155-6
Beard, Dan, 64

Beresford, Lord Charles, 63, 132, 144, 206, 210
Beveridge, William: *Unemployment*, 182
Birkenhead (ship), 125-6, 172
Blomfield, Lady Massie, 210-11
Boer War: B-P renowned in, 2; and British "decline," 3-4; effect on B-P, 13, 30; B-P in, 30-46; and "Boy Nature," 89; as stimulus to militarism, 196; *see also* Mafeking
Bompas Smith, H., 91, 94-5
Booth, General, 210, 230
Boys' Brigade: restricted appeal of, 6; influence on Scouting, 10, 52, 123, 230; and open-air life, 142; and militarism, 194-6, 201; origins, 231-4; Primmer from, 289n
Boys' Brigade Gazette, 63, 71, 236
Boys' Brigade Handbook, 231-2
Boys' Life Brigade, 235-6
Bray, R. A., 7, 140
Brendon, Piers: *Eminent Edwardians*, 283n
British Brothers League, 144, 297n
British Empire Union, 314n
Brooke, Rupert, 103
Browning, Robert, 16
Brownsea Island: 1907 Camp at, 4, 48, 52, 85-6, 88, 236, 289n
Buchan, John, 254
Burt, Cyril, 282n-283n
Bushido, 64, 176
Buxton, Sir Thomas, 173

Cadet Corps, the, 201, 237-41
Canada, 65
Cantlie, James, 141
Carlyle, Thomas, 250
Carrington, Sir Frederick, 26, 28
Carrol, Lewis *see* Dodgson, Charles
Carthusian, (magazine), 314n
Catholic Boys' Brigade, 235
Cecil, Lord Edward, 53, 162, 170, 229
Chamberlain, Joseph, 82
Chapman, Kate, 173
Charterhouse School, 2, 17-19, 88, 95, 238
Chesney, George: 222; *The Battle of Dorking*, 212
Childers, Erskine: *The Riddle of the Sands*, 212
Christ Church College, 20
Chronicle (Eton College magazine), 54-7, 60-63, 71, 175, 197, 287n
Church Lads' Brigade, 10, 234
Churchill, Winston, 210
city dwelling: and British "decline," 139-42, 295n-296n
class system, 8-10, 89-90, 117-8
Cole, Police-Sergeant, 173
Commission of Youth and Race, 145
Conan Doyle, Sir Arthur: 210, 287n; *The*

Construction and Reconstruction of the Human Body, 143
Confessions of the Kibbo Kift, 249-50
Connaught, Duke of, 20, 260
Conrad, Joseph, 255, 311n
Constabulary, South African, 44-6, 64, 92-3, 123-4
Contemporary Review (journal), 135
Cramb, J. A., 311n
Crichton-Browne, James, 149
Cromer, Lord, 210
Cronjé, Piet, 36-7
Curzon, Lord, 210

Daily Chronicle (newspaper), 25-6, 42
Daily Express (newspaper), 82
Daily Mail (newspaper), 213
De Mille, Cecil B., 51
Declining Birth Rate, (1916), 146, 148-9
diet: and British "decline", 141-2
Digby, Kenelm: *Broadstone of Honour*, 64
discipline: and good character, 8
Dodge, General, 167-8
Dodgson, Charles (Lewis Carroll), 20, 22
Douglas, Major, 250
Dragoon Guards, 5th, 29
du Maurier, Guy: *An Englishman's Home*, 214
Dulwich College, 95, 100-102
Dunraven, Earl of, 144, 297n
duty: in Scout Law, 117; and Scout ethos, 162, 171-2, 174
Duty and Discipline movement, 209-10

education: and class, 92; *see also* public school ethos
Elles, General Edmund, 206
Elliot, General, 174
Elliott, Newlyn, 173
Empire, British, 2-3, 132-5
Empire Day, 161-2
Epictetus, 64
Eton College, 17, 60, 104; *see also Chronicle*
eugenics, 150-60, 189
Eugenics Education Society, 151
Eugenics Review, (journal), 151
Evans, I. O.: *Woodcraft and World Service*, 242
Evans-Gordon, William, 144
Everett, Percy, 82-3, 185, 192, 304n-305n

Fabian Tract No. 131, 146-8
Farrar, J. A., 222-3, 308n-309n
fighting: and Scout ethos, 162; *see also* militarism
Fisher, Lord: *Memories*, 306n
Fitchett, : 287n; *Deeds That Won the Empire*, 176
Forest and Stream (magazine), 65
Fox, G. Malcolm, 131
France, 203

Freeman, Arnold: *Boy Life and Labour*, 8-9
Frontiersman, 208-9

Galton, Sir Francis, 150-52, 298n
games: and the public school ethos, 96-104, 291n-292n
Gee, Walter Mallock, 234
George, Eric, 198-9
Germany, 3, 175-6, 203, 205, 275-6, 300n, 306n-307n
Gibbon, Edward, 133
Girl Guides, 11
Glasgow, 52
Glasier, J. Bruce, 223
Godalming, 19
Goldsmid, A. E., 234
Gordon, Charles George, 280-81
Gould, Stephen Jay, 298n
Gray (hero), 173
Green Shirt movement for Social Credit, 251
Grenfell, Julian, 103
Grootboom, Jan, 257-8

Haggard, Sir Rider, 145
Haig-Brown, Dr, 18
Haldane, J. F. B., 211
Hall, G. Stanley, 242, 250
Hamilton, Angus, 37-9, 41
Hamilton, Ian, 44, 198, 238
Handbook for Girl Guides, 11, 293n-294n
Hardwick, Albert, 173
Hardy, Thomas: *Jude the Obscure*, 304n
Hargrave, John: 129-30, 197, 244-9; *The Great War Brings It Home*, 244-5
Harmsworth, Alfred, 213
Harris, Edith, 173
Harrow School, 17, 95, 104
Headquarters Gazette, 11, 129, 194, 238, 300n
Henty, G. A., 233-4, 254
heroism: and Scout ethos, 126-8, 173
Hibbert, Christopher, 178
Hill, James, 231
Hill, John, 231
Hillcourt, William, 13, 37, 53-4
Hirst, F. W.: *The Six Panics and Other Essays*, 211
Hitler Jugend, 276
Hobson, J. A., 2, 149
Hore, Colonel, 32
Horsfall, T. C., 224
Hussars, 13th, 2, 20, 29, 88
Huxley, T. H., 16

Imperial Defence Committee, 204, 221
India, 2, 20-24, 29, 119; *see also* mutiny, Indian
Inge, W. R., 149
Inter-Departmental Committee on Physical Deterioration, the, 134-9, 197

Isle of Wight, 20
Italy, 273

Jahn, 64
Japan: industrial expansion of, 3, 58-9; and Bushido, 64, 176; and hara-kiri, 126-7; and Empire, 133-4; B-P on, 172, 175; Shee on, 203, and seizure of Port Arthur, 205
Jewish Lads' Brigade, 234-5
Jones, Paul, 95, 100-104
Jowett, Benjamin, 16, 19-20, 22

Keary, Peter, 188
Kenya, 51
Khartoum, 281
Kibbo Kift Kindred, 244, 248-9, 251-2
Kiernan, V. G., 126, 305n
King Edward VII School, 91
Kipling, Rudyard, 97, 112, 165, 216
Kitchener, Lord, 44-5, 210
Kruger, President, 36-7

labor movement *see* socialism
Ladies' Home Journal (magazine), 65-7
Lads' Drill Association, the, 207
Lane, Sir Reginald, 206
Langley, Mrs, 173
Lawrence, Pethick, 141
LeQueux, William: 133, 212; *The Invasion of 1910*, 213-14
League to Combat Anti-Semitism, the, 271
Legion of Frontiersmen, the, 200, 207-8, 217-18
Legion of the Unemployed, 250
Livy, 64
Lloyd George, David, 3
London, 17, 19
Loyal British Waiters Society, the, 209
loyalty: and Scout Law, 115-16; and Scout ethos, 162
Lynch, Walter, 172-3
Lyttleton, Rev, 206

MacIllwain, Captain, 194
McLaren, Kenneth, 47-8, 85
Mafeking, 18, 30-46, 61, 93, 162-3, 170, 190, 241, 285n
Mafeking Cadet Corps, the, 53, 162-3, 229
Manning, Cardinal, 280
Marchant, James, 149
Martin, Hubert, 276
Masterman, C. F. G., 131-2
Matabele, the, 26-8
Matthews, Bessie, 173
Maurice, Sir Frederick, 3, 135-6, 196-7
Meath, Lord, 134-5, 155, 161, 206-7, 210-11, 297n, 304n, 307n
Mendel, Georg, 150
Miles, Eustace, 98-100

militarism, 13, 57-8, 71, 162-5, 191-229, 299n, 305n
Mills, Elliot: 295n; *The Decline and Fall of the British Empire*, 133-4
Milner, Lord, 44-5, 210
Moral Education League, 151
Morning Post (newspaper), 11-12, 281
Munroe, H. H. (Saki): *When William Came*, 218-21
Murchison, Lt., 42-3
Mussolini, Benito, 272-5, 315n
mutiny, Indian (1857), 2; *see also* India

Napoleon III, Emperor of France, 237
Nation in Arms (previously *National Service Journal*; journal), 131, 199, 202, 212, 215, 224-5
National Council for Public Morals, 144, 152
National Defence Association, 200
National Service Journal. see *Nation in Arms*
National Service League, 58, 155, 199, 202-12, 308n
National Sunday School Union, 236
Neath, Lord, 277
Neilly, Emerson, 40-41
New Age, (journal), 250
New Statesman (journal), 148
Newbolt, Henry: "A Ballad of John Nicholson," 301n-303n; "Vitaï Lampada," 97
Newcastle Journal, 199
News of the World (newspaper), 315n
Newton, Lord, 202
Newton, W. Douglas: *War*, 216
Nicholson, General John, 178, 300n-301n
Nightingale, Florence, 280
Norwood, Cyril, 95-6

obedience, 126-30; *see also* loyalty
observation: and Scout ethos, 166-7, 169
Official History of the War in South Africa, 37
Order of Woodcraft Chivalry, 242-4, 252
Oswell, William Cotton, 263
Oxford, 19-20

Packenham, Thomas: *The Boer War*, 40
Pall Mall Gazette (journal), 40-41
Parslow, Mr (Mafeking), 42
Paton, John, 236
Paul, Leslie: 251; *Republic of Children*, 252
Peacock, J. F., 211
Pearson, C. Arthur, 4, 81-7
Pearson, Karl: 151-9; *The Grammar of Science*, 152
Pearson's Weekly (magazine), 82, 84
Pelham, H. S.: 98; *The Training of a Working Boy*, 7-8, 89-90
Pestalozzi, 64

Philipps, Roland, 103
physical regeneration, 131-60, 207
Pickford, Sir Alfred, 268
Playne, Caroline, 306n
Plumer, Colonel, 32, 40
Pocock, Roger, 200
Portsmouth, 20
Pounds, John, 64
Powell, Agnes *see* Baden-Powell, Agnes
Powell, Augustus, 17
Powell, Baden (B-P's father), 15-16
Powell, Baden (B-P's brother) *see* Baden-Powell, Baden
Powell, Frank *see* Baden-Powell, Frank
Powell, George *see* Baden-Powell, George
Powell, Henrietta (B-P's sister), 16
Powell, Henrietta Grace *see* Baden-Powell, Henrietta Grace
Powell, Jessie, 16
Powell, John, 16
Powell, Robert Stephenson Smyth *see* Baden-Powell, Lord Robert Stephenson Smyth
Powell, Warrington *see* Baden-Powell, Warrington
Prempeh, King of the Ashanti, 24-5, 255-7
Primmer, Arthur, 289n
Protocols of the Elders of Zion, 268
public school ethos, 90-92, 94-107; *see also* individual schools

Quick, Fleet Engineer, 210

race: and British "decline," 144-57; Scouting and, 253-76; *see also* eugenics
Review of Reviews (magazine), 82, 212
Rhodes, Cecil, 28
Richard I, King of England, 172
Roberts, Lord, 32, 34-7, 42-4, 46, 63, 133, 204-7, 210, 213, 223-5, 286n-287n, 300n-301n, 306n
Rome, 133-4
Roosevelt, Theodore, 169
Roseberry, Lord, 12, 210
Rowntree, Seebohm, 182
Royal Arsenal Co-operative Society, 251
Royal Commission on Alien Immigration (1903), 144
Royal Commission on the War in South Africa (1903), 35
Rugby School, 17
Ruskin, John, 16-17
Russell, Charles, 9, 89-90
Russia, 278
Rustenburg, 43-4

Sadler, Sir Michael, 94, 241
Saint John's Ambulance Brigade, 230
Saki *see* Munroe, H. H.

Saleeby, C. W., 158-9, 298n
Salvation Army, the, 230
Sandhurst, 20
Sandow, Eugene, 142-3
"Sapper," 254
Scanner, David, 173
Schreiner, Olive, 29
Scott, Sir Francis, 24
Scout, (magazine, 83-4, 280
Scouter, (magazine), 269-70
Scouting: history, 1; origins, 3-14, 52-7; as "character factory," 6-7; motto, 17, 71, 163-4, 193; militarism of, 57-8, 71, 162-5, 191-229; and "knightly code", 59-63, 120-23, 174-6; organization of, 61-2; aims, 63-4; influence of Woodcraft movement on, 65-81; Pearson publicises, 81-7; and public school ethos, 104-7, 180; and "Scout Law," 108-30; as force for regeneration, 131-60; ideology, 161, 185, 192; and sexual continence, 185; and Scout Defence Corps, 228-9; context, 230-52, 277-81; and race, 253-66, 313n; and religion, 266-76; *see also* under Baden-Powell, Lord Robert Stephenson Smyth
Scribner's (magazine), 65
Serapis (ship), 20
Seton, Ernest Thompson: 13, 64-81, 197, 200, 242, 288n; *The Birch-bark Roll of the Woodcraft Indians*, 69, 71-5, 77-9; *How to Play Indians*, 67; *Two Little Savages*, 68
sexual continence, 186-90, 304n
Shakespeare, William, 13
Shaw, William, 297n
Shawnee Indians, 65
Shee, George: *The Briton's First Duty*, 202-4
Smiles, Samuel: 125; *Character*, 125; *Duty*, 125; *Self-Help*, 125; *Thrift*, 125
Smith, H. Bompas *see* Bompas Smith, H.
Smith, Horace, 211
Smith, John, 16, 177-8
Smith, John (hero), 173
Smith, Sir William, 52-4, 63-4, 123, 196, 230-31, 237
Smyth, A. W., 139-40
Smyth, H. A., 24
Smyth, William Henry, 16
Snyman, Commander, 37
Soames, Olave *see* Baden-Powell, Lady Olave
Social Credit movement, 250
Social Credit Party of Great Britain, 251
socialism, 114, 183-4, 303n
Society for the Suppression of the Immigration of Destitute Aliens, 297n
Soutter, H. W., 260
Spartans, 64

Spectator, (magazine), 214, 303n
Springhall, J. O., 309n
Stanley, Dean, 16
Stead, Alfred: *Great Japan*, 59
Stead, W. T., 212
Stent, Vere, 93, 285n
Strachey, Lytton: *Eminent Victorians*, 280-81

Tecumseh, Chief, 65
Thackeray, William, 16
Times (newspaper), 37-8, 195, 214, 299n
Tit-Bits (magazine), 82
Townroe, B. S.: *A Nation in Arms*, 215-16
tracking, 168-9
Trail, (magazine), 129, 245-8

union movement, 3; *see also* socialism
United States of America, 3, 65
urban degeneracy *see* city dwelling
Uwini, Chief, 28

Vane, Sir Francis Fletcher, 197, 206

Webb, Sidney, 146-8, 152, 189
Weil, Benjamin, 285n
Weismann, August, 150
Westlake, Aubrey, 242
Westlake, Ernest, 242
White, Arnold, 144, 160, 210, 297n
Wilkinson, Rupert: *Prefects: British Leadership and the Public School Tradition*, 92
Williams, Hanbury, 38
Wilson, H. W., 213
Wilson, Reginald, 314n
Winchester School, 17
Wingfield-Stratford, E., 90
Wodehouse, P. G.: 221; "The Swoop, or How Clarence Saved England," 216-17
Wolsley, Lord, 30, 32, 35, 311n
Woodcraft Chivalry, 243-4
Woodcraft Folk (Federation of Co-operative Woodcraft Fellowship), 251-2
Woodcraft movement, 65-81, 129, 200, 242
Woodruff, Philip, 293n
World War I: development of Scouting after, 13, 254; and English militarism, 58; Paul Jones in, 95, 100-104; B-P on, 157, 176, 227, 305n
Worsley, T. C., 94, 103
Wyndham, George, 133

Y M C A, 10, 61, 230, 236
Yellin, Mr, 269-70
youth movements, 7-8, 13-14, 230-52, 309n; *see also* individual movements

Zulus, 64

A graduate of Harvard College with a Ph.D. in English literature from Columbia University, Michael Rosenthal is currently associate dean of Columbia College. He has contributed
frequently to *Partisan Review, Raritan,* and the *New York Times
Book Review,* and is the author of *Virginia Woolf.*